MONDAY 14th ~~#~~ MAY 2001
2nd YEAR Psychology.

PERSONALITY

PERSONALITY

IN SEARCH OF INDIVIDUALITY

Nathan Brody

Department of Psychology
Wesleyan University
Middletown, Connecticut

ACADEMIC PRESS, INC.

Harcourt Brace Jovanovich, Publishers
San Diego   New York   Berkeley   Boston
London   Sydney   Tokyo   Toronto

ACADEMIC PRESS, INC.
1250 Sixth Avenue
San Diego, California 92101

United Kingdom Edition published by
ACADEMIC PRESS INC. (LONDON) LTD.
24-28 Oval Road, London NW1 7DX

Library of Congress Cataloging-in-Publication Data

Brody, Nathan.
    Personality :   in search of individuality / Nathan Brody
    p. cm.
    Bibliography: p.
    Includes index.
    ISBN 0-12-134845-8 (alk. paper)
    1. Personality. 2. Individuality. I. Title.
BF698.B6934   1988   87-24218
155.2—dc19   CIP

Cover photograph © Albano Guatti / Stock Market

PRINTED IN THE UNITED STATES OF AMERICA
88 89 90 91   9 8 7 6 5 4 3 2 1

Contents

5. The Biological Basis of Personality

6. Conscious and Unconscious Influences

Preface

Fifteen years ago I finished a book surveying research and theory in personality (Brody, 1972). I find it useful, as I write this preface, to reflect on the continuities and discontinuities in my own views about the field.

In several respects this book is similar to my earlier book. Both books emphasize empirical research. I continue to believe that personality may be studied in an empirical manner and that the ardent pursuit of research can lead to understanding. I have tried to deal with a limited number of topics, and I have tried to present several studies in detail. It is often the case, particularly in books dealing with fields that are not usually data intensive, such as personality, that the details of the data obtained in a study are not presented or are glossed over. Further, summaries of the data presented in the discussion part of an article by the author(s) of the paper are considered the definitive presentation of the import of the data. I find that frequently data are used to address issues that have risen independently or subsequent to the publication of a particular article. Further, commonly the interpretation placed on the data by the researchers who obtained the data is not fully justified by a detailed examination of the results. Accordingly, I have tried to discuss a limited number of studies in detail, including the presentation, on occasion, of the data obtained in these studies, in order to reach some conclusion about the import of a study.

There are also continuities between substantive positions that I have taken with respect to issues in the field of personality. The past 15 years have been marked by vigorous attacks on trait theory. The attacks and various responses to them are dealt with in Chapters 1, 2, and 4 of this book. Happily, as I write this preface, I am convinced that we have come in large measure to an empirical resolution of the trait–situation debate. I have tried to sketch that resolution in some detail. While there are differences in emphasis between trait theorists and their critics, I do not believe that there are any longer any true disagreements about substantive issues. Thus, the last 15 years have been marked by considerable clarification with respect to the nature of traits and of the limits and virtues of a trait approach to personality. I do not think that a currently defensible view of trait theory is in any way discordant or in disagreement with trait theory as it existed 15 years ago. It is merely that we have attained marginally increased understanding of the issues.

While our increased understanding of issues in trait theory has been only incremental, I believe that we have made truly significant progress in the understanding of the behavior genetics of personality. I argued 15 years ago that personality was influenced by genotypes. That argument was largely based on conjecture and the promising results of a few studies—the most important of which was Shields's study of monozygotic twins reared apart (Shields, 1962). That study, which has always seemed to me to be among the most important empirical contributions to the study of personality, was substantially ignored in American personality research. In the past 15 years, there has been a great deal of interest in the study of the behavior genetics of personality, particularly in American psychology. We have accumulated large bodies of substantive data on twins. Data from family studies, adoption studies, and studies combining longitudinal observations with behavior genetic techniques have provided an extensive new base for explorations of genetic and environmental influences. This research has, in my view, amply supported the tentative suggestions of the importance of genetic influences, and, at the same time, indicated a number of areas in which our knowledge is deficient. The awareness of new developments in behavior genetics has led to increased publication of the results of these investigations in journals devoted to the study of personality and development, and these results have slowly filtered into the consciousness of many American psychologists who were heretofore skeptical of the importance of behavior genetic investigations. In short, I believe that it can be argued that we have made genuine progress in our understanding of genetic and environmental influences on personality.

An additional area that has been the subject of increased empirical attention is the study of conscious and unconscious influences. Empirical investigations of unconscious influences in the 1950s and 1960s were flawed and subject to a variety of methodological criticisms. Recent research has been more rigorous, less easily dismissed, and is rooted in contemporary cognitive experimental psychology. It is also true that there is renewed empirical interest in the influence of phenomenal states on behavior. Thus, we have a simultaneous increase in interest in conscious and unconscious influences. While the role of conscious and unconscious processes in a mature psychology of personality remains philosophically, empirically, methodologically, and theoretically vexed, I believe that there are abundant new literatures that address this perennially complex issue. I have presented some tentative suggestions for my own resolution of some of these issues. My own views on these issues have changed considerably over the last 15 years.

Each of the three substantive issues discussed above has been marked by a different kind of progress or, if not progress, change. Trait theory has been reaffirmed with a better understanding of its limits and strengths. The behavior-genetic study of personality has made major empirical advances and has increased enormously in the sophistication of its data base, methods, and accordingly, the subtlety of the questions that it addresses. Our understanding of the influence of conscious and unconscious processes has also been deepened by a profusion of new data and theory. Here we are, in my view, somewhat further removed from the development of a completely adequate solution, but our awareness of the complexity of the issues and the richness of the theoretical and empirical data base with which we have to contend has clearly increased.

The previous discussion should provide some insights into the topics that will be dealt with in this book. However, a more formal outline may be useful to the reader. Chapter 1 is a presentation of trait theory and considers some of the recent criticisms of a trait approach to personality. It presents data indicating that some of the criticisms have been overstated. Chapter 2 presents longitudinal research and considers stability and change in personality. Chapter 3 deals with the behavior genetics of personality. It attempts to relate the results of behavior-genetic research to the evidence of the cross-situational generality and longitudinal stability of traits. Chapter 4 considers a number of suggested emendations and refinements of trait theory and again attempts to support the general utility of a broadly based trait theory. Chapter 5 considers three, somewhat related theories of the biological basis of traits developed by Eysenck, Gray, and Zuckerman. Chapters 1–5 all deal more or less directly with trait theory. Chapter 6 presents research and theory on conscious and unconscious influences on behavior. Although that issue is only tangentially relevant to trait theory, I believe that some resolution of it is necessary for a complete understanding of personality.

It is always a pleasure to acknowledge the assistance one has received in writing a book. Much of this book was put into its final form during a sabbatical generously provided by Wesleyan University during the fall semester of the 1986–1987 academic year. During this sabbatical I was in London, where I benefited from conversations with Hans Eysenck, Adrian Furnhan, and Jeffrey Gray. I have benefited from a number of conversations over the years with Howard Erlichman. My former colleague Jim Conley has increased my understanding of longitudinal research in personality.

PERSONALITY

1

Traits and Situations

Introduction

Personality psychology may be defined as the study of individual differences. People differ in an infinite variety of ways—from the structure of their nervous systems to their thoughts and feelings in a particular social situation. It is the task of the personality psychologist to systematically describe these differences and to study their significance for an understanding of individual lives. How is this to be done? We may begin with the observation that our language contains an extremely large set of terms to describe individuals—perhaps as many as 30,000 (Allport and Odbert, 1936). We use these words, or a subset of them at any rate, to describe ourselves and others. It is possible that our ordinary language may summarize observations of salient respects in which people differ and, as such, may provide a basis for constructing a more systematic understanding of personality.

Beginnings: The Study of the Ordinary Language of Personality

The study of ordinary language descriptions of personality is faced with an embarrassment of riches—there are simply too many terms available. However, a moment's reflection on this problem should inform us that many terms are at least roughly synonymous, and others may not be linguistically synonymous but may, in fact, have a high probability of co-occurrence. That is, words, such as

1

shy and *diffident,* may have at least marginally distinct meanings, yet such words may be linked as descriptors in that if we say of ourselves or others that we or they are shy, we may be likely also to assert that we or they are diffident.

If certain terms that may be used to describe personality are related in their meanings by being more or less synonymous or empirically linked in their probability of co-occurrence as descriptors, then it is possible to reduce the large number of terms to a smaller subset that eliminates the redundancies contained in the total set of descriptive terms.

The redundancies in the language used to describe personality may be discovered by asking individuals to describe themselves or another person on a large set of descriptors. Frequently, the descriptors consist of bipolar adjectives that are roughly opposite in meaning. Each individual, in effect, assigns a score to herself or himself on each of the descriptive dimensions.

Imagine a study of this type in which 100 individuals describe themselves on each of 200 dimensions. The initial data derived from the descriptions will consist of 200 scores for each of 100 individuals—20,000 numbers in all. These data may be used to describe a set of relationships among the descriptive dimensions that are used in the study. Consider a pair of dimensions on which each individual has assigned a descriptive score to himself or herself on each of the two dimensions. Note that we now have pairs of numbers that are linked in that each member of the pair is assigned to the same individual. The relationship between such pairs of numbers may be summarized by a statistic called the coefficient of correlation that varies between -1.00 and $+1.00$ and indicates both the direction and magnitude of the relationship between the pairs of numbers in the set. A correlation of $+1.00$ indicates a perfect positive relationship and would occur in our example if individuals who assigned a particular score to themselves on one descriptive term always assigned the same score to themselves on the second term. In such a case, knowledge of a person's self-assigned score on the first descriptor would always be adequate to predict a person's score on the second descriptor. A score of -1.00 would be obtained in this example if high scores on one descriptor perfectly predicted low scores on the other descriptor and vice versa. A correlation of $-.00$ would be obtained if there were no systematic relationship between scores assigned to the two descriptors. Thus, a coefficient of correlation may be used to summarize the relationship between pairs of numbers used by an individual to describe his or her personality. In this example the correlation may be understood as a statistical summary of the extent to which a person's description of himself or herself with respect to a particular dimension is likely to covary with the person's description on another dimension.

In our example it is possible to calculate a coefficient of correlation for all possible pairs of dimensions summarizing the relationships among all of the dimensions used in the study. Thus, it would be possible to calculate 19,900 correlations ($\binom{200}{2}$) to summarize all of the possible relationships. The 19,900 correlations obtained in our example do little to simplify and reduce the embarrassment of riches inherent in the large set of available personality descriptors. However, an examination of the set of correlations is likely to reveal that many of the correlations have a relatively high absolute number. Such correlations inform us that many of the descriptors may be empirically redundant. For example, if several descriptors all tended to correlate among themselves with high-positive values, we could infer that these descriptors form a cluster. In addition, we could replace an individual's description on each of the descriptors contained in such a cluster by a single score representing an individual's aggregate position on the set of clustered dimensions. Factor analysis is a statistical technique that may be used to reduce the set of all possible correlations to a set of clustered relationships that are defined by a set of measures that tend to be highly related to each other. The statistical procedures are arcane, but the basic notion is simple. Namely, the refinement of the empirical observation that some descriptive dimensions are empirically related to other descriptive dimensions.

It should be apparent that the technique of studying relationships among personality descriptors may be applied to ratings of others as well as to self-descriptions. One or more individuals may be asked to describe a group of individuals using a set of personality dimensions. Each individual who is described may be assigned a score on each dimension in the rating sheet. Scores on all possible pairs of dimensions may be correlated to obtain the relationships among ratings of personality dimensions, and these correlations may be subject to a factor analysis to discover the underlying clusters (or factors) needed to represent the total set of relationships among all of the dimensions.

In general outline, the method described above has been used in countless investigations of the structure of personality descriptors. And, despite inevitable disagreements about the details of the descriptive clusters that may be derived from some variant of the procedure described above, there are substantial agreements among many, if not all, psychologists engaged in this type of research. Consider the methods and results obtained by Norman (1963; Passini and Norman, 1966) in a classic study of the structure of trait ratings. Norman started with a set of 20 dimensions derived from a set of descriptive dimensions proposed by Cattell (1943), derived in turn from a large list of descriptors contained in Allport and Odbert's (1936) classic ''psycholexical'' study of personality. Norman found that the set of 20 descriptive dimensions, when factor analyzed, yielded five clearly defined factors, each of which was defined by four bipolar dimensions. Table 1.1 presents the five-factor solution obtained by Norman and also reports the *loadings* of each of the dimensions on the hypothetical factors assumed to represent the commonality existing among the subset of items that collectively define the factor. These loadings may be understood as a correlation

Table 1.1

Factor Matrix of Ratings[a]

Scales	Factors[b] I	II	III	IV	V
Extraversion					
Talkative–silent	80				
Frank, open–secretive	67		−32		
Adventurous–cautious	67		−42	37	
Sociable–reclusive	85				
Agreeableness					
Good-natured–irritable		67			
Not jealous–jealous	−30	65			
Mild, gentle–headstrong		70			
Cooperative–negativistic	46	67			
Conscientiousness					
Fussy, tidy–careless			72		
Responsible–undependable		57	61		
Scrupulous–unscrupulous		57	55		
Persevering–quitting, fickle		36	63		
Emotional stability					
Poised–nervous, tense		51		50	
Calm–anxious				77	
Composed–excitable				61	
Not hypochondriacal–hypochondriacal			−33	58	
Culture					
Artistically sensitive–insensitive					71
Intellectual–unreflective, narrow				30	69
Polished, refined–crude, boorish	54	36	32		20
Imaginative–simple, direct					72

[a]Based on Passini & Norman (1966). (Copyright 1966 by the American Psychological Association. Adapted by permission of the publisher and author.)

[b]Factor loadings less than .30 are omitted.

between each of the dimensions that defines a factor and the hypothetical factor. The relatively high-positive values reported by Norman indicate that each of the dimensions is substantially related to one of the hypothetical factors.

Norman's five-factor solution of trait rating data has been replicated a number of times and may be considered as a generally acceptable solution (see, e.g., Tupes and Christal, 1961). The solution is not dependent on the use of a particular set of descriptors. Norman (1967) used a more comprehensive set of descriptive terms and obtained an essentially similar solution. Comparable factors have also been obtained in studies based on the factor analysis of self-report data (Norman and Goldberg, 1966).

In addition, similar structural solutions have been obtained in studies of trait ratings in the German and Dutch languages (Goldberg, 1982). Eysenck and Eysenck (1983) have published data on a factor analysis of a self-report measure of personality—the Eysenck Personality Questionnaire—that they have developed, derived from factor analyses of translations of the test into a variety of different languages. They favor a three-factor solution that, we shall see, is related to Norman's five-factor solution. Eysenck and Eysenck found that the factors that are derived from different translations of their test are remarkably congruent. This rather cursory survey of the literature on personality description suggests that there exists a limited set of factors that repeatedly emerge in factor analysis of varied sets of personality descriptors. The same descriptors tend to emerge from self-reports and from ratings, and the factors that emerge are, at least to some extent, cross-culturally, or perhaps more precisely, cross-linguistically general.

The existence of a relatively general structure of descriptive dimensions or factors derived from descriptions of personality may or may not tell us something important about personality. We can ask whether the factors derived from self-descriptions and rater's descriptions tell us anything about personality as distinct from the language we use to describe ourselves and others. Ordinary language and its structures may have little or nothing to do with an adequate descriptive taxonomy for personality. It is clear that the structure of relationships obtained is a property of our language. Norman's five-factor solution reported in Table 1.1 was obtained in a study in which individuals rated strangers. Passini and Norman (1966) found virtually identical factor solutions in studies in which they compared ratings for individuals who were acquainted with the raters and ratings of individuals with whom the rater had no previous acquaintance. The Passini and Norman study demonstrates that the structure of descriptive ratings is inherent in our use of language and will occur even when there is no basis for assigning a description to an individual.

D'Andrade (1965) asked subjects to rate the similarity of the meaning of the personality descriptors used in the Passini and Norman study. Table 1.2 presents the results of his factor analysis of the similarity ratings. An examination of Table 1.2 indicates that the factor structure obtained from ratings of the similarity of the meaning of personality descriptors is virtually identical to the factor structure obtained from an analysis of trait ratings of strangers. And, both structures are virtually identical to the structure obtained from an analysis of ratings of individuals with whom the rater is acquainted.

Ratings of strangers do have different properties than ratings of individuals with whom one is acquainted. The ratings of strangers exhibit lower interrater

Table 1.2

Factor Matrix of Similarity of Meaning Ratings[a]

Scales	I	II	III	IV	V
Extraversion					
Talkative–silent	86				
Frank, open–secretive	93				
Adventurous–cautious	76		37	−30	
Sociable–reclusive	85				
Agreeableness					
Good-natured–irritable		67	−38	−40	
Not jealous–jealous		87			
Mild, gentle–headstrong	−70	36			−41
Cooperative–negativistic	32	04		−43	−49
Conscientiousness					
Fussy, tidy–careless	−80		−48		
Responsible–undependable	−41		−90		
Scrupulous–unscrupulous			−72	43	
Persevering–quitting, fickle			−80	−36	
Emotional stability					
Poised–nervous, tense		50		−67	
Calm–anxious		47		−79	
Composed–excitable	−59	44		−52	
Not hypochondriacal–hypochondriacal				−87	
Culture					
Artistically sensitive–insensitive				36	−71
Intellectual–unreflective, narrow			−30		−90
Polished, refined–crude, boorish	−53				−72
Imaginative–simple, direct					40

[a]Based on D'Andrade (1965).
[b]Factor loadings less than .30 are omitted.

agreement than ratings of acquaintances. That is, different raters describing the same person will tend to assign the same descriptors to the person if they are acquainted with the person. However, different raters do not assign the same descriptors to a person when one is not acquainted with the person who is being rated. It is also the case that agreements between factor scores derived from self-report descriptions and from external raters exhibit better agreement when the external raters are acquainted with the person being rated than when they are not. Norman and Passini report correlations between self-report and observer ratings on the five dimensions of personality ranging from .27 to .54. The correlations between ratings of strangers and self-report ratings are, of course, close to zero.

The fact that general factor scores derived from self-report descriptions of personality and from external raters' descriptions of personality tend to agree provides, at most, a necessary, but not a sufficient, condition for the view that the derived factors are valid descriptions of personality as opposed to the language we use to describe persons. It could be argued that the agreements among raters and between raters and individuals' self-descriptions may be based on nothing more than socially arrived at agreements about how a person is to be described. We may come to learn how people whom we know describe themselves, and we may accord some degree of validity to those descriptions. We may, therefore, develop a consensus description of a person that extends from self-description to descriptions by a community of acquaintances. However, this consensus may not be accurate, and it may not be the basis for understanding the structure of personality.

From Language to Action: Trait Theory

Traits as Ambiguous Dispositions

Our discussion of the structure of ratings and self-reports has been self-consciously presented as a discussion of the structure of the language used to describe personality. Is it possible to understand personality by using the structure of the language used to describe personality? One can assume that the descriptive factors derived from ratings and self-report studies serve to identify critical aspects of an individual's personality. On this view, an individual could be described in terms of his or her score on each of the factors obtained in a comprehensive factor analysis of personality descriptors. If one accepted Norman's five-factor solution, then one could describe a person by assigning a score to the person on each of these five factors. In order to use scores on descriptive factors as actual personality descriptors, it is necessary to assume that such descriptors inform us about the characteristic behaviors and actions of a person. The transition between descriptive factors and actual personality descriptions is usually made by assuming that factors define what are called *personality traits*.

A trait may be defined as a hypothetical entity that accounts for the tendency of an individual to behave in a similar manner in diverse situations. There are several additions and refinements that can be made in our definition of traits. It should be noted that traits are *diposition* terms. That is, they refer to characteristics of entities that are not invariably manifested. The expression of the disposition is contingent upon the presence of some set of eliciting conditions. For example, to say of an object that it is soluble in water is not to say that one will find the object in a dissolved condition. It is only to say that the object, given appropriate circumstances, will dissolve. So, too, to say of a person that he or she is aggressive, is not to say that the person will invariably be aggressive but only that the person has a capacity, or disposition, to behave aggressively under certain circumstances. It should be noted that the circumstances that result in the actualization of trait dispositions are not specified in the development of a descriptive system based on the factor analysis of self-descriptions or of descriptions derived from ratings.

Trait descriptions of personality are ambiguous in several other ways. They imply that the *sine qua non* for the postulation of the existence of a trait is its expression in varied situations. However, a trait description per se does not indicate the situations in which the trait will be expressed; nor, for that matter, are the characteristic behaviors whose occurrence will be considered as manifestations of the traits specified. Traits obviously involve some kind of generalization or aggregation of behaviors observed in different settings, but the rules for the aggregation remain unspecified and difficult to derive from our ordinary understanding of the words that form the foundation for the trait concept. One could specify aggregation rules that emphasize the number of different situations in which behavior considered to be a manifestation of the trait occurred. Such a rule implies that individuals who had a high score on a trait would be likely to manifest the trait in many more situations than individuals who score low on the trait. Alternatively, the set of situations that is defined as appropriate for the elicitation of those behaviors that are considered to be manifestations of the trait may be fixed, but individuals might vary in the frequency with which they express the behavioral manifestations of the trait in those situations. This latter rule leaves unspecified the weightings to be assigned to the different situations in the determination of a trait score. Are all appropriate situations to be weighted equally? Are certain situations assumed to be prototypical for the trait in the sense that they constitute more defining and critical contexts for the manifestations of trait behavior such that the failure to manifest the trait in such a situation might be highly indicative of a low score on the trait?

The above rules for the specification of traits are based on the frequency and distribution of occurrence of behavioral manifestations of a trait. They do not include any indication of the intensity of trait expression. Perhaps individuals who score high on a trait do not exhibit the behaviors characteristic of the trait more often, but do so with greater intensity when they do exhibit the relevant behaviors. Thus, we may be inclined to assume that a person is aggressive if he or she behaves in an extremely violent manner on a limited number of occasions.

The above specifications for the aggregation rules defining the relationship between trait descriptions and behavior are not mutually exclusive. All of the above rules may be involved in some unspecified weighting of the relationship between behaviors and traits. Thus, individuals who express behavior indicative of a trait in many different situations, and in situations where the behavior is considered defining of the trait, and who express the relevant behavior often, and who do so with great intensity when they express the behavior may be assigned high scores on a trait.

Ambiguities inherent in the understanding of the relationship between traits and their specific behavioral manifestations make it difficult to interpret the meaning of any given trait score. Consider some of the possible different ways in which individuals with the same trait score might manifest the behaviors indicative of a trait. Individuals may express a trait with characteristically different behaviors. Thus, one individual who is rated aggressive might manifest that aggression in terms of violent acts, while another individual who is aggressive might express that aggression by means of verbal sarcasm. In addition, factor scores represent aggregate component ratings on a variety of individual dimensions. Two individuals with the same trait score might have quite different patterns of scores on the component dimensions that collectively define the factor. The characteristic situations that elicit behaviors considered as manifestations of the trait may be different. One person may behave assertively with respect to people of the same sex who are younger and inferior in social status, and another person may behave assertively with respect to older people of the opposite sex who have superior social status. It is apparent that trait descriptions of a person occupy a realm of amorphous abstraction. Such descriptions may leave us with a vague sense of understanding of a person but not with a detailed specification of the characteristic behaviors and actions of a person. One could, of course, qualify the assignment of a trait description by specifying for each trait the characteristic behavioral manifestations of the trait and the characteristic situations in which those behaviors are manifested. Such a proposal, however, destroys the elegant simplicity and closure attained in a personality theory derived from trait descriptions. It is a relatively simple matter to assign a score on each of several traits to an individual based on self-report measures or on ratings of that individual. The specification of the more complete description required to understand the manifestations of the trait is not easily accomplished, and clearly cannot be based on the simple expedient of asking a person to describe himself or herself on some carefully chosen set of dimensions.

The ambiguities inherent in the ordinary meanings of trait descriptions can be elaborated to form a critique of the trait concept that results in its total rejection. There are several different theoretically and empirically linked lines of criticism of trait theory. Critics of trait theory have often been impressed with the results of social psychological investigations that demonstrate that an individual's behavior in a particular situation may be determined by the characteristics of the situation rather than by any personal disposition of the individual to behave in a particular way. For example, in a classic experiment on obedience, Milgram (1974) asked subjects to deliver extremely harmful electric shocks to an individual each time the individual made a mistake in a learning situation. The subjects were required to increase the level of the shock to the point where they thought it was beyond the pain threshold of the victim. Actually, no shock was delivered at all. Milgram claims that his subjects were not aware of the deception. Milgram found that under certain conditions, virtually all of the subjects were obedient and were willing to deliver extremely painful shocks to a stranger who appeared to be in extreme distress merely because they were asked to do so by an authority figure. Milgram's study provides powerful evidence of the importance of situational influences on behavior.

Explanations of the behavior of individuals in Milgram's study by appeal to a personal disposition to be obedient that varied among different individuals would be incorrect for many individuals, because virtually all of his subjects exhibited obedience to the demands of the experimenter. The appeal to personal dispositions to explain behavior in social settings has been called the *fundamental attribution error* by social psychologists who believe that most of the variance in behavior in a given situation is to be understood by the characteristic influence of the situation, rather than by the influence of varying personal dispositions that individuals bring to the situation (see Jones, 1979; Jones and Nisbett, 1972).

The emphasis on the characteristics of the social situation in controlling behavior was also influenced by the application of principles of social learning theory to personality (Bandura and Walters, 1963; Mischel, 1973). Social learning theorists are interested in the kinds of rewards or, in the technical jargon, reinforcements that individuals receive to behave in certain ways in particular situations. They note that whether or not an individual receives reinforcements may be contingent on the precise characteristics of the situation in which the behavior is emitted. Consider an example cited by Bandura and Walters. They found that there is often a tendency for adolescent boys who are severely punished for the expression of aggression in the home to behave in a physically aggressive way outside the home. They rejected a Freudian theory of displacement of these findings in favor of a social learning interpretation that indicates that such boys are often rewarded for the expression of aggression outside of the home. Thus, the tendency to behave aggressively may be shaped by the reinforcement history of the individual whose behaviors develop discriminative responsiveness to the contexts in which a given behavior will be rewarded or punished. Social learning principles thus support a view of behavior that emphasizes its responsiveness to the influence of a particular situation. Such a view tends to be antithetical to a broad trait theory and replaces a trait conception of personality with a view of the idiosyncratic reinforcement history of an individual that results in his or her expression of a set of discrete responses tied to particular situations.

Traits as Linguistic Artifacts

The hostility of social learning theorists and social psychologists to a broad trait theory conception of personality was accompanied by a number of alleged empirical refutations of trait theory. Shweder (1975; 1977; 1982; Shweder and D'Andrade, 1980; see also D'Andrade, 1974) has argued that trait conceptions of behavior do not accurately reflect the actual structure of observed acts. He argues that trait conceptions introduce illusory correlation into independent behaviors that are, in part, dictated by the semantic characteristics of our language. Thus they are, in his view, inherent in the structure of the meanings of an ordinary language system that does not accurately reflect facts of human action.

Shweder has presented an analysis of several sets of data in support of his assertion. In his studies Shweder obtains direct ratings of actual behavior. For example, raters are asked to observe a videotape of an actual behavioral interaction. The rater is required to keep a frequency count of actual behaviors. The raters are provided with a set of categories or descriptors that are assumed to serve as an adequate taxonomy for the exhaustive classification of each behavioral occurrence. The raters must assign each behavior to a particular category. Each category of behavior that is rated may be assigned a frequency score indicating the number of times it has occurred. These frequency scores may be conceived of as a record of actual behavior. The correlation between any two categories of behavior may be obtained if such records exist for a number of different individuals. Correlations among all possible pairs of categories may be obtained, and these correlations may be placed in a matrix of rows and columns in which the row and column headings refer to the behavior categories. The cell entries are the correlation values for any pair of categories. Let us call this the *behavior matrix*.

A second matrix of correlations with the same row and column labels can be obtained by asking raters to assign a rating on each category of behavior to the individuals whose behavior they have observed and rated in terms of frequency counts. This matrix of correlations corresponds to the typical trait rating matrix. Trait ratings are not ratings of specific behaviors. They are ratings of categories of behavior that refer in unspecified ways to the behaviors that are their constituents. This matrix is based on the recall or memory for specific actions. This second matrix may be called the *trait memory matrix*.

A third matrix with the same row and column labels may be obtained by asking subjects to rate the similarity of meaning of categories. Such a matrix— the *similarity of meanings matrix*—provides information about the meaning subjects assign to a category in terms of how similar or different they think its meaning is to other categories.

This procedure provides one with three different matrices of correlations where each matrix has identical row and column labels. It is possible to obtain a measure (actually a correlation) of the relationship between each pair of matrices. This is done by correlating the values of the correlations in each pair of matrices. Shweder has analyzed data, obtained in several different studies, that permit an analysis of the similarity of the three matrices described above. He finds that the correlation between the trait memory matrices and the similarity of meanings matrices are quite high and have an average value of .75. When individuals rate other individuals after observing their actions, they tend to assign ratings to them that reflect the assumed similarity in meanings of the descriptions. Thus, if raters assert that *dominance* is similar in meaning to *aggression,* they are likely to rate a person as aggressive if they rate the person as dominant.

The correlations between the actual behavior matrices and the trait memory matrices, and between the actual behavior matrices and the similarity of meaning matrices, are much lower. The average correlations are .25 and .26, respectively. Thus, trait ratings and the similarity of meanings assigned to traits are not closely related to the frequency of occurrence of actual behaviors.

Shweder argues that these results indicate that trait ratings that are inevitably based on recollections of the behavior of an individual who is being rated reflect the distorting influence of a language that is used to describe an individual's actions. This linguistic distortion introduces an ''illusory'' correlation and an artificial structure into the relationships among personality descriptors. Thus, in his view, traits are as much, or perhaps even more, a result of the structure of our language as they are of the actual relationships that exist among human actions. Shweder's analysis provides a critique of the trait concept that deals with very fundamental issues. If Shweder's analysis is correct, then it is likely that a personality theory based on traits contains fundamental errors and embodies semantically induced distortion at its very foundation.

Romer and Revelle (1984) have reported data that suggest that Shweder's analysis embodies a methodological flaw. Shweder's behavior matrix is assumed to represent an actual record of behavior that is free of linguistically induced distortions. Romer and Revelle indicate that the data-recording procedures used by Shweder and D'Andrade involve a particular choice of response format in which each behavior must be assigned to one and only one category. Thus, semantic relationships with respect to the meanings of a given behavior are excluded from their original behavior-encoding scheme. This procedure is, on reflection, quite arbitrary. A given behavior may have a multiplicity of relationships to a variety of other categories. Consider an example. Two individuals are talking, and one individual interrupts the second before the second person has a chance to complete his or her utterance. It is possible to imagine that a rater might describe the behavior of the person who interrupts the speech of a second person as domineering, if forced to choose a single category description. However, if given an opportunity to assign a multiplicity of ratings to the behavior, the rater might well be inclined to view the behavior as being indicative, at least to some extent, of impulsivity and insensitivity, and he or she would be rather unlikely to rate the behavior as being indicative of a shy and introverted dimension of personality. This example suggests that a single category rating of a behavior may not exhaust the meaning of a rating. The example further suggests that there is rarely a one–to–one relationship between a trait and any single behavioral manifestation of the trait. Ordinary social behavior may have a multiplicity of meanings, and each behavior may permit us to perform inferences about several different trait dimensions (see Block, Weiss, and Thorne, 1979).

Romer and Revelle report the results of a study in which they varied the coding procedures used by individuals to rate behaviors. They presented raters with descriptions of actions, and in one condition, they asked them to assign each action to a single descriptive category that best described the behavior. This condition replicates the behavior coding procedure used by Shweder. In a second condition they asked their raters to rate each behavioral event on each of the descriptive categories. Following the procedures used by Shweder, they also obtained trait memory ratings and similarity of meaning ratings. They replicated Shweder's results for the conditions in which behavior ratings were restricted to a single best category. That is, the trait memory matrix correlated highly with the similarity of meanings matrix ($r = .67$), and both of these matrices had lower correlations with the rated behavior matrix ($r = .40$ and $r = .45$). However, in the condition in which raters were required to assign a rating to each category for each behavior, the results were quite different. The correlation between the trait memory matrix and the similarity of meanings matrix ($r = .63$) was actually lower than the other two correlations ($r = .71$ and $.91$). Romer and Revelle's data suggest that Shweder's results are dependent on an arbitrary method of encoding data that artificially restricts the meaning of a given behavior. If we permit our complete understanding of the meaning of a behavior to be reflected in the original codings of a behavior, there is no evidence for a memory-induced semantic distortion in trait ratings. Romer and Revelle's analysis suggests that behavior may be viewed as containing a complex set of implications and that the notion of a theoretically denuded behavior frequency count of social actions involving an all-or-none categorical meaning for each observable behavior is artificial and arbitrary.

It may very well be the case that an understanding of the structures of meaning implied by ordinary social actions will require the development of a traitlike categorical structure that may be isomorphic with current schemes for trait categorization. Whether the relationship between a language descriptive of traits and a language descriptive of the meaning of individual social acts is one of identity or isomorphism cannot be confidently determined without additional research. It does appear reasonable to suggest, however, that semantic relationships will be required to construct an adequate language for the description of individual behavioral acts.

Situational Specificity and Behavioral Aggregation

Although the semantic-distortion objection to traits may be refuted, it is still possible that trait theory embodies an empirically false assumption with respect to the generality of behavior across varied situations. Recall that social learning approaches to personality emphasize the importance of reinforcement histories that lead to discriminative distinction among social situations. Such views emphasize the patterning of responsiveness to varied situations rather than the disposition to exhibit comparable behavior across situations. Mischel (1968, 1973) has been the most influential critic of the trait concept. His views were expressed in a book written in 1968 in which he argued that trait conceptions were generally incapable of predicting individual behaviors. He noted that most attempts at predicting particular behavioral actions from trait scores were rarely successful. And he coined the term "personality coefficient" to describe the typical correlation of .3 or less that was usually obtained in various attempts to predict measures of behavior from trait ratings. Because the magnitude of a correlation in terms of the percentage of variance of the predicted event that may be accounted for is defined by the square of the value of r, Mischel's analysis implies that personality traits rarely account for more than 10% of the variance of behavioral events. Mischel's critique of the trait concept was actually a revival of a traditional criticism of trait theory presented by Hartshorne and May (1928, 1929). They had studied children's responses to various situations in which it was possible to behave dishonestly. They noted that a child's tendency to exhibit dishonest behavior in one setting rarely predicted the child's tendency to behave in a dishonest way in another setting. The correlations among different situations in which dishonesty might be assessed were generally positive but quite low—for the most part below .2. They concluded on the basis of their research that it was a mistake to think of children as being honest or dishonest to some degree. They argued that the trait or personal dispositional analysis of dishonesty was mistaken. They preferred to describe the particular situations in which a child behaved in an honest or dishonest manner.

Mischel's critique of trait theory initiated considerable controversy. Epstein (1977, 1979a, 1979b, 1983a, 1983b, 1983c, 1983d) argued that Mischel's analysis of the predictability of behavior from traits was not convincing because of a fundamental statistical flaw inherent in his analysis. Epstein argued that a single measure of behavior was unlikely to provide an accurate index of an individual's behavior in a particular situation. Consider an example: I might want to obtain a measure of an individual's punctuality, and I might note whether an individual arrives on time or is late for some engagement—say a meeting of a faculty committee on which a particular professor serves as a member. The professor's behavior on a single occasion might not be indicative of her behavior in that situation on other occasions or, still less, of a general tendency to be punctual. Perhaps our mythical professor who is almost invariably punctual falls on the way to the meeting, injures herself and requires medical attention, and, as a result, arrives late. Or, with respect to a general tendency to punctuality, our professor might have a class that ends just before the time set for her committee meeting and is thus inevitably late for each meeting. This behavior might well be uncharacteristic of a general tendency to be punctual in other situations. This example points to an almost self-evident conclusion. One cannot assume that the behavior exhibited by a person in a given situation is characteristic of the behavior of that individual in the same or other related situations.

Epstein developed the logic of this objection. He noted that attempts to characterize what was typical of an individual's behavior in a single situation were analogous to trying to assess personality by a single-item test. There is a branch of statistical psychology called psychometrics that is concerned with the theory of measurement of individual differences. According to classical models of test theory, any measure may contain both error (i.e., random and unsystematic variations) and systematic true-score variance. The extent to which a measure contains true-score variance may be defined by a correlational statistic that is a reliability coefficient. The reliability of a single observation is generally low. One can increase the reliability (i.e., the extent to which measures provide an estimate that has less error variance) by aggregating (i.e., averaging) multiple observations. As long as each item or measure has some true-score variance, the true-score variance of the aggregate will increase as the number of items or measures increases. In fact, given a set of observations with a known reliability, the reliability of any increased set of observations with comparable individual reliabilities can be calculated by a formula called the Spearman–Brown prophecy formula. Epstein noted that the use of a single item to predict a single behavioral outcome violated classical principles of psychometrics. He advocated the use of an aggregating procedure involving multiple observations of the same behavior of the same individuals in order to obtain reliable measures of an individual's tendency to behave in a particular way in a particular situation.

Epstein provided empirical data in support of the principle of aggregation. In one of his initial studies (Epstein, 1977), he asked his subjects to keep a record of positive and negative emotional experiences each day for several weeks. The subjects assigned a daily positive and negative rating to each of their experiences. The correlations between the ratings assigned on any pair of days were quite low—generally below .20. However, the correlations for aggregated ratings were substantially higher. For example, Epstein averaged (i.e., obtained the mean rating) all of the ratings for each subject's most pleasant experience on all even days. He obtained a comparable average for all odd days. The correlation for mean pleasantness ratings on odd days with the mean ratings of pleasantness on even days was .81. Epstein's findings suggest that it is difficult to predict a measure of behavior based on a single behavioral observation because such measures are inherently unreliable. We cannot decide whether a person has the disposition to report intensely pleasant experiences by asking that individual to provide a single report about his or her most pleasant experience on a single day. However, if we ask an individual to provide ratings of his or her experiences on several occasions, an aggregated index of the pleasantness of the ratings is likely to be highly predictive of any other aggregated ratings of the pleasantness of that individual's experiences. Thus we would be entitled to assert that a person has a disposition to report pleasant experiences. The principle of aggregation is quite robust, and there are numerous examples in the personality literature demonstrating that measures of an individual's aggregate behavior predict an independent measure of an individual's aggregate behavior in the same situation (Rushton, Brainerd, and Pressley, 1983).

Epstein's analysis served to change the nature of the debate surrounding the trait concept. Mischel and Peake (1982) reported the results of a relatively large-scale analysis of the behavior of a group of college students attending Carelton College. They obtained a variety of measures of the behavior of individuals in different social settings over a variety of occasions. They presented an analysis of data on the trait of conscientiousness. They used 19 different measures of conscientiousness based on characteristics of the dispositions that were suggested by students. The behavioral measures of the dispositions included data on class attendance, study seminar attendance, neatness of assignments, and punctuality of handing in assignments. They were able to obtain aggregate measures for each of these alleged behavioral manifestations of conscientiousness. They had from 2 to 12 measures of each of the alleged behavioral manifestations of the trait.

Mischel and Peake's analysis of these data attempted to demonstrate that the aggregation principle did not provide a basis for the resurrection of the trait concept. They accepted Epstein's reasoning with respect to the benefits of aggregation for repeated observations of the same behavior in the same situation. They conceded that behavior could exhibit regularities when observed over many occasions. However, they argued that the demonstration of regularity and generality over time (i.e., longitudinal consistency of behavior of a given individual) had little or nothing to do with the essential issue in the debate—namely, the consistency of behavior across situations. They argued that an individual might tend to behave in the same way in the same situation but that his or her characteristic behaviors did not provide one with an adequate basis to predict the individual's behavior in a different situation that was presumed to reflect the same underlying trait or personal disposition. Behavior was temporally invariant and situationally variable. They found average correlations of the same behavior based on a single occasion correlated with the same behavior on another occasion .29. Aggregate measures of the same behavior correlated with other aggregates of the same behavior .65—demonstrating the typical benefits of aggregation. However, when they analyzed correlations involving observations of different behavioral manifestations of conscientiousness, the benefits of aggregation were far less apparent. They reported that the average correlation across situations for two single observations of behavior was .08. When they aggregated observations over the same situation and then correlated two aggregated measures of behavior in different situations, they obtained average correlations of .13. They argued that even when aggregation was used to obtain a more reliable estimate of an individual's characteristic behavior in a situation, there was little evidence that the behavior was related to the characteristic behavior of the same individual in a different situation, even though both situations were assumed to afford adequate measures of the same disposition.

The Mischel and Peake paper initiated considerable criticism and countercriticism (Bem, 1983; Conley, 1984a; Epstein, 1983b; Funder, 1983; Jackson and Paunonen, 1985; Mischel and Peake, 1983; Peake and Mischel, 1984).

Among the various issues that have been discussed, I find two of particular importance. Mischel and Peake were criticized for failing to aggregate behavior across situations. The average correlation of aggregated behavior in a single situation with a measure of aggregated behavior in another situation of .13 represents a relationship between pairs of situations. However, if the 19 situations they studied each represents an appropriate setting for the manifestation of the disposition, a more valid index of the underlying disposition might be obtained by aggregating behavioral measures across situations. Mischel and Peake report that such aggregated measures would yield correlations of .65. This finding appears to indicate that measures of behavior that are aggregated across situations can predict a different set of behaviors for which an aggregated measure could be obtained. Mischel and Peake object to this procedure. They argue that such aggregations are meaningless and distort the actual findings that demonstrate that even aggregated measures that have substantial reliability do not correlate highly across situations.

Actually, at this level, the debate is no longer about substantive issues but about the level of analysis one finds most appropriate for the study of personality. The logic of trait descriptions renders an aggregation across situations as perfectly rational and, indeed, even required by the meaning of the construct that is being assessed. By contrast, if one assumes that what is important about personality is the distinctive pattern of the expression of dispositional characteristics in different settings, then clearly it would be folly to obtain a measure that is aggregated across situations. Clearly, the issue of what constitutes an appropriate aggregation cannot be decided without examining additional sources of data that demonstrate the theoretical utility of different ways of measuring personality.

While the issue of appropriate aggregations is, theoretically, substantive rather than methodological, there is a more fundamental objection to the Mischel and Peake analysis that addresses the adequacy of their data base. Mischel and Peake do not provide an explicit rationale for the particular situational measures of conscientiousness they use. They rely solely on the opinions of a group of undergraduates to define the appropriate measures of conscientiousness. They do not have an explicit theory of the personal disposition they are measuring. In the absence of an explicit theoretical rationale for the development of measures, it is usually considered necessary to engage in a process of empirical exploration in order to develop an appropriate measure. Psychometric theory again provides explicit rationales and methods for the development of adequate measures of a disposition.

One can consider each of the 19 behavioral situations as a potential item to be included in a test of conscientiousness. There are a variety of item analysis procedures based on an examination of the relationships among the items. The empircal relationships among items provides the test constructor with a basis for deciding to include, or to exclude, the item. If a particular item is not related to other items, its inclusion in a test merely adds an error component. Factor analysis of item responses provides a basis for deciding which items to include and which items to exclude from the test.

Jackson and Paunonen (1985) have reanalyzed the Mischel and Peake data with particular emphasis on the adequacy of the 19-item measure of conscientiousness. A factor analysis of the 19 items indicates that the items do not form a unidimensional set. They note that there are different kinds of items included in the set. One group of behavioral items deals with what may be called studiousness and includes measures, such as the number of class readings completed, class attendance, and punctuality in turning in assignments. A second cluster of items deals with measures of neatness in different contexts. The second cluster of items is essentially uncorrelated with the first cluster. Jackson and Paunonen factor analyzed the 19 aggregated behavioral items and found one factor on which 12 of the items loaded. The average of the correlations among the 12 items with the highest loadings on the factor was .24. It is possible to correct correlations for the unreliability or error variance contained in each of the scores that enter into the correlation. This is called a correction for attenuation, and such corrected correlations may be thought of as the hypothetical correlation between scores that are without error. Corrections for attenuation of the average correlation value of .24 leads to a value of .40, suggesting some degree of cross-situational generality.

The remaining 7 items in the set of 19 correlated with items in the first set close to .00. This empirical analysis of the items indicates that the students' intuitions about the items to be included in a test of conscientiousness were not well founded. The flaws in the measurement of conscientiousness suggest that Mischel and Peake's data analysis was inappropriate and cannot be used as a basis for reaching a generalization about the cross-situational generality of personal dispositions. No trait theorist would assume that a personality disposition is manifested in any and all situations or that traits will exhibit cross-situational consistencies across an ill-chosen set of behavioral situations. In fact, Jackson and Paunonen's analysis suggests that with appropriate empirical refinement, a 12-item measure of conscientiousness derived from Mischel and Peake's data would have very substantial reliability and could be used to predict both individual and aggregated cross-situational measures of conscientiousness.

Jackson and Paunonen indicate that Mischel and Peake collected data that could be used to provide additional information about the relationship between trait ratings and behaviors, although they did not report their data in a form that would permit one to perform these analyses. Mischel and Peake obtained measures of self-ratings, peer ratings, and parent ratings on the trait of conscientiousness. They report that these several ratings exhibit positive relationships with an average correlation of .52 (see Peake, 1982). However, they do not present the relationships among the various trait ratings or from a composite or aggregation of the trait ratings and an aggregated index of their behavioral measures. The Jackson and Paunonen analysis suggests that the appropriate analysis required to determine how trait ratings relate to behavior would involve obtaining the correlations between trait ratings and a composite or aggregated score on the 12-item measure of conscientiousness.

Although Mischel and Peake do not report the appropriate data required for an investigation of the relationships between trait ratings and behavior, other extant analyses provide direct information about this issue. Moscowitz and Schwarz (1982; Moscowitz, 1982) have reported an appropriate analysis. They obtained behavior ratings for a group of children attending a nursery school on five different behaviors that were assumed to be indicative of dominance. They found that aggregating over occasions increased the reliability of the observations. The average correlations based on 1 week's observations were .34. Aggregating observations for the 8-week period increased the average reliability of each of the behaviors to .76. They also noted that the five separate behaviors assumed to be indicative of dominance were themselves related. In order to demonstrate this relationship, Moscowitz obtained all possible sets of averages of four aggregated behavioral measures and used that to predict each of the excluded aggregated behavioral measures. She obtained average correlations of .59, indicating that an aggregate measure of four different behaviors may be used to predict with considerable accuracy the remaining behavioral index. Each of the aggregated behavioral measures used by Moscowitz had less than perfect reliability, and each was based on a limited set of observations. It would not be inappropriate to correct the obtained average correlation value of .59 for the unreliability of measurement inherent in each of the measures. This correction would, of necessity, increase the magnitude of the correlation. Moscowitz's data suggest that there is considerable cross-situational consistency in the tendency to behave in a dominant way in the different behavioral manifestations of the disposition she studied.

Moscowitz also collected data providing information about the validity of the trait ratings of dominance. She obtained ratings of the dominance of each child in her study from their teachers and other knowledgeable informants. She obtained a correlation of .59 between teachers' ratings and her aggregated behavioral measure of dominance. These data provide direct evidence, at least for this particular context, that trait ratings may be used to predict relevant social behavior of groups of individuals.

The results reported by Moscowitz are not anomalous. Other studies in the literature indicate that frequency counts of aggregated measures of different behavior are substantially related to trait ratings. For example, Small, Zeldin, and Savin-Williams (1983) observed the behaviors of four different groups of adolescents in a wilderness camping situation that lasted for 3 or 4 weeks. They defined five behavioral acts that they assumed were indicative of what they called prosocial behavior—a trait of helping or assisting others. And they defined eight behavioral acts that they assumed were indicative of the tendency to behave in a dominant fashion. The average correlations among the set of alleged behavioral manifestations of the same underlying disposition in the four groups studied ranged from .59 to .83 for the prosocial or helpfulness disposition and from .42 to .85 for the dominance disposition. Their analyses indicated that individuals tended to behave in a similar manner over this brief time period in this setting and that the specific behaviors that were assumed to reflect the underlying trait disposition were substantially related. Thus, if a person scored high on a single behavioral manifestation of prosocial behavior, it was likely to be found that the person would score high on a different behavioral manifestation of prosocial behavior.

The aggregated behavioral indices of prosocial and dominance behaviors were substantially correlated with the trait ratings made by a camper's peers. The correlations between peer ratings and aggregated behavioral measures of prosocial and dominance behaviors were .73 and .85, respectively. These data provide clear support for the notion that peer trait ratings are related to the actual behavior of individuals.

Conclusion: Behavior and Traits

This brief review of studies relating trait ratings to frequency counts of behavior establishes that there are relationships between behaviors and ratings and that trait ratings do relate, at least in some contexts, to measures of behavior that are aggregated over different situations. However, this general conclusion does not provide an explication of the relationship between traits and behaviors. Trait theory has clearly evolved from an analysis of self-report and observer ratings. Could one derive personality dimensions from observations of behavior? Would a theory of personality derived from behavioral observations lead to the development of a set of dimensions that are analogous to the factor analytically derived dimension of personality? In what follows, I will try to address these issues in greater depth.

Heteromethod Aggregation

There is one approach to the use of behavioral measures of personality dimensions that provides a simple—and possibly a simplistic—solution to the question. We can assume that all procedures for the measurement of a person are fraught with error. Individuals may, for a variety of reasons, distort self-reports. They may understand questions asked them on an inventory in an idiosyncratic, and possibly incorrect, manner. They may choose to distort their reports about themselves in order to present themselves in a particularly favorable or unfavorable light. Even where individuals are rating themselves in a truthful way, they may provide incorrect information because their beliefs about their own behaviors are incorrect or even distorted for defensive reasons. A person may believe that he or she is kind and considerate, yet observers of another person may detect an underlying lack of concern and cruelty in the person's social actions of which the person may not be aware. We are not always knowledgeable with respect to the social impact of our own behaviors.

Just as self-reports of behavior may be less than accurate, any individual asked to rate a person's behavior may provide an inadequate rating for any of several reasons. The rater may have observed the person being rated in a limited number of contexts and thus may provide ratings that do not adequately summarize the behavior of an individual over all relevant social contexts. The rater may also fail to understand the meaning of the personality dimension being rated, or assign an idiosyncratic meaning to the dimension. In addition, the rater may assign characteristics to the ratee that are reflective of the particular personality structure of the rater rather than the personality structure of the ratee. For example, a rater who is extremely extroverted may tend to see everyone else as been less extroverted than he or she is and, as a result, tend to indiscriminately assign introverted ratings to other individuals. Or, perhaps giving credence to the Freudian concept of projection, a rater may assign undesirable characteristics to a ratee that are actually possessed by the rater but are, for defensive reasons, not in the rater's awareness. Thus, a rater who is unconsciously hostile might, on this notion, defend against his or her hostility by projection, that is by assigning the trait of hostility to others.

This brief gloss on the errors of personality ratings is not meant to be exhaustive or scholarly. Undoubtedly some or all of these distortions occur as well as many others. This discussion of errors in ratings leads to a simple conclusion. All measurement of an individual's personal characteristics is subject to error.

Behavioral observations related to personality also have sources of error inherent in them. Observers may not agree about the occurrence of a particular behavior. Observers may relate behaviors to any of several trait-related categories, and the agreement about the appropriate trait categories may be less than perfect. It is difficult, if not impossible, to sample all of the relevant behavioral contexts in which a trait may be exhibited. The behavior of individuals in a given context may be subject to the influence of hidden exogenous variables that are not under experimental control. For example, a room may be poorly ventilated, and the effects of the less-than-perfect atmosphere may lead individuals to become irritable and uncomfortable—thus changing their characteristic social behavior. The personality of the experimenters may influence the way in which experimental instructions are given to subjects, and this might influence their characteristic behavior and might have different effects on different individuals. Examples of the ways in which any given behavior may be influenced by exogenous variables that change the meaning of the behavior and influence both the ability to observe the same behavior in the same situation again and to relate the behavior to a particular trait may be endlessly multiplied. Any given behavioral observation is subject to a variety of effects that render its interpretation as a measure of a particular trait suspect.

There is an additional problem in the use of behavioral measures of personality. What behavior will be observed? How does one segment the naturally occurring stream of behavior into appropriate units of observation? Consider a simple example. Skinner's (1938) studies of operant behavior in the rat were based on a behavioral measure that involved the pressing of a bar with a given level of force sufficient to move the bar a given distance, leading to a change in a microswitch and the recording of a particular bar press. The level of force required to depress the bar and record a response was perfectly arbitrary and was dictated solely by the characteristics of the apparatus Skinner designed to measure the frequency of bar pressing. Moreover, Skinner made a quite conscious decision to ignore the ways in which the bar was depressed. Thus, typically, no record is kept of whether the rat leaned on the bar, swatted it with one paw, or used its teeth to depress the bar. All responses of a given level of force sufficient to depress the bar are considered equivalent members of the class. Even the decision to study the frequency of occurrence of bar-pressing behavior, however bar pressing is defined, is arbitrary. One could, for example, have chosen to study not the frequency of occurrence of a bar press, but the force with which a particular response is emitted (see Notterman, 1959). Actually, there are lawlike relationships between the force of a response and the occurrence of reinforcements or rewards—the force of the response tends to decrease over reinforced trials, while the probability of a response increases. In addition, the measurement of the force of an individual response involves several possible alternatives. One can, for example, measure the peak force of the response or the total effort expended in a response, which involves an integration of the force of the response over its duration. This brief excursion into the measurement of responses in a Skinner box only begins to sketch out some of the complexities of response measurement, even in a context as limited as a rat bar pressing in a Skinner box. The import of the example for the measurement of behavior in social contexts that may be relevant to the development of a theory of personality appears self-evident. It demonstrates that the term *behavior* is an undifferentiated and undefined notion. It is by no means obvious what behaviors should be measured, how they should be measured, and in what contexts they should be studied in order to understand individual differences in personality. The complexities in the measurement of social situations undoubtedly exceed those involved in the measurement of a rat's responses in a Skinner box.

This analysis suggests that all available procedures for the measurement of personality are inadequate. Self-reports, behaviors of various kinds including psychophysiological indices, and ratings are all subject to a variety of overlapping and distinct distortions. Given this analysis, the simple solution to the problem of the relation between trait ratings and behavior is to aggregate across methods of measurement on the assumption that the aggregated score based on different methods of measurement—a heteromethod measure—is likely to involve the removal of errors of measurement that are peculiar or idiosyncratic with respect to each method and to yield, at the aggregate level, a measure of a trait disposition that is more accurate and contains a smaller amount of error than any of its constituents. Thus, the best estimate of a person's score on a trait dimension could, on this analysis, be obtained by aggregating self-report ratings, ratings by several knowledgeable informants, and aggregated measures of behavior in several different contexts.

This approach also provides us with a specification of the meaning of a particular trait dimension with respect to its relationships to behaviors and trait ratings. A trait is not to be understood as referring exclusively either to behavior or to a rating. Rather, it is that entity that must be postulated to account for the commonalities that extend over ratings and behaviors. Of course, ratings themselves are to be understood as a complex judgment of the meaning of particular behavioral acts observed by the self or another. Although the rules permitting one to specify the exact relationships between observed behaviors and trait ratings are not specified or, indeed, may not be specifiable, trait ratings have an ultimate behavioral referent. Thus, the commonality between behavior and trait that defines the heteromethod aggregated trait score is compatible with our original definition of a trait as a disposition to behave in a similar way in different situations.

Behavioral Measures of Traits: Intelligence and the Theory of g

The use of a heteromethod aggregation procedure to obtain a general trait measure does not provide a clear analysis of the relationship between traits and behaviors. Rather, this procedure dissolves the issue by a methodological fiat. An alternative approach exists. One could, in principle, develop measures of traits by the observation of an individual's behavior on repeated occasions in diverse settings. Such research has, on occasion, been conducted. Mischel and Peake's research and the Moscowitz studies are both relevant examples. However, such a strategy has rarely been systematically pursued because of the cost and difficulty of obtaining a representative sample of an individual's behavior in many different settings and occasions. This procedure has been pursued for over 100 years, however, in research on the trait of intelligence, and we can look to this body of research to explicate the characteristics of a behaviorally based measure of a human trait. We shall explore analogies between research on the traits of intelligence and personality traits at several different places in this manuscript.

Research on intelligence (starting from its beginnings in the latter half of the nineteenth century with Galton's attempts to measure individual differences in sensory acuity) has always relied on behavioral measures rather than ratings (Galton, 1883). Intelligence tests, in contrast to personality tests, are not based on ratings. They do not ask an individual if he or she has behaved in an intelligent fashion in a particular setting. An individual is not, for example, asked to rate his or her vocabulary or someone else's vocabulary. One is able to derive a measure of an individual's vocabulary by providing a set of behavioral tests in which an individual is required to provide a correct definition for a word. All tests of intelligence involve the observation of behavioral responses of an individual to a standardized set of situations or tasks designed to sample an individual's intellectual functioning.

An explicit rationale for the definition of intelligence as a general trait was presented in 1904 by Spearman. In 1904 Spearman presented his two-factor theory of intelligence according to which all behavioral measures of intelligence had two components called g and s. General intelligence, or g, was that component of intelligence that was present in all possible measures of intelligence; s was a component of tests of intelligence that was present in each behavioral index of intelligence and was present only in that particular measure. One may think of s as error variance and g as true-score variance for the measurement of intelligence. Spearman's two-factor theory of intelligence is really a one-factor theory of intelligence.

Spearman's theory provides an explicit rationale for the consideration of intelligence as a trait. If Spearman's theory is correct, every measure of intelligence will be positively correlated with every other measure of intelligence, and the value of the expected correlation between any two measures of intelligence will be solely determined by the amount of g that they share in common. Measures of intelligence assumed to have high amounts of g will correlate with each other more than measures of intelligence with relatively low levels of g. Since s is specific to each measure, it does not contribute to the correlation between measures of intelligence.

Since Spearman's theory implies that all possible measures of intelligence are positively correlated, it is obvious that the theory assumes that intelligence is a trait that leads individuals to behave in a similar way in an indefinitely large number of situations. Spearman's theory and the research that has followed has not provided a clear definition of the boundary between tasks that are assumed to be measures of general intelligence and tasks that are not. Thus the precise boundaries of the situations that serve as elicitors of the disposition to behave intelligently are not known. However, the possible set of such situations is indefinitely large and may be assumed to comprise a rather heterogeneous set of behaviors including, among others, the ability to define words on a vocabulary test, to memorize digits and repeat them in backward order, to solve spatial reasoning problems, and to solve numerical problems.

It is interesting to note that Spearman's theory provides a definition of the trait of general intelligence that assigns a meaning to the trait that is partially independent of the behavioral manifestations of the trait. One may define g as a hypothetical entity that accounts for the positive relationship between all possible measures of intelligence, including measures not yet devised. As such, g contains meanings that transcend, and are not reducible to, any of its behavioral manifestations; g is independent of scores on tests of intelligence. One might develop an analogous argument for personality traits. Impulsivity may be defined as a tendency to behave in an impulsive way in many different situations, including those that an individual has not encountered. Thus, even a trait measure that is closely tied to specific behavioral referents, rather than ratings or judgments, will nevertheless contain meanings that transcend the specific behavioral measures and manifestations of the trait.

Spearman's theory implies that all measures of intelligence are not equivalent. Measures of intelligence differ with respect to the ratio of g and s they contain. One could say that measures of intelligence that contain high levels of g will be better measures than those that contain lower levels of g. The theory implies that an optimal measure of intelligence will be one whose individual constituents contain items or subtests that are highly saturated with g. Although Spearman's theory implies that all measures of intelligence measure one thing, the theory does not imply that all measures of intelligence are interchangeable or equivalent measures of g. It is possible to provide at least some empirical support for Spearman's view that tests or subtests of intelligence may differ in their g content. For example, among the subtests included in Wechsler's test of intelligence is a test called digit–symbol substitution. For this test subjects are presented with a row of symbols, and a digit is presented below each symbol. They are then given rows of symbols without digits and are required to write the appropriate digit below each symbol. Performance is measured by the number of correct digits that are written in a period of time. The test does relate to other subtests and hence may be considered to be, in part, a measure of g. However, factor analyses of the Wechsler tests (see Jensen, 1985) have consistently found that the digit–symbol test has relatively low loadings on the general factor that defines commonalities across the subtests. Thus, one can say that it is a relatively poor measure of g.

A similar analysis can be made of the extent to which various situations are related to personality traits. Hampson (1982) and Mischel (1979) have emphasized the notion that the situations that may serve to define a particular trait may form what is called a *fuzzy* set. That is, the set of behaviors or behaviors in particular contexts that express the trait may not be invariant across individuals. However, certain behavioral manifestations may be construed as being more prototypical or characteristic of the trait than others. Just as we are inclined to think of a robin as a more prototypical bird than a turkey, we may be inclined to think of certain expressions of a trait as more prototypical than others. One way of interpreting the concept of prototypicality for personality traits is to suggest that behavioral settings may have differential loadings on a factor that serves to specify the meaning of the trait in terms of commonalities in behaviors across situations. Variations in behavior in those situations that are found to have consistently low loadings on a trait factor are only weakly determinative of an individual's trait score. Variations in behavior in those situations with high trait loadings are more determinative of an individual's trait score. This latter class of situations may be described as being prototypical for the trait.

Is Spearman's theory correct? We are in a position to answer this question with some precision. An appropriate initial answer to the question is that the theory is only approximately correct. The theory is supported in a general way by the finding that all items on a test of intelligence, despite their superficial heterogeneity of form, tend to correlate positively. Item correlations are generally between .10 and .20 (Brody, 1985b; Brody and Brody, 1976; Green, 1978; Jensen, 1980). Moreover, test scores based on an aggregate score for several situationally homogeneous items—for example, a vocabulary test—will correlate positively, and often substantially, with the aggregated scores of items of a different kind—for example, memory for digits repeated backward. The correlations between such homogeneous tests in a representative sample of individuals is not atypically found to be between .5 and .6. Further, a composite measure of several different types of homogeneous aggregated subtests can be used to predict a remaining aggregated test score with no obvious overlap in content.

Paradoxically, one of the most convincing sources of data in support of the notion of general intelligence is contained in the extensive research on patterns of relationships among tests of intelligence presented by Spearman's strongest critic—Guilford (1964, 1967; Guilford and Hoepfner, 1971). Guilford wished to replace g with a theory of intelligence that postulated the existence of more than 100 independent factors. He developed a variety of tests designed to measure these factors and performed many factor analyses of tests in the intellectual domain. He found that 90% of the correlations among his tests were positive. This figure is misleading for three reasons. First, some of Guilford's tests had low reliability and could not correlate highly with any other measure. Second, Guilford often used samples of individuals who were selected for high intelligence—for example cadets in officer's training in the military. Such a group of individuals who tend to be relatively equivalent in their score on intelligence, when given a battery of tests, will, of necessity exhibit relatively low correlations among different measure of the trait for which they have relatively homogeneous scores. Third, some of Guilford's tests included attempts to measure aspects of intelligence that are of questionable relevance to a construct roughly defined as measuring abstract intellectual ability. For example, Guilford included measures of social skills or social intelligence in his test batteries. It may very well be the case that social intelligence is relatively distinct from general intelligence as usually conceived.

If one excludes samples that are relatively homogeneous for intelligence and tests of intelligence that have very low reliabilities or that measure aspects of intelligence that are of marginal relevance to the usual construal of the construct, virtually all of Guilford's tests demonstrate positive correlations, even when they are alleged to measure quite distinct special factors (see Brody and Brody, 1976). Thus, the body of data collected by Guilford provides one of the most comprehensive sources of support for Spearman's theory. The existence of positive relationships among virtually all measures of intelligence also provides support for a conception of intelligence as a general trait that is cross-situationally predictive. It is also the case that Spearman's theory has been conclusively disconfirmed. Indeed, Spearman himself was aware of the fact that his two-factor theory could not account for the pattern of correlations among tests of intelligence as early as 1906 (see Spearman, 1927). Recall that Spearman's theory implies that the only basis for a correlation between any two tests of intelligence is the amount of g they share. This implication is incorrect. Tests of intelligence that share some specific characteristic (e.g., they involve spatial reasoning) will tend to correlate more highly with each other than tests of intelligence that may be equally good measures of g but are quite dissimilar with respect to the kinds of intellectual problem they present (e.g., a vocabulary test and a spatial reasoning test). The g component is not the only factor present in matrices of correlations derived from batteries of diverse tests of intelligence. There are many different ways of supplementing g by the specification of more specialized factors of intelligence.

Vernon (1961) has presented a heirarchical model of intelligence that distinguishes between factors defined by tests of spatial and mechanical reasoning and a factor based on tests of verbal skills and more educationally relevant skills. The factors are themselves correlated. Cattell (1971) has proposed a related model in which he distinguishes between tests of intelligence that are assumed to be relatively good measures of an underlying biological capacity (fluid ability—g_f) and tests that are assumed to be more reflective of educational and cultural opportunities (crystallized ability—g_c). As in Vernon's two-factor scheme, g_f and g_c are positively correlated. Both Vernon's theory and Cattell's theory imply that one would have to supplement a theory of intelligence as a perfectly general trait with a theory that implies that individuals with the same score on g would tend to exhibit idiosyncratic patterns of behavior in different situations.

One can specify still more specific intellectual skills. Thurstone (1938) postulated the existence of such specific intellectual factors as numerical skills, inductive skills, spatial skills, etc. Each of these factors may in turn be split into specialized factors of different types of abilities—for example, different types of spatial skills. The existence of a heirarchical relationship between relatively specific and more general factors implies that relatively narrow traits defining similarities of behavior among a narrowly specified class of situations (tests of spatial reasoning that involve ability to visualize) coexist with traits that imply generalities across much broader classes of situations, culminating in g as the most general trait. Thus, a theory of traits with minimal situational specification (all situations measuring intelligence) can coexist with theories of traits emphasizing increasingly precise situational specifity.

The process of specifying narrower contexts for the specification of the way in which individual differences in intellectual abilities determine performance in particular situations can be extended to an analysis of the specific components of performance involved in a particular task. For example, Sternberg (1977) has developed models of the processes involved in analogical reasoning. He assumes that the solution to inductive reasoning problems involves several independent processes or task components including things, such as metacognitive components that involve planning for the control of the order in which different component processes will be executed, and various component processes, such as mapping the possible relation between the a and b terms of the analogy. Each of the component processes is assumed to be executed in real time. That is, each component process requires a particular amount of time to occur. One can estimate the time required to execute a process by presenting problems that are assumed to vary in the difficulty of executing one of the component processes. Individuals may be assigned a score on each of the components that are involved in the solution of a particular problem. These component score parameters may be used to predict solution times for individuals on a particular problem—often with considerable success. Sternberg reports correlations in excess of .80 between his individual difference estimates of the times required to execute a particular component process and overall solution time on a particular task. While Sternberg has had considerable success in developing models that predict individual differences in performance on a particular problem, it should be recognized that such models have quite restricted generality. They obviously do not purport to provide a basis for understanding performance on unrelated intellectual tasks. More critically, the models have had quite limited success in predicting performance on related tasks with different characteristics that are alleged to involve some of the same parameters. For example, Sternberg (1985) reported that the average correlation between components alleged to measure the same intellectual processes in analogy problems and in series completion and classification problems correlated with each other .32, and the average correlation of unrelated components across different tasks was .24. Thus, specific component scores for a given task tend to have quite limited generality. Such component scores for an individual might well be thought of as having a strictly intratask or intrasituational relevance.

Spearman's theory of g and Sternberg's componential analysis of analogies performance may be thought of as defining extremes of a continuum of models of the relationship between traits and behavior. The theory of g specifies the widest possible generality of individual differences across situations. Sternberg's models specify the narrowest possible construal of the generality of individual differences in behavior across situations. They are best thought of as providing an understanding of the behaviors of individuals in a particular kind of task. Note that the conceptions are not mutually exclusive, and they are both likely to be valid for different purposes. If one wants to make a prediction about the aggregate level of performance of an individual over the widest possible class of intellectual tasks, the specification of the individual's score on a general test of intelligence as an estimate of g is quite appropriate. If one wants to understand something about the determinants of variations in performance of a group of individuals on a particular task, characterization of individuals in terms of g may not be particularly informative. Traits of great generality predict performance on many tasks without great precision; specific analyses of the components of performance on a particular task predict performance on that task, or on minor variations of the task, without necessarily providing much information about performance on other, marginally different, tasks.

The specification of the processes of reasoning engaged by a particular intellectual task also allows for the specification of noncomparable processes across individuals. Performance on the same task may be determined by quite different intellectual abilities for individuals who use different approaches to the solution of a problem. Sternberg and Weil (1980) have provided a particularly apt demonstration of this phenomenon. By examining the pattern of errors in performance on a deductive-reasoning task, they were able to classify their subjects into two groups defined by the method of solution to the deductive-reasoning problems they used. One group was described as relying on a verbal approach to the solution, the other group as relying on spatial analogs for solution. Individual differences in spatial and verbal ability measures related to performance in quite different ways in these two groups. For subjects who were characterized as using a spatial method of solution, the correlation between their score on a measure of spatial ability and performance on the deductive-reasoning task was .60, and the correlation between verbal ability and performance for these subjects was .08. The corresponding correlations between spatial- and verbal-ability measures and performance for subjects classified as relying on verbal solution procedures were .28 and .76, respectively. The Sternberg and Weil data provide a clear example of the ambiguous nature of a behavioral situation. While the description of the situation or task presented to a subject is clear and unambiguous, the meaning of the task, or more precisely, the kinds of processes engaged by the task, may be quite different for different individuals. It is not difficult to think of parallels between this example and examples of the ambiguity of situations with respect to personality traits. A given behavioral setting, for example, a party, may engage quite different traits in different individuals. A party might make one person aware of a sense of neurotic shyness and inadequate social skills, while another person may respond to the party in terms of impulsive exhibitionism, and still another may view the party as an occasion for the expression of aggressive tendencies. It is not only the case that behavior in the same situation may differ as a function of individual differences in position on one or more common traits, but the traits engaged by the same situation may be different in different individuals. Individual personalities may have much to do with determining the meaning of situations and the personal dispositions engaged by a situation. The boundary between situation and personal disposition is fluid in the sense that part of the meaning of a situation is determined by the individuals in the situation.

Research on intelligence provides particularly clear evidence for an additional way in which the relationship between trait and situation is ambiguous. As we shall see when we review longitudinal research on traits, traits may have a selective influence on the kinds of situations one encounters. Since intelligence tests or other tests that are highly correlated with them are used to select individuals for social roles, the social settings one encounters are likely to be, in part, a function of one's trait characteristics. Students who score high on intelligence tests are likely to perform well in school and to be placed in academically more rigorous classes. This is likely to place them in situations in which they are surrounded by other students with relatively high intelligence test scores. This may have some influence on friendship patterns and on the kinds of social activities they are involved in after school. Analogously, individuals who are socially extraverted may be likely to spend more time in social activities with other individuals. Thus, traits may influence the situations one is likely to encounter as well as the characteristic behaviors one exhibits in a particular situation.

Summary

Traits may be defined as personal dispositions to behave in comparable ways in many diverse situations. We postulate the existence of traits to account for the commonalities we observe among self-reports, the ratings of informed observers, and appropriately aggregated measures of behavior in diverse settings. We assume that the heteromethod trait commonalities that are observed derive from broad dispositional tendencies of individuals to behave in common ways in diverse settings. While these commonalities, irrespective of the method used to assess them, all have ultimate behavioral referents, it is clear that trait dispositions contain meanings that are more general than their specific behavioral referents.

The relationship between behavior in specific situations and traits is vexed and indeterminant for several reasons. The set of situations in which a trait may be exhibited is always potentially larger than the set of situations in which the disposition to exhibit trait-related behaviors has been or could be observed. Traits may be manifested in different situations and in different ways by individuals having the same general trait score. Put another way, this assertion is equivalent to the assertion that an individual difference psychology based on traits cannot account for all of the variations in behavior that exist. Indeed, a trait psychology emphasizing extremely general dispositions can coexist with an individual difference psychology that emphasizes narrower commonalities and even with an individual difference psychology that deals with the parameters that determine performance on a single task. Broadly defined, traits will tend to erode the detailed specification of situations in the attempt to render them equivalent for the purpose of generalization across situations, and thus trait psychology is an incomplete specification of individual difference psychology. The relationship between traits and situations is problematic for two other reasons. First, the meaning of a particular situation may be different for different individuals, and the influence of personal dispositions on situationally specific behaviors may be different for different individuals who respond to the same situations differently. Second, traits may influence the kinds of situations one encounters.

The analogies we have developed between a trait-oriented approach to intelligence that is essentially derived from behavioral measurement and trait theory in personality that is more typically derived from ratings and self-reports suggest that the essential features of a trait theory are not inherently different, whether one searches for commonalities in behavior across situations by actual behavioral measurement or by asking individuals to rate their own or someone else's behavior. Both approaches coalesce on a common view of the meaning of traits.

2

Trait Stability and Change

Trait Stability

Stability of Intelligence

The clearest understanding of stability and change in traits derives from research on general intelligence. We have much more extensive data and a far clearer understanding of issues surrounding stability and change for intelligence, construed as a general trait, than for personality traits.

Intelligence as measured by omnibus tests (i.e., tests that aggregate scores from several different behavioral situations) is among the most enduring of personal dispositions. A score on a contemporary test of intelligence may be thought of as a ranking of an individual relative to his or her age cohorts. Such rank–order positions remain relatively stable over large parts of the human life span. The results of longitudinal studies over the adult years have been summarized by Conley (1984b). His review of 10 studies in which the period elapsing between separate testings ranged from 7 to 40 years indicates that the test–retest correlations for scores on intelligence tests ranged from .62 to .94. Thus adults tend to exhibit invariance with respect to their age cohorts in scores on tests of general intelligence.

It should be noted that the relative invariance of intelligence-test scores over time also implies the existence of relatively high time-lagged, cross-situational generality for the trait of intelligence. Let us develop this point. Different omnibus tests of intelligence correlate substantially with each other, although they may be constructed from subtests that share little obvious surface similarity. (For a review of correlations among standardized tests of intelligence see Matarazzo, 1972). This implies that the relatively high correlations obtained when the same test of intelligence is administered with large time intervals between administrations would also be obtained for different time-lagged omnibus tests sharing little or no obvious surface content. This conclusion is based on an obvious chain of reasoning in which it is assumed that if A relates substantially to B, and B relates substantially to C, then A should relate to C.

The correlations between measures of intelligence given at different times can be increased by correlating aggregates of test scores based on separate administrations of a test. In his analysis of the Berkeley Growth Study—a study in which a group of individuals was repeatedly tested in intelligence beginning with infancy—Pinneau (1961) reports that a measure of intelligence that is the aggregated-test score of administrations at ages 10, 11, and 12 correlated .96 with an aggregate score of intelligence tests administered at ages 17 and 18. This finding suggests that, for the Berkeley sample, there was virtually no change at all in an individual's score relative to his or her cohorts over the high school years.

Evidence for the cross-situational generality of general intelligence as a trait is also clearly present in longitudinal studies of intelligence before the adult years. Intelligence tests given to children of different ages are clearly noncomparable with respect to surface content. One does not use the same items to assess intelligence in a 7-year old and a 13-year old. Absolute levels of intelligence change greatly, but positions relative to one's age cohort remain relatively invariant. Because the items used to assess intelligence are grossly different at different ages during the years when intelligence is developing, evidence of positive correlations between tests administered at different ages is evidence of both longitudinal stability and cross-situational generality of the underlying trait or disposition of intelligence. Table 2.1 presents data from the Berkeley study demonstrating the predictive relationships between intelligence tests given early in life and intelligence test scores at age 18. Note how quickly during the course of development the trait becomes substantially predictive of an individual's behavior on a new set of tasks administered at a different time.

Table 2.1 also indicates that intelligence tests given in the first few years of life are not predictive of later intelligence (McCall, 1979, 1981). The lack of correlation between tests given early in life and later scores may be explained in a variety of ways. The development of the underlying disposition may follow irregular growth rates early in life and be subject to spurts and plateaus. Rapid and irregular changes in the disposition being measured may make it difficult to assess the underlying disposition. Many of the environmental influences on the development of intelligence—particularly the influence of formal schooling and the interactions between underlying ability and more formal tuition—are not operative during the first few years of life, and thus the determinants of early intellectual ability are, in part, different from the determinants of later intellec-

Table 2.1

Correlations between Average Intelligence Test Scores Obtained
at Different Ages in the Berkeley Growth Sample[a]

Average of months or years	Correlation with average of ages 17 and 18
Months	
1,2,3	.05
4,5,6	−.01
7,8,9	.20
10,11,12	.41
13,14,15	.23
18,21,24	.55
27,30,36	.54
42,48,54	.62
Years	
5,6,7	.86
8,9,10	.89
11,12,13	.96
14,15,16	.96

[a]Based on Pinneau, 1961.

tual ability (see Gottfried and Brody, 1975). It may be difficult to assess intellectual ability in a very young child. The limitations in the development of the child's intellectual ability impoverish the capacity of the test constructor to design items and situations that might be reflective of the level of underlying intellectual ability of the child. This latter possibility suggests that an underlying continuity in intellectual ability may be present earlier in life than has been demonstrated in studies of the predictive relationship between tests of ability given in the first 2 years of life. There is, in fact, some recent research that suggests that there are predictive relationships between some measures of infant performance and later intellectual ability. Lewis and Brooks-Gunn (1981) have published research on a measure of responsiveness to stimulus change in 3-month-old infants. In their procedure, infants are repeatedly presented with the same stimulus, leading typically to a reduced pattern of attention. The reduction in attention, for example, looking at a stimulus, after repeated presentations of the same stimulus is a ubiquitous occurrence that is indicative of habituation. If the stimulus is changed, there is usually an increase in attention, for example, looking at the stimulus, that is indicative of dishabituation. Lewis reported that the magnitude of response recovery after stimulus change in 3-month-old infants is correlated with 2-year-old intelligence test scores .52 and .40 in two different studies. This correlation is higher than that which is usually obtained by omnibus tests of infant intelligence at age 3 months and 2 years.

In a related study, Fagan and McGrath (1981) reported correlations between measures of infant memory recognition obtained at 4 and 7 months of age and measures of intelligence at 4 and 7 years of age ranging between .37 and .57 (see also McCall, 1981). These results suggest that measures based on laboratory techniques might extend the evidence for some continuity or predictive relationships between measures of intelligence at different ages to the first years of life. Whatever the ultimate predictive status of measures of infant intelligence, there is no doubt that intelligence-test scores, construed as a trait, rapidly develop predictive relationship to later scores on the trait during the preschool-age period and become increasingly predictive of adult performance.

Stability of Personality

Stability of Personality Traits: Self-Reports

Do trait measures of personality change? Conley (1984b) has analyzed data on the test–retest correlations of personality trait ratings and trait measures derived from self-reports based on personality inventories for the traits of extraversion, neuroticism, and impulsivity. His comprehensive review indicates that the correlations in different studies range from .26 to .84 for periods extending from 10 to 40 years. The trend in these data derived from an examination of many different studies is for the test–retest correlation to decline as the period of time between administrations of the test increases. If one corrects the correlations for unreliability based on the notion that a single administration of a test provides a less than perfect index of a person's score on the trait, the test–retest correlation for a 1-year period becomes .98—suggesting that individuals do not exhibit large scale changes in personality over what is a relatively brief proportion of an adult lifespan. However, if one extrapolates these results over the adult lifespan, one would expect larger changes in an individual's test scores. Thus, Conley's analysis indicates that corrected test–retest correlations for a 40-year period would be .45—suggesting, in spite of some invariance in major personality traits, considerable change over the course of an individual's adult years. The comparable analysis for intelligence test data implies a 1-year test–retest reliability of .99 and a 40-year test–retest reliability of .67. Thus, on this analysis, personality traits are only marginally less consistent over time than measures of intelligence.

In order to evaluate this conclusion, we will examine some longitudinal studies of personality. Costa and McRae (1980) have reported data on the longitudinal stability of the traits of extraversion and neuroticism and a trait called "open-to-experience," which they have extensively studied in a sample of middle-class men of different ages who have been studied for a 12-year period. They classify their sample into young (ages 17–44), middle (44–59), and old age (60–85). The test–retest correlations for their self-report measures on these traits for a

6-year longitudinal study ranged from .75 to .77 for subjects in the different age groups. Thus, during the adult years, they find little difference in stability as a function of the age at which the adult is initially tested. For a 12-year longitudinal study the correlations ranged from .72 to .75. Thus, their data suggest little or no decrease in test–retest stability when the time elapsed between administrations is increased from 6 to 12 years. Also, the correlations they obtained are quite high when one notes that these are uncorrected values.

Costa and McRae's results demonstrating relatively high stability in normal samples for self-report measures of such personality traits as extraversion are not anomalous. Leon, Gillum, Gillum, and Gouze (1979) report data for a 30-year test–retest study of responses on the Minnesota Multiphasic Personality Inventory—a test used to measure various forms of psychopathology. However, the test does permit one to obtain a general measure of extraversion. The test–retest correlation for a 30-year period for a composite social introversion score was .74.

The test–retest stabilities of self-report measures of personality may over- or underestimate true trait stability. The high stabilities reported by Costa and McRae, for example, might be attributable to the development of a relatively invariant self-description of personality that does not mirror underlying true changes in personality. Because self-reports about traits are considerably removed from the actual behavioral referents of the traits, information about relative invariance of self-reports does not provide confident knowledge about the stability of the ultimate behavioral manifestations of the trait.

McRae and Costa (1982) have presented data addressed to this issue. They obtained spouse ratings of personality for subjects participating in their study. They assumed that spouses' ratings would be more reflective of true changes in personality than self-report ratings, if the latter ratings are, in part, reflective of a crystallized self-image that is resistant to change. If this analysis is correct, they reasoned that correlations between self-ratings and spouse ratings for personality traits would exhibit divergence with age and should thus be higher in relatively young samples than in older samples. They found no evidence of this divergence. They did find, however, that spouse ratings exhibited some degree of agreement with self-ratings. They obtained correlations ranging from .37 to .85 between spouse ratings on their trait measures for male and female subjects. The McRae and Costa data are not completely convincing. While spouses may be likely to observe changes, the greater period of interaction and mutual influence experienced by older spouses who have lived together for an extensive period of time might produce agreement with respect to their respective personalities.

Just as there is reason to believe that longitudinal studies of self-report measures of personality might exaggerate the extent of continuity in underlying trait dispositions, there is also reason to believe that such measures might exhibit change where none had occurred. Individual items on a test of personality might have a different relationship to the trait construct that the items assess at different ages. Consider the item—"Would being in debt worry you?"—an item that loads on a trait dimension called by Eysenck, "psychoticism." A person might feel quite differently about the level of debt he or she has at different points in his or her life, depending upon job prospects and the like. It might very well be the case that the loading of the item on the factor would remain invariant over age groups (although really definitive data on this point is probably not available), yet the meaning of an item for the individual might change with life circumstances. It might well be that over all periods of time and in all equivalent circumstances individuals who score high on psychoticism are more cavalier in their attitude toward debt. Granting this, it should also be noted that the item might mean different things to a person at different times, and a person's response to the item might change for reasons having little or nothing to do with change in the underlying trait, defined in terms of behavior on a representative sample of situations appropriate for the measurement of the trait.

Stability of Personality Ratings

Ratings of individuals obtained at different times by different raters that are made independently without knowledge of the previous rating are not as contaminated as self-reports. That is, they are not subject to the development of spurious stability due to the crystallization of a self-image that is not isomorphic with the true behavior of an individual.

Haan (1981) has reported data on the stability of ratings derived from a Q-sort for a longitudinal sample studied from ages 14 to 47. The Q-sort technique requires subjects to sort a set of descriptive adjectives (typically 100 such descriptors) into nine piles or groups ranging from those that are most descriptive of the individual to those that are least descriptive. An equal number of descriptors must be assigned to each grouping. The technique forces descriptions to be made on an individual basis because one does not compare a person's position on a descriptive characteristic to some implicit group of individuals. Rather, descriptors are assigned in terms of their differential relevance to the individual whose personality is being described. Statistical analysis of scores derived from Q-sort descriptions has indicated that certain descriptive categories are associated with others and that one can define clusters of Q-sort descriptors. Block and Block (1980a,b) have placed particular emphasis on clusters they call *ego control* and *ego resiliency*. The former cluster is related to what is generally considered to be impulsivity by trait theorists, and the latter is related to neuroticism—or what Norman calls adjustment—although the connotations of the various terms are not quite identical. Table 2.2 presents data obtained by Haan in two different cohorts for the test–retest stability of scores on ego control in female and male subjects. The data indicate that short-term stability between ages 14 and 17 and between ages 37 and 47 appears to be somewhat higher than long-term stability between

Table 2.2

Longitudinal Stability Correlations in Q-Sort Ratings:
Measures of Under- Overcontrol in Two Cohorts[a]

Cohort no.	Sex	Correlation according to age group (years)			
		14–17	17–37	37–47	14–47
1	Male	.58	.30	.44	.48
	Female	.52	.26	.56	.32
2	Male	.72	.54	.45	.30
	Female	.67	.21	.53	.36

[a]Based on Haan, 1981.

ages 14 and 47. Nevertheless, there is some evidence for stability from the early adolescent period until middle age, with correlations ranging from .30 to .48.

Block and Gjerde (1985) have reported longitudinal data for children aged 3 to 14 on the Q-sort measure of undercontrol used by Haan. The measures they obtained were based on independent ratings. Table 2.3 presents their data. An examination of these data indicates that the correlations for both boys and girls between ratings obtained at ages 3 and 4 tend to exhibit declining correlations with ratings at later ages. However, ratings obtained at age 7 exhibit considerable longitudinal stability and no evidence of a difference in relationship to ratings obtained at ages 11 and 14. Note that for males, the correlation of independent ratings obtained at age 7 and at age 14 is higher than the correlation of ratings obtained at ages 7 and 11. These data suggest considerable stability from ages 7 to 14 in the ratings.

Olweus (1978, 1979) has surveyed literature on the stability of trait ratings of aggression in children and young adults. In his studies of aggression, based on peer ratings or teacher ratings, he finds uncorrected 1-year test–retest stabilities of .65 for a rating of the tendency to start fights. He studied children who were

Table 2.3

Longitudinal Consistency of Undercontrol Indexes from Age 3 to Age 14[a,b]

Age	Undercontrol index by age (years)				
	3	4	7	11	14
3	—	.67 ****	.50 ***	.41 **	.38 *
4	.86 ****	—	.50 ***	.31 *	.31 *
7	.57 **	.44 **	—	.53 ****	.74 ****
11	.40 **	.43 **	.60 ****	—	.65 ****
14	.47 **	.26	.55 ****	.61 ****	—

[a]Based on Block & Gjerde, 1985.
[b]Females above diagonal, males below diagonal.
*$p < .05$, **$p < .01$, ***$p < .001$, ****$p < .0001$.

nominated by teachers as bullies or what he called *whipping boys*—that is, boys who were the victims of aggression. He had a second teacher nominate children into the same categories—bullies, whipping boys, or neither—one year later. The boys attended different schools in different settings, having left elementary school for junior high. Table 2.4 presents Olweus's data indicating the similarity of categorization of the boys made by the different teachers. Olweus's data suggest considerable continuity for a 1-year period of aggressive behavioral tendencies for boys in school.

Olweus (1979) has reported a careful survey of literature related to agreements among independent ratings of aggression. His survey indicates that the test–retest correlation declines as a function of the time between ratings and that the test–retest correlation declines when the initial rating is made at an early age. He estimates that the corrected test–retest correlations of ratings for aggressive tendencies range from .80 to .40. The lower correlations are estimated values for a 21-year longitudinal period.

Backteman and Magnusson (1981) obtained independent ratings from teachers of 10- and 13-year-old Swedish children in a longitudinal study on six different personality dimensions. They reported average test–retest correlations of .52 for boys and .48 for girls.

Mussen, Eichorn, Honzik, Bieher, and Meredith (1980) obtained independent ratings of a small sample of women at ages 30 and 70. They reported test–retest correlations of .34 and .24 for trait ratings of neuroticism and sociability, respectively, over this 40-year period.

Trait ratings of personality are more likely to be representative of cross-situational stability of behavior over time than are self-reports. Independent raters rating an individual at different times in his or her life are likely to observe the individual in different settings and contexts. Thus, these correlations are more likely to be reflective of cross-situational generality of behavior. However, there are few studies available in which the longitudinal stability of ratings is considered where raters have observed an individual in quite different social contexts. Ratings that are indicative of the stability of behavior in a school setting, for example, are not necessarily indicative of the behavior of an indi-

Table 2.4

Longitudinal Classification of Boys in Aggressive Behaviors[a]

	Grade 7		
Grade 6	Bully	Neither	Whipping boy
Bully	24	9	2
Neither	9	200	15
Whipping boys (victim)	1	10	16

[a]Based on Olweus, 1978.

vidual at home. Nor do ratings by teachers in schools necessarily provide us with information about an individual's behavior in job settings. We could, in principle, obtain information about the stability of trait dispositions by correlating aggregated ratings of an individual at different times made by raters who have had an opportunity to observe the person in diverse settings (e.g., peers, family members, teachers, and employers). An alternative procedure that is still more utopian would involve aggregating observations in a set of situations deemed to be appropriate to assess a particular trait on two different occasions. In effect, this would involve the use of procedures of measurement for the study of stability in personality traits that are analogous to the procedures used to study the stability of the trait of general intelligence.

Stability of Heteromethod Measures of Personality

The study of heteromethod relationships is one way of overcoming the limitations of any given method. One can consider the relationships between two or more different methods of measuring the same trait at a given time as reflective of the true-score variance of the latent or hypothetical trait that is postulated to account for the congruence among different methods of measurement of the same trait. Suppose that, for at least one of the methods of measurement that have entered into the calculation of heteromethod measurement on a trait, data exist that measures the same trait on a second occasion. One can compare the heteromethod correlation of a trait at the same time with the heteromethod correlations employing the same or similar methods of measurement obtained at different times. The correlations based on a single time period estimate the true-score variance on the trait at a particular time, and the correlations for different times (holding constant methods of measurement) are estimates of the true-score variance of the latent trait over time. The ratio of the former to the latter correlations provides an estimate of the stability of the latent trait.

We will review studies that provide evidence for the longitudinal stability of personality based on heteromethod stabilities, including studies that permit us to compare heteromethod single-occasion measures with the comparable heteromethod measures obtained on different occasions.

Olweus (1979) reported substantial 1-year time-lagged heteromethod correlations between teacher ratings of the aggressive behavior of children and frequency count observations of the actual aggressive behavior. He reported correlations of .81 for these data.

Harrington, Block, and Block (1983) have reported the results of a longitudinal study of creativity relating teachers' ratings of creativity at age 11 and responses to a behavioral measure of creativity given to 4- and 5-year-olds. Their behavioral measure was an index of the number of high-quality, different kinds of responses that children could think of in divergent thinking tasks that required children to think of the number of different things that fulfilled some criterion.

They found that their behavioral index correlated with a creativity rating on a Q-sort made by the children's teachers at age 11 by .45. The correlation between their behavioral index of creativity was higher with the Q-sort rating of creativity than with any other personality characteristic included in the Q-sort. Also, the correlation they obtained was not attributable to individual differences in intelligence. That is, scores on the divergent-thinking index predicted creativity ratings after controlling for individual differences in intelligence test scores at age 11. The Harrington, Block, and Block study suggests that there is some continuity in behaviors indicative of creativity that extends from childhood to preadolescence.

Funder, Block, and Block (1983) have reported data on the longitudinal stability of the dimension of under- and overcontrol. They obtained independent Q-sort ratings from teachers of the same children at ages 3, 4, 7, and 11. They derived a composite index of under- or overcontrol from these data at each time period. Scores on this index were compared to a composite measure of behaviors on two different laboratory tasks exhibited by a child at age 4 on two occasions that were separated by one week. One of their behavioral measures involved responses to a situation in which a child was presented with an attractively wrapped gift and then given a task to perform before opening the gift. They noted such things as the time taken for the child to open the gift after completing the task and the occurrence of verbal responses directed toward the gift. The second task they studied involved a moral transgression in which children were shown a set of attractive toys that they were told belonged to someone else and they should not play with. The psychologist then left the room ostensibly to seek the permission of the owner of the toys for the child to play with them. The tendency of the child to play with the toys was noted.

Table 2.5 presents correlations for male and female children as well as for the combined sample for the composite behavioral index and Q-sort ratings on overcontrol for the same children at different ages. Table 2.5 indicates that there are higher and more consistent relationships for boys than for girls. This table

Table 2.5
Correlations between Behavioral Index of Delay of Gratification at Age 4 and Q-Sort Ratings of Overcontrol[a]

	Correlation as a function of age (years)			
Subjects	3	4	7	11
Girls	−.05	−.17	−.41	−.11
Boys	−.43	−.31	−.47	−.43
All subjects	−.28	−.25	−.46	−.32

[a]Based on Funder, Block, & Block, 1983. (Copyright 1983 by the American Psychological Association. Adapted by permission of the publisher and author.)

also shows that the correlations between these measures taken at approximately the same time (age 4) tend to be lower than the correlations between the behavioral index and trait ratings made at different times.

How are the data in Table 2.5 to be interpreted? It is possible to focus on the magnitude of the correlation between the behavioral composite and the Q-sort ratings and view these data as an instance of the .3 to .4 correlation between behavior and trait ratings noted by Mischel. However, such an analysis might miss some important facets of these data. First, we can note that as a behavioral measure of impulsivity or inability to delay gratification, the composite behavioral index derived by Funder, Block, and Block is not ideal. It is based only on responses to two behavioral tasks, and it is based on tasks that may be said to incorporate rather different components since one task involves a moral transgression, or failure to obey an adult instruction, and the other does not. In addition, the tasks sample the behavior of a young child on only two occasions rather than on several occasions. It appears almost self-evident that a more comprehensive index obtained from observations of a child's performance on several different tasks administered on several different occasions would provide a more accurate index of the child's behavioral tendencies. The correlations in Table 2.5 may be thought of as underestimates of the true relationship between aggregate behavioral measures of impulsivity and Q-sort ratings related to this trait.

The correlations obtained at different times also provide evidence of the replicability of the obtained relationship between the behavioral index and the Q-sort rating of undercontrol since each of the ratings is independent and made in the absence of knowledge of previous ratings.

Perhaps of greatest interest in these data in the absence of any difference between time-lagged heteromethod correlations and heteromethod correlations obtained at the same time. If taken literally, this result suggests that the latent hypothetical trait that may be postulated to account for the relationship between behavior and ratings remains invariant from ages 3 to 11.

Conley (1985) has also presented data that permit comparisons to be made between heteromethod correlations obtained at the same time and at different times. Conley's data involve correlations between self-report measures of neuroticism, impulsivity, and extraversion and ratings of these traits that are composites of ratings made by five acquaintances just before a person's marriage for a sample of approximately 400 individuals first studied as young adults and studied again 20 and 45 years later.

Table 2.6 presents data indicating the correlation between composite-trait ratings and self-report measures of neuroticism, social extraversion, and impulsivity obtained between 1935 and 1938, and correlations between those obtained some 20-odd years later separately for male and female subjects. The data appear to be quite consistent for male and female subjects. The correlations between composite-trait ratings and self-report measures obtained at the same

Table 2.6

Heteromethod Contemporaneous and Time-lagged Correlations for Personality Traits[a]

	Males		Females	
Traits	Same time	Time-lagged	Same time	Time-lagged
Neuroticism	.48	.43	.39	.30
Extraversion	.52	.36	.48	.41
Impulse Control	.36	.30	.38	.29

[a]Based on Conley, 1985. (Copyright 1985 by the American Psychological Association. Adapted by permission of the publisher and author.)

time are a bit low, but this is probably attributable to the use of self-report measures that were not as well developed as those currently available. Of greater interest in these data are the relationships between the time-lagged heteromethod correlations and the contemporaneous heteromethod correlations. The latter correlations are only slightly larger than the former correlations. There are a variety of statistical procedures that can be used to obtain estimates of the magnitude of the ratios of heteromethod contemporaneous to heteromethod–time-lagged correlations. When applied to these data, they suggest that approximately 60–80% of the true-score variance on the latent trait remained invariant over the 20-year time period studied by Conley.

Very few longitudinal studies report data that permit comparable comparisons, and thus it is difficult to reach any firm conclusions about the extent of stability of personality traits when the trait score is based on heteromethod composites. In addition, there are no studies of the stability of personality traits that involve samples of behavioral observations in a standardized set of representative situations that were studied at different times. Thus, there are no studies of the longitudinal stability of personality traits that are comparable to studies of the longitudinal stability of intelligence as a general trait. The available data do permit us to suggest that there is considerable stability in personality traits, even when measurements are separated by a period of years. What the available data do not permit us to do is to infer something about the relative stability of personality traits and intelligence as a trait. Measurements of the latter trait are clearly more stable than measurements of personality traits, but true relative stabilities of the underlying traits remain indeterminate.

Traits and Socially Relevant Outcomes

Intelligence and Education

If traits are relatively enduring dispositions and are related to behavior in a variety of social situations, then we would expect that traits are related to a variety of social indicators that may be construed as the end result of an extended social interaction. Again, research on intelligence provides a particularly clear example of the way in which personal dispositions determine the outcomes of an individual's extended interactions with institutions and situations. Ever since the inception of intelligence tests in the first decades of this century, it was assumed that intelligence as measured by tests was related to performance in school. We can describe this relationship with some precision.

Omnibus tests of general intelligence correlate with measures of an individual's performance in school. The correlation through the elementary and high school levels is approximately .5 and is lower at the college level, chiefly as a result of a restriction in range of talent. That is, individuals whose scores on tests are low are not in college, and this restriction in sample or "range of talent" tends, of necessity, to decrease the correlation between intelligence test scores and indices of academic achievement (Lavin, 1965). The correlation is ubiquitously obtained and is not in dispute. It is also true that it is possible to obtain scores on intelligence tests before school entry, and, in this sense, intelligence as a trait may be said to be logically, or at any rate, chronologically, prior to school entry and therefore to act as a determinant of school performance.

Intelligence tests also relate to an additional educational outcome—the number of years of education attained. Longitudinal studies indicate that tests of intelligence given to preadolescents correlate with the number of years of education that they attain. For example, Benson (1942) administered intelligence tests to a sample of sixth graders and obtained a correlation of .57 with the number of years of education eventually obtained. The relationship between scores on intelligence tests and years of education is important since the number of years of education obtained by a person is the single most important predictor of an individual's social status. Studies of social mobility in American society have implicated individual differences in intelligence as a mediating variable in determining intergenerational social mobility (Jencks, 1972). Parental education and social status correlate weakly with the intelligence test scores of children— $r = .3$ to .4. However, parental social background has very little independent influence on the number of years of education that a child obtains after one controls for differences in intelligence test scores. Variations in intelligence have a relatively strong influence on the number of years of education obtained. Thus, a child's eventual social status in American society is more nearly reflective of his or her childhood intelligence test score than it is of his or her parents' social status (Duncan, Featherman, and Duncan, 1968).

The relationship between individual differences in intelligence and school performance helps to explain the relationship between social status and the outcomes of education. This latter relationship has led to a good deal of comment and controversy. We shall briefly review this topic in order to develop some ideas about the ways in which traits relate to an individual's behavior.

A number of large-scale surveys of the outcomes of education (see Jencks,

1972) have reported a very strong relationship between educational achievement (as assessed by tests measuring knowledge of the curriculum presented in public schools) and the social status of pupils in a particular school. These relationships were based on analyses in which a school was taken as the unit of analysis rather than the individuals in a school. Schools may be characterized by indices of the aggregated social background of pupils in the school and by the aggregated educational performance of pupils in the schools. Large-scale surveys of schools have indicated that these two aggregated indices are substantially correlated. In a survey of these data, Jencks argued that the data indicate that there is very little significant variation among schools in their ability to determine what pupils learn. He argued that variations in what was learned among schools were substantially determined by variations in the characteristics of pupils attending a school. The input determined the output. Bowles and Gintis (1976), using a Marxist perspective, have argued that schools act to reinforce social status and, in effect, are programmed to fail students of low social status and to assign them to low-status occupations. Rutter (1983) has argued that these conclusions are overdrawn. He believes that schools do not invariably produce the same level of academic achievement for pupils of the same social status.

We can get some idea of the issues in this debate by examining data obtained by Brookover, Beady, Flood, Schweitzer, and Wisenbaker (1979) that, they argue, suggest that variations in academic achievement among schools is related to the quality of the school. Brookover et al. surveyed a group of schools in the state of Michigan. They obtained information about the social background of pupils in these schools as well as their aggregated performance on tests of knowledge of the curriculum. They also obtained data on a composite variable called *school morale* that was based on attitudes of pupils and teachers to the possibilities of academic success. They found that their school morale variable was correlated more highly with school success than the social background of pupils attending the school and they also argued that schools characterized by different social climates and atmospheres could produce quite different learning outcomes among students with comparable social backgrounds. Brookover et al. presented the results of a number of statistical analyses designed to explicate the relationship among social status, school morale, and educational achievement. They used step-wise multiple correlations to study the increments in predictability of educational achievement when variables were added to the equation.

Table 2.7 presents these data. Table 2.7 indicates that the social status of pupils attending a school and, independently, the racial background of pupils attending a school, jointly predict 76% of the variance in the educational outcomes of the schools. Knowledge of the school social climate adds 7% to the predictable variance in educational achievement. Thus, these data suggest that social-status variables account for 10 times more variance than school morale in determining the educational achievement of different schools. Of course, one

Table 2.7

Percentage of Variance in School Achievement
Related to School Characteristics[a]

Variables	Percent
Socioeconomic background	46
+ Percentage of Whites	76
+ School climate	83
Climate first	73
+ Socioeconomic background	75
+ Percentage of Whites	83

[a]Based on Brookover, et al., 1979.

could object to this assertion. If one began with school morale as the first variable in the prediction equation and entered pupils' social status and race as prediction variables after school climate, the amount of predictable variance attributable to school climate would be a great deal larger than the amount of variance attributable to pupils' social status or race. However, this latter order of entry of variables is not a logical or preferred way of developing the prediction equation. In the United States, pupils are assigned to public schools by geographical residence. The social climate of a school cannot determine the social background of pupils in the school. On the other hand, a school's social climate can, in principle, be determined by the characteristics of pupils who enter a school. Therefore, it is logical to begin the analysis with the social status and race of pupils entering a school before moving on to an examination of the influence of the school's characteristics. When the analysis is done this way, the Brookover et al. data suggest that most of the variance in educational outcome is determined by the characteristics of pupils who enter the school. One could add that one reason for this effect is that schools with large percentages of pupils with low socioeconomic status develop a climate that is not conducive to the development of academic achievement. In any case, while there is a debate about possible variations in educational outcome associated with variations in school, there is no doubt that social background variables account for a substantial portion of the variance in educational outcomes among different schools.

The relationship between the social background of pupils in a school and their educational achievement may be understood, in part at any rate, by referring to individual differences in intelligence. Both social class background and independently of social class, racial background, correlate with intelligence-test scores (see Brody and Brody, 1976; Jensen, 1980). Race and social class do not predict educational outcomes to any significant degree if they are considered in a prediction equation after intelligence scores are entered. In addition, intelligence test scores are more substantially related to educational performance than either race or social background. Thus, it is possible to explicate the relationship between social status and background variables with reference to intelligence and to develop a model that assumes that social and racial status are correlated (although not substantially) with intelligence test scores, including intelligence test scores given before school entry. Intelligence test scores are predictive of what pupils learn in a school. Indeed, if one were to obtain the aggregated intelligence test score of pupils entering a school for each of a large number of schools, one could predict with substantial accuracy the aggregated academic achievement of pupils in the school. Since variations in the disposition that is measured by tests of intelligence appear to mediate the relationship between social status and educational outcome, one could assert that educational outcomes among schools that vary in the social backgrounds of their pupils could be made more equal if one could change the relationship between individual differences in intelligence and social background, or if one could find some way of modifying scores on intelligence tests or on the trait that is indexed by such scores. Alternatively, one could change this relationship if one could change the relationship between what is learned in the schools and individual differences in intelligence.

Cronbach and Snow (1977) reviewed the literature on Aptitude X Treatment Interactions. They were particularly interested in the possibility that certain types of instruction would benefit individuals who are low in intellectual ability, while other methods of instruction would benefit individuals who are high in intellectual ability. They also investigated the possibility that different instructional methods interact differentially with different components of intelligence. Two rather striking conclusions are suggested by their comprehensive review of the literature. First, most of the interactions of instructional methods with measures of ability are between general ability measures, rather than between specialized abilities and instructional methods. Thus, with occasional exceptions, a more differentiated view of intellectual abilities has not been found to be the most useful basis for individualizing the curriculum. Second, there are very few, if any, disordinal interactions with ability such that certain instructional treatments lead to poorer performance for individuals of higher ability than for individuals of lower ability. Snow and Yalow (1982) have summarized the more recent literature on this issue. They found that there are treatments that benefit individuals with high intellectual ability and lead to poorer performance of individuals with low intellectual ability. Most of these treatments may be characterized as providing more opportunities for students to develop their own ideas and to deal with more complex materials. A number of instructional procedures appear to benefit individuals of low ability without harming individuals of high ability. Many of these may be described as providing students with structured information that relieves them of the burden of organizing materials for themselves. There are few, if any, replicated findings that suggest that instructional conditions exist that permit individuals of low intellectual ability to exceed the learning performance of individuals of high ability.

Essentially similar conclusions may be derived from Bloom's analysis of mastery-learning procedures (Bloom, 1974). Bloom notes that one of the reasons for the ubiquitous correlation of measures of general intellectual ability and school achievement is that individuals of high ability are able to master concepts more rapidly than individuals of low ability. Schools typically do not provide enough time for individuals of low ability to acquire the concepts that are necessary to master new materials and, hence, slower students tend to develop cumulative deficits. Under mastery-learning procedures, students are given sufficient time to master a concept before being introduced to a new concept. Under such procedures Bloom asserts that the correlation between intelligence test scores and the acquisition of knowledge in school settings is reduced. However, Bloom does not claim that mastery-learning procedures eliminate individual differences in general ability. He asserts only that the acquisition of conceptual knowledge may be made less dependent upon individual differences in general intelligence. Possibly educational changes in instructional formats may help students with lower ability develop greater mastery of the educational program of the schools. No known instructional formats exist, however, that will eliminate individual differences in general ability as an index of the ability to acquire more complex intellectual skills. The matter has been expressed well by Cronbach and Snow (1977), who conclude their review of the relationship between general ability and treatment interactions for instruction as follows:

> We once hoped that instructional methods might be found whose outcomes correlate very little with general ability. This does not appear to be a viable hope. Outcomes from extended instruction almost always correlate with pretested ability unless a ceiling is artificially imposed.
>
> The pervasive correlations of general ability with learning rate or outcomes in education limits the power of ATI findings to reduce individual differences. (Cronbach and Snow, 1977, p. 500.)

This analysis of the relationship between intelligence and educational outcomes provides us with additional information about the relationship between social situations and traits that is the fulcrum of the debate within personality psychology about the place of the trait concept. Traits exert an influence on social institutions and change the nature of the feedback received by an individual from social institutions.

Rehberg and Rosenthal (1978) have reported the results of a longitudinal study of the educational plans of a group of high school students. Their investigation focused on the determinants of the decision to enroll in postgraduate education. They obtained data from their subjects when they were in the 9th, 10th, and 12th grades, and one year after leaving high school. They obtained information about the social class backgrounds of the pupils in this study, their intelligence, the educational aspirations of the pupils' parents and friends, the choice of curriculum of the pupils, and their academic achievements as well as their ultimate decision to continue their education. Their study provides a relatively comprehensive picture of the ways in which social background, ability, and feedback received from the school shape the educational decisions of pupils. It is beyond the scope of this book to present in detail the results of their investigation. Their analyses do indicate that individual differences in intelligence influence the outcome of the critical educational decision in several different ways. Intelligence is an important determinant of educational achievements, and educational achievements influence educational aspirations. School counselors, in encouraging or discouraging students to continue their education, are influenced by the educational performance of the children and, at least in this study, are not at all influenced by the social class background of pupils. Educational aspirations influence one's choice of curriculum, and this, in turn, may exert an influence on friendship patterns and the influences of one's peers on one's educational aspirations. What is of great interest in the Rehberg and Rosenthal data is evidence of the changing influence of intelligence on educational aspirations and the decision to continue to obtain additional education. Rehberg and Rosenthal found that social class had a diminishing influence on the decision to continue education from the 9th to the 12th grades, and intellectual ability had an increasing influence. The Rehberg and Rosenthal study provides a detailed picture of the way in which a trait influences the responses individuals receive from a social institution. Their study deals with a limited period in a person's life. If their analyses had been extended to the beginning of one's education, it is quite likely that additional information about the impact of individual differences on a number of intermediate events that structure the educational experience of an individual could have been obtained. A child's interest and liking for school are undoubtedly shaped by the response of the school to the child. Children of high intellectual ability are likely to receive rewards and encouragement in school and develop an interest in school. Parental aspirations for children's education may be shaped by parental responses to their children's academic progress. This analysis suggests that the trait of intelligence continually interacts with educational experiences and determines and changes the feedback that the individual receives from the school. The extended interaction between the trait of intelligence and the experience of schooling has much to do with the ultimate educational experience of an individual.

The Rehberg and Rosenthal study contains a number of features that are rarely duplicated in longitudinal studies of personality. It had a large sample, it was longitudinal, and it included trait data, as well as information about a number of potential social influences on an individual.

Personality and Socially Relevant Outcomes

The data we have reviewed have provided clear evidence that intelligence as a trait does relate to important social outcomes in a person's life. We shall consider analogous data for personality. The Kelly longitudinal study is a longitudinal study covering the adult life span of a large sample of couples, which included aggregated trait ratings made by five acquaintances at the start of the study. Kelly and Conley (1987) have reported data from the Kelly longitudinal study relating trait scores to divorce and marital satisfaction. They also analyzed data on attitudes toward marriage, retrospective reports about the early social environment of the couples, and data about the number and kinds of stressful life events that occurred during the adult life of the couples. They found that the aggregated scores on personality traits were more predictive of their indices of marital satisfaction and divorce than information about social attitudes, characteristics of the spouse's family life, or the number of stressful life events experienced by the individuals. They found that before their marriage males who were rated by their acquaintances as either neurotic or impulsive and females who were rated as neurotic were less likely to have satisfactory marriages than males and females who were not assigned these trait ratings. For example, they compared 110 stably married couples to 50 divorced couples on their trait measures. Stably married and satisfied couples had trait rating scores that were approximately one-half a standard deviation lower in male neuroticism, one-half a standard deviation higher in the male partner's impulse control rating, and slightly more than one-half a standard deviation lower in the female partner's neuroticism rating than the ratings assigned to the male and female partner of couples who subsequently divorced. These data, which are supported by data from other studies covering shorter periods and using self-report measures of personality, suggest that personality traits are related to the likelihood that an individual will be able to enter into a satisfactory marital relationship. It is also noteworthy that, at least for this data set, trait ratings were more predictive than other kinds of data, including data relevant to the social experiences of the individuals in the study. It should also be noted that these data are subject to a severe limitation with respect to their generality. They are based on a single cohort of individuals who were middle class and whose marriage occurred when they were young adults in the 1930s. Divorce is more frequent today, and there is no way of knowing whether or not the personal dispositions that were predictively related to the development of a successful marriage are in fact similarly related to contemporary marriages.

Conley and Angelides (in press), using the data from the Kelly longitudinal study, have also reported relationships between trait ratings on personality characteristics and the subsequent development of alcoholism and serious emotional disorders among males. They found that 40 of the 233 males in their study were judged to have developed serious emotional disturbances. At the time of entry into the study only three of their subjects indicated that they had emotional problems. Thus, in large measure, this study deals with the prediction of subsequent emotional disorder developing over the adult life span from measures of trait ratings obtained during the early adult years. It was found that the 40 males who were classified as developing alcoholism or emotional disorders were assigned neuroticism ratings that were approximately three-quarters of a standard deviation higher than males who did not develop alcoholism or an emotional disorder. Males assigned to the alcoholism group differed from males assigned to the emotional disorders group in their scores on impulse control. The group of alcoholics had impulse control ratings that were approximately one standard deviation lower than males who were judged to have developed an emotional disorder. Trait-rating data were more predictive of the development of emotional disorders or alcoholism than information about early stresses experienced or life stresses that occurred after the measurement of trait ratings.

The data obtained from the Kelly longitudinal study provide information about the way in which personal dispositions measured early in adulthood are related to socially relevant outcomes. Such outcomes as alcoholism, emotional disorder, and divorce are clearly not specific behavioral measures. However, such outcomes may be construed to be a result of an extended period of social interaction with the environment. These data suggest that, over time, the influence of the personal dispositions that are indexed by trait ratings relate to the way in which individuals behave in many different contexts, and cumulatively, these interactions eventually lead to the development of behavior patterns that result in divorce, alcoholism, or the judgement that someone is emotionally disordered.

There are also studies relating personality and intelligence to academic success. Kipnis (1971) has reported a series of studies relating scores on a self-report measure of impulsivity to academic success. In studies of college students he found that impulsivity was related to academic success and seemed to moderate the influence of individual differences in intelligence on school success. He reported that, among individuals who score low in intellectual ability, there is very little relationship between impulsivity and academic performance. However, among individuals who achieved high scores on tests of academic aptitude related to intelligence, there was a relationship between impulsivity scores and academic success. Table 2.8 presents data from one of Kipnis's studies indicating a relationship between intelligence as indexed by Scholastic Aptitude Test (SAT) scores, impulsivity, and college grade point average. The data reported in Table 2.8 indicate that individuals who score high on impulsivity and who have high SAT scores tend to have lower grade point averages than individuals who have high SAT scores and score low on impulsivity. Kipnis also reported that individuals who are impulsive are more likely to flunk out of college than individuals who are not impulsive. Smith (1967) also reported data indicating that impulsivity related to academic success in college. He found a correlation of .47 between peer ratings of impulse control before college entry and grade point average.

Evidence for a relationship between personality characteristics and school success is also present for temperamental variables. Matheny, Dolan, and

Table 2.8

Mean Grade Point Average for Individuals
Differing in SAT Scores and Impulsivity[a]

SAT scores	Impulsivity	
	High	Low
High	2.23	2.63
Low	1.70	1.81

[a]Based on Kipnis, 1971.

Wilson (1976) have reported a twin study in which school authorities were askeu to nominate children from a large cohort of twins who were experiencing academic difficulty and who thus formed an index group. A control group was formed from the same cohort. At a median age of 10 the children who were nominated were described as having reading-test scores that were 1.9 grade equivalents lower than the children in the control group. It was found that at age 6 twins in the index group had Wechsler intelligence test scores that were 8 points lower than the twins in the control group. These results suggest that the differences in academic performance between the index and the control children are not likely to be attributable to differences in their intelligence. The standard deviation of grade equivalent scores at an average age of 10 is not given in the report. However, it is unlikely to be very much larger than 1. Differences in reading score and the general school difficulty exhibited by the index twins relative to the control group twins cannot be accounted for by the relatively small difference they exhibited on intelligence test scores. Matheny, Dolan, and Wilson, however, report that the index twins were significantly different from the control twins on measures of temperament derived from the preschool-age period. The index twins were reported to be overly active (87% versus 26% for the control group), distractable (89% for the index versus 22% for the control group children), and were more likely to be described as experiencing feeding and sleeping problems. It was also found that the variables that differentiated between the index twin cases and the control cases were heritable; the concordance rates for monozygotic-twin pairs for these variables was higher than the concordance for dyzygotic twins. These results suggest that there are temperamental variables that are genetically influenced that moderate the relationship between intelligence and academic achievement.

There are also data available relating personality traits to illness. Kobasa, Maddi, and Kahn (1982) have reported a longitudinal study relating the occurrence of stressful life events to illness. They studied 259 middle-level supervisors and executives in a utility company for 3 years and obtained a measure of a personality variable they called *hardiness*, defined as a commitment to change, a belief in one's ability to control the outcomes of events that influence a person's life, and a commitment to one's work. They then obtained data on the occurrence

Table 2.9

Scores on Change in Illness Occurrence
as a Function of Hardiness[a]

Life stress	Hardiness	
	High	Low
High	553	1254
Low	368	387

[a]Based on Kobasa, Maddi, & Kahn, 1982.
(Copyright 1982 by the American Psychological
Association. Adapted by permission of the pub-
lisher and author.)

of life stresses and on an index of self-reported change in health and illness over
this period. Table 2.9 presents their data. Table 2.9 indicates that the occurrence
of life stress was associated with an increase in the occurrence of reports about
illness. However, this effect was substantially attributable to subjects who had
earlier described themselves as being low in hardiness.

These data suggest that enduring personality characteristics might moderate
and influence the impact of life stresses on illness. There are, however, some
limitations to these data. First, all the information is based on self-reports.
Second, the personality dimension that is related to response to life stress is one
that has not generally been studied, and it is not based on the systematic investigation of trait ratings. It should be noted that one of its components, a belief that
one can control events, has been related to neuroticism (Eysenck and Eysenck
1985, Chapter 4).

Trait Change

Cohort and Maturational Effects: Personality

In this review of research on relationships between traits and behaviors, we have
implicitly considered traits to be enduring personal dispositions and have considered ways in which such dispositions influence the impact of the social world on
the individual. It is possible to reverse this process and to consider traits as, in
effect, the dependent variables in personality research. Here one is concerned not
with traits as enduring personal dispositions but with change in personality traits.
We will review several different types of investigations concerned with changes
in personality and intelligence.

It is possible to distinguish among three different kinds of changes that might
influence traits in a longitudinal study. First, there are cohort effects. Individuals
who are born at different time periods may have different experiences that might
alter personality. Cohorts born at the turn of the century were young adults

during the depression. Those born after World War II have not experienced the depression and grew up during a period of relative prosperity. Various social changes with respect to women, minority groups, and homosexuals, which are roughly dated from the 1960s, may alter personality characteristics for individuals who have experienced these changes at different periods of their lives. Second, there are maturational or age-related changes. Personality traits may change in systematic ways as people age. For example, Levinson, Darrow, Klein, Levinson, and McKee (1978) have argued that males experience a midlife crisis that may profoundly alter their personality. Third, there are time-of-testing effects, which may be either short-lived or extend over a period of time. Periods of great social change or trauma might produce changes in traits such that individuals exhibit temporary changes in personality.

One can obtain data with respect to all of these potentially existing changes by studying individuals of different ages in a longitudinal study. Suppose one studied two groups of adolescents who were 12 years old and 14 years old in 1980 and then studied the same individuals in 1982. Evidence for age-related maturational changes would be obtained if there were differences in test scores for 14-year olds as compared to 12-year olds, irrespective of the time of testing or of the time of their birth. Cohort effects would be exhibited by evidence that adolescents born in 1966 were different from adolescents born in 1968, irrespective of the time of testing or the age at which they were tested. Time-of-testing effects would be exhibited by differences in characteristics associated with testing in 1980 as opposed to testing in 1982, irrespective of the age of the individuals being tested at a particular time. There might also be interactions involving two or more of these variables. Thus, age changes might be different for different cohorts.

Nesselroade and Baltes (1974) have reported a study of 2000 adolescents who were born in 1954, 1955, 1956, and 1957 and tested in a longitudinal design in 1970, 1971, and 1972. They obtained data on several dimensions of intelligence and personality. While the results are complex and slightly different for each of the dimensions of personality that were studied, certain generalizations can be made as to the relative influence of different kinds of changes on personality. First, there were very few significant interactions among the variables, suggesting that maturational, cohort, and time-of-testing effects did not interact with each other. Cohort and age effects were, for the most part, weak and absent. Thus, over the age ranges studied and the time-of-birth effects investigated, there were few, if any, systematic changes in personality. Sex differences were relatively large and were significant for 9 of 10 personality traits and were absent only for the trait of tough-mindedness or autonomy. There were significant time-of-testing effects for at least 6 of the 10 personality dimensions studied, but they were much smaller in magnitude than the effects of sex. The largest effects were obtained for self-report measures of intelligence and impulsivity. Impulsivity generally declined between 1970 and 1972.

The Nesselroade and Baltes study was designed to test for cohort and time-of-testing effects and their interactions. Their data indicate that for the most part neither of these variables was a major source of variance in personality. They do report test–retest stability correlations that were somewhat variable for different traits and different subgroups. Averaged over all dimensions, the test–retest correlations for the 1970–1971 and the 1971–1972 testing were .56 and .60 for males, respectively, and .60 and .65 for females, respectively. The 2-year test–retest stabilities were .49 and .54 for male and female subjects, respectively. Although Nesselroade and Baltes were primarily interested in changes in personality traits and did not analyze their data in such a way as to permit a direct comparison of the relative importance of stability and change in personality, it is possible to get some idea about these issues from an examination of their data. Imagine that one, given information about a person contained within the data set obtained by Nesselroade and Baltes, wanted to predict a person's score on a particular personality trait. Consider the following information: a score obtained by the same person on the same personality trait on a different occasion; the sex of the person taking the test; the time when the test was taken; the age of the person taking the test (*N.B.*, this last piece of information, when combined with the previous piece of information, provides one with cohort information). These variables would provide one with information of decreasing utility in terms of their predictive relationship to the test score. While it is difficult to be precise about the relative importance of these variables, there is no doubt that information about the previous test score is dramatically more predictive than any other information contained in the data set.

It is not only the case that the cohort and time-of-testing effects were relatively weak—the evidence for their existence at all is less than convincing. Nesselroade and Baltes only had self-report data. We do not know if comparable effects would have been obtained in observor ratings or in other forms of measurement. Since the time-of-testing effects they obtained were relatively weak, it is entirely possible that they were method specific.

This analysis of the Nesselroade and Baltes study is not undertaken in order to assert that personality traits do not exhibit maturational, cohort, or time-of-testing effects. I might add parenthically, however, that I have not seen good heteromethod data that convincingly demonstrate the existence of such effects. Rather, the analysis is meant to indicate that studies of personality change that neglect personality traits are, in effect, in the dangerous position of overlooking the clearcut and dramatic evidence for stability of personality and of focusing on effects that may be ephemeral and epiphenomenal. It would be better to include prior trait scores as variables in the analysis in order to provide information about the relative importance of stability and change as well as the possibility that events that are presumed to cause change, which are related to cohort effects, or the like, may interact with personality characteristics in such a way that the effects are different for individuals with different personality trait characteristics.

Such an analysis is compatible with an analysis of traits that suggests that they influence the impact of the social environment on the individual.

Costa and McRae (1980) have also expressed skepticism about the development of a comprehensive understanding of personality change that uses measures of trait change as an outcome variable. They report an analysis of Levinson's view of the male midlife crisis. When they examined the subjects in their longitudinal study, they found little evidence for the existence of a midlife psychological crisis. They found that there was a subset of subjects in their study who could be described as experiencing a midlife crisis. However, their data indicated that this subset of individuals could also be characterized as having enduring neurotic tendencies and that evidence of high neuroticism as assessed by self-report measures was present several years before the occurrence of a midlife crisis.

Cohort Effects: Intelligence

The critique presented above does not constitute a systematic survey of the literature on the possiblities for change in traits over the life span. We shall attempt a more systematic survey of change in traits again by starting with research on intelligence. Clearly, intelligence changes early in life. This is self-evident. Does intelligence change over the adult life span of an individual? It was once thought that scores on intelligence tests declined with age and that scores on tests of intelligence would show gradual declines from young adulthood through the fifth and sixth decade of life, and then they would begin to decline quite rapidly. There was considerable evidence for this view based on the results of cross-sectional studies in which intelligence tests were administered to individuals of different ages at the same time (see Wechsler, 1958). Schaie and Strother (1968), however, succeeded in demonstrating quite convincingly that scores of tests of intelligence do not exhibit substantial declines with age. They studied individuals of different ages longitudinally. If one looks at intelligence-test scores as a function of age, there was clear evidence for declines. However, when they looked at their data longitudinally, there was little or no evidence for decline. Thus, the declines that had been obtained were not age related or maturational but were cohort effects. Individuals born at the turn of the century tended to have scores on intelligence tests that were approximately one standard deviation lower than individuals born in the 1930s. The increases in scores in intelligence tests are probably attributable to secular changes in educational opportunity. High school graduation has become the norm for the American population. Only a minority of the cohorts born in 1900 were high school graduates. Evidence for cohort related changes in performance on tests of intelligence is also present in the comparison of test scores for army recruits in World War I, World War II, and the Korean War (see Flynn, 1984). There appears to be relatively clear cut evidence for a significant increase in performance on tests of intelligence. The increase is relatively large in magnitude—approximately one standard deviation.

The newer data on changes in intelligence tests as a function of age suggest that scores in intelligence tests remain relatively constant over the life span. That is, individuals do not exhibit large and inevitable declines over much of the adult life span. There is, however, some evidence for declines in the seventh, eighth, and ninth decade of life (see Baltes and Schaie, 1976). It is also the case that the pattern of declines may be different for different subtests, with tests relying on knowledge and experience, such as tests of vocabulary and comprehension, exhibiting little or no decline and with tests of spatial reasoning exhibiting small declines at an earlier age. Thus, for most of the adult life span, individuals not only remain relatively invariant with respect to their position relative to age cohorts in intelligence, but they tend to perform at about the same level on tests of intelligence.

Educational Experience and Changes in Intelligence

We have implicated educational experience as an explanation of cohort effects in intelligence-test scores. If this analysis is correct we should expect to find that variations in educational opportunities do influence performance in tests of intelligence. There is evidence for such an effect. Harnquist (1968a,b) studied a sample of Swedish students who were assigned to an academically rigorous secondary education designed to prepare them for university education and pupils assigned to a less academically rigorous educational experience designed to be terminal. Adjusting for initial differences in test scores, he found that the pupils assigned to the more rigorous educational experience did in fact increase their scores on intelligence tests more than pupils on the less academically rigorous track. The differences were calculated to be approximately 0.4 of a standard deviation.

Jensen (1977) has attempted to find evidence for the *cumulative deficit* hypothesis—defined as a decline in intelligence test scores associated with inferior schooling. The hypothesis implies that children provided with inadequate educational experience will exhibit increasingly large deficits relative to adequately educated children the longer they are in school. He used a sibling control design to study this issue. If the hypothesis is correct, then older siblings provided with inferior education will score lower on tests of intelligence than their younger siblings with comparable educational experiences. He used a sample of black children attending schools in California to test the cumulative deficit hypothesis. This research was based on the assumption that black children are likely to experience inferior education. He found no evidence of systematic declines in intelligence with age in this study. In a subsequent study, using a sample of black children attending schools in a rural area of Georgia, he found clear evidence for systematic declines as a function of age differences in siblings. The declines were large and over the course of a child's educational experience were estimated to be approximately one standard deviation in magnitude.

These studies suggest that gross variations in educational opportunities do affect intelligence. If variations in educational experience can affect scores on intelligence tests, it is reasonable to believe that systematic attempts to alter the educational experiences of children would lead to changes in intelligence. There have been several such attempts made for children in the preschool age period.

Several studies reported gains of 10–15 points in intelligence test scores as a result of a 2- or 3-year preschool intervention (see Weikart, 1967, for a typical study of this type). While these studies appear to suggest that the provision of adequate early intellectual enrichment can lead to relatively substantial increments in intellectual ability, we now have reasons to interpret these results with more caution. Many of these results may be attributable to rather superficial test-taking skills that are relatively more important determinants of test performance among young children than they are of older children or adults. Also, some of these results may be attributable to motivational changes (see Zigler, Abelson, and Seitz, 1973). The possibility that 10–15 point increments in test performance for preschool children growing up in poverty may not be of great importance is suggested by the results of a study by Jacobsen, Berger, Bergman, Millham, and Greeson (1971). They found that preschool-age children exposed to 20 hours of training in solving two choice-discrimination problems of increasing complexity had a 13.3 point increase in intelligence test score as assessed by the Stanford–Binet. The largest increments in intelligence test score were obtained by the children who initially had the lowest intelligence test scores. We are not inclined to assume that 20 hours of instruction in two choice-discrimination problems dramatically altered intellectual ability. A more sensible interpretation of these results would require us to question the meaning of low scores on intelligence tests for preschool-age children with impoverished backgrounds. The potential ease of manipulation of test scores for very young children leads us to interpret the findings of 10- to 15-point increments in intelligence test scores obtained for intellectual interventions of 2-years duration cautiously. There is an additional reason to be skeptical of these findings. The typical result for these studies is that the intellectual gains fade over time (see Bronfenbrenner, 1975; Zigler and Valentine, 1979; Zigler and Seitz, 1982). The decline in intelligence test scores to the point where the experimental group is no longer substantially different from the control group may occur because of the failure of the public schools to provide adequate intellectual enrichment for children who have been intellectually enriched in the preschool period. However, one finds the fadings of intelligence test gains as a result of enrichment even where children exhibit some gains in intellectual achievement in schools (see Zigler and Valentine's assessment of the benefits of Headstart programs, 1979). These results suggest that the fading of intelligence test scores is not so much attributable to inadequate intellectual stimulation provided by the schools, as to the possibility that the score increases obtained during the preschool-age years did not reflect true gains in ability.

More dramatic gains in ability were reported by Heber and Garber (1970) in a study in which a group of black children, whose mothers had intelligence test scores below 70, were exposed to an intensive intellectual enrichment program starting shortly after birth. The preliminary reports of the outcomes of this project indicated gains of over 30 points in intelligence test scores relative to the control group at age 4. These children had a mean test score of 120. Clarke and Clarke (1976) reported, on the basis of a personal communication, that the intelligence test scores of the experimental group of children had faded to 106 shortly after school entry. The results of the Heber and Garber research, although widely cited as demonstrating the possibility of dramatic gains for children from deprived backgrounds who are provided intensive intellectual interventions starting shortly after birth, have never been presented in refereed journals. All the information about the study has been gleaned from personal presentations at meetings and from a variety of technical reports. Moreover, the principal investigators have not responded to requests for technical details of their research (Page, 1975; Beller, 1979). And, more recently, there have been suggestions that the results may be fraudulent (see Sommer and Sommer, 1983).

Ramey and Haskins (1981a) have reported the results of an early intervention program starting at 3 months of age. They reported a 14-point increment in Binet test IQ scores for their experimental children compared with their control group children at 36 months of age. However, by age 5 the differences between the experimental and the control groups had faded to 7 points and were only marginally significant (Ramey and Haskins, 1981b). The results of the Ramey and Haskins study require longer follow-up for full evaluation. However, the preliminary data reported above suggest that the changes in intelligence test scores as a result of intensive interventions were marginal. To my knowledge no one has reported gains in intelligence test scores as a result of preschool interventions that are of enduring significance or even that persist as far as the third grade. This assertion should not be construed as a negative statement about the value of such preschool interventions. There is at least preliminary evidence that some of these programs have had a positive impact on the school performance of children (see Zigler and Valentine, 1979). But these benefits occur independent of changes in intelligence test scores. The only intervention in the preschool period that has been found to produce increments in intelligence test scores is adoption. Scarr and Weinberg (1976) have reported that a group of black children adopted by white middle-class parents had intelligence test scores of 106 at age 7. Similarly, Schiff et al. (1978) reported that 26 children whose biological mothers had working-class backgrounds who were adopted by middle-class parents before 6 months of age had intelligence test scores of 111.5—over 16 points higher than the intelligence test scores of their sibling controls who were raised with their biological mothers. Of course, adoption is a dramatic intervention that can have a substantial impact on the kind of environment to which a child is exposed. The adoption studies suggest that the provision of optimal intellectual environments will result in changes in intelligence test scores over and above those that would be obtained if the adopted children experienced a less stimulating environment. Of course, adoption is not a socially viable program for the production of intellectual improvements for children whose parents are poor and uneducated. The research reviewed here supports the vague common sense view that abilities are not subject to a "quick fix" but that they are modifiable slowly over time as the result of the provision of optimal environments.

There have also been studies of attempts to provide adults with intensive, but relatively brief, learning experiences in an attempt to increase their performance on tests of intellectual ability. Some of these studies are little more than clinical reports (e.g., Whimbey, 1975). Others are more systematic. For example, there have been several attempts to increase the scores of individuals on the Scholastic Aptitude Test. Messick and Jungeblut (1981) have published a comprehensive review of this literature. Their analysis of the literature indicates that the average increment in SAT scores as a function of coaching is a nonlinear function of the duration of training. Small increments are achieved rather quickly, but the rate of gain in test scores then slows, and longer and longer periods of instruction are necessary to produce equal increments in scores. While a gain of approximately one-tenth of a standard deviation in score would require approximately 12 hours of instruction, a gain of one-third of a standard deviation would require approximately 260 hours of instruction. These results are based on fitting regression lines to a variety of studies that are often, in various ways, flawed. They do suggest, however, that SAT scores, which are highly related to measures of general ability, are not easily changed by exposure to intensive intellectual training.

Our review of studies of the stability and change in intelligence may be summarized as follows: (1) There is considerable evidence of stability through the life span; (2) There is very little evidence that experimental procedures exist that can produce changes in intelligence; (3) Enduring and profound interventions in the character of the educational experiences of individuals can, cumulatively, lead to changes in intelligence. Evidence from studies of the effects of adoption, from cumulative deficits in very deprived educational settings, and the effects of enduring enriched educational experiences have all been found to alter intelligence.

Can Personality Traits Be Changed?

We have less systematic information permitting us to reach conclusions about changes in personality. I am not aware of any data indicating cohort effects for personality traits. Are individuals more or less extraverted or neurotic than they were 50 years ago? We simply don't know. Similarly, we can ask whether personality changes systematically over the life span. Do individuals become more or less neurotic with age—more or less extraverted? Again, we don't know. Nor do we have evidence for systematic changes in personality traits as a function of gross variations in environmental experiences. Studies of intelligence suggest that variations in the educational background of families that rear individuals influence intelligence, and thus adoption is an important influence on intelligence. When we come to review the behavior genetics of personality, we shall argue that several different sources of data suggest that there are little or no effects of the family-of-rearing on personality traits, and thus adoption should not be expected to have an influence on personality traits. Again, for intelligence, we can argue that variations in the quality of schooling do cumulatively influence intelligence. We have little evidence that permits us to say with confidence that variations in the environment of a particular kind are likely to lead to changes in various personality characteristics. In short, we do not know if there are systematic changes that occur in personality traits, and we do not know what, if any, systematic variations in the environment produce changes in personality traits. There is perhaps one respect in which there appears to be some degree of congruence between our knowledge of change in intelligence and our knowledge of change in personality traits. We have seen that efforts to change intelligence have yet to yield convincing evidence of enduring changes. It is possible to argue that systematic efforts to change personality have produced equally unconvincing evidence of change.

Therapy and the Attempted Modification of Personality

Just as there are efforts designed to remediate intellectual deficits, there have been attempts to change personality characteristics that are considered to be undesirable from one or another perspective. Various forms of therapy exist that are presumed to be capable of changing personality. Behavior therapies tend to be focused more narrowly and attempt to change relatively specific behavior patterns that are considered undesirable. Various forms of psychotherapy attempt to create more fundamental alterations in personality. The distinction is fundamental with respect to evaluating therapy as a technique for producing changes in personality traits. Consider an example: A depressed person enters therapy and, as a result of a therapeutic intervention, the person's depression is reduced. Has the person's personality changed? From a trait perspective, depression is a behavioral index or manifestation of an underlying trait disposition. One could assume that certain trait dispositions exist that increase the likelihood over the life span that a person will become depressed. From this perspective, even if one grants the efficacy of the therapeutic intervention, it is not obvious that the previous personality has altered in the sense that the disposition predisposing the individual to become depressed has altered. What would constitute evidence for an alteration of the trait disposition? One would have to have long-term, follow-up observations that demonstrate that the person has a significantly reduced likelihood of developing subsequent depressions and other undesirable behavioral manifestations that may be assumed to be manifestations of the underlying disposition. This point is analogous to the typical psychoanalytic complaint about behavior therapy. Evidence for the reduction, in what may be construed as a symptom, of an underlying disorder does not constitute evidence of profound change in personality, nor does it necessarily put the individual at decreased risk for the development of other undesirable manifestations (symptoms) of the underlying personality disorder. Or, to use an example from research on intelligence, attempts to remediate the intellectual deficits of individuals with very low intelligence quotients have been reasonably successful when they focused on a given task or problem. However, the benefits of the remediation decline rapidly as the characteristics of the task change. Thus, it is relatively easy to change a specific behavioral manifestation of a trait and relatively difficult to change the trait in such a way that one changes the broad dispositional tendency for the trait to be manifested in diverse settings.

Irrespective of one's view of what we shall see is the vexed question of the efficacy of various forms of therapy, evidence for the occurrence of profound changes in traits in the sense outlined above does not exist or, if it does exist, it is certainly not abundant. Such evidence would require monitoring individuals who have received some form of therapy for several years in order to ascertain whether they are at significantly reduced risk for exhibiting a class of behaviors presumed to be related to the trait that was assumed to be implicated in the development of their initial difficulties. The evidence for outcomes of therapy that we do have is usually confined to relatively brief, follow-up investigations.

Quite apart from the question of the extent to which therapy alters traits, we can ask what is the status of the evidence that various forms of therapy are capable of changing individuals. Before 1952, as Eysenck (1952) pointed out in an historically important article, the evidence for the efficacy of therapy, particularly of various forms of psychotherapy, was substantially anecdotal. Studies using control groups were virtually nonexistent. Reports about improvements as a result of treatment should, of course, be treated with extreme caution for a variety of reasons. The data in support of such claims are rarely systematic and objective. Since individuals enter therapy typically in a period when they believe that things are quite bad for them, we can expect, given the usual ebb and flow of events, that on retesting they would report being improved. More formally, as long as the test–retest correlation for stability of behavior is less than 1.00 (and it always is), we would expect that individuals who are at a very low ebb in their psychological state when entering therapy will be found to be improved when they are retested at some later date.

Eysenck's expressed skepticism about the evidence for the benefits of psychotherapy was instrumental in the initiation of systematic research efforts that typically involved the random assignment of individuals seeking therapy to a wait-list control group in order to see if individuals who receive therapy improve or change relative to individuals who do not receive therapy. Smith, Glass, and Miller (1980) published a review of more than 500 controlled outcome studies of various forms of therapy, and critics of their book (e.g., Wilson and Rachman, 1982) argued that they had omitted many relevant studies of the outcomes of behavior therapy. The interpretation of this literature has also engendered considerable controversy, and various individuals who have summarized this literature have taken different views of the evidence it provides for the efficacy of various forms of therapy (see Meltzoff and Kornreich, 1970). Smith, Glass, and Miller used a procedure for the evaluation of a body of research called *meta-analysis* in order to attempt to resolve the controversies surrounding this issue. Meta-analysis is a statistical procedure that, in effect, averages the results of many different studies to reach a conclusion about the results obtained in the entire set of studies. The procedure is based on the notion that statistical indices, whether of mean differences between groups, or correlations, or percent differences, may be converted to a common metric called an *effect size* that may be thought of as a standard deviation of the difference between groups treated differently. Smith, Glass, and Miller obtained outcome measures from more than 500 studies involving a comparison between a group given some form of therapy and a control group. They converted all of the outcome measures to measures of effect size and then averaged the effect-size indices and obtained a value of .81. This analysis appears to suggest that when averaged over all forms of therapy and all methods of assessing therapy, including ratings by therapists, friends, and independent psychiatric assessments, behavioral measures, and self-reports, therapy tends to change individuals in desirable directions, and the magnitude of expected change is approximately 0.8 of a standard deviation.

Although on the surface the Smith, Glass, and Miller analysis appears to provide definitive evidence for the ability of therapy to produce change, a number of additional issues may bear on an evaluation of the expected changes that are attributable to various forms of therapy. Prioleau, Murdock, and Brody (1983; see also Brody, 1983b; Brody, 1985a) have performed an additional analysis of the studies included in the Smith, Glass, and Miller survey. Their analysis was confined to the subset of studies that dealt with psychotherapy, rather than behavior therapy. In one sense this restriction is apt for our present purposes since one can argue that it is psychotherapy, rather than behavior therapy, that attempts to create fundamental changes in personality traits.

They further restricted the subset of studies they considered by including in their analysis only studies that involved a comparison of psychotherapy with placebos. Most of the studies evaluating psychotherapy have used wait-list controls. Such studies typically assign a random sample of individuals to a control group who are usually told that there are no facilities available for treatment but facilities will be available at a later time. Such individuals are then evaluated after a period of time and compared to individuals who have received therapy. Individuals in a wait-list group do not believe that they are receiving treatment. Individuals who believe that they are receiving treatment generally improve even if the active ingredient in treatment is removed. The classic example of such effects and their control is found in the evaluation of drug therapies. Typically, when evaluating a drug, one randomly assigns treated individuals to a group receiving a chemically inert pill in order to ascertain whether the changes that occur are attributable to the effects of the chemical interventions or to the mere belief that one is receiving treatment. It is generally accepted that placebo effects do cause change in a variety of conditions, and it is generally considered reasonable to use placebos as controls.

Prioleau, Murdock, and Brody analyzed the subset of studies included in the Smith, Glass, and Miller analysis that involved comparisons between psychotherapy and various treatments considered to be placebos. They found 32 such studies, and their meta-analysis resulted in a calculation of an effect size of .42—a value in exact agreement with the earlier results of the Smith, Glass, and Miller findings. Thus, approximately one-half of the changes attributable to psychotherapy could be attributable to placebo effects. Prioleau, Murdock, and Brody noted that the majority of their 32 studies did not involve comparisons between patients who sought therapy and placebo controls. Most of the studies were best described as analogue studies of solicited subjects who were recruited to serve as subjects for the purpose of an investigation of therapeutic outcome. Such subjects do not constitute a representative sample of individuals who seek therapeutic intervention. The latter group generally are more distressed. In any case, generalization about changes attributable to therapeutic interventions cannot be confidently reached by investigations of solicited subjects since the populations from which these samples derive are fundamentally distinct. Among the 32 studies included in their analysis, they were able to find only 3 studies in which comparisons were made between patients who sought and were provided psychotherapy and patients assigned to a placebo group. Brill, Koegler, Epstein, and Forgy (1964) randomly assigned psychiatric outpatients to a group who received 20 sessions of psychoanalytically oriented therapy and groups who were given pill placebos or psychoactive drugs in a *double-blind* design in which neither the patient nor the physician was aware of the drugs provided to the patients. They also had a wait-list control. Changes in the patients were measured by self-reports, therapists' reports, personality test scores, independent psychiatric ratings, and ratings by friends or spouses. All of the outcome measures exhibited comparable results. All of the treatment groups improved relative to the wait-list control group. There were no differences among the treatment groups. Thus, psychotherapy was no more effective than a pill placebo in inducing personality change.

Lorr, McNair, and Weinstein (1963) used a similar pill placebo design in a study comparing brief psychotherapy (only four sessions) with pill placebos for psychiatric outpatients. Their therapists were experienced. They had only two outcome measures—ratings of improvement by patients and therapists. They found essentially similar outcomes for patients given brief psychotherapy and patients assigned to a pill placebo treatment.

Gillan and Rachman (1974) studied a group of multiphobic patients who were provided with 15 hours of psychotherapy administered by experienced therapists and compared them with patients randomly assigned to placebo treatments who were either given training in muscle relaxation (a procedure not generally thought to be effective for the treatment of phobia) or were asked to think about situations that were likely to induce anxiety that was related to their phobias. They had several different measures of outcomes, including self-report measures of personality, therapist and independent ratings of phobia and depression, and an actual behavioral measure of response to a phobia-inducing situation, including measures of psychophysiological responsivity. They found that the therapy group and the placebo groups were essentially similar in these several outcome measures. It is also interesting to note that another group of subjects, given a behavior therapy treatment in which relaxation was associated with the imagined phobic situations, was improved relative to the placebo controls, indicating that the placebo controls had not received certain essential features of effective treatment for multiphobics. Gillan and Rachman also reported the results of a follow-up investigation. They found, on follow-up, that there were no differences among the multiphobics assigned to the different treatment conditions. The benefits of behavior therapy relative to placebo conditions were short-lived, and psychotherapy in this study, with an unusually wide-ranging set of outcome measures, was not superior to placebo treatments.

In addition to the three studies described above, culled from the set of more than 500 studies included in the Smith, Glass, and Miller review, Prioleau, Murdock, and Brody were able to find another study comparing psychotherapy to placebo treatment. McLean and Hakstian (1979) reported data for 37 randomly assigned clinically depressed outpatients who received 8–12 hours of insight-oriented psychotherapy from licensed psychologists and psychiatrists. Psychotherapy was the treatment of choice for these professionals. Outcome was assessed by the use of 10 self-report measures derived from analyses of questionnaire data. The placebo treatment was administered to 38 randomly assigned patients who received 10 hours of muscle relaxation therapy. Subjects were informed that the muscle relaxation treatment was therapeutically relevant, although McLean and Hakstian asserted that they considered the variable as a placebo since there was no compelling rationale for the view that treatment of depression by muscle relaxation is therapeutically efficacious. At the end of the therapy, in a comparison of the patients assigned to the psychotherapy and the placebo treatment groups, there were no appropriate differences on any outcome measure, although a group of subjects randomly assigned to a behavior therapy treatment condition were discernibly improved relative to the relaxation therapy patients. The relaxation therapy patients had slightly better outcomes than the psychotherapy patients. Three months after the termination of psychotherapy, there was again no discernible difference in outcome.

In a number of ways, McLean and Hakstian's study was well designed. It used trained psychotherapists with a commitment to the virtues of psychotherapy; it included a well-defined patient group, and it had a follow-up. It had two limitations. There was exclusive reliance on questionnaire and self-report data (although arguably the instruments used are well standardized and have some validity for the particular target population). In addition, it is conceivable that the placebo treatment might include a number of complex aspects (e.g., following instructions) that extend beyond an expectancy manipulation. However, if considered in conjunction with the results of the three other studies of outpatients, this study appears to buttress the view that psychotherapy does not lead to outcomes that are more favorable than those attained by placebo treatment for outpatients.

It might be argued that this survey of the literature is partial and incomplete. While this may not be an exhaustive review of studies comparing psychotherapy to placebo treatments, I am not aware of any other studies. It should also be noted that the available literature covers only a small subset of therapies and does not include the long-term psychotherapy favored by traditional psychoanalytically oriented therapists. Perhaps very long-term therapy produces relatively enduring changes in personality structure that will lead to an enduring change in neurotic behaviors.

It is possible to argue that the placebo effect is the basic ingredient in all successful psychotherapy. That is, a belief that one is doing something about one's problems and is engaged in an activity that is likely to lead to improvement in one's life may replace despair with hope and might lead one to develop an altered sense of one's ability to control one's life. The sense of efficacy or belief in the capability of change has been postulated to be a central mediating event for many kinds of behavior change (Bandura, 1977).

It should be noted that if one accepts this analysis, several ingredients that are usually considered to be essential to changes induced by traditional psychotherapy are discarded. For example, gaining insight into one's motives, experiencing and analyzing the meanings of one's emotional responses in the therapeutic setting, and, indeed, carried to its extreme logical conclusion, participating in *any* process of human interaction with a therapist may be discarded in favor of an assertion that taking a pill will change a person's life.

Even if a placebo-induced belief in the possibility of change is viewed as the essential ingredient in the creation of therapeutically induced change, it may be that the magnitude of change induced by such placebo-induced beliefs is small. We shall return to the issue of the influence of belief on action later in this book (see also Brody, 1980; 1983a). We shall argue that changes in beliefs do not invariably change behavior. Moreover, it is difficult to believe that the mere belief that one is engaged in a therapeutic enterprise is sufficient to cause a profound alteration in personality traits that will lead to enduring changes in the way in which an individual responds to the world.

What can we conclude about stability and change in personality on the basis of this brief review of outcome research? It is clear that the available evidence does not suggest that psychotherapy is capable of inducing relatively enduring changes in personality traits or, perhaps, more precisely, in neuroticism. This does not mean that psychotherapy does not produce such changes or could not, but it means only that the available evidence does not convincingly indicate that psychotherapy does produce such changes. There is nothing in the available data that would lead one to believe that personality traits may be substantially changed or remediated on the basis of therapeutic interventions. In this respect, the data for personality traits appear to be at least crudely analogous to the data base related to experimental attempts to change general intelligence. Intelligence and personality traits are relatively enduring dispositions that are not easily changed.

3

Behavior Genetics

Introduction

In a trait-centered approach to personality, traits are conceived of as enduring dispositions that determine an individual's response to diverse situations. Such an approach assigns logical and chronological priority to traits. If one searches for personality characteristics that endure through time and that remain invariant over the lifespan, one is led ineluctably to those dispositions that are present from the origin of life at the moment of conception, that is, to genetic dispositions. The trait approach to intelligence, ever since its inception in the 1860s, has been intertwined with a conception of the influence of genetic characteristics. Because genotypes do not change, their continued influence might provide a basis for the existence of enduring, relatively invariant personal characteristics. There is another reason why intelligence as a trait has always been intimately connected with behavior genetic research. Intelligence is often defined as the ability to acquire knowledge. Such a definition implies that a person who is not intelligent cannot acquire knowledge. In fact, a person may be intelligent and not acquire knowledge. The person may not have been exposed to appropriate tuition, or the person may have been exposed to appropriate tuition but, for a variety of personal reasons, may not have benefited from the tuition. Note that such a conception assigns a causal (but not a unicausal) prior directional influence of ability (i.e., intelligence) on achievement. Ability may be a cause of what one achieves. Achievement cannot, in the first instance, cause one to have ability—achievement logically presupposed ability. Since ability must, by definition, be present before achievement, it is natural to approach ability from a genetic point of view. This is not logically required. One could assert that ability develops early in life as a result of early experiences and, once crystallized, becomes a basis for the determination of achievement.

We shall argue that evidence for genetic influences on traits provides one of the strongest sources of support for assigning a central role in personality to traits. Curiously, American critics of the trait concept (e.g., Mischel) typically ignore the evidence for a genetic basis of individual differences of traits.

We shall consider the origins of traits. In particular we shall review research that provides a basis for understanding the ways in which heredity and environment influence a person's trait dispositions. We shall see that contemporary behavior-genetic research is focused at least as much on an understanding of the impact of the environment on personal characteristics as it is on explicating the influence of genotypes on phenotypes.

Twin Studies

Methodology and Basic Findings

We shall review twin studies, family studies, and adoption studies. Twin studies are based on differences in the degree of resemblance on personality characteristics of monozygotic (MZ) and dyzygotic (DZ) twins. The basic idea behind such studies is quite simple. Monozygotic twins are genetically identical. Hence, any differences between them must be attributable to the influence of the environment. Dyzygotic twins are not genetically identical—they are as similar as siblings. Therefore, differences among pairs of DZ twins are attributable to both environmental and genetic effects. If MZ twins resemble each other more than DZ twins, it is possible to infer that the lesser degree of resemblance among DZ twins is attributable to the variability of their genotypes. Hence, one can infer that variations in genotypes are related to the phenotype, which is measured in the twin study.

There is a crucial assumption in the use of the twin method as outlined above. The use of the twin method assumes that the variations in the environment experienced by MZ twin pairs are equal to the variations in the environment experienced by DZ twin pairs. If MZ twin pairs, by virture of their greater similarity in physical appearance, are treated more alike than same-sex DZ twin pairs, the greater similarity among MZ twins in some phenotypic characteristic may be attributed to the greater environmental similarity they have experienced, rather than to their genetic identity. The environmental critique of twin studies is plausible. There is evidence that MZ twin pairs do experience a more similar environment than DZ twin pairs in some respects. For example, Smith (1965) found that MZ twins were more likely than DZ twins to have the same friends.

Although the environmental objection to twin studies is plausible, there are several possible objections to it. First, evidence that MZ twin pairs experience more similar environments in some respects than DZ twin pairs is not a critical objection, unless one can show that the greater similarities they experience influence the phenotypic characteristic that is being assessed. This is rarely done. In addition, the greater similarity of environment experienced by MZ twins may itself be attributable to genetic influences. If individuals select friends who share their interests and personal characteristics, and if interests and personal characteristics are influenced by genetic characteristics, then the greater similarity of environment experienced by MZ twins may itself be a reflection of the influence of genotypes on the environment. Second, studies that have attempted to assess variations in intrapair similarity in the environment experienced by twins have generally found that such variations are not related to the degree of similarity of twin pairs for personality characteristics (see Loehlin and Nichols, 1976). Third, Scarr and Carter-Saltzman (1979) have reported that a significant minority of parents, perhaps as many as one-third, are mistaken with respect to the true zygosity as determined by objective assessments (typically using blood-typing) of their twins. They found that the degree of resemblance of twins was determined by true zygosity rather than believed zygosity. Thus, even where same-sex DZ twins are sufficiently physically similar to lead their parents to believe that they are MZ twins, the physical similarity does not lead to similarity in measures of personal traits that are equivalent to the similarity of MZ twin pairs. In addition, where MZ twin pairs are sufficiently dissimilar in appearance to lead their parents to mistakenly believe that they are DZ twins, this does not lead to a reduction in their phenotypic trait similarity relative to other MZ twins correctly identified as such by their parents. Fourth, studies of MZ twins reared in different homes exist. These studies indicate that MZ twins reared apart tend to have scores on personality tests that are as similar to each other as MZ twins reared in the same home. These data strongly suggest that the evidence of greater similarity among MZ twin pairs than DZ twin pairs in measures of personality is not attributable to differences in the extent to which they are treated more alike by their parents.

There are many twin studies comparing MZ and DZ twins on the traits of neuroticism and extraversion as assessed by self-report questionnaires. The existence of this body of research is largely attributable to the influence of Hans Eysenck, who suggested in the 1950s that extraversion and neuroticism were the most important personality traits and that they both had a genetic basis (see Eysenck and Prell, 1951; 1956). In addition, Eysenck developed a series of self-report questionnaires designed to measure these traits. Because of Eysenck's influence, many researchers in this area have used one of the questionnaires developed by him. Not only are there many such studies, there are also studies with very large samples—in some cases with samples of more than 12,000 twin pairs (see Floderus-Myrhed, Pedersen, and Rasmuson, 1980). The results are, for the most part, remarkably consistent. Monozygotic twins are invariably found to be more alike than DZ twins on measures of extraversion and neuroticism. The correlations for MZ twins are usually about .50, whereas those for same-sex DZ twins are approximately .20. Several details of these data are noteworthy.

The correlation between pairs of MZ twins reared in the same home on personality traits is considerably lower than the test–retest correlation for administration of the test to individuals after a brief period of time. (Test–retest correlations for these personality trait measures are approximately .84.) By comparison, the test–retest correlation for group tests of intelligence is approximately .87, and the correlation for MZ twins reared together is approximately .86. These data suggest that MZ twins are less similar in their responses to personality questionnaires than they are in their scores on tests of intelligence. The existence of differences between MZ twins reared together leads to an important implication about the influence of the environment on personality traits. We can distinguish between two kinds of environmental influences, that is, within-family and between-family environmental influences. *Between-family* influences are environmental influences attributable to variations in the environment experienced by individuals who are reared in different families. When we think of the environmental impact on personality, we usually think of between-family influences. Most of our theories of socialization that emphasize variations in child-rearing practices are theories of between-family environmental influences. *Within-family* environmental influences are attributable to variations in the environment experienced by individuals growing up in the same family. The term within-family is a misnomer. It does not necessarily refer to influences on an individual that occur within the context of the family. Note that the definition refers to variations, that is, differences, in the environment experienced by individuals growing up in the same family. These variations might be attributable to the influence of the family. For example, one child might be treated more leniently than another child in the family. However, the variations might also be attributable to events occurring outside the family. For example, two individuals growing up in the same family might have different friends, and the interactions they have with their friends might influence their response to personality questionnaries.

The existence of differences in scores on personality questionnaires among pairs of MZ twins reared together implies that there must be within-family environmental influences on these measures. This assertion is almost self-evidently correct. Differences among MZ twins reared together cannot be attributable to between-family environmental influences because they are reared in the same family. They cannot be attributable to genetic influences. This leaves within-family influences as the only possible basis for the existence of such differences.

If differences in the degree of similarity between MZ and DZ twin pairs are explained by reference to differences in genetic similarity, then genetic influences must also determine scores on personality tests.

In behavior genetic studies of variations in human characteristics, it is traditional to partition the total variability in a phenotypic measure (i.e., in the observed characteristic) into separately defined components of variance that contribute to the total variation in scores on the trait. We have identified two sources of variation in scores on questionnaire measures of neuroticism and extraversion—genetic influences and within-family influences. These two sources of variations may be used as a first approximation to fitting a model to these data—that is, to partitioning the variance in trait scores. These two sources of variation account for *all* of the variance in the trait. There is no residual variance left to be attributable to between-family environmental influences. This leads to a conclusion that many psychologists find counterintuitive. If there are no between-family environmental influences on a particular trait, it follows that variations in environmental experiences that are associated with being reared in different families do not lead to differences in personality traits, as assessed by questionnaires. Although this conclusion appears counterintuitive, we shall see that it is supported by other data.

The twin data may also be used to derive an estimate of the proportion of total variability in the phenotypic trait measure that is attributable to variations in the genotypes of members of the population. This estimate is called a heritability estimate, and it is the estimate that is generally referred to in discussions of the relative importance of genetic and environmental influences on a particular trait. It is no simple matter to calculate heritability estimates. Contemporary calculations tend to use different sources of data (e.g., twin studies, family studies, and adoption data), and information from different kinds of studies are not always in agreement. Also, heritability estimates can vary appreciably, depending upon assumptions one makes about such things as assortative mating—that is, the extent to which individuals mate with individuals who are similar with respect to the genotypes that influence phenotypes. If assortative mating exists, then siblings, including DZ twins, will resemble each other genetically more than would be expected if mating occurred among individuals who are genetically unrelated. Assortative mating assumptions are only one of a complex set of assumptions that must be dealt with in developing a procedure to calculate heritability, and different assumptions can produce quite different heritability estimates.

In addition to the difficulty involved in the calculation of heritability estimates, these estimates are subject to a popular misinterpretation. Heritability estimates should be considered as properties of a particular population from which individuals are sampled, rather than as properties of the trait. Thus, it is incorrect to say that a percentage of the variation of a trait, such as extraversion, is attributable to variations in genotypes. To the assertion that some percentage of variation in the trait of extraversion is attributable to variations in genotypes, the correct formulation of a heritability estimate would add the phrase "in a particular population". What is the significance of this distinction? The qualification of heritability estimates to a population is necessary because different populations or groupings of individuals may have different distributions of genotypes. If genotypes that influence a trait are not equivalent among different populations, then one might expect to find differences in heritability estimates. More fundamentally, the influence of a genotype on a phenotype may be dependent on the kinds of environments that an individual experiences. If individuals in different groups or populations experience different environments, then it is possible that the influence of genotypes on phenotypic measures would vary. The disease phenylketonuria provides a good example of a variable influence of genotypes on phenotypes. The disease is carried by the presence of two recessive genes leading to an enzyme deficiency that, in ordinary circumstances, results in mental retardation. It is now standard practice to test for the presence of the disease at birth and to provide special phenylalanine-restricted diets to individuals who have the disease. Children with phenylketonuria who are provided with this special diet tend not to develop mental retardation. The example indicates that a genetic influence may be modified by an environmental intervention. The genotype remains invariant, but its influence on the phenotype is variable, depending on the nature of the environment. This example helps us to understand why heritability estimates are specific to a particular population. Heritability estimates are not invariant. Changes in the environment experienced by different generations, or by different groups of individuals, might change the influence of genotypes on phenotypes.

Now that we have considered the meaning of heritability estimates and briefly discussed some of the difficulties involved in their calculations, we are in a position to indicate that the twin data suggest heritabilities of approximately .50 for the personality traits of extraversion and neuroticism. If one corrects these data for the existence of unreliability of measurement in the personality questionnaire data, the heritability estimates increase to approximately .55. Thus, these data imply that a substantial portion of the variance in scores on personality questionnaires appears to be attributable to variations in genotypes.

In summary, our analysis of twin data on personality suggests that trait scores are determined by variations in genotypes and environmental variations that occur within families, and not at all to between-family variations.

Monozygotic Twins Reared Apart

Research on MZ twins who are reared apart in different families provides support for the conclusion that between-family variance does not influence a person's score on self-report measures of extraversion and neuroticism. Although, for obvious reasons, studies of MZ twins reared apart are not plentiful and never constitute a representative sample of the population, there now exist at least five studies of this type, all of which found that MZ twins reared apart are as similar in self-report trait measures of personality as MZ twins reared in the same home. One study was done in the 1920s and used outmoded measures (Newman, Freeman, and Holzinger, 1937), two studies were presented only as preliminary reports (Langinvainio, Kaprio, Koskenvuo, and Lohnquist, 1983; Pedersen, Friberg, Floderus-Myrhed, McClearn, and Plomin 1983) and two studies provided perfectly adequate reports of their methods and procedures. Shields (1962) studied 44 pairs of MZ twins who were reared separately. They were not, for the most part, separated from birth, and some were reared in collateral branches of the same family. The average degree of separation in their first 18 years of life was 11 years. While their rearing conditions were not totally independent, there is no doubt that the MZ twins reared apart in Shields's study did experience substantial divergence in family backgrounds, which exceeded the divergence experienced among the group of 44 MZ twins reared together that constituted the comparison group. Table 3.1 presents the correlations obtained by Shields for MZ twins reared apart, MZ twins reared together, and a sample of DZ twins reared together in his study. An examination of these data indicates that MZ twins reared apart were, if anything, slightly more similar than MZ twins reared together. The difference, given the relatively small sample, is best thought of as being attributable to chance variations.

Lykken (1982; see also Bouchard, 1985) has reported data in a similar study for a sample of 28 twin pairs who were all separated in the first year of life. Lykken and his colleagues did not use a specific version of the Eysenck personality questionnaires, but they used a paper and pencil test developed at the University of Minnesota. Two of the factor-derived trait scores on this measure, positive affectivity and negative affectivity, are related to extraversion and neuroticism. Negative affectivity, defined as a tendency to experience negative affect, is correlated with neuroticism. Positive affectivity, defined as the tendency to experience positive affect, is positively correlated with extraversion. The data obtained from the Minnesota twin study as reported by Lykken are also

Table 3.1

Correlations for MZ Together, MZ Apart, and DZ Twins in Two Studies[a]

Study	MZ apart	MZ together	DZ together
Shields			
Neuroticism	.53	.38	.11
Extraversion	.61	.42	.17
Minnesota twin study			
Negative affectivity	.65	.67	.43
Positive affectivity	.57	.63	.02

[a]Based on Shields, 1962 and Lykken, 1982.

presented in Table 3.1. Note again that the findings indicate that MZ twins reared apart are as similar in their scores on self-report measures of personality as MZ twins reared together in the same family.

Nonadditive Genetic Influences

There are a number of other findings in twin studies of personality that provide suggestions about the role of genetic and environmental influences on the development of personality traits. On a simple "additive" genetic model, one would expect that the correlation between DZ twins would be one-half the value of the correlations for MZ twins. If we ignore the influence of assortative mating, we expect that the genetic correlation between DZ twins is .5, and the genetic correlation between MZ twins is 1.00. Assortative mating inflates the genetic correlation of DZ twins. If the environmental factors acting on these two kinds of twins are more or less equivalent, the difference in their genetic similarity should lead to DZ correlations that are one-half the value of MZ correlations.

Correlations between MZ and DZ twins for extraversion do not support the simple additive genetic studies. Dyzygotic correlations tend to be less than half the value of the correlations obtained for MZ twin pairs. Henderson (1982) reviewed 30 twin studies in which measures of extraversion were obtained and found that, in all of the studies, the value of the DZ correlation was less than half the value of the MZ correlation. Data obtained from the Minnesota study indicates near zero correlations for DZ twins on positive affectivity. Data on large samples of twins that permit one to fit various behavior genetic models to twin data has led to the rejection of the hypothesis that the personality trait of extraversion is determined by within-family variance and additive genetic variance. For example, Eaves and Young (1981) reanalyzed data on 12,858 same-sex Swedish twin pairs and were able to reject a model of simple additive genetic influences (Floderus-Myrhed, et al. 1980). Martin and Jardine (1986) reached the same conclusion in their analysis of 3810 Australian twin pairs. For example, they reported correlations between MZ and DZ pairs of .53 and .50 for male and female twin pairs on extraversion, and corresponding correlations of .19 and .13 for DZ twin pairs (see Loehlin, 1986). The rejection of a model of simple additive genetic influences for extraversion may be explained by a variety of genetic or environmental hypotheses. If genetic dominance exists such that one of the two possible genes at a particular location exerts a larger influence on the phenotype than the other, it would tend to reduce the similarity of DZ twin pairs on the phenotype. A second source of genetic divergence among DZ twin pairs is epistasis. The term *epistasis* refers to genetic influences that derive from nonadditive combinations of genes at different loci. Genotypic influences on a phenotype might depend upon the configural influence of several different genes, and the combined effects of these independent genes might not be predictable from a knowledge of their individual effects. Epistatic influences tend to decrease the resemblance of DZ twins on a phenotype. Lykken (1982) has coined the term "emergenesis" to describe an extreme form of epistatic influence in which the influence of genes on a phenotype is determined by the configural properties of a set of genes. Similarity on several members of the set does not create similarity on the relevant configural or emergent property of the total set of genes. He argues that positive affectivity fits an emergenetic model. Such a model is supported when DZ correlations tend toward zero for traits for which MZ correlations are relatively high.

The presence of nonadditive sources of variance attributable either to dominance or epistasis will tend to decrease narrow heritability. *Narrow heritability* is a term used in animal genetics and refers to the degree to which traits breed true, that is, the degree to which offspring resemble parents. To the extent that there are nonadditive sources of variance on a trait, we would expect that children would not resemble parents on the trait. The broad heritability of a trait refers to the total genetic influence on a trait and includes both additive and nonadditive genetic influences. The twin data for extraversion, therefore, provide support for a genetic model that implies that broad heritability exceeds narrow heritability and further implies that parent–offspring relationships should be relatively low.

There are environmental explanations for relatively low correlations among same-sex DZ twin pairs. Dyzygotic twins who are marginally different growing up in the same family might come to see themselves as being quite different. Thus, their self-reports might exaggerate the actual differences between themselves. Monozygotic twins, being more alike, would be less likely to exaggerate their personality differences. If this hypothesis is correct, one would expect that the variability of scores among DZ twin pairs would exceed the variability of scores of MZ twins. This does not appear to be the case (see Henderson, 1982). Monozygotic twins might experience environmental pressures that lead them to be alike and cause them to behave in very similar ways. This line of reasoning appears to be refuted by the data on MZ twins reared apart, as well as by the other arguments previously cited against an environmental explanation of MZ–DZ differences in general. In the absence of evidence in favor of an environmental explanation for relatively low same-sex DZ twin scores on self-report measures of extraversion, an explanation in terms of the existence of nonadditive genetic variance appears to be plausible. It should also be noted that the existence of relatively low correlations for DZ twins supports the conclusion that there are no between-family environmental influences on personality. That is, same-sex DZ twins who are reared in the same family and who share some degree of genetic similarity are not substantially similar in personality. If scores on personality tests were shaped by the characteristic socialization experiences provided to children reared together, then one should find high degrees of similarity among DZ twin pairs.

Heritability of Other Personality Characteristics

Our discussion of the heritability of self-report measures of personality traits has dealt exclusively with the heritability of extraversion and neuroticism. Are other traits equally heritable? Loehlin and Nichols (1976) have argued that all personality traits tend to exhibit roughly comparable heritabilities. A possible explanation for this result derives from the pervasive nature of dimensions such as extraversion and neuroticism. Factor analyses of self-report measures of traits tend to find that narrowly defined personality characteristics are related to each other and that there are broadly based pervasive general factors analogous to the existence of g in the intellectual domain. The pervasive influence of extraversion and neuroticism in self-report questionnaires tends to influence the heritability of other, more narrowly defined personality factors. Evidence also exists for the heritability of other, more narrowly defined personality trait characteristics. For example, Rushton, Fulker, Neule, Blizard, and Eysenck, (in press) have reported the results of a twin study of self-report measures of altruism and aggression. They reported MZ correlations of .53, .54, and .49 for the three measures of altruism, and they noted corresponding correlations of .25, .20, and .14 for DZ twin pairs. For two self-report measures of aggressive tendencies, they obtained MZ correlations of .40 and .42; corresponding DZ correlations were .04 and .20, respectively.

There is also evidence for the heritability of various measures of interest and attitudes. For example, Lykken (1982) reported that a measure of *husbandry*, defined as an interest in building, fixing, and decorating things, appears to act as an emergenetic trait. Using this measure, he reported correlations of .65 for MZ twins reared apart, .55 for MZ twins reared together, and −.07 for same-sex DZ twins. Martin and Jardine (1986) have obtained evidence for the heritability of the social attitude of conservatism. There are innumerable additional examples scattered throughout the literature. Thus, when twins describe their personal characteristics and even, on occasion, when they describe their recreational interests and attitudes, one finds higher MZ correlations than DZ correlations on their self-report measures.

We have discussed twin research using self-report indices. There is a lack of research on the heritability of personality traits using other types of measures, such as ratings, behavioral measures, or heteromethod aggregated indices, for adult subjects. Thus, we do not know what behavior genetic studies of heteromethod measures of personality traits might indicate. There are rating studies available of temperamental characteristics in infants and young children. However, these characteristics may be weakly related, or not related at all, to measures of traits obtained from adults. Buss and Plomin (1984) have developed a rating scale to assess infant temperament, from which they derive measures of emotionality, activity, and sociability. Emotionality is defined primarily in terms of negative affect and is, at least conceptually, linked to neuroticism. Sociability is linked to social extraversion and is defined as a preference to be with other people. They found that twin studies using parental ratings have typically reported MZ correlations of these temperaments exceeding .5 by the second year of life, and DZ correlations close to .0. One obvious artifact in these data is that ratings by parents of twins are clearly subject to contrast effects. Parents' perceptions of, and reports about, their twins are derived principally from their observations of the twins. Their ratings may tend to exaggerate small differences because of the presence of contrast effects. In order to control for such effects, Buss and Plomin compared ratings made by the fathers and mothers of twins. In their design each parent rated one member of the twin pair separately. The results were quite comparable. Even this did not really eliminate the possible source of contrast effects bias because each parent was still forming a view of the temperament of each of his or her children by observing their actions, and contrast effects resulting in an exaggerated view of differences between the twins could still occur.

Wilson and Matheny (1986) have used behavior ratings of infant twins based on observations of their performance in response to standardized testing situations. Ratings of each twin were made independently and thus were not subject to the influence of possible biasing contrast effects. These researchers factor analyzed behavior ratings based on observations of the twins and were able to define three factors (Matheny, 1980). One factor was called goal directness and included ratings of goal direction and orientation to the test. A second factor contained ratings for fear, cooperation, emotional tone, and social responsiveness. A third factor was an activity and energy factor. At 24 months there was clear evidence for divergence of MZ and DZ twin pairs. On these factors they found average MZ correlations of .53 and average DZ correlations of .13. While the DZ correlations are not .00, as in Plomin and Buss's analyses of parental ratings, they are still quite low and also well below one-half the value of the MZ correlations.

Wilson and Matheny (1986) have also obtained data, based on an extensive set of observations, on the response of infants to a standardized set of laboratory observations. Ratings were made while infants were presented with a variety of tasks and play activities and while they interacted with the experimenters under standard protocol conditions. Factor analyses of these ratings resulted in the extraction of an emotional tone factor, an attentional factor, a factor of cooperativeness with the staff, and an activity factor. For their relatively small samples at 24 months of age (approximately 30 MZ and 30 DZ twin pairs), there were no significant differences in factor scores for three of the factors. Monozygotic twins had higher correlations on their emotional tone factor than DZ twins. The correlations were .81 and .40, respectively. Note, for this measure of infant temperament, DZ twin correlations are approximately half the size of MZ correlations.

Goldsmith and Gottesman (1981) have reported the results of a twin study using ratings of responses to a standardized laboratory assessment. They found evidence for the heritability of five of nine factors, which they obtained from ratings of twins at three different ages: 8 months, 4 years, and 7 years. Table 3.2 presents these data. The DZ correlations they obtained tended to be above zero. These data, combined with the results of Wilson and Matheny, suggest that ratings based on laboratory behavioral observations are not in agreement with the results of the parental ratings of young twins summarized by Buss and Plomin, which indicated near zero correlations for DZ twins. How are these discrepancies to be explained? Parental observations are more extensive and are based on a broad sampling of situations. They tend to focus on general behavioral characteristics. Laboratory ratings are relatively specific and narrow in their scope. However, because they have been made independently, they are not subject to potential contrast effects. Possibly the independent ratings, based on aggregated observations of behaviors in young children, would resemble parental reports of very low DZ correlations. On the other hand, moderate agreement among DZ twins fits most of the research reports for older twins. It appears reasonable to conclude that the twin data we have on ratings in young children is in at least rough agreement with research on self-report questionnaires. Both sets of data do provide evidence for higher MZ than DZ correlations, and neither set of data provides much, if any evidence, of between-family environmental influences.

Table 3.2

Twin Correlations for Factors Derived from Behavior Ratings at Three Ages[a]

Factors	MZ	DZ	R_{MZ}-R_{DZ}
	Age 8 Months		
Vigorous Activity	.57	.35	.22*
Interest in/responsiveness to people	.28	.20	.08
	Age 4 Years		
Spontaneous Activity	.41	.37	.04
Task Persistence	.56	.25	.31*
Irritability/Negative mood	.45	.17	.28*
	Age 7 Years		
Active Adjustment:			
Spontaneous/Friendly	.55	.22	.33*
Fearful/Inhibited	.36	.21	.15*
Task Persistence	.29	.24	.05
Agreeable/Co-operative	−.02	.09	−.11

[a]Based on Goldsmith & Gottesman (1981).
*$p < .05$.

Twin studies may also be used to study the behavior genetics of change and development. Early measures of temperament exhibit considerable instability, and infant temperament scores are not invariably predictive of temperament scores obtained at a later date. For example, Wilson and Matheny (1986) reported that factor scores on emotional tone, derived from ratings of behavior in laboratory settings, correlated .38 from 9 to 12 months and .36 from 12 to 18 months. However, the correlation for the 18- to 24-month period was .62. These data suggest considerable instability for measures obtained in the first year of life, with a pattern of increasing stability with increasing age. Wilson and Matheny studied change in development for measures obtained at 12, 18, and 24 months of age. When they correlated change scores over this period, they found that MZ twins exhibited greater concordance in change than DZ twins. The correlations for change over this period were .73 and .47 for MZ and DZ twin pairs, respectively. These data suggest that infant temperament changes are in part the result of a genetically influenced maturational process. Wilson (1983) had earlier reported comparable data for infant scores on mental development. That is, changes in scores on tests for the first 2 years of life exhibited greater concordance for MZ twin pairs than for DZ twin pairs. Also the concordance for MZ twin on IQ increased over time and that for DZ twins decreased. Thus, there was an increase in the heritability of IQ as IQ scores became more stable and predictive by age 7. These analyses suggest that one reason that early measures of traits may be relatively unpredictive of later measures of traits is that there is considerable variation in the rate at which individuals develop their more stable adult characteristics. Further, the data suggest that some of the changes are themselves under genetic control.

Covariance Analysis

We have seen that twin studies may be used to gain information about the behavior genetics of change. Twin studies may also be used to investigate the relationship between different traits and characteristics. The outcome variable to be analyzed in such investigations is the correlation or association between two different measures or human characteristics. Behavior genetic analyses of the covariance between traits is directed toward partitioning the covariance between characteristics with separate genetic and environmental influences. Martin and Jardine (1986) have used their large sample of Australian twins to study the relationship between neuroticism, as assessed by the Eysenck Personality Questionnaire, and measures of the specific level of depression and anxiety experienced by an individual at the time the questionnaire is filled out. The latter two measures are presumed to be state measures and, as such, fluctuate over time. They analyzed the relationship between these characteristics and they were able to fit a model that was based on the assumption that the covariance among these characteristics was determined by additive genetic factors and within-family environmental factors. There was no evidence for nonadditive genetic covariance or for between-family environmental influences. They also partitioned the additive genetic variance components into those that were common to their three measures, and those that were specific to their three measures. Their analysis suggests that the additive genetic components that are associated with the relationships among the traits are, for the most part, common to these traits. Table 3.3 presents the results of the genetic analysis of the covariance among these measures. An examination of the data reported in Table 3.3 indicates that most of the variance in the traits from the additive genetic component is attributable to components of variance that are common to all three measures. This suggests that the additive genetic characteristics that predispose an individual to neuroticism are the same as those that predispose an individual to report anxiety symptoms and depression. Some of the additive genetic variance that is presumed to influence neuroticism (16 and 12% in females and males, respectively) is specific to neuroticism. This implies that there are additive genetic influences on neuroticism that do not necessarily predispose an individual to report the presence of anxiety and depression. In addition, there are additive genetic influences that account for a small proportion of the variance of reported depression (6 and 9% for females and males, respectively) that are specific components and that are independent of neuroticism.

The within-family environmental influences, in contrast to additive genetic influences, consist in roughly equal magnitudes of sources of variance common to all three traits and of sources of variance that are specific to each of these traits.

The Martin and Jardine analysis of covariance structures is congruent with a view of traits that construes neuroticism as a trait that may influence the develop-

Table 3.3

Proportions of Variance for Specific and General Sources of Variance for the Covariances of Neuroticism, Anxiety, and Depression[a]

Sex	E_1 (Within-family) Environment		V_A (Additive genetic) Component	
	General	Specific	General	Specific
Females				
Neuroticism	20	29	35	16
Anxiety	35	27	35	03
Depression	33	31	30	06
Males				
Neuroticism	22	32	34	12
Anxiety	31	35	30	04
Depression	33	35	23	09

[a]Based on Martin & Jardine, 1986.

ment of specific behavioral states and symptoms. It also indicates that the specific environmental events, whatever they may be, that lead an individual to develop neuroticism may be quite distinct from the specific environmental events that lead to the development of either anxiety states or depression.

While the model suggested by the Martin and Jardine analysis is quite reasonable and comprehensible, we should accept it with caution. Note that the three measures were all based on self-reports from the same individuals and were obtained at the same time. Thus, method specific variance might inflate the reported correlations between the measures. It would be quite interesting to know whether comparable results would be obtained from heteromethod methods of measurement. Of course, given the large sample size required, the use of such techniques might be quite difficult. The Martin and Jardine results also illustrate a potentially interesting extension of behavior genetic analysis into the study of relationships among traits or other human characteristics.

Pathological Characteristics

In addition to the twin studies dealing with normal personality, there are also twin studies of pathological personality states. These are relevant to our concerns because psychoses, such as schizophrenia, may be thought of as lying at an end point on a continuum with normal personality. That is, there may be an underlying trait disposition, such as schizothymia, that, at its extreme, results in a diagnosis of schizophrenia. In studies of the genetics of such characteristics one treats the condition as a categorical event, that is, as being present or absent and notes the degree of concordance or agreement among different categories of individuals.

Gottesman and Shields (1982) have very carefully surveyed the behavior genetic literature dealing with schizophrenia. They found slightly lower concordance rates for newer studies that are somewhat better controlled than for older studies. For the five newer studies they found concordance rates among MZ twins ranging from .35 to .58, with a weighted mean concordance of .46. The comparable data for DZ pairs ranged from .09 to .27, with a weighted mean of .14. The newer twin studies exhibit good agreement and provided evidence for the heritability of schizophrenia.

These studies suggest a pattern of heritability for schizophrenia that is quite comparable to that reported for continuously varying personality traits. Note that the lack of perfect concordance for MZ twins suggests that schizophrenia is influenced by within-family environmental events. The discrepancy between MZ and DZ concordance values suggests that schizophrenia is influenced by a genetic component. Also the total variance in the phenotype may be partitioned into genetic and within-family environmental components, thus leaving no remaining variance for between-family influences.

The conclusion that the occurrence of schizophrenia is not influenced by the particular type of family that one is reared in is buttressed by studies of MZ twins reared apart and, as we shall see, by adoption studies. Gottesman and Shields report that there are nine known cases of MZ twins reared apart where schizophrenia is present in at least one member of the twin pair. Given the lack of a systematic sample, they are inclined to view these nine cases as isolated case histories. Nevertheless, it is interesting to note that seven of the nine cases are concordant for schizophrenia. These data, at least marginally, support the conclusion that between-family environmental influences are not an important source of variance in the etiology of schizophrenia.

There are a number of other twin studies of concordance for different psychopathological conditions, such as manic-depressive illness and alcoholism. These studies generally show higher concordance for MZ than DZ twins. I shall not review this literature. However, there is one set of studies that indirectly implicates personality characteristics. Christiansen (1977) has reviewed twin studies on the heritability of criminality. He found a pattern of results that was quite comparable to that obtained for schizophrenia. For male criminals he estimated an MZ concordance rate of .52 and a DZ concordance rate of .22. The comparable concordances for female MZ and DZ twins were .35 and .14, respectively. In addition, there were eight known cases of MZ twins reared apart where at least one was criminal. Four of these eight cases were concordant for criminality. The data on criminality fit the pattern of results of twin studies of personality traits and of schizophrenia. The discordance among MZ twins reared together suggests substantial within-family environmental influences. The MZ vs. DZ difference suggests genetic influences. And the combined effects of both of these sources of variances provide little or no evidence for the influence of between-family sources of variance. In addition, the data on MZ twins reared apart, however fragmentary it may be, is compatible with the conclusion that between-family sources of variance are not substantial sources of variance. The genetic influences on criminality are probably mediated by personality characteristics that influence the way in which an individual responds to his or her environment.

Family Studies

Personality in Natural and Adopted Families

Studies of the relationships between members of the same family also provide sources of information about genetic and environmental influences. Studies of adopted children provide an additional way of assessing the independence of genetic and environmental influences. Studies of the relationships between parents and children and between siblings rarely report correlations for personality trait scores in excess of .3, and they occasionally report correlations that are substantially lower. Insel (1974) reported parent–offspring correlations of .21 and .24 in neuroticism and extraversion, respectively. The comparable correlations for siblings were .34 and .27. Ahern, Johnson, Wilson, McClearn, and Vanderberg (1982) reported parent and sibling correlations averaging .15 for a variety of self-report trait measures. These data indicate that siblings resemble each other about as much as DZ twins in self-report measures of personality and that children do not greatly resemble their parents in scores on self-report measures of personality traits.

What do these data tell us about environmental and genetic influences on personality? Clearly not very much. Children growing up in the same family share genes with their parents and siblings. And siblings share a common family environment. It is interesting to note that a shared family environment does not creat substantial similarity among siblings. These results become more clearly interpretable when one adds information about the relationship between parents and children and among siblings in adopted families. These comparisons isolate the effects of common family experiences from the influence of genetic similarities of members of the same family. Scarr, Webber, Weinberg, and Wittig (1981) have reported the results of a study comparing parent–child and sibling correlations on self-report measures of personality in adoptive and biological families. They reported correlations between biological parents and their children on extraversion and neuroticism of .19 and .25, respectively. The correlations between siblings in these families for extraversion and neuroticism were .06 and .28, respectively.

Comparable correlations in adoptive families were different. The midparent (i.e., averaged across parents) score on extraversion and neuroticism correlated with their adopted children's score on these traits .00 and .05, respectively. The correlations between adopted siblings were also close to zero.

Loehlin, Willerman, and Horn (1985) have reported correlations for a cluster of traits on the California Personality Inventory that together define an extraversion factor for adopted children and their biological and adopted families. Their data are presented in Table 3.4. Note that on the scales that combine to form a general extraversion factor, children have low correlations with their adopted parents. However, there is some resemblance between adopted children and their biological parents. They also found near zero correlations between adopted siblings for personality characteristics.

These data lead to a number of conclusions that tend to buttress the results of twin studies. Children do not substantially resemble their parents in scores on personality trait measures. Children reared in the same family tend not to resemble each other substantially on such measures. These relatively low correlations are compatible with the assumption of weak or nonexistant effects of common family environmental effects. The relationships that are obtained appear to be substantially mediated by genetic effects. Note that there are near zero correla-

Table 3.4

Parent–Child Correlations for Extraversion Scales in Adopted Children[a]

	Adopted parent		Biological parent	
	Father–child	Mother–child	Father–child	Mother–child
Scale	(N = 240)	(N = 253)	(N = 52)	(N = 53)
Dominance	.04	−.04	.13	.25
Status	.20	.09	.18	.18
Sociability	.08	.01	.20	.15
Social prescence	.18	.06	.42	.26
Self–acceptance	.04	.07	.20	.42

[a]Based on Loehlin et al., 1985. (Copyright 1985 by the American Psychological Association. Adapted by permission of the publisher and author.)

tions for personality trait measures for children reared in the same home who are not genetically related and near zero correlations between adopting parents and their adopted offspring. The existence of a relationship between biological parents and their adopted offspring is strongly supportive of an additive genetic relationship for these trait measures. Indeed, it is difficult to explain such relationships in any way other than by assuming a genetic influence on a trait.

Plomin and DeFries (1985), have reported additional data for measures of infant development on the relationship between biological parents and their adopted children. The Colorado Adoption Study has reported relationships between the characteristics of biological parents, adopted parents, and adopted children on a variety of measures of development for the first two years of life. In addition, Plomin and DeFries have obtained similar measures in a sample of control families who have not adopted children. Their data for measures of infant temperament indicated that infants' temperamental characteristics are not easily predictable from a knowledge of parental characteristics. Neither the characteristics of the adopting nor of the biological parents are strongly related to infant temperament. This conclusion holds even for measures of infant temperament that are based on aggregates of different kinds of data. Thus, the evidence for genetic or between-family environmental influences on infant temperament is not strong. The Colorado Adoption Study, which is longitudinal, plans to obtain data from their sample of infants when they are older, and it is entirely possible that measures of older children will provide stronger evidence of various genetic and environmental effects. The sample is large and a relatively rich source of heteromethod data will be obtained. The study promises to provide extensive information about the genetic and environmental influences on the development of personality and intelligence.

Although most of the obtained relationships are weak, the Colorado study does provide evidence for various kinds of parental influence on children's early development. Data based on laboratory ratings of infants are, for the most part, not predicted by measures of the personality traits of biological, adoptive, or control parents. However, there are some relationships between parental charactertistics and parental ratings of infant temperament. In control families there are significant correlations between parental self-report measures of extraversion and their children's ratings on sociability, .22 and .17 for mother and fathers' scores, respectively. The correlations for adopted families between parents' extraversion scores and their ratings of children on sociability are nonsignificant, that is, −.08 and .14 for mother and fathers' scores, respectively. The absence of a relationship between these variables in adoptive families indicates that one cannot assume that the relationship is mediated by environmental influences. The corresponding correlation for the biological mothers[1] is .02. Therefore, the significant relationship reported for control families is not mediated by genetic relationships between parents and children. Thus, the relationship in control natural families between parental extraversion and their ratings of their children's sociability is essentially unexplained.

There is a significant correlation ($r = .20$) between the biological mothers' scores on neuroticism and the ratings of her biological children on emotionality by the children's adoptive parents. This relationship is interesting for several reasons. First, the ratings and the self-report measures of personality are not contaminated and are made by different individuals. Second, the relationship cannot be explained environmentally. Postnatal contacts of mothers with their biological children are quite limited. Third, the relationship between the adoptive mothers' neuroticism scores and parental ratings on the emotionality of their adopted children is only .07. The corresponding correlation for the parents and children in the control group is .10.

The data indicating a possible genetic relationship between the biological mother's neuroticism and her child's emotionality indicate substantial genetic continuity of influence on neuroticism. A correlation between the biological mother's personality characteristic and her adopted infant's scores is dependent on three types of genetic relationships. There must be a genetic influence on both the infant measure and the adult measure. Furthermore, the genetic influences that are present for both infants and adults must be related. Thus, given reasonable estimates of the genetic influences present in both infant ratings and adult trait scores, the relatively low correlations would imply substantial genetic continuity of influence for infant and adult measures. That is, the genes that would influence adult trait scores are the same genes that influence infant ratings. While this scenario might be correct, there are several reasons why it should be thought of, at best, as a kind of demonstration of what one might infer from an analysis of the data collected by Plomin and DeFries. Several other analyses fail to provide

---

[1]Data exist for only a subset of the biological fathers. Therefore, the correlation reported for biological fathers is based on too small a sample (35–36) to be reliable.

support for this type of genetic continuity. The absence of a significant correlation between adult neuroticism scores and children's ratings on emotionality in control families does not fit this analysis. Also, the failure to obtain comparable relationships between ratings derived from laboratory measures reinforces arguments opposed to drawing strong conclusions from a correlation of .20 between infant emotionality ratings and their biological mothers' neuroticism scores.

Pathological Characteristics

Information about the relationship between personality characteristics of biological parents and their adopted children can also be gleaned from studies of criminality and schizophrenia. The first systematic adoption study of schizophrenia was reported by Heston (1966). He studied a sample of 47 children of schizophrenic mothers whose children were given up for adoption early in life. He found that five of the sample were diagnosed as schizophrenic. The age-corrected probability of developing schizophrenia in this sample was 16.6%—a figure that is comparable to that obtained for children whose mothers are schizophrenic and who were reared by their own mothers.

More systematic studies with larger samples have since been done in Denmark. The Scandinavian countries maintain extensive social register data, which are accessible to researchers and permit them to study relationships between biological and adopted parents and their children. Rosenthal et al. (1968, 1975) started with a sample of 5500 adopted children. They then obtained information from social registers about the biological parents of the adoptees and ascertained that 69 of the children had a biological parent who was schizophrenic. The 69 children formed an *index* group. These researchers also formed a *control* group of 79 adoptees whose biological parents were not schizophrenic and who were matched with the index group on sex, age-at-adoption, and social class of the adoptive home. The adopted children were interviewed by a psychiatrist who was unaware of the status of their biological parents. Thirty-two percent of the index children were rated as having schizophrenic tendencies, compared with 16% of the control children who were also rated as having schizophrenic tendencies.

Kety, Rosenthal, Wender, Schulsinger, and Jacobson (1978) used the Danish social registers to gather data for a study of adoptees who were diagnosed as schizophrenic. They then formed a matched control group of adopted children. Afterwards, they searched the social registers for information about the biological and adopted parents of the control and index children. Kety et al. found that a history of schizophrenia was present in 12.1% of the biological parents of the schizophrenic children compared with 6.2% of the control children's biological parents. These researchers also found that 1.6% of the adoptive parents of the schizophrenic children were schizophrenic compared with 4.4% of the adoptive parents of the control children. These data indicate that children whose biological parents are schizophrenic are at increased risk to develop schizophrenia even if they do not interact with their biological parents.

The Kety et al. and the Rosenthal et al. studies support the existence of additive genetic influences on schizophrenia and are congruent with the results obtained in twin studies. Also these data suggest that there is no between-family environmental influence on the origin of schizophrenia. Children whose biological parents are schizophrenic appear to be at roughly equal risk for the development of schizophrenia, whether they are reared by their biological parents or not. And, adopted children who develop schizophrenia are more likely to have biological parents who are schizophrenic than control adopted children who do not develop schizophrenia, but they are not more likely to have adopted parents with a history of schizophrenia. Thus, the elevated risk for schizophrenia among children of schizophrenic mothers appears to be entirely a matter of genetic influence.

Hutchings and Mednick (1977) have reported an adoption study of criminality using Danish social register data. They began their study by gathering data on all biological fathers in Copenhagen who had a child given up for adoption. They then studied files on criminality to ascertain whether any of these parents had ever been convicted of a serious criminal offense—an offense that roughly corresponds to a felony conviction. Next they examined the criminal records of the adoptive fathers of the children and obtained data on the criminal status of all of the adopted children. These data permit an analysis analogous to a *cross-fostering* design used in animal behavior genetics. That is, one can study children whose biological fathers were or were not criminal and who were reared in families where the fathers did or did not have a history of criminality. Table 3.5 presents their data. The examination of the data in Table 3.5 indicates that children whose biological fathers were criminals are at increased risk of being convicted of criminal activity compared with children whose biological fathers were not criminals. Children reared by fathers with a history of criminality are not at increased risk to develop criminal behavior if their biological parents were

Table 3.5

Percentage of Criminal Records in Adopted Male Children in Relation to Criminality of Biological and Adoptive Fathers[a]

| | Biological father | | | |
| | Has criminal record | | No criminal record | |
Adopted father	%	N	%	N
Has criminal record	36.2	58	11.5	52
No criminal record	22.0	219	10.5	333

[a]Based on Hutchings & Mednick, 1977.

not criminal. These data suggest that there are genotypes that predispose an individual to develop criminality and that the family environment created by criminal fathers, in the absence of appropriate genetic predispositions, does not lead to an increased tendency to develop criminal behavior. The data in Table 3.5 also provide evidence suggesting a possible interaction effect of genetic and environmental influences. That is, for the relatively small subset of children whose biological parents have a history of criminality and who are reared in adoptive families where the fathers have a history of criminality, the risk of criminality is elevated compared with children whose biological fathers are criminals and who are reared in homes where the adoptive fathers are not criminals. These data suggest that the environment may potentiate the impact of genetic predispositions. However, given the small size of this sample ($N = 58$), this conclusion should be accepted cautiously.

Even with the relatively large number of cases studied by Huchings and Mednick, it was not possible to distinguish among types of criminal activities. Criminal activity was studied using an undifferentiated grouping, and distinctions among criminal activities, such as those involving violent and impulsive acts of aggression, and other activities, such as fraud and nonviolent theft, were not made. Thus it is probable that the criminals as a group are heterogeneous with respect to their personality traits.

It is also likely that criminals as a group relative to noncriminals may be characterized as being high in such traits as extraversion, neuroticism, and psychoticism (see Eysenck and Eysenck, 1985). Criminal activity is probably related to personality. It is highly unlikely, if not ludicrous, to assume that there are genes for criminality. What these data probably mean is that there are personality characteristics of individuals that predispose them in a variety of different ways to be convicted of criminal activity. Such personality characteristics are, in turn, influenced by genetic variables.

Conclusions: Genetic and Environmental Influences

Our review of behavior genetic studies of personality leads to certain conclusions and raises questions for further analysis. The studies we have reviewed provide evidence for the pervasive influence of genetic characteristics on personality and on various forms of psychopathology that are related to individual differences in personality. There are certainly gaps in our knowledge—particularly the virtual absence of studies of personality ratings by peers and of measures aggregated across different methods of measurement for older children and adults. Nevertheless, it is quite clear that genetic influences are important in creating differences among people.

While the evidence for genetic influences appears to be relatively clear, the evidence for the influence of environmental characteristics on personality appears to be quite difficult to assess. While we know that genetic influences are important, we really do not know with any degree of confidence how important they are. Twin studies suggest that broad heritability for personality traits as assessed by self-report questionnaires are approximately .50 and, depending on correlations for unreliability in the data, they may be a bit higher—approximately .55. Family studies, on the other hand, suggest somewhat lower heritability. Family studies underestimate broad heritability if nonadditive sources of variance exist. On the other hand, our estimates of heritability are estimates for the heritability of measures of personality traits, not of traits per se. If there are sources of variance in self-report measures of personality that are not influenced by genetic variance and are not related to true latent trait scores, then the true heritability of personality traits could be higher than the heritability of scores of self-report tests of personality. It should be noted that corrections for errors of measurement, as indicated by the fact that a person may not obtain the same score on two separate administrations of the test, are not relevant to the issue of the heritability of latent true scores on personality traits. Consider an example. There may be individuals in the population who answer the question "Do you like going out a lot?" consistently in the affirmative. This answer is assumed to be indicative of extraversion. Let us assume that there is a subset of individuals for whom the answer does not represent a veridical assessment of their preferences, but it is merely a reflection of what this group considers is a conventionally appropriate response to the question. While this item might be a valid index of extraversion for most people, for the subset of hypothetical individuals it would not be a good item. Moreover, some individuals might have a sense of their own behavioral tendencies that is not correct. Again, they might be consistent in their responses, but wrong. Their misperceptions might not be related to genetic characteristics. Such systematic sources of error in the relationships between obtained scores on questionnaires and true latent trait scores probably exist. Heteromethod trait measures tend to cancel out those sources of variance that are idiosyncratically present in one source of measurement. It is possible that behavior genetic analyses of such measures might indicate that a larger percentage of the variance in personality traits is genetic.

How Do Genotypes Influence Phenotypes?

In addition to uncertainty surrounding the "true" value of the heritability of personality traits, we know little about the ways in which genotypes influence phenotypes for personality traits. In order to speculate about the way in which genotypes for personality interact with the environment to create phenotypic personality characteristics, it is useful to speculate about the nature of the genetic disposition that influences psychological development. It is possible to define genotypic dispositions in a broad, or a narrow, fashion. We have argued in

Chapter 1 that traits can mean quite different things in different individuals and, indeed, each individual may express a similar trait in rather idiosyncratic ways. Perhaps what one inherits is a disposition that predisposes an individual to develop a generalized trait score, and the idiosyncratic modes of expression of the trait result from the idiosyncrasies of the extended interactions between genotypes and the environment. Individuals who are sociable might inherit a broad disposition to be responsive to other individuals. Neurotic individuals might possess a biological capacity for fear and anxiety that is influenced by specific experiences and is transformed into an individualized version of neurotic behavior. In this interpretation of genetic influences, one starts with a broad genetic disposition that is then particularized and individuated in the course of interactions with the environment.

However, it is also possible that what one inherits is a disposition to respond and behave in relatively specific ways that then influence one's general personality characteristics. There are several lines of suggestive evidence in support of a model of specific inheritance. Recall our review of the covariance analysis of Martin and Jardine (1986) for the relationship between neuroticism, anxiety states, and depression. Their analysis suggests that specific components of depression are heritable that are independent of neuroticism. There may be genetic predispositions to respond in quite specifical pathological ways. For example, Öhman (1986) has argued that the frequency of occurrence of various phobias does not reflect the likelihood of having encountered phobic stimuli in one's personal experiences. He believes that many phobias occur because of preexistent biological preparedness to respond with fear to certain stimulus objects. It is not hard to imagine that individuals might differ in such biological preparedness for genetic reasons. The development of quite specific phobic reactions might lead an individual to be described as neurotic. In this example, the disposition that is inherited is not a general neurotic tendency, but it is a disposition to develop quite specific behavior patterns that increases the likelihood of a person's being described as neurotic.

Relatively little behavior genetic research has been addressed to the patterning of trait expressiveness, but there is at least some suggestive evidence that genotypes might influence the idiosyncratic pattern of trait expressivity. For example, Dworkin (1978, 1979) reported the results of a twin study using an S–R inventory of anxiety. The inventory asks individuals about their characteristic anxiety responses in a variety of different situations. This type of inventory permits one to obtain measures of the situations that elicit anxiety for a particular individual. For a relatively small sample, he reports higher MZ correlations than DZ correlations ($r_{MZ} = .36$, $r_{DZ} = .19$) for situations that elicit anxiety. The sample is small and the differences are not large, but the results are suggestive.

The psychologists involved in the Minnesota twin study of separated twins (Bouchard, 1985, and Lykken, 1982) have noted a number of instances of rather unusual concordances for specific behaviors among separated twins. For example, one female twin pair was concordant for a tendency to wear a large number of rings.

How are we to explain such unusual agreements? One could, of course, dismiss such events as mere accidents. After all we do not have good base-rate data for the occurrence of such events. If we examine comprehensively two individuals chosen at random, we might discover all sorts of unusual coincidences in their actions. On the other hand, the Minnesota psychologists are struck by the frequency of occurrence of such concordances. We can imagine ways in which they might come about. Perhaps a tendency to wear several rings might be influenced by physical characteristics. Genotypes might exist that predispose an individual to develop hands that are viewed as attractive and that are capable of moving in a graceful way. A genotypically influenced predisposition toward expressive exuberance combined with the particular shape and form of hand movements might lead a woman to adorn her hand with several rings. This example is not meant to be thought of as a literal or a well worked out example of the details of a process leading to a genotypically influenced tendency to wear many rings. Rather, it is taken as being indicative of an emphasis on the possible heritability of relatively specific characteristics, which may lead individuals who share genotypes to develop congruence on relatively general traits.

It should be noted that a model of genotypic influence on personality traits that emphasizes the heritability of relatively specific, narrow traits does not exclude the possibility of the heritability of broad, general dispositions. Both types of processes may coexist.

We have discussed genetic and environmental effects on personality traits as if they were, at least partially, independent of each other. Obviously, genetic influences act in an environmental context. We can speculate about the way in which genotypes might combine with environmental influences to produce phenotypic scores on measures of personality.

Genetic influences can exert both a passive and an active influence on the environment (Scarr, 1981; Scarr and McCartney, 1983). A child, born with a propensity to be fearful, might very well see the world as a frightening and dangerous place. This would be an example of a passive genetic–environmental relationship in which the perception of the environment is influenced by genotypes. Genotypes may also influence the occurrence of environmental events. Children may be aware of the fears of a genotypically fearful child, and that, in turn, may lead them to bully that child. Thus, a child's fearfulness may actually cause the environment to become more threatening. Finally, there is an active genetic–environmental relationship in which individuals choose environments that are compatible with their genotypes. The genotypically fearful child might select less threatening environments and seek to avoid situations that are likely to elicit fears. In her analyses of these types of genetic relationships, Scarr suggests that development proceeds from a passive to an active genotypic relationship.

This analysis helps us understand why it is difficult to predict adult characteristics on the basis of children's behavior patterns. The influence of the genotype on the phenotype may be quite limited early in development because children have limited opportunities to structure their environments in ways that are compatible with their genotypes. Also, the range of environmental events that have been experienced is limited, and thus, the opportunity for genotypes to filter and structure the environment is quite limited. A possible example of the differential effects of genotypes at different stages of development may be found in research on the Home Scale—a measure of the environmental stimulation for cognitive development based on home observations and parental reports (Caldwell and Bradley, 1978). Gottfried and Gottfried (1984) have summarized research using the Home scale to predict intelligence test performance in the preschool-age years. Their review indicates that the Home scale consistently predicts preschool-age IQ, even when one controls for parental socioeconomic status, intelligence, or education. This suggests that the scale measures aspects of the environment that influence intellectual development. Longstreth et al. (1981) found that the Home scale did not predict performance on intelligence tests when one controlled for mother's IQ during the preadolescent period. How do we account for the discrepancy in these findings? It is possible that the home environment is an important influence on early intellectual development but that its influence fades as the school becomes the most important source of intellectual socialization. It is also possible that the effects of the partial control for genotypic influence, which is achieved by statistically controlling mother's IQ, has different effects at different stages of development. Wilson's (1983) research suggests that the influence of genotypes on the intelligence test score phenotype is larger at preadolescence than at the preschool-age period. This may be attributable to an increased influence of genotypic characteristics on environmental events. The wider scope for active genotypic interactions with the environment might explain the greater relevance of genotypic controls for parental IQ in the Longstreth study. This account is speculative. It is, however, illustrative of a way of thinking that emphasizes the role of genotypes in structuring the impact of the environment on the individual.

There is stronger evidence for genotypic mediation of environmental effects. Plomin, Loehlin, and DeFries (1985) have summarized results obtained from the Colorado adoption study of relationships between various measures of environmental influence, including those derived from the Home scales and measures of children's early development. They found a consistent pattern of differences in the relationship between environmental measures and early development in adopted families and in their ordinary control families. For example, there were 10 significant correlations between measures of the home environment and measures of early behavioral problems. The average value of these 10 correlations for the control families was .23, and the corresponding average correlation was .07 in the adopted families. Similarly, there were 14 significant correlations between measures of the home environment and measures of infant temperament. The average of these 14 correlations was .20 for the control families and .06 for the adopted families. Similar differences exist for measures of early infant development. Children and parents are genetically related in natural families, but they are not genetically related in adopted families. Apparently the genetic covariance (i.e., shared genetic variance) between parents and children creates an environment whose influence is different than it would be in the absence of genetic covariance. This result suggests that obtained relationships between what appears on the surface to be purely environmental influences and individual differences may involve suppressed genetic influences that are not apparent. Unless one uses adopted families as a control, it is possible to overlook subtle ways in which the genetic covariance of parent and child influences the creation of an environment with a particular influence on the psychological development of the child.

Covariance and Interaction

In addition to genotypic mediation of environmental influences, there can be relationships between genotypes and environments. This is called genetic and environmental covariance. Formal behavior-genetic analyses of intelligence generally assume that some portion of the variance in the phenotype for intelligence is attributable to the covariance of genetic and environmental influences. It is easy to understand such an influence. Parents who are likely to provide their offspring with genes that predispose them toward the development of high IQ are also likely to provide their offspring with an environment that is conducive to the development of high IQ. Do such influences exist for personality? We don't know. There is no obvious mechanism for such genetic–environmental covariance influences. Since there is apparently no between-family environmental influence, it is hard to see how the genetic influences of parents could be correlated with their environmental influences.

In addition to genetic–environmental covariance, formal behavior-genetic models also allow for the existence of what is called genotype by environment interaction. Genotype by environment interactions exist when genotypes and environments combine in nonadditive ways. In such a case, one could not predict phenotypes completely from knowledge of either environmental or genetic influences alone. One would have to know the particular combination of genetic and environmental influences to which an individual had been exposed in order to predict the phenotype. It is easy to imagine such interactions. Perhaps a child with a genotypic predisposition toward violence would become extremely violent and aggressive in a family where the father is aggressive and would learn to sublimate aggressive tendencies in a family without an adult aggressive model. One can suggest many other examples. We have relatively little evidence that such interactions occur. Recall that the Hutchings and Mednick's (1977) data on criminality provided some evidence for a genetic by environmental interaction when they found that adopted children whose biological parents were criminal were at an increased risk for criminality if their adopted fathers appeared on the criminal register. Since children whose biological fathers were not on the criminal register were not at increased risk for criminality, even if their adopted fathers had a criminal record, these data suggest that there is a significant, genetic by environmental interaction effect for criminality. However, these results were based on a small sample.

Loehlin, Horn and Willerman (1981) have reported evidence suggesting a paradoxical interactive relationship between genotypes and the environment. They found a negative correlation between biological mothers' adjustments, as measured by the MMPI taken during their pregnancies and ratings of their adopted offsprings' adjustments. Thus, poorly adjusted biological mothers tended to have well-adjusted offspring when they were raised in adopted homes. Plomin and DeFries (1985) reported a similar relationship. For example, they found that the biological mothers' hysteria scores correlated $-.11$ with their adopted offsprings' tendencies to have sleeping problems at 24 months of age. The correlations between these measures in control families was .16. These results suggest that the same genotypes might lead to quite different effects in different environments. Loehlin, Horn, and Willerman suggest that what one might inherit is a genotype for reactivity, or sensitivity, to the the environment. If one then encountered an adverse environment, one might develop behavioral problems. In the assumed supportive environment of an adoptive home, children with a "hyper-responsive" genotype might be less likely to develop behavioral problems. This account is rather speculative. The Loehlin, Horn, and Willerman study is based on a small sample, and the Plomin and DeFries results are based on rather small correlations. In addition, when Loehlin et al. (1985) attempted to replicate these results using a sample of older children, they failed to find an inverse relationship between the biological mothers' adjustments and their adopted children's reported adjustments. Thus, the effect may be nonexistent or, if it exists, it may be short lived and observable only in infancy.

Studies of adoption provide the most direct method for obtaining evidence of genotype by environment interactions because they permit, in principle, the study of independent variations among genotypes and environment analogous to the cross-fostering design of animal genetics. However, there are relatively few studies of the relationships between biological parents (typically mothers) and their adopted offspring. Such literature as we have does not provide abundant evidence for genotype by environment interactions. Plomin and Daniels (1984) summarized the results of 32 tests for interaction. They studied variations in the characteristics of biological mothers and adoptive mothers and their effects on infant temperament. They concluded that they were unable to find any evidence for such interactions.

Environmental Influences: Within-family Effects

We have considered direct, indirect, and interactive influences of genotypes on personality traits. We have not considered the influence of environmental factors that are independent of genetic influences. Our review of behavior-genetic research has suggested that the environmental influences on self-report measures of personality, and other personality measures, are within-family influences. It should be noted that the behavior-genetic methods used are quite capable of discovering between-family influences, if they exist. Behavior-genetic studies of intelligence commonly find that some portion of the environmental influences are between-family influences. It is also interesting to note that Martin and Jardine (1986) found evidence for between-family environmental influences on a measure of conservative political attitudes in the same twin study in which they failed to find evidence for between-family influences on personality traits. They found that 15 and 21% of the variance on conservatism in males and females, respectively, was attributable to a between-family environmental influence. This result occurred because DZ correlations were more than half as large as MZ correlations. They also found that additive genetic influences account for 49 and 38% of the variance for females and males on conservatism.

If behavior genetic research can detect between-family environmental influences, and appropriate research has failed to do so, it might be reasonable to assume that personality traits are influenced by within-family environmental events.

A theory of the environmental influences on personality traits that excludes between-family environmental influences excludes most of the events that are thought to influence personality development. Such a theory excludes social class variables and many subtle enviornmental effects that are linked to class and affluence. For example, it excludes variations in diet, in adequacy of medical care, and in the physical characteristics of the home. It excludes whether one grows up in a home that is sufficiently spacious to provide one with one's own room. It excludes family size and the composition of the family with respect to number, gender, and spacing of siblings. It excludes the social and ideological beliefs of the parents. And, it excludes parental behaviors and characteristics. The entire emotional climate of the home and the emotional states of the parent, as well as their enduring personality characteristics, do not appear to influence their offspring's personality. Parental beliefs about childrearing that result in tendencies to treat children in similar ways are excluded as potential influences on personality traits.

In a less obvious way, the exclusion of between-family environmental influences also excludes many potential influences that occur outside of the family. For example, family background influences the schools a child is likely to attend, and the characteristic values and attitudes of children attending different schools are likely to be quite different. Children form friendships with children they meet in school and in their neighborhoods. Thus, a model that excludes between-family environmental influences also excludes the influence of the characteristic social class background and values of the friends that a child is likely to make and who serve as potential influences on personality traits.

Although many potential environmental influences are excluded by the assumption that all environmental influences on personality are within-family influences, there are many potential environmental influences that can be considered. It should be noted that the term *within-family environmental influences* is a misnomer. It includes all influences that create differences among individuals growing up in the same family. As such, it encompasses influences that occur within the context of the family as well as influences that are external to the experiences of a child within his or her own family. It should also be noted that the within-family influences that exist should also be capable of creating differences among twins reared together. Obvious within-family differences, such as birth order, are not operative in the case of MZ twins in any ordinary sense. One could not, therefore, assume that birth order effects account for a substantial portion of variance in personality. A similar analysis suggests that prenatal events that might be assumed to create differences among siblings are not a major source of within-family environmental influences. Various stressors and biological influences experienced by a mother during pregnancy could effect the characteristic prenatal environment of the fetus. In principle, differential experiences associated with each pregnancy could be a source of variation in the influence of the environment experienced by siblings within the same family. However, since twins (whether MZ or DZ) derive from the same pregnancy, they are likely to experience similar prenatal environments. Since DZ twins are not conspicuously more alike than siblings reared together, this would imply that differential prenatal environments are not an important source of variance for the development of individual differences in personality traits.

Are postnatal events within a family important? Children within the same samily may have different roles. One child may be the black sheep of the family or outcast. Another child might be favored. One child may be closer to one or the other parent. Parents might treat same-sex children within a family differently. Children within the same family might have quite different attitudes toward their parents. In addition to relationships between children and parents, children might be influenced by their own relationships. Sibling rivalry and competition might influence personality.

While all of the above possible influences are plausible, it should also be noted that we have very little evidence that these are the sorts of things that do lead to differences in scores on personality traits. Rowe and Plomin (1981) have developed a questionnaire measure of sibling relationships in an initial attempt to study such within-family environmental differences. They noted three interesting findings about such differences. First, parents reported that they intended to create, and generally succeeded in doing so, roughly comparable environments for their children. Using this same measure, Daniels and Plomin (1985) reported correlations for sibling experiences, obtained from parental reports, varying from .38 to .65 on different components of a scale of sibling experience. Siblings reported much larger discrepancies in experiences, with correlations ranging between .18 and .26 on different components of sibling experiences. Thus, siblings reported that they were treated quite differently. The exact meaning of this difference is not easily understood. Perhaps parents do intend to treat their children equally, and their reports reflect their intentions. It is also possible that, in the course of interactions with their children, small differences in treatment develop. Children's perceptions of their environment are influenced by contrast effects, and thus are subject to exaggeration. However, the effective environmental influence might well be the perceived one. Children do not constantly and directly experience the ways in which children growing up in other families are treated by their parents. However, they do constantly and directly interact with their own parents. A child's sense of his or her treatment is thus plausibly derived from his or her perception of the relationship between his or her treatment and that of his or her sibling. These perceptions, then, could come to define the way in which the environment influences personality.

Daniels and Plomin (1985) also reported that sibling perceptions of differences appear to be of the same order of magnitude for adopted and biological siblings. This suggests that the differences in reported divergences in sibling experiences are not a function of genetic differences between siblings.

Do reported sibling differences relate to personality trait characteristics? Daniels and Plomin (1985) reported that correlations between several dimensions of related sibling divergences are related to reported differences in adjustment of the siblings as indexed by self-reports, teacher reports, and parent reports. Differences in reported sibling experiences account for between 6 and 13% of the variance in differences on various indices of adjustment. How is this finding to be interpreted? Note that the relationships are relatively weak, and the percentage of variance accounted for is based on multiple correlations of several derived indices of reported sibling differences. Thus, the value may be somewhat inflated. Nevertheless, even if one has accounted for only 10% of the variance, given all the error variance in reports of adjustment differences, the results are impressive. Does this mean that sibling differences in environmental experiences are causally related to adjustment differences among siblings? Not necessarily. It may be that differences in adjustment cause reported differences in experiences. In order to understand this relationship, we need to know more about the origins of differential treatment of siblings. Parents do not, generally, intend to treat their offspring differently. However, younger children might be treated differently by parents on the basis of their previous experience with older children.

However, this effect would not be present for twins. If parents intended to treat their offspring in similar fashions, why do differences in actual or perceived treatments emerge? One could assume that differential treatments emerge as a result of genetic or constitutional differences among siblings. Differences in the way children respond to parental treaments might lead parents to treat them differently (Bell, 1968). Daniels and Plomin (1985) attempted to rule out such an explanation by noting that reported sibling differences are about the same magnitude for biological siblings and for adopted siblings. However, this explanation, while reasonable, is not entirely convincing. Recall that the correlation in personality trait scores for biologically related siblings is usually about .20. Thus, their genetic similarity is not sufficient to create a great deal of similarity in phenotypic trait characteristics. As a result one would not expect to find dramatic differences in the reported similarity of treatments of biological and adopted siblings. A more critical test of the importance of perceived variations in parental treatment and experiences of siblings can be obtained by studying MZ twin pairs. It is interesting to note that the study of MZ twins has always been associated with those psychologists who have emphasized the role of genetic influences in understanding individual differences. However, it is the study of such twins that provides potentially the clearest, least-confounded basis for understanding the influence of the environment on personality. Loehlin and Nichols (1976) noted that the reported discrepancy between the experiences of MZ twins and their discordance for measures of personality are not related. However, their survey of differences in the experiences of siblings (i.e., twins in their study) was not as systematic and detailed as the reported differences studied by Daniels and Plomin. What can be concluded about the relationship between differences in sibling experiences and differences in personality traits among siblings? First, we can conclude that a promising beginning has been made by the development of an instrument that surveys reported differences. Second, the instrument has not been used sufficiently to establish its predictive utility. Third, the reported relationships are weak, and the available data have yet to rigorously exclude possible genetic mediation of the obtained relationships between personality and reported divergences in sibling experiences.

Within-family environmental influences encompass influences that occur outside of the family setting. These might include the influences of friends, sexual relationships, teachers, books, religious experiences, accidents leading to injury and disability, etc. We can conjecture that there are virtually limitless numbers of potential events and experiences in a person's life that might influence his or her personality characteristics. We have no empirically adequate information about this type of potential influence. We do not even know if such influences act in a random or systematic fashion. It has been suggested that the environmental events that influence a person's life are different for each individual and are, for all practical purposes, random, unrepeatable events whose influence is dependent upon the confluence of a series of unique occurrences. A combination of a particular psychological state, manifested by a pattern of thoughts that might be influenced by physiological events, associated with a particular environmental occurrence may change the course of an individual's psychological development. Such a model of environmental influences was proposed by Meehl (1972) in comments he provided for a book dealing with the genetics of schizophrenia written by Gottesman and Shields (1972).

Meehl suggested that the findings of discordance for schizophrenia among MZ twins was in some ways more interesting than the findings of increased concordance of MZ twins relative to DZ twins. When one examined discordant MZ twin pairs, it was difficult to find any set of events that could account for the discordance. This led Meehl to suggest that the environmental events that produced schizophrenia in a genetically vulnerable individual were different for each schizophrenic and were, for all practical purposes, the effects of random concatenations of events. Loehlin and Nichols (1976), commenting on their failure to find correlations between reported discrepancies in experience among MZ twins and discrepancies in their scores on self-report measures of personality, also suggested that the environmental events that influenced personality traits were essentially random and different for each individual.

Is a theory of the environment that emphasizes random, unpredictable influences on personality characteristics viable? In one sense, it is clearly not a preferred theory. Scientists abhor random and unpredictable events and prefer to discover systematic order in the world. However, it might be possible to gain additional empirical information about such events. One could ask individuals to describe the events that they believe have influenced their lives. One might then try to examine such events. While the important events in a person's life might be unique to that individual, they might nevertheless be classifiable. Studies of MZ twins might provide information about classes or types of events that are associated with MZ twin discordances for various measures of personality. Psychologists interested in the environmental events that shape personality have generally ignored the results of behavior-genetic research that suggested an absence of between-family environmental influences, and they have not attempted to find such events. Psychologists engaged in behavior-genetic research in personality have focused, until recent years, on demonstrations of the importance of genetic variables. Consequently, there has been relatively little systematic effort expended to understand the impact of within-family environmental events on personality. Therefore, it is premature to assume that systematic generalization, based on classification of relatively unique and unrepeatable events, is not attainable. However, it should be noted that attempts to gain information about such events will probably initially be heavily dependent upon the use of self-report measures. If individuals are not aware of the events that have had a profound impact on their psychological development, it will be exceedingly difficult to study such events.

Summary

We do know that genotypes influence personality traits. The influence of genotypes on traits may extend to changes in development early in life and to the patterning and expressiveness of trait behaviors. Genotypes may influence general traits, as well as quite specific behavioral tendencies, and the covariance structure of the relationship between traits. While we have increasing evidence of the importance of genotypic influences, we know much less about environmental influences. Detailed models of the way in which genotypes act upon the environment are without firm empirical support. We know little of the environmental events that shape personality traits other than that they are within-family events. Evidence for genetic and environmental covariance and genetic by environmental interactions is virtually nonexistent. What we do know is that by some ill-defined process individuals who are genotypically identical develop similar personality characteristics. The process by means of which this occurs is both biologically and behaviorally mysterious.

The evidence for the existence of genetic influences on traits also serves to buttress a trait conception. The fact that some portion of the variance of trait scores is genotypic argues that traits are not merely a linguistic artifact. Moreover, genotypes exist chronologically prior to the interaction of the organism with the social world. As such, they provide a rationale for the view that traits exist prior to situations. This provides an additional justification for a view of personality that assumes that individual characteristics determine behavior in social settings. This suggests that what is fundamental to a trait theory is the view that one cannot understand the social actions of individuals unless one understands the characteristics that individuals bring to situations. And, since those characteristics appear to involve a genotypic component, this suggests that the study of personality is ultimately rooted in the biological nature of the organism. One cannot directly inherit a response to a social situation, but one can mediately inherit a set of physical characteristics, including a nervous system with varying characteristics. Thus, the ultimate justification for a trait theory is based on the view that traits are genetically influenced characteristics that are rooted in the biological characteristics of an individual. As such, traits may be construed as biologically, chronologically, and methodologically prior to social settings. Such a view of traits neither denies, nor precludes, the study of the social environment. It merely insists that that study must proceed in the context of a recognition of the characteristics that the individual brings to the environment.

4

Traits: Summary, Refinements, and Emendations

Introduction

In Chapters 1, 2, and 3 we reached three general conclusions about traits: (1) There are general traits that influence a person's behavior in a variety of situations. (2) Traits endure through time and are not easily changed. (3) Traits are influenced by genotypes.

In this chapter we shall consider a number of suggested refinements in trait theory. We begin with a sketch of two different theories or specifications of general traits: Eysenck's theory based primarily on self-report measures that specifies a three-dimensional theory of traits, and the five-dimensional theory of traits derived from Norman's research on trait ratings. We shall consider the relationship between these descriptive systems and a number of possible emendations and refinements in such descriptive systems.

Traits: Two Descriptive Theories

In order to develop a trait description of personality it is necessary to specify the total set of descriptive traits that may be used for this purpose. Although factor analysis may be used to develop descriptive systems, it is generally conceded that factor analysis does not provide a unique solution to the development of a descriptive system. The factors that specify traits are clearly a function of the descriptors that are analyzed, and different input variables will result in different solutions. In addition, factor solutions for a given set of inputs are not unique. The development of the dimensional structure of factors and their relations to each other are not uniquely specified by the statistical manipulations of inputs. Some of these complexities will become apparent when we consider two trait-descriptive systems for personality: Norman's five-factor theory and Eysenck's three-factor theory.

Eysenck's Descriptive Theory

Eysenck's descriptive trait theory has evolved over a 40-year period. Although the descriptive system has changed, there are several respects in which there is considerable continuity between the system developed in 1947 and recent versions of the descriptive system (see Eysenck 1947, 1953, for older statements of the theory, and Eysenck and Eysenck, 1985 for the most recent statement of the descriptive aspects of the theory). There are at least four respects in which Eysenck's descriptive theory of traits has remained constant over time. First, Eysenck has always insisted that a system based on a limited number of general traits is more valid than one based on many narrowly defined traits. For example, he has criticized Cattell's attempt to measure and define 16 different personality factors in his 16 PF test of personality (see Cattell, Eber, and Tatsouka, 1970; Eysenck and Eysenck, 1985, pages 122–129). Eysenck argues that systems based on narrow factors are difficult to replicate in various factor analyses and ignore evidence of relationships among the narrow factors. However, factor analytically derived trait descriptions based on very general factors are replicable and are repeatedly discovered in investigations using different tests and item pools. Thus, Eysenck has consistently expressed a preference for a system based on a limited number of very general traits.

Second, there has been considerable substantive continuity in the system. The traits of extraversion and neuroticism have been considered as central in the descriptive system since its inception.

Third, the theory has attempted to provide a descriptive system that relates various forms of psychopathology to trait dimension that may be used to describe normal personality. For example, individuals who are likely to develop either obsessive or compulsive states and phobias are assumed to be low in extraversion and high in neuroticism.

Fourth, Eysenck has been involved with the development of several self-report tests of personality that provide measures of traits.

The current version of Eysenck's descriptive system postulates the existence of three fundamental traits of personality—extraversion, neuroticism, and psychoticism. Scores on these traits are assumed to be unrelated. This version, in effect, provides a three-dimensional descriptive system for personality. Each of the traits is itself a compound of several more narrowly defined traits. Psychoticism is related to aggressive, cold, egocentric, impersonal, impulsive, antisocial, unempathic, creative, and tough-minded characteristics. Neuroticism is related to anxious, depressed, tense, irrational, shy, moody, and emotional characteristics, as well as guilt feelings and low self-esteem. Extraversion is related to sociable, lively, active, assertive, sensation-seeking, carefree, dominant, surgent, and venturesome characteristics.

The description of neuroticism and its characteristics has remained relatively invariant in the Eysenck system. However, the descriptions of both extraversion and psychoticism have changed.

Extraversion was originally defined as an amalgam of the traits of sociability and impulsivity. Two arguments were advanced for the inclusion of both sociability and impulsivity within the general factor of extraversion. First, as with all lower order traits that were linked to form a general trait, there were empirical relationships between the narrower traits. Second, in their behavior genetic study of the covariance of impulsivity and sociability, Eaves and Eysenck (1975) found evidence for a genetic influence on the covariance of the traits. This implied that there are genes that influence the relationship between the traits, and thus there is a genetic basis for their linkage.

Eysenck's description of extraversion as a compound of impulsivity and sociability has changed. The changes are primarily related to the development of theory and measurement related to psychoticism as a trait. Eysenck traditionally argued that there was a dimension of psychoticism that was unrelated to neuroticism and that a unidimensional continuum of psychopathology in which neurotic behaviors were to be construed as a less extreme form of pathology than psychotic behaviors was incorrect. Neurotic behaviors and psychotic behaviors were construed by him as anchoring separate independent and uncorrelated dimensions of behavior. The early versions of the Eysenck personality questionnaires, however, did not contain a measure of the trait of psychoticism whereas the new versions do. In the latest versions of the system impulsivity is aligned with psychoticism. Interest in dangerous and thrilling activities is assumed to measure a trait called venturesomeness that is assumed to be a component trait of extraversion. Impulsivity proper, as indexed by an item that asks whether one is or is not an impulsive person, is now assumed to be a component trait of psychoticism.

The decision to separate impulsivity from sociability in Eysenck's descriptive system is supported by empirical research that indicates that impulsiveness can itself be split into separate components and that these components relate differentially to psychoticism and extraversion as measured by the Eysenck Personality Questionnaire. Eysenck, Pearson, Easting, and Allsopp (1985) obtained data relating venturesomeness and narrow impulsivity to extraversion and psychoticism. They reported data for two samples of young adults and older adults on these measures. Venturesomeness as indexed by endorsement of items referring to an interest in taking risks, and in sports such as parachute jumping, was uncorrelated with narrow impulsivity, as indexed by a tendency to endorse such items as "Are you an impulsive person?"

Table 4.1 presents the correlations for males and females in two different samples for these variables. The correlations reported in Table 4.1 indicate that venturesomeness and impulsivity are relatively unrelated and that impulsivity is more related to psychoticism than to extraversion. Venturesomeness is more substantially related to extraversion than to psychoticism.

The analysis of the relationship between impulsivity and its changing position within Eysenck's descriptive system is illustrative of some more general properties of the system. Just as general traits may be divided, narrow traits may be divided. Also, narrow traits may be related to more than one general trait. Thus the independence and clarity of the descriptive system emerges at the more abstract level of general traits.

A second possible reason to treat impulsivity as separate from sociability derives from research relating extraversion to performance in experimental situations. Revell Humphreys, Simon, and Gilliland (1980) have suggested that relationships between extraversion and performance in experimental situations may be mediated by what is the impulsivity dimension of extraversion.

Eysenck's Descriptive Theory and Five-Dimensional Theory

Eysenck's measures of personality traits are based on self-report measures. Virtually all of the factor analytic research cited in support of the current three-dimensional descriptive version of the theory is based on analysis of various questionnaire measures. Factor analyses of peer-ratings have often supported some version of the five-factor solution for trait ratings proposed by Norman (see Digman and Inouye, 1986). To what extent can Eysenck's system be reconciled with the five-dimensional descriptive structure proposed by Norman? Two of the factors are, of course, directly comparable. Both descriptive systems contain an extraversion factor. Neuroticism is described in the Norman taxonomy as emo-

Table 4.1

Correlations between Psychoticism, Extraversion, Impulsiveness, and Venturesomeness in Two Samples[a]

	Sample 1 adults		Sample 2 children	
	Male	Female	Male	Female
Psychoticism and Impulsiveness	.46	.45	.31	.47
Psychoticism and Venturesomeness	.22	.11	.02	.26
Extraversion and Impulsiveness	.39	.22	.10	.22
Extraversion and Venturesomeness	.37	.44	.60	.67
Impulsiveness and Venturesomeness	.24	.11	.17	.22

[a]Based on Eysenck et al. (1985).

tional stability. The remaining three dimensions within the Norman system are less easily aligned with Eysenck's three-dimensional system. Eysenck views the dimension described as culture as an aspect of intelligence—a trait that he would recognize as a fundamental dimension of personality. He indicates that it is entirely a matter of convention whether one includes general intelligence as a personality trait or not. In any case, Eysenck would accept a descriptive system that assumes that intelligence is a fundamental personality trait.

The attempt to relate the dimension of culture to intelligence is not, as far as I know, supported by an empirical demonstration that there is a substantial correlation between individual differences in intelligence test scores and an aggregated score of peer-ratings of the dimensions that constitute the culture factor within Norman's five-factor descriptive system. An examination of these dimensions (see Table 1.1, chapter 1) indicates that on the surface they include meanings that are not normally included in our understanding of the meaning of intelligence. Such characteristics as imaginativeness and artistically sensitive are, arguably, closer in meaning to creativity than to intelligence. Recall that Eysenck considers creativity to be a component trait of psychoticism. Thus, while there is little doubt that individual differences in intelligence may be properly construed as a dimension of personality, it is not transparently clear that individual differences in the culture dimension are to be construed as being a proxy for intelligence.

Eysenck argues that agreeableness is not a primary trait (see Eysenck and Eysenck, 1985). He believes that it is a trait whose locus within his dimensional system is defined by its relation to several other traits. In particular, he views agreeableness as a trait that is defined by high scores on extraversion and low scores on neuroticism and psychoticism.

Conscientiousness may be considered a dimension related to impulsivity and related to psychoticism as a trait.

These suggested relationships between Eysenck's three-dimensional system and Norman's five-dimensional system are based largely on intuition and on inspection of various scales. Obviously, such intuitions are not a substitute for empirical investigation of the actual relationships. Fortunately, Costa and McRae (1985) have collected data including peer-ratings and self-reports on four of the five Norman dimensions and scores on the Eysenck Personality Questionnaire. They substitute for Norman's culture dimension a dimension called openness to experience. Open individuals are assumed to be imaginative, artistic, aware of their inner feelings, intellectually curious, and possessed of nondogmatic values. The dimension may be viewed as a somewhat broadened dimension of culture included in Norman's typology. Eysenck has suggested that openness, as defined by Costa and McRae, may be related to psychoticism. Open individuals may be low in psychoticism. Table 4.2 presents the correlations between scores on the Eysenck Personality Questionnaire and self-report and peer-ratings on each of

Table 4.2

Correlations between Eysenck Personality Questionnaire Scores
and Peer- and Self-Ratings on Five Dimensions of Personality[a]

	Scores on Eysenck's Personality Questionnaire[b]		
Self-Reports	N	E	P
Neuroticism (Adjustment)	.75	−.05	.25
Extraversion	−.18	.69	−.04
Openness	.01	.15	.05
Agreeableness	−.18	.04	−.45
Conscientiousness	−.21	−.03	−.31
Peer-Ratings			
Neuroticism	.41	.01	.17
Extraversion	−.01	.48	.08
Openness	.07	.17	.14
Agreeableness	−.02	−.14	−.25
Conscientiousness	−.05	−.14	−.20

[a]Based on Costa and McRae (1985). N = Neuroticism; E = extraversion;
P = psychoticism.

the five dimensions derived from the Norman descriptive system with the substitution of openness for the culture dimension. An examination of Table 4.2 indicates that there is quite substantial agreement between the measures of extraversion and neuroticism. These data reinforce the view that these two traits may be construed as the least problematic, best established, and most general dimensions of personality. Openness is a trait that is not, contrary to Eysenck's assertion, substantially related to psychoticism. The question of the relationship between openness and intelligence remains to be explored. There is some evidence for a view of psychoticism as being related to agreeableness and conscientiousness, although it should be noted that the correlations between psychoticism and these traits as defined by peer-ratings are relatively low, i.e., respectively, −.25 and −.20. This discussion of the relationship between dimensional systems based on peer-ratings and Eysenck's three-factor dimensional system suggests that they are not equivalent. Such dimensions as narrow impulsivity, aggression, dominance, conscientiousness, and agreeableness all figure prominently in current personality research. Whether they are all subsumable under the dimension of psychoticism remains to be determined in additional research relating scores on the psychoticism dimension to various peer-ratings and other behavioral manifestations of the traits.

Is Personality to Be Described by a Limited Number of General Traits?

In this section we shall consider if a descriptive system based on a limited number of general traits provides an adequate basis for a description of personality. Buss and Craik (1985) argue that there exists an indefinitely large number of traits that are not related to the major dimensions of personality. They present, as an example of one such trait dimension, calculating. They demonstrate that respondents agree that a number of behaviors are prototypical exemplars of the characteristic. For example, making a friend in order to obtain a favor is considered a prototypical exemplar of the trait. One can form a composite index of the trait. Individuals can be asked to describe themselves with respect to the frequency with which they engage in those behaviors that are more or less prototypical for the trait.

Buss and Craik make a number of theoretical and empirical claims about the trait calculating. First, they report that individuals exhibit moderately high test–retest stability on a composite index derived from their endorsements of the behaviors that collectively define the trait. They report a test–retest correlation of .65. Second, observers (in their case, spouses) also report stability in their ratings of the composite trait behaviors that define the trait.

In addition, Buss and Craik claim that calculating is not related to other traits. They indicate that the only measure they have found in the existing personality literature with which the trait of calculating appears to share conceptual overlap is Machiavellianism, a trait studied by Christie, whose meaning is congruent with the ordinary language meaning of the trait (see Christie and Geis, 1970). Buss and Craik indicate that their calculating index derived from the frequency of endorsement of prototypical trait-defining behaviors is uncorrelated with Christie's test of Machiavellianism. Buss and Craik also suggest that there are other traits that may be defined in terms of their prototypical behavioral manifestations that are not well represented among current general trait conceptions. They mention as examples, jaded and ingenuous. And they suggest that it would be premature to assume that personality is to be defined by a limited set of general trait dimensions.

Is the Buss and Craik argument persuasive? I think not. First, note that they do not establish that their index of the trait calculating is unrelated to other general traits. They merely report that their index is not correlated with a trait measure with which it has some conceptual overlap, Machiavellianism. Would their trait index correlate with any of the traits defined by Norman's five-dimensional system or Eysenck's three-dimensional system? We do not know. In any case Buss and Craik report only minimal exploration of the independence of their index from other trait measures.

Second, there is no evidence that self-reports of calculating behaviors correlate with actual measures of behavior or with independent ratings of the trait. It is interesting to note that they report test-retest stabilities for self-report measures of calculating and spouse-ratings of the trait. Both measures were obtained for the same subjects. They do not report the correlation between the spouse-ratings and self-report measures of the trait. This is a curious omission. If there were agreements between self-reports and spouse-reports there would be additional evidence in favor of the trait.

Third, the prototypical behaviors that define calculating are not behaviors per se, but are descriptions of the reasons or motives for a particular act. A considerable body of evidence suggests that human beings are not particularly accurate reporters of the reasons for their actions (see Nisbett and Wilson, 1977). This is an issue we shall subsequently discuss. Whether or not one believes that human beings are generally knowledgeable of why they do what they do, it is still the case that the behavioral referents of the reasons for an action need to be specified in order to define the relationship between the trait and its behavioral referents. Note that the prototypical referents of calculating are not behaviors. How is one to know from an observation of the fact that a person has made a friend that the friendship was made in order to extract a favor from the new friend? I suspect that interrater agreements for inferences about the reasons for actions may be much lower than agreements about the occurrence of the actions themselves. Thus, the ultimate behavioral referents of this trait may be difficult to specify.

The above analysis of Buss and Craik's hypothesis that calculating is an example of a trait that is unrelated to any other trait suggests that the evidence presented for this assertion is less than convincing. To assert this is not to assert that their hypothesis is wrong. It is quite possible that calculating and many other narrower traits would be useful addenda to the set of traits available to describe individuals. The search for additional traits might enrich the description of individuals to permit a more differentiated and subtle sense of personality. However, it is necessary to demonstrate that such traits are actually predictive of behaviors and that they have heteromethod validity before postulating their existence.

Idiographic Characteristics: Qualification of Trait Descriptions

All of the traits that we have considered are what are called "common traits." That is, they are meant to apply to all individuals in the population. Individuals may differ in their position on the trait dimension but not in terms of whether the dimension does or does not apply to them at all. Allport (1961) has argued that the traits that are most defining and descriptive of an individual are those that are not common. He argues that the most defining traits are those that apply uniquely to an individual. Are there such traits? Allport does not specify how such traits are to be discovered. Nor, for that matter, is he particularly clear about what kinds of traits apply uniquely to an individual. He gives as an example the "unique sexual cruelty" of the Marquis de Sade. The example is problematic. The trait as described is derived from the combination of common traits, sexuality and cruelty. Both of these are, self-evidently, dimensions that apply to all individuals. One could of course argue that the Marquis de Sade was characterized by an extreme position on both of these dimensions. But that is not a unique condition. One might say that any person who is extreme on both of these dimensions would behave in a manner that is similar to the Marquis de Sade. It should also be noted that a descriptive system based on common traits that permits individual variations in trait scores can serve to identify the unique individual. The probability that two individuals will have exactly the same set of trait scores can be made infinitesimally small as long as one permits some variation in the scores assigned to each of a limited number of common traits.

Not only is a theory of common traits compatible with a virtually infinite degree of human uniqueness, but it is also the case that the notion of a unique trait leads to a *reductio ad absurdum*. If the trait applies to only one person, then it cannot be described in terms that apply to more than one person. This would require one to invent a new language to describe each person or, perhaps, to develop the skills of a poet to describe an individual. Either of these expedients would render the scientific study of personality impossible.

There is a sense in which common traits apply, to use Allport's terminology, idiographically—that is, to the unique individual. We have indicated that two individuals with the same trait score may have different patterns of expression of the trait. Thus, common traits do generalize or abstract from the idiosyncratic details of behavior to reach a level of generality that loses the details of an individual's behavior. There is a good deal of polemics surrounding this issue but relatively little attempt to address it empirically. There is a way of gaining empirical information about the limitations of a theory of common traits. Individuals can be presented with a large list of trait terms and asked to select from the list those that are most defining. This selection procedure does not derive a set of truly idiographic traits since the descriptors selected apply in principle to all persons. If one selects a small number of descriptors from a relatively large set, however, it is the case that the selected descriptive terms are partially idiographic in that they may be assumed to be most defining for an individual, and the subset of defining descriptors will be quite different for different individuals. Amelang and Borkenau (1984) have reported the results of a study that employed a related methodology. They presented their subjects with a list of 45 trait terms and asked them to rate each term with respect to the extent to which the term applied to them. They then divided their sample of 389 adults into two equal-sized groups on each trait—those who rated the trait as descriptive or appropriate for them and those who rated the trait as relatively nondescriptive or inappropriate for them. They then compared self-ratings with the average of three peer-ratings on each of the traits. The average correlation overall between self-reports and the aggregated peer trait ratings was .35 for traits that were assumed to be appropriate and defining for an individual. The comparable average correlation for the subgroups who rated the traits as relatively inappropriate for them was .23. Note that the gains in predictability were relatively modest. One reason why ratings of trait appropriateness do not add dramatically to the heteromethod agreement about traits is that the judgment of the extent to which a trait is an appropriate descriptor for an individual is neither stable nor something that different raters can agree about. Amelang and Borkenau obtained test–retest stability correlations for appropriateness ratings for 13 different traits for a group of 46 of their subjects. They found an average correlation of .36 for test–retest stabilities of appropriateness ratings for 13 traits. This figure should be compared with an average test–retest stability correlation of .71 for trait ratings themselves. In addition, the average trait agreement between self- and aggregated peer-ratings for this subset of subjects for 13 traits was .40. The average self- and peer-rating correlations for the appropriateness ratings was .07. These data suggest as we have seen previously that individuals exhibit stability in their trait descriptions and that there is some agreement between self- and peer-descriptions. Individuals do not exhibit stability in their ratings of whether a trait is or is not appropriate as a descriptor of their personality, however, and self-reports about appropriateness do not agree with observer ratings of the trait as a descriptor.

Cheek (1982) reported the results of a similar study in which he obtained correlations between self- and peer-ratings on the traits of extraversion, agreeableness, conscientiousness, and stability. He asked his subjects to indicate whether or not the trait was one that was appropriate to them. He divided his sample on each trait by their ratings of appropriateness and found that where subjects rated a trait as appropriate, the average correlation between self- and peer-ratings was .47, and where subjects rated the trait as inappropriate the average correlation between self- and peer-ratings was .38.

Amelang, Kobelt, and Frasch (1984) have reported results for a study of agreements between aggregated peer-rating scores on a self-report measure of extraversion and neuroticism for subjects who differ in their ratings of appropriateness of the traits. They reported peer-self correlations of .58 and .25 for extraversion and neuroticism, respectively, for the subjects who describe these traits as appropriate descriptors. The comparable correlations for their low appropriateness subjects were, respectively, .23 and .13.

Note that both the Cheek and Amelang, Kobelt, and Frasch studies indicate that increments in heteromethod predictability can be obtained for common traits by using a self-report rating of the extent to which the trait is an appropriate or important descriptor for an individual. Note that the increments to predictability attained by selecting common traits appear to be at least as large if not larger than the increments for predictability attained by selecting more narrowly defined traits from the list of 45 traits used in the Amelang and Borkenau study. These findings suggest that the use of appropriateness or importance ratings will not be a useful procedure to define idiographic traits. Rather, such ratings might more appropriately be a useful moderator or addenda to a trait-rating for those traits that are commonly applied to all individuals. It is also the case that the increments to predictability that may be attained by the use of such methods are limited by their apparently low test–retest reliability.

There have been a number of proposals in the literature that attempt to qualify trait-ratings in order to improve their predictability. Bem and Allen (1974) were the psychologists most responsible for initiating the search for various ratings that would enhance the predictability of trait-ratings by specifying a group of traits that were particularly appropriate for some subset of individuals. They assumed that one could identify a subset of individuals who were consistent, and hence predictable, from their trait scores. They reported evidence suggesting that individuals who reported themselves as being consistent did exhibit higher heteromethod correlations for their trait-rating scores than individuals who did not rate themselves as consistent on the trait. There have been several reported failures to replicate these results, however, in relatively thorough and large-scale research efforts. For example, Chaplin and Goldberg (1985) collected self-report data, observer-rating data, and objective data for eight different traits. They found that heteromethod correlations were no higher for traits on which individuals rated themselves as consistent than for traits on which individuals rated themselves as inconsistent. Similarly, Cheek (1982) and Amelang and Borkenau (1984) failed to replicate Bem and Allen's findings.

Kenrick and Stringfield (1980) used a variant of this procedure. They asked their subjects to select, from a list of 16 traits derived from Cattell's 16 PF test, the trait on which they were most and least consistent. They then obtained heteromethod agreement indices for self- and peer-ratings for those traits that individuals selected as being the ones on which they were most consistent and least consistent. They found heteromethod agreement correlations of .47 for the traits on which subjects asserted that they were most consistent and .24 for those traits that were selected as being least consistent. Although Kenrick and Stringfield's procedure does indicate that the selection of a single most consistent trait may lead to increments in predictability, the effects are again not dramatic.[1]

There is one additional trait-rating variable that has enhanced the heteromethod predictability of traits. Individuals who have rated themselves as relatively observable on a particular trait have generally exhibited higher heteromethod correlations than individuals who have rated themselves as unobservable on a trait. In three of the studies in which ratings of appropriateness or impor-

---

[1]The correlations are those reported by Kenrick and Braver (1982). The original correlations reported in the Kenrick and Stringfield (1980) article were based on an improper analysis. These correlations also may have been inflated by failure to control for a correlation between consistency and extremity of ratings.

tance were used as a trait rating—Cheek (1982), Amelang and Borkenau (1984), and Amelang, Kobelt, and Frasch (1984)—ratings of observability were also obtained. Self-report ratings of trait observability appeared to enhance hetero-method trait agreement indices as much as, or slightly more than, ratings of the appropriateness of a trait. Amelang and Borkenau split their sample on each trait into individuals who rated themselves as observable and unobservable on the trait. They found that the average correlation for 45 different traits for individuals who rated themselves as observable was .41. The corresponding correlation for individuals who rated themselves as unobservable on each of the traits was .20. (Compare these correlations with the values of .35 and .23 obtained for appropriateness ratings in the same study.)

Cheek reported correlations between self-report and peer-ratings for four traits of .50 for individuals who rated themselves as observable on a trait and .35 for individuals who rated themselves as relatively unobservable. (Compare these correlations with the values of .47 and .38 reported earlier for ratings of appropriateness.)

Our review of research on trait-ratings has established that at least modest increments in predictability may be obtained by using trait-ratings of appropriateness and observability. Amelang and Borkenau (1984) have reported very low test–retest correlations and self-observer agreements for such ratings. Because ratings of observability and appropriateness are not highly stable, it is surprising that they provide any increment to predictability at all. This suggests that the true increment to predictability that is attainable is larger than that which has been obtained. Quite apart from technical and methodological implications, these results raise a number of theoretical questions. What are the meanings of such trait-ratings, and what do they tell us about the meaning of traits?

Trait appropriateness is inherently ambiguous. Consider some of the possible meanings inherent in ratings of appropriateness. Individuals might avoid those situations that permit the assessment of prototypical behaviors. Or, individuals might be exposed to such situations but fail to exhibit behaviors that are indicative of their position on the trait. Of course, a rating of the extent to which a trait is appropriate may simply reflect one's own sense of oneself. That is, it might mean that an individual simply does not think of himself or herself in these terms. This meaning, however, which, on the surface, appears to be the most obvious or self-evident meaning of the appropriateness rating, cannot exhaust the total meaning of the rating since a purely private or personal meaning would not account for the differential predictiveness of the ratings. That is, individuals who rate themselves in different ways on the appropriateness or importance of a trait must behave differently in order to influence the correlations between self- and peer-ratings on the trait.

Ratings of the observability of a trait also pose theoretical problems of interpretation. An individual might be unobservable on a trait for the same reasons that a trait may differ in appropriateness. That is, individuals may avoid those situations that permit a prototypical assessment of the trait or not engage in those behaviors that permit the prototypical assessment of the individual on the trait. There is, again, an interesting private or personal meaning that is compatible with the word "observable." Perhaps individuals mean that there is a discrepancy between their actions and beliefs. Could one not act in ways to satisfy convention or social roles and yet believe that one's actions are not reflective of one's true self? It would appear that to assert that one is not observable on a trait is to imply either that one does not engage in trait-relevant behaviors or that one does, but that they are not reflective of one's true position on the trait. In the former case, one's self-ratings would be meaningless. In the latter case, one's self-ratings would not be predictive of peer-ratings on the trait on the assumption that peers have greater access to behaviors than they do to private beliefs about the discrepancy between one's actions and an inner sense of self. This discussion suggests that we need to know more about the meanings and behavioral referents of such trait-ratings as observability of traits in order to understand why they influence the relationship between self-reports and peer-ratings.

Just as a particular trait may be more or less predictive for a particular individual, individuals may differ in the extent to which they are predictive. That is, predictability may itself be a trait. Amelang and Borkenau (1984) reported that self-report ratings of consistency on the traits of friendliness, conscientiousness, assertiveness, and honesty were positively and substantially correlated, ranging from .36 to .63, with an average correlation of .48. Thus individuals who said they were consistent on one trait tended to say that they were consistent on other traits.

Because trait-ratings for consistency are substantially related, it is natural to aggregate such ratings across traits. Amelang and Borkenau divided their sample on the basis of their aggregated consistency score and then compared self-report scores to peer-ratings on these traits. They found an average correlation between self-ratings and peer-ratings of .57 for individuals who described themselves as consistent on the traits and a corresponding average correlation of .37 for individuals who described themselves as inconsistent. These data suggested that individuals may differ in the extent to which their self-ratings are in agreement with peer-ratings.

Scheier, Buss, and Buss (1978) used a measure of private self-consciousness as a basis for dividing subjects into individuals who differ in predictability. Their measure of predictability was derived from a self-report scale that was assumed to measure a person's tendency to be aware of his or her inner psychological states (a trait like characteristic). Individuals who pay attention to their inner psychological states and are aware of them are assumed to behave in a way that creates greater concordance between their inner states and their actions (see Carver and Scheier, 1981). Scheier, Buss, and Buss (1978) assumed that trait ratings would be more predictive of actual behavior for individuals who were high in self-consciousness. They asked their subjects to rate themselves on the trait of aggressiveness, and they obtained a behavioral measure of aggression by asking subjects to deliver shocks to a ''victim'' who had angered them in an experimental situation in which the subject was instructed to use shocks to assist the victim to learn. They divided their subjects into two groups whose scores on their measure of self-consciousness were in the upper third and the lower third of the distribution. They found that the correlation between self-report measures of aggression and their behavioral measure of aggression was .66 for subjects in the upper third of the distribution of the self-consciousness scale, and the corresponding correlation for subjects in the lower third of the distribution was .09. These data provide rather dramatic support for their hypothesis.

Cheek (1982) found that scores on self-consciousness did not moderate the relationship between self-report measures and peer-ratings of traits. One reason for the differences in results is that the aggression measure was obtained in a laboratory setting and was highly artificial. Under conditions of laboratory measurement individuals who are self-conscious might pay particular attention to the kinds of implicit demands inherent in the social situation and thus accentuate the congruence between their actions and their own sense of their psychological characteristics. However, they might be less inclined to attend to subtle cues for behavior in the external world in ordinary situations that are less likely to heighten their sense of the social requirements of the situation. Thus, congruence between their sense of themselves and their actions may be variable and may in part be limited to rather special situations. Whether or not this analysis is correct, it is the case that the inconsistency in the data reported above indicates that additional data are required before it can be confidently asserted that individuals who are high in self-reported consciousness have trait-ratings that exhibit higher predictability.

This review of the characteristics of persons that relate to their predictability suggests that modest increments in predictability may be obtained by distinguishing between individuals who are more or less predictable. It is also the case that nothing in these results or in the results of the analyses of differential predictability of traits for certain individuals supports the view that common traits are not in fact common. That is, none of the so-called moderator variables that influence the predictability of traits results in the elimination of predictability for common traits for subsets of individuals or subsets of traits. Rather, these results may best be viewed as indicating ways to refine and add to the predictability of common trait-ratings.

The Idiographic Paradox

Although I have suggested that common traits apply to, and may be used to make predictions about, all individuals, it is possible to argue that predictions derived from common traits may be correct when viewed in their aggregate meaning as applying to all individuals and, simultaneously and paradoxically, incorrect, or more technically, meaningless, when applied to one individual. Lamiell (1981, 1982) has argued that correlations between trait-ratings and behaviors do not permit one to infer anything about the individual case. Consider some examples. It is possible to study the stability of a trait by obtaining trait-ratings on two different occasions. If the test-retest stability correlation is .00, it is conventional to say that the trait is not stable. If we look at the two scores obtained for each individual, however, we are likely to find that some individuals have the same score, some individuals have increased their score, and some individuals have decreased their score. Thus, a generalization based on a group of individuals does not apply to the individual case. What about the case in which there are test-retest stabilities that are greater than zero? A correlation of 1.00 does, of course, apply to all individuals in a sample. It would imply that an individual's position on the trait relative to all other individuals in the group would be invariant—and this assertion would apply to each individual in the group. As the correlation decreases from a high absolute value, however, the extent to which generalizations are true about the individuals in the group decreases. Thus, a relatively high positive correlation still permits exceptions to the rule of predictability. Subsets of individuals might exhibit dramatic changes in their position vis-à-vis other individuals in the group. Thus, the statement that scores on a trait remain stable over time to some degree as indexed by a test–retest correlation should be understood as being differentially true. That is, we should understand the statement as being a statement of what is likely to be true for most individuals, recognizing that any given individual may exhibit a deviant pattern. It should be obvious that the same analysis applies to the interpretation of heteromethod trait relationships. If we obtain correlations of .40 or .50 between self-ratings and peer-ratings on traits, as we commonly do, this does not mean that there is an equally modest predictability obtained for self-ratings to peer-ratings for all individuals in our sample. Some individuals in the sample may have self-ratings on a trait that are perfectly congruent with peer-ratings, and other individuals may have self-ratings on the trait that are substantially at variance with peer-ratings.

Lamiell's analysis indicates that we have developed methods for studying individual differences that, strictly speaking, do not apply to the individual. To what extent is it possible or desirable to develop a psychology of personality that does apply to the individual case? It may be argued that the deviations from the general case are aberrant and of little interest. It is possible to assert that deviations from aggregate predictability for all individuals represent random error. When we correct correlations for attenuation and derive a "true score" correlation between two measures (assumed to represent the relationship between the variables if all fluctuations in scores within each variable are attributable to random error), we are, in effect, assuming that individual deviations from the aggregate or common pattern for all individuals are merely error or random perturbations of no particular interest. This solution to what we may call Lamiell's paradox is not completely satisfying. First, it is almost self-evidently fictitious. At least some individual deviation must be lawlike and, in any case, we should recognize that the assumption that all deviations are not lawlike is arbitrary and extreme. Second, the paradox is not removed by the error assumption since, in most cases, disattenuated correlations are less than 1.00 and we are again faced with the paradox that correlations tell us what is likely to be true of some subset of individuals but not of all individuals in the sample.

To assert that the assumption that all individual deviation from some pattern of relationship in error is an extreme assumption is not to deny that it is a reasonable assumption in some subset of cases. Consider an example. The correlation between a child's score on an intelligence test and grades in school is usually .50. Let us assume that one child in our sample exhibits an extremely discrepant score. Perhaps his or her intelligence test score is very low and his or her grades are quite high. Is this child an exception to the rule that one cannot acquire knowledge unless one has the ability to do so that is usually invoked to explain the obtained correlation? Perhaps not. One can think of a myriad of reasons why the intelligence test score might not reflect the true ability of the child. The child might, for example, have been emotionally troubled on the day the test was administered. The example suggests that individual variations that occur in the pattern of group predictability may sensibly be thought of as resulting from individual aberrations that in effect cause certain individual measurements to fall outside implicit boundary limits that exist for a particular scientific theory. Consider a second related example. The test–retest correlation for intelligence is quite high. Any given individual might exhibit quite large changes. Consider the case of a person incurring brain injury whose IQ score exhibits a large decline. The generalization that intelligence test scores remain stable over time carries with it any of a number of implicit boundary conditions that are usually not specified. Among these is an obvious notion that individuals remain physiologically intact. These examples demonstrate that at least some deviations of individual predictability from group predictability are not meaningful or of general scientific interest because they fall outside implicitly understood boundary conditions for the validity of the scientific generalizations that constitute the explanation of the aggregated common relationship.

The relevance of a generalization derived from common relationships for a group of individuals to the individual case may be enhanced by considerations of multivariate relationships. The analysis of individual correlations does not do full justice to the possibility of extending group generalizations to the individual case. Let us again consider the example of the relationship between intelligence test scores and grades in school. We have presented data indicating that the relationship may be influenced by a person's score on impulsivity. If we were to develop a multivariable prediction equation, it might, given the results obtained by Kipnis for impulsivity as a trait, reflect the moderating influence of impulsivity.

This procedure, in effect, qualifies the relationship between two variables by considering an individual's position on one or more additional variables that might serve to modify or change the relationship between the original variables. Note that there is nothing in this procedure that requires one to use measurements that are not based on correlations based on groups of people. Multivariable prediction based on common correlations qualifies the meaning of particular correlations and implicitly restricts the generality of relationships to subsets of individuals. As one increases the number of variables and the complexity of possible relationships among them, the class of individuals to which the predictions apply becomes increasingly narrow. That is, if the prediction equation contains several variables and combinations of variables, the equation may simultaneously be understood as applying to all individuals and to subsets of individuals defined by the particular configuration of scores they have on the several predictor variables entered into the equation. Such a procedure, however, must inevitably result, even in its narrowest predictive class, in generalization about a group of individuals. One cannot derive a prediction from group correlations for an individual with a particular combination of scores that is based on the notion that the configural relationship among all the variables ultimately determines the predictive relation of any given variable. One cannot determine the changes to be made in the predictors for N-1 variable set when the nth variable is entered into the equation unless one has data for groups of individuals who share configurated values on all the variables. As one increases the number of common variables whose combinations must be considered, one rapidly finds that the number of individuals whose scores must be sampled (in order to find a suitable number of individuals whose scores are sufficiently similar on several variables to permit a configurated prediction for them) increases quite rapidly. Thus, while it is in principle possible to develop prediction equations for increasingly narrower subsets of individuals, such a procedure is neither practical, because of the limitations of sample size, nor adequate for the unique case, because one can use this procedure only to generalize about classes of individuals.

It should be noted that empirical literature exists concerning the use of complex configural predictions (see Meehl, 1956; Wiggins, 1973). In most situations, complex equations consisting of many variables and many complex relationships among the variables do not enhance predictability. It is almost always the case that a prediction equation based on two or three variables, without weightings for particular combinations or configural relationships among variables, is as or more accurate than more complex equations that in effect continually serve to modify and narrow the class of individuals to which a predictive relationship applies.

The use of multivariable prediction equations to individualize predictions to subsets of individuals is based on the use of common personal characteristics. It is also possible to individualize trait measurements themselves by deriving measures that are, in various ways, based on samplings of a single individual's response patterns. Q-sort methodology provides an example of the derivation of trait-ratings based on a single individual's response pattern. Recall that Q-sort methodology requires an individual to rate a large set of descriptors in terms of the extent to which they apply to a person. Usually the individual must place an equal number of descriptors into one of several categories. If an individual rates a particular descriptor as being extremely descriptive of himself or herself, this does not imply anything about an individual's position on the descriptor relative to other people. For example, if a person rates himself or herself as creative, this does not mean that the individual is creative relative to other people. It means, technically, only that the individual finds creative more descriptive of his or her personality than other possible descriptors included in the set. This type of measurement in which the individual's descriptions, scores, or ratings, and so forth are assigned relative to other descriptors, scores, or ratings that are assignable to that individual is called ipsative measurement.

Clearly, ipsative measurements are, in a strict sense, relativized to the individual case. It is not clear, however, that this difference is, in anything other than a strictly logical sense, of great importance in the empirical or theoretical interpretation of this type of measurement. Q-sorts generally provide a large set of descriptors to an individual that are meant to approximate an exhaustive set of potential descriptors. The set is exhaustive not in the sense that all possible terms are included. It is exhaustive in the sense that the set is assumed to contain a relatively complete set of nonredundant descriptors. Thus, those descriptors not included are likely to be redundant with descriptors that are included. If this is correct, what implication does this have for the interpretation of a Q-sort descriptor? In our example, the person who describes himself or herself as creative relative to other descriptions is probably creative relative to other individuals as well. It is theoretically possible that this last assertion is false. If a person is not well described by most of the other descriptors, including descriptors that are opposite in meaning, a person might say validly that he or she is creative although the person is low on creativity. For this to be true, however, one would have to assume that Q-sort descriptors are not equally exhaustive sets for all individuals, or, perhaps, that individuals differ in the variability of the extent to which a descriptor applies to them. Therefore, the person who validly rates himself as creative but is in fact relatively noncreative in comparison to other people can only be understood as being nonvalidly described by the other available descriptors in the set. In effect, such a person might be described as not being describable at all by the large set of possible descriptors available on the Q-sort. The person therefore lacks a personality or lacks a personality that is readily descriptive in terms that are available to describe other people. This analysis suggests that Q-sort methodology may be thought of as providing a methodological injunction that forces a person to concentrate on the descriptiveness of individual descriptors for a particular individual. The descriptive ratings that are obtained, however, are probably substantially related to ratings that involve a comparison of an individual to other individuals. It is also the case that Q-sort ratings are frequently related to nonipsatized measures. For example, we have discussed research relating Q-sort ratings to measures of delay of gratification. Correlations between such measures are, in Lamiell's sense, true of aggregates of individuals but may not be descriptive of any given individual.

It is possible to develop measures of personality dispositions that are more individualized than Q-sort measures. Such measures should be based on a comparison of an individual to himself or herself on a particular characteristic. There are several ways to do this. If one obtains multiple measures for a single individual on a single characteristic, it is possible to establish scale values for that individual. For any given occasion an individual may be assigned a score on that characteristic that indicates whether the individual is high or low relative to his or her own previous performance on the scale. One could, for example, obtain measures of mood and determine the negativity in an individual's mood state on repeated occasions. Such data permit one to reach several generalizations whose range of application may be limited to a particular individual. Consider some possibilities. One could study the sequential dependencies or periodicities in a particular individual's mood-ratings. An individual's variations in negative moods might be random. Another individual might exhibit any of a variety of sequential dependencies. For example, an individual might exhibit an alternating sequence of negative and nonnegative mood states with a particular periodicity— say, on alternate days.

It is possible to study the covariation within an individual for individually derived scores. For example, if one obtains measures of the negative moods of an individual and the positive moods of an individual aggregated over several occasions, one could investigate how these individually derived scores covary. Zevon and Tellegen (1982) have obtained data indicating that aggregated positive mood scores are independent of aggregated negative mood scores. However, this is a generalization that is true of a group of individuals when considered as an aggregate. Any given individual might exhibit intraindividual lawlike regularities of covariation between individually measured mood scores. Consider some possibilities. A particular person might have a positive correlation between his or her individualized aggregated positive and negative mood scores. Such an individual would tend to report that he or she has relatively intense positive moods during periods when he or she has relatively intense negative moods. Another individual might have a negative correlation between individualized negative and positive mood scores. Such an individual would be unlikely to report himself or herself in a relatively high negative mood. Still a third individual might have a zero correlation between his or her positive and negative moods.

Note that in the above examples the correlations express different relationships for different individuals between two sets of measures that are based solely on scores that assign a value to an individual that is relativized to repeated measures of that individual's behavior. Such relationships express laws based on individual measures whose range of applications is strictly limited to an individual. The dispositional characteristics are common terms, but the scores on these dispositions and the relationships among such dispositions are idiographic.

The idiographic study of the person need not be construed as antithetical to more traditional homothetic methods of investigation. Having discovered lawlike relationships for idiographic characteristics of a person one can inquire whether or not such relationships are replicated in each individual case and in studies that measure personal dispositions in traditional nomothetic ways. Zevon and Tellegen (1982) have reported the results of an interesting study that deals with the relationship of idiographic and nomothetic dimensions of mood. They asked their subjects to repeatedly describe their moods on a comprehensive list of 60 mood adjectives at random intervals over a three-month period. They then created idiographic mood measurements and conducted what Cattell (1952) called a P-factor analysis separately for each person. The factor analyses were based on the correlations of ratings scores on all possible pairs of adjectives for each subject. The units for each paired comparison were the separate occasions on which a person rated his or her moods.

Zevon and Tellegen note that previous nomothetic factor analyses had indicated that there was evidence for a two-factor solution in which positive moods were independent of negative moods. Each of the factors was bipolar with positive moods ranging from delighted to sleepy and sluggish states and the negative mood factor defined by such descriptors as distressed at one pole and contented at the other. Zevon and Tellegen report that they were able to replicate the same two-factor solution on an idiographic basis for 20 of their 23 subjects. One subject's mood ratings were not congruent with the two-factor solution derived from nomothetic measurements. This subject's mood ratings were better defined by a three-dimensional factor structure. However, there was some evidence for a third, less well-defined factor in the nomothetic research. Thus, this subject's data were not incongruent in a fundamental way with results obtained from nomothetic measurements. This leaves two subjects whose factor ratings did not fit the nomothetically derived model. Zevon and Tellegen obtained semantic relationships among the descriptors for several of their subjects. They found that semantic relationships among the adjectives were deviant for the two subjects whose idiographic factors were not congruent with the nomothetic factor structures. This analysis helps to explain why these subjects produced ratings with an idiosyncratic factor structure. However, this analysis also raises as many questions as it answers. Why did these two subjects exhibit deviant semantic structures? Perhaps their moods were really organized in a different way and their use of language reflected the reality of the structure of their moods.

The Zevon and Tellegen analysis indicates dramatically that idiographic descriptions are not necessarily incongruent with nomothetic descriptions. The analysis provides one way of resolving what we have called Lamiell's paradox. That is, while it is conceptually correct to assert that relationships between nomothetic measures do not permit assertions about what is true for any given individual, it is not necessarily true that nomothetic relationships are not *empirically* equivalent to idiographic relationships.

The positive and negative mood dimensions are substantially related to the traits of extraversion and neuroticism as measured by the Eysenck Personality Questionnaire. Tellegen (undated) reports that positive and negative mood factors correlate with traits called Positive and Negative Affectivity as measured by the Differential Personality Questionnaire (DPQ). The DPQ factors of positive affectivity and the Eysenck extraversion score have substantial loadings on the same general extraversion factor and the negative affectivity factor score from the DPQ loads on the same factor as the neuroticism score on the Eysenck scale. These data suggest that the two most important common traits, extraversion and neuroticism, may be recoverable on the basis of idiographic measurements. Of course, there may be idiographic personality dimensions that are not isomorphic with common dimensions. However, I am not aware of any empirical research that supports the existence of idiographic traits.

We can summarize this discussion of the limitations of a common trait approach to personality. Marginal improvements in the predictability of trait-ratings may be obtained by relativizing prediction to subsets of individuals or traits. Evidence suggests, however, that a limited number of common traits are, at least to some degree, descriptive of all individuals and are even, apparently, recoverable on the basis of idiographic measurement. Personality descriptions based on a small set of common traits provide a limited and even an impoverished descriptive system. It is a serviceable system, however, and there is no compelling empirical justification for the rejection of such a system. Indeed, we have no compelling empirical justification to enrich the system by adding limited traits or by substantially qualifying the range of application of existing traits.

More about Personality and Situations

It is generally accepted among personality theorists that trait approaches to personality are incomplete. At the very least, a trait approach should be supplemented by a consideration of the kinds of situations in which we would expect to find a relationship between a trait and behavior. In what follows we shall consider several approaches to the specification of situations and the way in which they relate to personality characteristics.

S–R Inventories and Interactionism

There is a deceptively simple approach to studying the relationship between traits and situations that was introduced by Endler and Hunt (1966). They suggested that personality inventories should be qualified to include measurement of situations and response styles for the expression of a particular personality disposition. They constructed an S–R inventory of anxiety—(a self-report personality test)—that asked subjects about their characteristic modes of responses or way of expressing anxiety in specific situations. This type of test permits one to partition the variability of the scores into several components of variance. The person variance represents the traditional trait measure and reflects differences among individuals summed over all responses and situations. Situational variance is represented by the characteristic differences in situations summed over individuals and modes of responses. Situational variance would be reflected in the S–R inventory of anxiety if situations differed in the characteristic level of anxiety they elicited. Response variance refers to differences in different modes of the expression of anxiety summed over individuals and situations. There are also interactions or nonadditive combinations of any two sources of variance. Thus, person by situation interaction variance refers to differences in the situations in which individuals express anxiety. The total variance of all the responses may be partitioned into its components and a quantitative measure of the importance of trait, situation, and response variance and their interactions may be obtained. Following Endler and Hunt's pioneering work there have been many studies attempting to provide quantitative estimates of the importance of traits, situations, and their combination (see Furnham, 1986 for a comprehensive summary of these studies). These studies have generally indicated that trait variance and situational variance account for relatively small portions of the total variance—usually about 10%—and their interaction accounts for a substantial portion of variance. It is not unusual to find as much as 50% of the variance represented by the interaction of traits and situations, implying that it is not possible to predict an individual's expression of a particular behavioral disposition from a knowledge of his or her characteristic personal disposition aggregate (or trait level) or from a knowledge of the characteristic level of expression in that situation. Rather, different individuals express their personal dispositions in different situations, and it is necessary to have information about both the person and the situation in order to predict the characteristic response of a person to a situation. The interactionist position that is derived from this type of analysis is plausible—indeed, it may almost be compellingly obvious (see Bowers, 1973; Ekehammer, 1974 for an explication of the "interactional" argument). I shall argue, however, that results of the S–R inventory studies do not really provide compelling evidence in favor of the interactionist position.

S–R inventories may be made to yield virtually any result with respect to the relative importance of person (trait) variance, situation variance, and their interaction by varying the selection of situations. Consider an example. Suppose I wish to study compliance as a personality trait, and I choose to include on an S–R inventory the following two questions: (1) If you see a policeman at a crowded intersection directing traffic, are you likely to stop for a red light when you are driving a car? (2) If you were ordered by your high school teacher to shoot your parents, would you do so? Virtually all people would answer yes to question 1 and no to question 2. An analysis of variance of an S–R inventory containing such questions would indicate that virtually all the variance is attributable to situations since virtually all people respond in an identical way to such questions. This example is not intended to argue that existing S–R inventories have preordained results by virtue of their choice of extreme or irrelevant situations. It is, however, meant to indicate that the relative importance of different components of variance is very much a function of the nature of the situations that are selected for analysis.

There are also a number of statistical problems inherent in the analysis of S–R inventory data. The usual analyses do not provide appropriate indices of the importance of trait variance. If there are average differences in the level of expression of a trait disposition in different situations but individuals maintain the same rank order in their level of expression of the trait, trait variances will be underestimated by the usual procedures used. A second statistical problem concerns the importance attributable to interaction effects. The percentage of variance attributable to the interaction of situations and responses is actually a combination of the interaction effect and of error variance. Thus, the true importance of the interaction is exaggerated.

There are two additional difficulties in the S–R inventory approach. Furnham (1986) has indicated that the results of these studies vary depending on whether the S–R inventory is based on self-reports or on observer-ratings. Individuals tend to fill out the inventories in a way that minimizes trait variance. In effect, they report their behavior as being discriminatively responsive to situational influences. Observers tend to assign more variance to traits assuming that individuals tend to exhibit similar behaviors in different situations.

Perhaps the most fundamental limitation of this approach is that it studies the responses of all individuals to a standard set of situations. However, it can be argued that there is a relationship between traits and the situations that individuals choose to enter. Several studies indicate that traits relate to the kinds of situations and activities that people select. Furnham (1981) has found a number of relationships between extraversion and the leisure activities of individuals. Individuals who scored high on extraversion report that they seek to engage in situations in which they can be with other people and meet new people more than individuals who score low on the scale. Introverts, in contrast to extraverts, prefer activities in which they can organize and arrange things.

Although the S–R inventories do not provide a definitive answer to the relative importance of situations and trait variance, the recent comprehensive summary of these studies provided by Furnham, who reanalyzed the available studies, indicates that trait variance is somewhat larger than was originally indicated in the earlier studies. He reports that trait variance accounted for 20.3%, situational variance 9.9%, and the trait × situational variance accounted for 20.7% of the total variance. This last figure is a nondecomposable compound of both true interaction variance and error variance. What is perhaps of greater interest is the attempt to use the information contained in these inventories to predict how people will respond to different situations. Endler (1982) attempted to classify individuals' responses to anxiety in terms of situations that are likely to elicit anxiety. He designed an inventory that permitted one to distinguish between those individuals likely to experience anxiety in situations that elicit changes and those experiencing anxiety in situations that involve social evaluation (see Endler and Okada, 1975). He then studied the reported response of individuals to situations that are assumed to elicit specific types of anxiety. For example, Flood and Endler (1980) obtained measures of the current state of anxiety in a group of athletes just before a practice session and before a track and field meeting. They assumed that athletic competition would arouse anxiety in individuals who are high in social evaluation anxiety and not in groups who differed in other types of anxiety. Table 4.3 presents their data. They found a significant interaction between social evaluation anxiety and differences in the level of the state of anxiety reported in practice situations and in athletic competition. An examination of Table 4.3 indicates that subjects who reported that they became anxious in social evaluation situations reported larger increases in their state of anxiety during the athletic competition than subjects who were low in social evaluation anxiety. There were no significant interactions between individual differences in other types of situational anxiety and these two situations. These results should be accepted cautiously for two reasons. First, an examination of Table 4.3 indicates that there were comparable patterns of change for other types of anxiety even if the results were not quite statistically significant. Thus, the results for individual anxiety in situations that are physically dangerous or in situations that elicit interpersonal anxiety are quite comparable to the effects of social evaluation anxiety. These results do not provide dramatic evidence for a discriminative response for individuals characterized by different patterns of situationally elicited anxiety. Second, these results are all based totally on self-reports. In effect, individuals are asked in what situations they become anxious and then are asked if they are anxious when confronted with a situation that is presumed to elicit that type of anxiety. Evidence indicating that one could predict

Table 4.3

Reported State Anxiety in Response to a Practice
Situation and an Athletic Competition[a]

	Scores	
Anxiety traits	Practice	Competition
Interpersonal		
High	46.2	58.2
Low	40.0	53.1
Physical Danger		
High	47.8	61.3
Low	36.7	49.4
Ambiguous		
High	45.4	61.5
Low	39.5	51.5
Daily Routines		
High	47.8	57.1
Low	40.4	58.0
Social Evaluation		
High	46.9	64.1
Low	40.0	49.2

[a]Based on Flood and Endler (1980).

the behaviors of individuals in different situations from an S–R inventory of anxiety would be more convincing.

Kendall (1978) reported data providing somewhat clearer support for the interaction of different types of anxiety and situations. He asked subjects to report their anxiety when shown movies of automobile crashes (designed to elicit anxiety related to physical danger) and in response to a situation in which they were presented with a difficult cognitive task. He found that subjects who were high in evaluation anxiety reported high levels of state anxiety in response to the cognitive task and low levels of state anxiety in response to the movie about automobile crashes. Subjects who reported themselves high in anxiety about physical danger reported high levels of anxiety in response to the noise of automobile crashes and low levels of anxiety in response to the cognitive task. The Kendall study provides particularly clear evidence for an increase in predictability that may be attained by specifying the types of situations that are likely to elicit anxiety in individuals who respond to particular social stresses.

Situational Determinants of Trait Predictability

Are there properties of situations that enhance the predictability of traits? In Chapter 1 I indicated that psychometric theory could be used to provide guidelines for a behaviorally or situationally based measure of traits. A particular situation may be conceptually relevant to a trait but, for purely psychometric reasons, the correlation between trait scores and behavioral measures obtained in the situation will tend toward zero. Coefficients of correlation are a function of the "range of talent," or variance, of the two variables that enter into the correlation. If the variance is small and restricted on one of the variables, the correlation between them will be low. This statistical relationship has direct relevance to understanding the relationship between trait scores and situationally specific behavior. A situation may be conceptually related to a trait, but there may be little or no variability in the behavior exhibited by individuals in the situation. In such a case, knowledge of a person's trait score would be useless as a predictive variable. Alternatively, we might say in such a case that the situation is not diagnostic with respect to an individual's personality characteristics. This suggests that a necessary property of any situation that is related to a trait is that different individuals must exhibit variability of behavior in the situation.

The selection of situations that are relevant to a trait may involve some degree of empirical analysis and should not be done on the basis of intuition or common opinion. Recall our discussion of Jackson and Paunonen's (1985) reanalysis of the Mischel and Peake (1982) study in which they were able to show that the situations selected to represent conscientiousness were factorially complex. The set of situations alleged to be conceptually related to a trait must be empirically investigated in order to cull from the set those situations where the intuitions of the investigator about the relevance of the situation to the trait are incorrect.

There are several investigations extant in the literature that provide general information about the situations that are likely to be relevant to a trait; Buss and Craik (1980) asked subjects to rate a series of acts with respect to how prototypically they were, that is, how indicative or characteristic they were of the trait of dominance. For example, a prototypical dominance act would be monopolizing conversations. A low-prototypical act, not highly indicative or characteristic of a dominant individual, would be the act of flattering someone. Prototypicality ratings provide one way of judging the relevance of a given behavioral action in some situation to a trait. In effect, they represent a consensus among a group of individuals who provide ratings about the loading or relevance of an act to the trait. Buss and Craik report that a trait measure of dominance had a correlation of .67 with the self-reported frequency of performing acts that were judged to be high in prototypicality for dominance. The corresponding correlation for acts judged to be low in prototypicality for the trait was .05. These data indicate that one cannot study the relationship between traits and behaviors without using some procedure to cull or evaluate the relevance of the behaviors to the trait that is being investigated. Factor analysis of behavioral measures to establish the "loadings" of behavioral items on the trait factor and prototypicality ratings may both be understood as procedures to investigate the relevance of items to the trait construct.

Monson, Hesley, and Chernik (1982) studied the relationship between extraversion and talkativeness in experimentally created social situations that differed in the variability of observed behaviors. They instructed subjects in one situation to behave in an extraverted way and in an introverted way in another situation. In a third situation subjects were given no special instructions to behave in either an introverted or an extraverted manner. They found that the correlations between extraversion scores and their behavioral measure were relatively low in the situations in which subjects were instructed to behave in an extraverted or introverted manner ($r = .10$ and $.38$, respectively). In the situation that was not artificially constrained, the correlation between extraversion and behavior was higher, $r = .58$. It was also the case that the variability of behavior was higher in the unconstrained situation. These data indicate that under conditions of maximal social pressure and constraint the variability of behavior may be reduced and the resulting correlations between traits and situations are likely to be low. Social psychologists attempt to create situations that will enable them to predict behavior and to create homogeneous responses among all individuals exposed to such situations. There is no doubt that with sufficient experimental ingenuity it is possible to succeed at this task. However, generalizations about the importance of trait variance derived from such experimental manipulations that are, in effect, designed to eliminate trait variance may have limited ecological validity. That is, they are not necessarily representative of the relevance of traits to behavior in situations that are not artificially constrained to limit response variability.

Diener and Larsen (1984) used a different procedure to study patterns of consistency of individual behavior across situations. They asked 42 subjects to describe their affective states and behavioral tendencies in response to signals generated by a beeper that they wore. They were signaled on two randomly chosen times each day for a 6-week period. This procedure, called experience sampling, has a number of interesting properties (see Hormuth, 1986). It permits one to obtain measures of the characteristic moods and thoughts of a person at randomly selected intervals. In addition, it is possible to relate these responses to the various situations in which individuals find themselves when signaled. The situations that are studied are not those arbitrarily selected by the psychologist but rather are situations that are selected by the individual. Thus, one major criticism of the S–R inventory approach (namely that personality may influence the situations one selects) is circumvented.

Diener and Larsen classified the situations in which individuals found themselves when they responded to signals as being ones in which the subjects were alone, with others (social), novel, or typical. These data permit one to study the cross-situational consistency of responses in various naturally occurring situations. Diener and Larsen find considerable evidence for consistent affective responding. The correlation over all situations for positive and negative affect scores are .79 and .81, respectively. These values, when corrected for reliability, become .95 and .93. These data suggest that the tendency to report experiences of positive and negative affects are a traitlike characteristic that is expressed quite consistently in the varied situations that individuals find themselves. These data should be contrasted with a self-reported tendency to desire the company of other people. This sociable tendency has a cross-situational consistency correlation of .34. Thus, individuals are not consistent in their desire to be alone or with other people.

The extent to which individuals are consistent in their trait dispositions in the Diener and Larsen data varies over situations. Correlations for reports about affective states within each of the classes of situations studied vary from .72 to .86 for the social, alone, and typical situations. However, affective states for individuals are less consistent in different novel situations. The correlations for novel situations are .61 for positive affect and .48 for negative affect. Although these correlations are quite high, they are lower than the consistency obtained within other classes of situations. A similar result was found for sociable behavioral tendencies. The correlation of scores for novel situations was .29 and the corresponding correlation for the other three classes of situations ranged from .49 to .71. These data indicate that one could predict an individual's tendency to be sociable or to experience positive and negative affect from a knowledge of his or her characteristic responses in similarly classified situations with greater accuracy for situations classified as social, alone, and typical than for situations described as novel.

Diener and Larsen (1984) also report the results of an analysis of person (trait) and situational variance for different types of situations. Table 4.4 presents these data. Note that Table 4.4 indicates that traitlike variance is more important for reports of negative affect than for positive affective scores. Thus individuals are consistent with respect to the level of negative affect they report, irrespective of the situation in which they find themselves. Also, the level of negative affect that individuals experience is apparently not greatly influenced by the classification of situations that college students (the subjects in this study) are likely to encounter in their everyday lives. Of course, there are situations that are likely to elicit great negative affects, but fortunately, they are not frequently encountered. By contrast, positive affects do appear to vary in a lawlike way among different classes of situations that people encounter.

The Diener and Larsen study provides a method for studying traitlike consistencies in different situations that represent a random sample of an individual's activities. The study provides very strong evidence for the importance of traitlike variance for reported positive and negative affective states. Even within this demonstration, however, the study also provides information about the limits of traitlike generalities, providing evidence of the kinds of situations in which individuals are likely to be somewhat inconsistent in their affective responses. It is among this latter class of situations that the study of person by situational

Table 4.4

Aggregated Cross-Situational Consistency Correlations for Different Responses[a]

Response	Situations		
	Social/Alone	Novel/Typical	Work/Recreational
Affect			
Positive	.58 (.72)[b]	.67 (.75)	.70 (.77)
Negative	.70 (.81)	.80 (.90)	.74 (.81)
Bodily feelings			
Aroused	.50 (.62)	.56 (.77)	.60 (.69)
Energetic	.24 (.33)	.43 (.69)	.34 (.47)
Feeling well	.57 (.68)	.60 (.70)	.77 (.90)
Behavior			
Physically active	.11 (.15)	.58 (.76)	.47 (.54)
Productive	.29 (.40)	.56 (.71)	.16 (.19)
Behavioral predispositions			
Sociable	.10 (.13)	.15 (.20)	.01 (.01)
Cheerful	.13 (.17)	.47 (.55)	.37 (.47)
Cognitive/judgmental			
World beautiful	.80 (.90)	.84 (.89)	.78 (.86)
Self-esteem	.41 (.54)	.62 (.69)	.58 (.74)
Satisfied with life	.92 (.94)	.96 (.99)	.97 (.98)

[a]Based on Diener and Larsen (1984). (Copyright 1984 by the American Psychological Association. Adapted by permission of the publisher and author.)

[b]Values in parentheses are corrected for unreliability.

interactional rules specifying the situations likely to elicit a particular affective response in a particular class of individuals is likely to be rewarding. It should also be recognized that the use of a signaling procedure does not easily lend itself to the use of methods of data collection other than self-report measures. Thus, strictly speaking, Diener and Larsen's data provide us with evidence of the consistency of individuals' reports about their affective experiences and behavioral tendencies.

Aries, Gold, and Weigel (1983) studied the situational settings that were likely to elicit behaviors that are related to individual differences in dominance. They obtained a measure of dominance derived from the California Personality Inventory. They then formed a number of groups and observed the actual interaction patterns of individuals and the extent to which they behaved in ways that were indicative of dominant behavioral tendencies. They found that their dominance scale was able to predict both single behavioral indices and an aggregated behavioral index as long as individuals were observed in single-sex groups. The average correlation between the single behavioral indices and dominance trait scores was .31. The correlation between an aggregated behavioral index of dominance and the trait scores was .67 for male subjects in all-male groups and .65 for female subjects in all-female groups. The comparable correlation was .02 for the relation between trait scores and dominance behavior in mixed-sex groups. These data provide information about the kinds of behavioral situations that relate to self-reported dominance. It is difficult to know why dominance traits do not predict dominance behavior in mixed-sex groups. Does the meaning of the behaviors change as the settings change? Do other traits determine dominance behaviors? Or, is the tendency to behave in a dominant way something that is learned in single-sex contexts? In any case, the study provides a clear example of the necessity of specifying the class of situations and behaviors that may be construed as relevant manifestations of a trait.

Personality and Situational Interdependence

I have discussed research that indicates that personality may influence the situations people choose to enter and that situations may be differentially related to a trait. However, neither of these kinds of studies addresses fully the interdependent relationship between traits and situations. We can argue that personality may shape and influence the impact of situations. In Chapter 2 I reviewed evidence suggesting that over extended periods of time personality traits influenced the impact of the environment on an individual and in effect structured the environment itself. Snyder and Ickes (1985) have also suggested that individuals change the social world they encounter and in effect create their own behavioral environment. They note that the writer John Updike suggests that different writers impose their world views and personalities on their ordinary social encounters. To be in the presence of John O'Hara, for example, is to be aware of a cruel complex of stoic pain and social irony.

Malloy and Kenny (1986) have developed a model and a technique that permits one to study the way in which individuals influence the social environment they confront. They analyze experimental situations in which groups of individuals engage in a series of interactions with other individuals. With these designs the influence of the person as an actor on other individuals can be assessed. Let us consider some of their examples. In an unpublished study that they discuss by De Paulo, Kenny, Hoover, Webb and Oliver female undergraduates were required to interact with three different partners on four occasions. Each actor was asked to estimate the impression she made on each of her partners after each interaction. An actor component of the model refers to the female undergraduate's description of the impression she made with each of her partners in similar ways. The partner component represents a measure of the extent to which different individuals interacting with the same female undergraduate assume that they made a similar impression on that person. This is a measure of the capacity of the person to elicit common responses from other individuals, that is, to influence the nature of the interaction. Finally, a relationship component refers to changes in the assumed impression that is made with each partner. The researchers' analysis indicates that most of the variance in this situation is derived from actor variance, which accounted for between 57 and 71% of the variance on different measures of impression. Partner variance is near zero for all measures. The relationship component accounts for between 25 and 40% of the variance and 25–50% of that variance is error. This analysis indicates that female undergraduates tend to believe that they make a consistent impression on all individuals. Individuals do not elicit consistent responses from their partners with respect to the impressions partners believe they have made on them. They also found that a self-reported measure of social anxiety correlated with the actor effect, with correlations for different measures varying from $-.39$ to $-.63$, indicating that socially anxious people believe that they have made negative impressions on the individuals with whom they have interacted. These data do not indicate that individuals elicit common responses from others in this type of situation. Rather, they suggest that people believe that they make a common impression on others and this belief is related to their scores on a trait measure.

In a second unpublished study (by McGillan) described by Malloy and Kenny, individuals were asked to interact with a member of the same sex and the opposite sex. The interactions were videotaped and rated for dominance. They found that 30% of the variance was actor variance, 7% was partner variance, and the remaining 63% of the variance was attributable to the relationship of each pair. An indeterminant portion of the relationship variance was error variance. The behavior ratings indicated that actor variance was more than four times as large as partner variance. These ratings suggest that persons tend to differ in the extent to which they are interpersonally dominant. On the other hand individuals do not consistently elicit dominance behaviors from different individuals.

McGillan correlated the actor and partner components with a self-report measure of masculinity. Masculinity scores correlated .52 with the actor component and $-.51$ with the partner component. Thus, individuals who describe themselves as masculine tend to be dominant in their social interactions and to elicit submissive behaviors from their various partners. The correlation of $-.51$ with the partner component of variance is interesting since that component is quite small.

Miller, Berg, and Archer (1983) had 40 women in a sorority indicate the extent to which they were willing to disclose high and low intimacy topics to each other. For both high- and low-intimacy items there were no partner effects. Thus there were no individuals who consistently elicited disclosure from their sorority sisters. Actor variance was 14 and 39% of the total variance for high and low intimacy categories, respectively. Of the remaining relationship variance, approximately 85% was estimated to be true variance. These data suggest that individuals have only a weak characteristic tendency to disclose intimate details of their lives to their friends and acquaintances. Nor do individuals differ at all in the extent to which they elicit intimate disclosures from others. Disclosure, particularly of highly intimate details, is a function of the particular dyadic relationships.

The social relations model provides a way of distinguishing between the extent to which individuals respond consistently to other individuals and the extent to which individuals consistently elicit the same responses from their interactants. The techniques involved are relatively new and have not been widely used. In the three studies reviewed here in no case is there evidence of partner variance. Thus, there is no evidence for the view that individuals are capable of eliciting common responses from the several people with whom they interact. However, this does not imply that individuals are not able to elicit common responses from others. That conclusion would be premature given the available data.

For two of the three studies there was evidence of consistent responses of individuals to their several partners and further evidence that these consistent responses were related to scores on personality inventories. In one case there was relatively little evidence of consistent trait (actor) variance.

Summary

We have examined several different kinds of research that in various ways was designed to provide a clearer understanding of the relationship between traits and situations. Considered collectively these studies may be viewed as suggesting emendations and corrections in a simplistic view of traits that implies that individuals are consistent in their behaviors in all situations. Clearly, certain traits are marginally more predictive than others. Traits may not be related to behaviors in a variety of situations that might intuitively seem to provide an appropriate setting for the manifestation of the trait. It is apparently necessary to empirically investigate the range of situational applicability of each trait. Moreover, the range may marginally differ among individuals who share a position on a common trait, thus requiring the specification of situationally restricted trait measures.

Although it is clear that there are many potential restrictions on an unmodified trait position, I am impressed with the extent to which a limited number of common traits predict behaviors in a variety of situations. Mischel's personality coefficient of .30 is clearly a fiction derived from badly designed research and measurement error. It is apparent that there are many situations in which traits do not relate to behavior. And, of course, situations powerfully determine and shape our actions. When we turn from situations to a focus on individual differences, however, we find that we can ascribe important differences in the characteristic behaviors of individuals in different situations to their differences on a limited number of common traits. And while increased predictability can be obtained by qualifying traits to include situational specificities that are particular to subsets of individuals, or by more precise specification of the situations that are related to a trait, it is not clear that these additional qualifications or emendations are substantially necessary. I would guess that if traits were carefully measured and if we obtained prototypical, empirically derived, multi-situational measures on behavioral indices, we would be content with the assertion that common traitlike variables are quite consistently related to a variety of behaviors, and that the improvements in predictability attained by introducing traits of limited situational generality might be marginal.

5

The Biological Basis
of Personality

Introduction

In this chapter we shall consider theories of the biological basis of traits. We have argued that traits are influenced by genotypes. Genotypes cannot directly influence social behavior, but they might plausibly influence the structure of an individual's nervous system. Therefore, the evidence of genotypic influences on traits leads to a consideration of biologically based theories of traits.

H. J. Eysenck, more than any other psychologist, has been at the forefront of the attempt to develop a biologically based theory of traits. He views personality psychology as providing a mediating link between the biological and the social sciences. He has attempted to develop theories that relate traits to genotypically influenced characteristics of the nervous system. Eysenck's theories attempt to relate nervous system characteristics to the response of individuals to social situations. Thus, the theories provide a link between biological and social aspects of behavior.

Eysenck's Biological Theory

Description

Eysenck's first biological theory, developed in 1957, was based on Pavlov's concepts of excitation and inhibition (Eysenck, 1957). Eysenck abandoned the theory 10 years later and replaced it with a theory of arousal based on a specific model of brain functioning (Eysenck, 1967). Eysenck's theory has generated a considerable body of empirical work in the last two decades. Although, as we shall see, the empirical work has not always provided clear cut support for his theory, Eysenck has not proposed fundamental modifications of the theory.

Eysenck assumes that individual differences in extraversion are related to differences in the functioning of the ascending reticular-activating system. Stimulation of this system is assumed to produce a widespread pattern of excitation or arousal of the cerebral cortex. Introverts are assumed to have a more active ascending reticular system than extraverts and are thus assumed to be chronically more aroused than extraverts. Introverts are not only assumed to be chronically more aroused than extraverts, they are also assumed, by virtue of the functioning of their reticular system, to be more responsive to stimulation. Thus, they are assumed to be both more aroused and more arousable.

The effects of arousal of the ascending reticular system on the actual level of cortical arousal are complex. Eysenck assumes that measurable indices of cortical arousal, such as the EEG, are potentially influenced by the operation of a Pavlovian mechanism called *transmarginal inhibition*. This mechanism is presumed to create inhibiting influences that decrease stimulation once an upper threshold or limit of stimulation has been reached. These inhibitory mechanisms are assumed to reduce the level of cortical arousal. Since introverts have a hyperarousable nervous system, they are more likely to reach the level of arousal required to initiate the operation of transmarginal inhibition at a lower level of stimulation than extraverts. Figure 5.1 illustrates Eysenck's assumptions about the effects of stimulation on cortical arousal in extraverts and introverts. The assumption of the existence of transmarginal inhibition implies that the chronically higher level of arousal of the ascending reticular system assumed to characterize introverts does not invariably result in a chronically higher level of cortical arousal. However, the theory does appear to unambiguously imply that under low levels of stimulation introverts will be more aroused than extraverts and, under intense levels of stimulation that elicit transmarginal inhibition, extraverts will be more cortically aroused than introverts.

Eysenck has also proposed a physiological theory of neuroticism. Individual differences in neuroticism are assumed to be related to differences in the functioning of what he calls the *visceral brain,* consisting of a linked set of brain structures including the hippocampus, amygdala, cingulum, septum, and hypothalamus. This brain system is assumed to control the emotions. Eysenck (1967) uses the term *activation* to describe the level of activity in the visceral-brain system. Neurotic individuals are assumed to have hyperarousable visceral-brain systems. That is, they are likely to respond to events that are capable of eliciting emotional reactions intensely and with greater activation of the visceral brain than individuals who are not neurotic. Activation of the visceral-brain system leads to activation of the sympathetic nervous system. Various psycho-

LOW LEVELS :- Introverts More aroused than Extraverts.
HIGH LEVELS :- Extroverts More Cortically Aroused than Introverts.

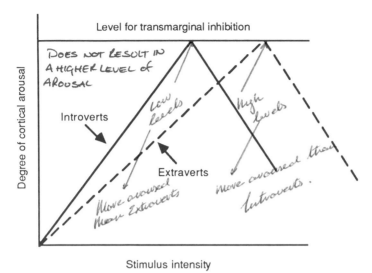

DOES NOT RESULT IN A HIGHER LEVEL OF AROUSAL

Low levels

High levels

More aroused than Extroverts

More aroused than Introverts.

Figure 5.1   The relationship between stimulus intensity and cortical arousal in introverts and extraverts in Eysenck's theory.

physiological measures that are assumed to reflect the activity of the visceral brain and the sympathetic nervous system, such as the galvanic skin response, may be used to index the level of activation of the visceral brain system. Thus, Eysenck's theory implies that there should be relationships between neuroticism and psychophysiological indices of emotional reactivity.

At the level of personality description, Eysenck's theory postulates independence of the two major dimensions of neuroticism and extraversion. At the physiological level the mechanisms are interactive. Eysenck assumes that the activation of the visceral-brain system will lead to the activation of the ascending reticular-arousal system. Individuals who are neurotic are assumed to be hyper-responsive to stress-inducing situations. Such situations are assumed to lead to a hyperaroused visceral brain system that, in turn, is likely to lead to a high level of arousal of the ascending reticular system. By contrast, arousal of the ascending reticular system is not assumed to lead to the activation of the visceral system.

It is apparent, even from this brief gloss, that Eysenck's model of cortical arousal is one of considerable complexity. The level of cortical arousal is influenced both by the assumed effects of the visceral-brain system on the ascending reticular system and by the potential operation of transmarginal inhibition.

In order to evaluate Eysenck's theory we shall consider research relating psychophysiological measures to individual differences in personality dimensions. We shall then consider Eysenck's attempt to relate his biologically based theory to various behavioral manifestations, including manifestations of the social behavior characteristic of individuals who differ in their scores on personality dimensions.

Extraversion and Arousal

There is a relatively large body of research relating individual differences in extraversion to various psychophysiological indices of arousal. In order to evaluate this literature, it is useful to distinguish among three levels of analysis. First, we can distinguish between indices of chronic arousal and indices of responsivity. Chronic arousal refers to the level of arousal exhibited by an individual over some period of time. Thus, a measure of the average skin conductance level or the average level of EEG alpha level over some period of time may be assumed to index the general arousal of an individual. Responsivity refers to measures that index change in arousal in response to some stimulus. For example, one can present a novel stimulus to a person and measure the change in his or her skin-conductance level. This is called a *skin-conductance response*. Similarly, one can measure the evoked response of the EEG to the presentation of a stimulus. Finally, it is possible to study changes in responsivity to stimuli that differ in properties, such as intensity or arousal potential.

Extraversion has been related to psychophysiological indices of chronic arousal, responsivity, and differential responsivity as a function of variations in the nature of the stimuli presented to an individual. Hypotheses relating psychophysiological measures to extraversion have been developed for each of these three general types of measures. Investigators have considered whether or not introverts are more chronically aroused than extraverts; whether or not introverts are more responsive to stimuli than extraverts; and, whether or not introverts are more physiologically responsive than extraverts to stimuli that are either low or high in arousal potential.

Eysenck asserts that introverts will be more chronically aroused than extraverts, that introverts will be more responsive to stimulation than extraverts, that introverts will be more aroused than extraverts under conditions in which they are presented with low-arousal-potential stimuli, and extraverts will be more aroused than introverts under conditions in which they are presented with high-arousal-potential stimuli. It should be apparent that these hypotheses are not compatible unless additional assumptions are made. Consider hypotheses about chronic arousal. Presumably, chronic arousal refers to an aggregated measure of arousal. Whether or not introverts will be higher in chronic levels of arousal than extraverts depends on the ratio of low-arousal-potential contexts to high-arousal-potential contexts they encounter. Only under conditions in which the aggregated measure of chronic arousal is taken in contexts in which low-arousal-potential situations predominate will introverts have higher arousal than extraverts. Much the same analysis holds true for measures of responsivity to stimuli. If the level of arousal prior to the presentation of the stimulus is high, or if the stimulus has high arousal potential, introverts will not be more responsive than extraverts to stimuli. Once one postulates the existence of transmarginal inhibition as an explanatory concept, one can no longer derive hypotheses about chronic levels of arousal or about the level of responsivity of introverts and extraverts to stimuli without making additional assumptions relevant to the possible activation of transmarginal inhibition. Thus, although Eysenck has continued to assume that introverts and extraverts differ in chronic arousal and chronic responsivity to stimuli, these hypotheses are not derivable from his theory. The clearest hypothesis that is derivable from the theory relates the arousal potential of stimuli to the level of arousal of introverts and extraverts.

Studies relating psychophysiological indices to extraversion have been renewed a number of times (see Eysenck and Eysenck, 1985; Gale, 1973, 1983; O'Gorman, 1977; Stelmack, 1981). They have yielded inconsistent results. For example, Stelmack (1981) reviewed 11 studies relating EEG indices of cortical arousal to extraversion. He classifies these studies as follows: introverts exhibited higher cortical arousal than extraverts in five studies, extraverts were more aroused in two studies, and there were no significant differences in the remaining studies. Similar inconsistencies have been reported in the use of evoked-response measures to stimulation. Burgess (1973) and Rust (1975) failed to find a relationship between extraversion and the magnitude of the evoked response to stimulation.

There appears to be more support for the hypothesis of differential arousal as a function of the arousal potential of the stimuli to which an individual is exposed. Gale (1983), in his review of 33 studies relating extraversion to the EEG, indicates that it is important to consider the nature of the situation in which EEG indices of arousal are obtained. In some studies individuals are asked to lie quietly with their eyes closed. In other studies individuals are given complex and demanding tasks to perform. Gale suggests that extraverts find the situation in which they are asked to lie quietly with their eyes closed stressful. Thus, the situation is likely to be more arousing for them than for introverts. Studies in which individuals are presented with demanding problems may have high-arousal potential and may lead to transmarginal inhibition resulting in a decrease in the cortical arousal of introverts. This analysis suggests that introverts would be more likely to be more aroused than extraverts under conditions which have low to moderate arousal potential. Gale classified EEG studies relating extraversion to arousal into studies in which the situation was minimally, moderately, or highly arousing. Introverts were more cortically aroused than extraverts in each of the eight studies classified as moderately arousing.

The clearest evidence of an interactive relationship between extraversion and various arousal-inducing manipulations is contained in a series of studies performed by Smith and his colleagues. Smith (1983) has reviewed the literature relating extraversion to various indices of arousal based on the galvanic skin response. He indicates that there are considerable inconsistencies in the literature. It is by no means the case that introverts are invariably more aroused and responsive. However, there is clear evidence in a series of studies reported by Smith and his colleagues that introverts exhibit higher skin-conductance arousal than introverts in situations that are low in arousal potential.

Wigglesworth and Smith (1976) measured the initial skin-conductance response to 80 and 100 decibel (db) tones. Figure 5.2 presents their data. An examination of the data reported in Figure 5.2 indicates that introverts exhibit a greater level of arousal than extraverts only when the stimulus intensity is low. At high levels of stimulus intensity extraverts have higher skin-conductance responses than introverts.

Smith, Wilson and Davidson (1984) studies the effects of caffeine on skin responses in their experiment. They reasoned that caffeine would act as an arousing drug. Introverts given caffeine would be more likely to reach a level of stimulation that elicits transmarginal inhibition, and they would thus exhibit a decrease in skin-conductance responses. Figure 5.3 presents their data. Figure 5.3 indicates that introverts have larger skin-conductance responses under placebo conditions. Extraverts exhibit higher levels of responsiveness than introverts when they are given caffeine. The data exhibit a dose–response interaction effect. Extraverts exhibit increasing levels of skin-conductance responses as

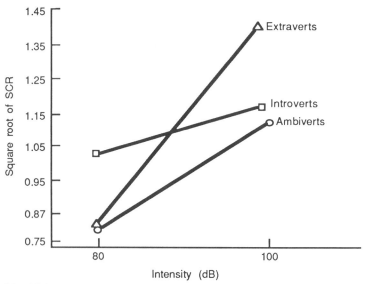

Figure 5.2   Clinical response amplitude as a function of extraversion and stimulus intensity. (Based on Wigglesworth and Smith, 1976.)

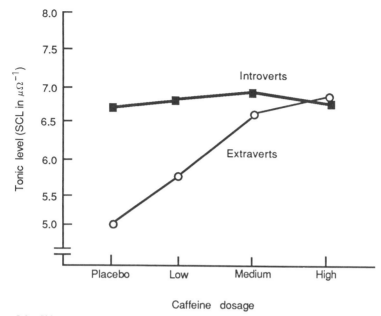

Figure 5.3   Skin-conductance responses as a function of extraversion and caffeine dosage. (Based on Smith, Wilson, and Davidson, 1984.)

caffeine doses increase; introverts do not exhibit increases in levels of skin-conductance responses as caffeine doses increase.

Gilbert and Hagen (1985) have reported interactions between extraversion and dose responses to another drug, nicotine. Eysenck (1973) has suggested that nicotine can increase arousal when arousal is low and decrease arousal when it is high. If introverts are more aroused than extraverts under conditions of low or moderate arousal, we should expect that under these conditions nicotine would decrease the arousal level of introverts more than extraverts. Gilbert and Hagen (1985) presented mild emotional stimuli to their subjects and recorded skin-conductance responses. They varied the does level of nicotine in cigarettes that their subjects were required to smoke. Figure 5.4 presents their data. Figure 5.4 indicates that introverts were more responsive than extraverts when provided with low-dose nicotine cigarettes, and extraverts were more responsive than introverts when given cigarettes with relatively high-nicotine content.

The studies we have reviewed appear to provide relatively clear-cut support for Eysenck's theory relating extraversion to arousal, provided one takes into account the complexities introduced by a consideration of the influence of trans-marginal inhibition. However, there are a number of additional empirical complexities that are not easily accommodated by the theory.

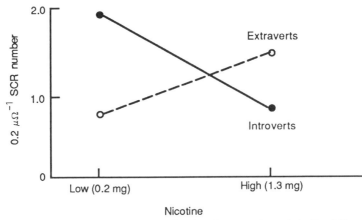

Figure 5.4   Skin-conductance responses as a function of extraversion and nicotine delivery. (Based on Gilbert and Hagen, 1985.)

If one assumes that transmarginal inhibition is likely to be present in any situation in which there is a high potential for arousal, then the failure to find evidence of a reduced response to stimulation among introverts in a situation with high-arousal potential must count as evidence against the theory. There are experimental situations where one would expect transmarginal inhibition to oc-cur where there is no apparent evidence of its presence. For example, Stelmack and Mandelzys (1975) measured pupil size in response to the presentation of neutral, affective, and taboo words that were presumed to elicit an emotional response (Figure 5.5). Pupil size is presumed to be a measure of arousal. Figure 5.5 indicates that introverts had larger pupil size than extraverts, suggesting that introverts were more aroused than extraverts. The presentation of taboo words produced larger pupil responsivity among introverts than among extraverts. These data do not unambiguously fit Eysenck's theory. If introverts exhibit high arousal under neutral conditions, we should expect that the presentation of arous-ing stimuli, such as taboo words, would lead to a hyperaroused state and the occurrence of transmarginal inhibition. Thus we would expect that introverts would be less responsive to the taboo words than extraverts, since they would be more prone to the effects of transmarginal inhibition. In effect, in Stelmack and Mandelzys' experiment, extraverts exhibit less responsivity to taboo words and might be said to be more subject to the operation of transmarginal inhibition. Of course, one could always argue that the level of stimulation appropriate for the operation of transmarginal inhibition had not been reached. This argument, however, leaves transmarginal inhibition as a *deus ex machina* hypothesis that is invoked at will when necessary to explain certain patterns of results, and is

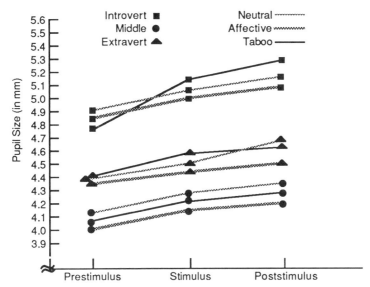

Figure 5.5   Mean pupil size of extraversion groups to neutral, affective, and taboo words. (Based on Stelmack and Mandelzys, 1975.)

otherwise ignored. It is obviously necessary to provide independent specifications of the conditions in which transmarginal inhibition will be present.

Relationships between extraversion and psychophysiological indices of arousal are complicated by the possibility that the relationships may be mediated by impulsivity rather than sociability. For example, in their study relating caffeine and extraversion to electrodermal responses, Smith, Rypma, and Wilson (1981) obtained separate measures of the impulsivity and the sociability components of extraversion. They found that the interactions of extraversion with caffeine were attributable to the influence of the impulsivity component, rather than the sociability component, of extraversion. This result is not anomalous. Frith (1977) studied pupil responsivity to light flashes in introverts and extraverts and found that his results were mediated by the impulsivity component of extraversion.

Other studies relating extraversion to a variety of experimental tasks that are thought to reflect the influence of arousal exist where the critical component of extraversion that mediates the relationship is impulsivity rather than sociability. For example, Eysenck and Levey (1967) reported that it was the impulsivity component of extraversion, rather than the sociability component, that was related to differences in classical eyelid conditioning. Similarly, Revelle et al. (1980) have reported data indicating a complex pattern of interactions between the impulsivity component of extraversion, caffeine ingestion, and time of day when testing occurred in determining an individual's score on a test of intellectual ability.

One of the few studies relating the sociability component of extraversion to arousal-inducing situations was reported by Eysenck and Eysenck (1967), who studied the salivary response to lemon juice. They found that introverts salivated more than extraverts to the presentation of lemon juice. When their subjects were required to swallow the lemon juice, they found that extraverts salivated more than introverts. They interpreted their results by appeal to the principle of trans-marginal inhibition. The greater intensity of stimulation caused by swallowing the lemon juice was assumed to produce transmarginal inhibitions leading to a reduction in level of arousal among introverts. Eysenck and Eysenck reported that it was the sociability component of extraversion, rather than the impulsivity component, that was responsible for these results.

These results create a number of difficulties for Eysenck's theory. The problem is compounded by the changing status of impulsivity within Eysenck's descriptive system. Narrow impulsivity, as opposed to venturesomeness, is now assumed to relate more substantially to psychoticism than extraversion. Although many investigators reporting research relevant to Eysenck's theory have not reported separate results for the impulsivity and sociability components of extraversion, there is at least suggestive evidence, among the subset of investigators who have separately analyzed their data for the two formerly linked components of extraversion, that it is the impulsivity component that is more likely to mediate relationships between extraversion and direct and indirect indices of arousal.

Whatever the vexed status of impulsivity as a mediator of the relationship between personality and direct and indirect indices of arousal, the possibility that sociability is not related to arousal poses a major difficulty for Eysenck's theory. Sociability is clearly the more central defining component of extraversion. In addition, as we shall see, Eysenck attempts to derive individual differences in sociability from his arousal theory of extraversion. If sociability does not relate to arousal, the social and biological components of Eysenck's theory become disconnected.

The relationship between extraversion and arousal is also complicated by the influence of neuroticism. Eysenck's theory implies that activation of the visceral-brain system is likely to lead to arousal of the reticular activating system. Thus, neuroticism should influence the relationship between arousal and extraversion. There are studies that have examined the relationship of neuroticism and extraversion to psychophysiological measures. Some of the obtained results do not fit neatly into Eysenck's theory. A good example of some of the complexities obtained in such studies can be seen in research on sedation thresholds. Eysenck (1967) assumes that introverts would be more difficult to sedate than extraverts. The hypothesis follows from the assumption that introverts are likely to be hyperaroused and thus would require a higher does of a depressant drug, such as sodium amytal, to attain a behaviorally or physiologically defined threshold of sedation. Such drugs are usually administered under conditions in which special efforts are made to relax the subjects. If these relaxation efforts are successful, an assumption that may not always be valid, then transmarginal inhibition should not be operative, and the hypothesis should be a correct deduction from Eysenck's theory. While there is some support for the hypothesis, a number of complexities occur when the influences of extraversion and neuroticism are jointly considered. Claridge, Donald, and Birchall (1981) have summarized the results of several studies of sedation thresholds. They divided their subjects into nine groups by dividing both extraversion and neuroticism scores into upper, middle, and lower thirds of their respective distributions of scores. Figure 5.6 presents their data. Note that these data indicate that there is a complicated interaction of extraversion and neuroticism. For individuals in the middle third of the neuroticism distribution, there is clear support for the hypothesis that introverts have higher sedation thresholds than extraverts. However, the hypothesis does not hold for individuals who are either low or high in neuroticism. Moreover, appeal to the interaction of the activation of the visceral brain or the influence of transmarginal inhibition will not explain this particular pattern of results. The fact that the relationship between extraversion and sedation threshold is, in some respects, similar for individuals who are either low or high in neuroticism precludes any direct interpretation of these results within the framework of Eysenck's theory.

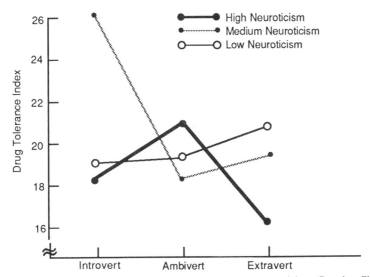

Figure 5.6   Drug tolerance index as a function of extraversion and neuroticism. (Based on Claridge, Donald and Birchall, 1981.)

There is an additional difficulty in interpreting the relationship between extra-version and arousal. There are data suggesting that introverts and extraverts have different circadian rhythms. Blake (1967) reported that introverts had higher body temperatures in the morning (an index of arousal) than extraverts, and extraverts had higher body temperatures than introverts in the evening (see also Eysenck and Folkard, 1980; Folkard, 1975; Larsen, 1985). Revelle et al. (1980) found complex interactions between time of day, impulsivity, caffeine ingestion, and performance. Most of the research relating extraversion to arousal occurs during the day rather than in the evening. It is not known whether or not the results indicating relationships between extraversion and arousal are perfectly general relationships or are limited with respect to the time of day in which the research is conducted.

We have considered the relationship between arousal and extraversion. Are there relationships between psychophysiological measures and other personality dimensions? Eysenck's theory does postulate a relationship between neuroticism and activation of the visceral-brain system. There have been a number of at-tempts to relate neuroticism to psychophysiological indices, and some rela-tionships have been reported, but for the most part the findings are inconsistent, and there are frequent nonsignificant findings. Stelmack (1981) has summarized studies relating neuroticism to psychophysiological indices, and he concludes that the results are not sufficiently consistent to permit any inferences about the physiological basis of neuroticism. Eysenck accepts Stelmack's summary of the data (see Eysenck and Eysenck, 1985, p. 234). Thus, theories about the physio-logical basis of neuroticism are without empirical foundation in the psycho-physiological literature.

Psychoticism and Psychophysiology

Eysenck has not proposed a physiological theory of psychoticism, and there is relatively little research relating psychoticism to psychophysiological measures. Claridge (1981; Claridge and Birchall, 1978) has suggested that psychoticism might be related to a dissociation or "uncoupling" of nervous system responses that leads to a breakdown of control systems that provide for the modulation and integration of different functions. He has provided some tentative evidence in support of this notion. In one of his studies he measured skin-conductance levels during an experimental session. He also obtained four EEG-evoked-potential measures of the tendency to augment or reduce the EEG response to different levels of stimulation. He obtained the correlation for each of his subjects between a measure of change in skin-conductance level over the experimental session and a measure of change in the tendency to augment or reduce the EEG response to stimulation. A positive correlation for a subject would indicate that increases in skin-conductance level are accompanied by an increased tendency to augment stimulation. He also obtained a measure of the mean skin-conductance level over the experimental session. He then obtained a correlation between mean conductance levels and the covariation or correlation between changes in skin-conductance level and changes in the tendency to augment or reduce stimulation. The correlation was $-.72$. This correlation indicates that subjects who had a low-average level of skin conductance tended to exhibit increased EEG augmentation of stimulation as skin-conductance levels increased. Subjects who had a high-average level of skin conductance tended to reduce EEG-evoked responses to stimulation as skin-conductance levels increased. These relationships suggest the existence of a kind of homeostatic regulatory system in which cortical arousal, as indexed by the evoked potential response, is modulated by changes in general arousal, as indexed by skin-conductance levels. When autonomic arousal is low, increases in arousal are accompanied by increased cortical responses. When arousal is high, increases in autonomic arousal are accompanied by decreases in cortical responses.

In an additional study of the relationship between changes in skin-conductance level and changes in the evoked response to stimulation as a function of average skin-conductance level, Claridge obtained scores on the Eysenck Personality Questionnaire. For his sample of 44 subjects who were low on psychoticism, he obtained the same inverse relationship between changes in skin-conductance level and changes in evoked responses as a function of average skin-conductance level that he had obtained earlier. For this group of subjects the correlation was $-.45$. For the group of subjects who were high on psychoticism the correlation was $-.09$, indicating, in Claridge's view, a breakdown in the physiological regulatory system. For a subset of eight subjects who scored high on psychoticism and low on extraversion the correlation between changes in the EEG and changes in skin-conductance level as a function of average skin-conductance level was $.87$. That is, for this small subset of subjects the physiological regulatory system was nonhomeostatic. For those subjects whose skin-conductance levels were low, increases in skin conductance were accompanied by decreases in augmentation, and for those subjects with high-average skin-conductance levels, increases in skin-conductance levels were accompanied by increases in cortical augmentation of stimuli.

Claridge's research is one of the few attempts to relate individual differences in psychoticism to psychophysiological measures. It is important also for its attempt to relate personality to the pattern of relationships among psychophysiological indices rather than to a single indicator. It is also the case that Claridge's results have not been the basis of an extended research program. They are, at this stage, more properly construed as suggestive, rather than definitive.

We can conclude that, apart from Claridge's research, there is little or no research that provides an understanding of the physiological basis of psychoticism.

Extraversion and Performance

Eysenck attempts to relate his physiological conception of personality dimensions to the behavior of individuals in diverse experimental and social settings. Our brief review of studies relating extraversion to psychophysiological measures implies that the performance of individuals differing in extraversion should vary on tasks in which performance varies as a function of cortical arousal. More particularly, we should expect that introverts would perform best in tasks in which arousal is related to performance, where the tasks have been structured to be low in arousal potential, and extraverts would perform best in tasks that are structured to be high in arousal potential.

Research using several different experimental paradigms provides support for the interactive relationship between extraversion and arousal potential. Shigehisa and Symons (1973) studied auditory thresholds among individuals differing in extraversion. In addition, they varied the intensity of a visual stimulus presented to an individual while they were determining auditory thresholds. Figure 5.7 presents their data. An examination of the data presented in Figure 5.7 indicates that there was little difference in auditory thresholds under conditions of weak visual stimulation. However, as visual intensity increased the performance of extraverts improved (i.e., they had lower auditory thresholds) and the performance of introverts declined.

Geen, McCown, and Broyles (1985) studied the performance of extraverts in

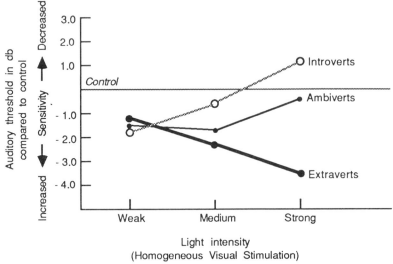

Figure 5.7   Auditory thresholds as a function of extraversion and intensity of visual stimulation. (Based on Shigehisa and Symons, 1973.)

Table 5.1

Values of d' as a Function of Extraversion
and Noise Intensity[a]

	Mean d'[b]	
	Low noise	High noise
Introvert	3.42[1]	1.30[2]
Extravert	1.71[2]	1.81[1,2]

[a]Based on Geen, McCown, and Broyles (1985).
[b]Cells having common superscripts are not significantly different.

a visual vigilance-detection task in which subjects were required to report the occurrence of a visual signal. Vigilance tasks require one to maintain attention over long periods of time in a situation that typically provides relatively low levels of stimulation. Geen and his colleagues stimulated their subjects with 65db or 85db noise. They used a signal-detectability analysis to derive estimates of their subjects' sensitivity to visual signals (d') (see Swets, 1964).

Table 5.1 presents the results of this analysis. An examination of these data indicates that the performance of introverts declined under conditions of high-noise stimulation, while introverts performed better than extraverts in low-noise conditions.

Eysenck and Levey (1967) studied classical eyeblink conditioning. This is a classical conditioning task in which the (unconditioned stimulus) UCS is a puff of air delivered to the eye. They found that introverts conditioned more rapidly than extraverts when the puff of air (UCS) was relatively weak in intensity, and extraverts conditioned more rapidly when the puff of air delivered to the eye was relatively strong. Eysenck and Levey also indicate that it was the impulsivity component of extraversion rather than the sociability component that was responsible for the interaction between extraversion and the intensity of the conditioned stimulus in determining the rate of conditioning.

In addition to data indicating that the performance of individuals in tasks varies as a function of the stimulation present in the task, there is evidence that extraverts prefer a higher level of stimulation while working on tasks. Geen (1984) permitted subjects to choose the optional loudness level of noise they preferred while performing a learning task. Extraverts preferred a higher level of
~~lation~~ than introverts. Not only do extraverts prefer a higher level of stim-
~~are~~ able to tolerate intense aversive stimuli better than intro-
(1976) asked subjects to endure electric shocks of
 e 5.8, which presents their data, indicates that extra-
gh-intensity shocks better than introverts. As the shock

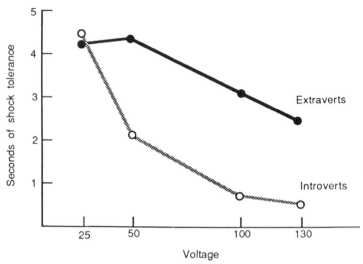

Figure 5.8   Duration of shock tolerance as a function of extraversion and voltage level. (Based on Bartol and Costello, 1976.)

intensity increased, the ability of extraverts to tolerate the shock increased relative to the ability of introverts to tolerate the shock (see Barnes, 1975, for a
review of related studies).

Eysenck's arousal theory may be used to derive the social behavior of individuals differing in extraversion. The critical assumption required for the derivation is that the presence of other people tends to increase arousal.

There is some evidence in favor of the view that the mere presence of others
can lead to increases in arousal. Zajonc (1965) has developed an analysis of the
behavioral effects of the presence of others. He argues that individuals experience an increased state of arousal in the presence of other individuals that
changes their behavior. Markus (1978) conducted a study supporting Zajonc's
position. In her experiment, female subjects were required to put on clothes in
preparation for an experiment in which all subjects were to be dressed alike. The
subjects performed the task alone; they performed it while being watched by
another person; or they performed it in a condition in which another person was
present but working on some experimental apparatus with his or her back to the
subject. Markus measured the time required to perform familiar acts of dressing
and the time required to perform unfamiliar acts of dressing. She assumed that
increases in arousal would increase the probability of occurrence of dominant
responses, thus leading to more rapid performance of familiar, overlearned act⸱
of dressing, and greater difficulty, due to interference from dominant but inc⸱
rect responses, in performing unfamiliar acts of dressing. Her results are pr⸱

ed in Table 5.2. Note that subjects in the condition representing mere presence (incidental audience) demonstrated the theoretically expected effects of an increase in arousal. The results of the Markus study demonstrate that the presence of other people, even in a condition where they are not observing or evaluating a person, can serve to increase arousal and to influence behavior. These data and other related findings support Eysenck's position that the presence of other human beings creates a high-arousal-potential situation. Introverts apparently prefer situations that are low in arousal potential. Thus introverts might very well learn to avoid situations in which they are with other people. One might assume that introverts would be particularly wary of meeting new people or of being placed in social situations in which they are forced to interact with many individuals. Thus, Eysenck's attempt to relate the social behavior of introverts and extraverts to their characteristic psychophysiological response to stimuli that differ in arousal potential has some empirical support.

Evaluation of Eysenck's Theory

Does Eysenck's arousal theory provide a satisfactory account of the physiological basis of individual differences? The theory provides an empirically supported account of only one of the three dimensions included in the descriptive account—extraversion. Psychophysiological accounts of neuroticism, as we have seen, have not been supported, and Eysenck has not presented a physiological theory of psychoticism. Thus, the evaluation of Eysenck's physiological theory reduces to an evaluation of the theory of extraversion.

There are several difficulties with Eysenck's physiological theory of extraversion. There are internal inconsistencies in the theory. The inconsistencies derive in part from the operation of transmarginal inhibition. The psychophysiological data and the data on the influence of stimulation on performance provide evidence for the hypothesis that introverts are more aroused than extraverts under

Table 5.2

Mean Time (in seconds) to Complete Well-Learned and Transfer Responses[a]

| Responses | Conditions[b,c] | | |
	Alone	Incidental audience	Audience
Well-learned	16.46[1]	13.49[1,2]	11.70[2]
Transfer	28.85[3]	32.73[4]	33.94[4]

[a]Based on Markus (1978).
[b]$N = 15$ observations per cell.
[c]Means with different superscripts are significantly different.

conditions of low-arousal potential, and extraverts are more aroused than intro-verts under conditions of high-arousal potential. The explanation of these results requires the assumption that transmarginal inhibition automatically reduces arousal level when arousal potential is high. The experimental situations in which arousal potential appears to be at its highest levels are those in which pain tolerance is assessed. If transmarginal inhibition is present in these situations, we would expect that introverts would exhibit greater tolerance for pain as the intensity of the pain stimulus increases. However, the Bartol and Costello study, as well as other studies reviewed by Barnes (1975), indicates that extraverts exhibit higher pain tolerance than introverts. These data are inconsistent with research indicating lower psychophysiological arousal among introverts under conditions of high-arousal potential. What appears to be consistent across all of these studies is that introverts avoid and dislike intensely stimulating situations and find them aversive. If introverts find highly stimulating situations aversive, it is possible that they have acquired or developed mechanisms that occasionally lead to the reduction of stimulation under conditions of high stimulation. This account involves a subtle reinterpretation of Eysenck's theory. That is, arousal theory is not used to derive the response of introverts and extraverts to intensely stimulating conditions. If differences in the aversiveness of situations that have high-arousal potential is the basic explanatory notion invoked to explain the behavior of introverts, then the psychophysiological differences may in part be explained by the aversiveness of different levels of stimulation. If the psycho-physiological differences between extraverts and introverts are seen as a conse-quence of their response to different levels of stimulation, rather than the cause of differential responsivity, then the explanatory program that begins in neu-rophysiology and ends in social behavior is questionable. That is, both social behavior and physiological responsivity might derive from different responsivity to different levels of stimulation. In order to maintain a reductionist explanatory program for social behavior that derives such behavior from explicit neu-rophysiological models, one would need a neurophysiological model that is rooted in affective differences in the response to stimulation.

We have examined several empirical inconsistencies and difficulties that arise in the attempt to relate Eysenck's theory to specific empirical results. There are, however, rather more fundamental criticisms of the theory that, in part, derive from its time of development. When Eysenck attempted to present a theory of the biological basis of individual differences he was, quite obviously, restricted to the physiology and experimental psychology available to him. His first theory, developed in the 1950s, which we have not considered here, was based on Pavlovian concepts and placed classical conditioning at the forefront of experi-mental concerns. In the 1940s and 1950s classical conditioning was of central concern to many experimental psychologists, and a theory attempting to relate individual differences to neurophysiological concepts deriving from the study of conditioning appeared to be congruent with many of the research theories and interests of contemporary psychologists.

Eysenck's revised theory, presented in 1967, was similarly regnant with the central neurophysiological and experimental concepts available at the time it was presented. However, neurophysiology and experimental psychology have changed in the last 20 years, and Eysenck's theory appears to be based on concepts that are somewhat dated and that in some instances have been abandoned, or at least dramatically modified, as a result of subsequent work. Thus they may be viewed as an imaginative attempt to integrate the study of personality with concepts from neurophysiology and experimental psychology that are no longer central to the latter disciplines. In what follows, I shall attempt to justify this rather sweeping conclusion.

Eysenck's theory derives from ideas about the concept of arousal that were current in the 1940s, 50s, and 60s (See Dufy, 1962; Lindsley, 1957; Moruzzi and Magoun 1949). These ideas include a distinction between the goal-directed properties of motivated action and the energy and force with which an action is undertaken. Arousal as a property of behavior referred to the nondirected component of the energy or force with which an action was undertaken. It was assumed that various motivational states had a common dimension of arousal. Thus, an organism could be characterized by its position on a unidimensional continuum of arousal that varied from states of deep sleep to hyperexcitement and manic behavior. There were assumed to be many different sources of arousal including stimulating drugs, noise, and the arousal contributed by various motivational and emotional states. Since different sources of arousal have a common organismic effect, they also would have a common behavioral effect. All sources of arousal had common neurophysiological effects identified with changes in the ascending reticular-activating system, which in trun produced common psychophysiological changes as well as common behavioral consequences.

The assumption of common behavioral consequences of the instantiation of a common state of arousal was supported by the development of theories relating arousal to performance in diverse experimental tasks. It is interesting to note that Eysenck still refers to these theoretical concepts in his recent comprehensive theoretical statement of his theory (Eysenck and Eysenck, 1985). The Yerkes–Dodson law is a very general formulation of the relationship between arousal and performance in diverse tasks (Yerkes and Dodson, 1908). The Yerkes–Dodson law asserts that the relationship between motivation (arousal) and performance is summarized by an inverted U function. That is, low levels of arousal and high levels of arousal are accompanied by poor performance, and intermediate levels of arousal lead to optimal levels of performance. The Yerkes–Dodson law is actually two laws. The second law asserts that the optimal level of arousal or motivation for performance in a task is inversely related to task complexity. Thus, for very simple tasks that involve the repetition of simple overlearned tendencies, the optimal level of arousal related to task performance is relatively high, and for complex tasks where successful performance requires the discovery of novel concepts, the optimal level of arousal is relatively low. The Yerkes–Dodson law may be derived from a theoretical principle developed by East-erbrook (1959). Easterbrook suggested on the basis of a review of diverse bodies of empirical research that arousal was inversely related to the *range of cue utilization*. Cue utilization refers to the number of different elements or compo-nents of the potential range of stimuli present that are noticed or apprehended by an individual. Under conditions of intense arousal there is a narrowing or funnel-ing of attention, and individuals are alleged to focus on a small number of cases. The first part of the Yerkes–Dodson law is derivable by assuming that for any task the attentional focus of an individual can become too narrow to support optimal performance at very high levels of arousal, and at very low levels of arousal cue utilization may become too diffuse and broad, such that individuals are not able to focus on task-relevant cues. The second part of the Yerkes–Dodson law is derivable from Easterbrook's principle by assuming that the number of cues that must be used to produce optimal performance is directly related to task complexity. Optimal performance in complex tasks may require an individual to sample relatively rare and unusual cues and to notice and re-spond to many different aspects of the environment. The demands on cue utiliza-tion may be much lower for simple tasks. As arousal increases cue utilization decreases, and individuals are assumed to be increasingly unlikely to perform well in complex tasks.

The set of ideas briefly sketched above provides a very general and coherent model relating diverse arousal manipulations to the instantiation of a central state, defined in neurophysiological terms, that relates to performance in an extraordinarily diverse set of situations. Thus, the identification of a fundamental dimension of personality with such a comprehensive and powerful model was a singular intellectual achievement that provided a powerful integration of person-ality and experimental psychology and neurophysiology. Unfortunately, the cen-tral ideas forming this integration are subject to empirical and theoretical criticisms.

On the neurophysiological level the concept of a unidimensional continuum of arousal is no longer accepted as a central unifying concept. There are several partially dissociated arousal systems in the brain (see Routtenberg, 1968). The notion that there are individual differences in the intensity of response to stimula-tion is complicated by the results of studies reported by Haier (1984) using positron-emission tomography—a device that permits one to observe activity in different areas of the brain following the ingestion of a radioactive substance. Haier indicates that there is a cortical gradient of augmentation of the response to a stimulus such that certain areas of the cortex exhibit cortical arousal to stimula-tion, and other areas exhibit cortical inhibition. Theoretical understanding of the chemistry of neurotransmitters suggests that there are chemically and anatomically independent arousal systems in the brain that respond to different neurotransmitters. Such partially independent systems do not fit a model of a unidimensional arousal system. Thus, new developments in measurement of brain activity and understanding of neurochemistry have led to the increased irrelevance of a concept of a unidimensional arousal system.

The concept of a unidimensional continuum of arousal has run into similar difficulties at the level of psychophysiology, in which attempts are made to study measurable changes in indices of arousal, such as changes in electrodermal responses, EEG, and heart rate. Different indices of arousal are only weakly correlated. Changes in indices of arousal follow quite different time courses. For example, body temperature as an index of arousal changes over a period of hours. Heart-rate changes occur over a period of seconds. Not only is it the case that different indices of arousal change over different periods of time, but it is also the case that the indices exhibit changing relationships to one another over time, in part as a function of the kinds of activities with which an individual is involved. Thus, there are changing patterns of relationships among various indices of arousal at different times.

We have argued that the concept of a unidimensional continuum of arousal should no longer be construed as an adequate representation of the underlying neurophysiological state of an organism as indexed by a variety of psychophysiological measures. It can also be argued that the effects of diverse sources of arousal can no longer be summarized by such simple, overreaching principles as the Yerkes–Dodson law. There are two principal difficulties in the application of the Yerkes–Dodson law to understanding the effects of arousal on performance in various complex tasks. First, different ways of manipulating arousal almost invariably are found to have subtly different effects on various measures of performance in complex tasks (Brody, 1983a; M. W. Eysenck, 1982). In addition, contemporary cognitive psychology has attempted to provide measures of several independent components of information processing that are involved in the performance of tasks. Thus, statements about the effect of arousal on the overall quality of performance fail to capture the nuances of the effects of several sources of arousal on task performance. A good example of the effort to precisely specify the effects of a source of arousal (noise, in this instance) is seen in the results of an experiment reported by Hamilton, Hockey, and Rejman (1977). They reported the results of a study that demonstrates differential influences of noise on different components of task performance. In this study subjects were asked to state which letter followed a particular letter in the alphabet. Subjects were asked to indicate the next letter or the second, third, or fourth letter following a particular letter. This aspect of their experiment measured the rate required to perform mental operations where the results of the operations need not be stored or retained in memory. In addition, they varied the task by presenting subjects with a single letter, two letters, three letters, or four letters. Where more than one letter was presented, the subject could not give a response until all of the responses were given simultaneously. Thus the subject was required to hold in memory, or store, the results of intermediate processing. Table 5.3 presents an outline of the experimental conditions, and Figure 5.9 indicates the results of the experiment, presenting the ratio of the time required to complete the task under conditions of quiet and noise. Note that Figure 5.9 indicates that individuals were able to process information more rapidly under noise, rather than quiet, conditions provided that the subject was not required to store information or retain in memory the results of previous information processing. However, as the retention components of the task became increasingly demanding, performance deteriorated under noise.

Another example of the attempt to link a presumed source of arousal (individual differences in extraversion, in this instance) is found in the results of a study reported by M. W. and M. C. Eysenck (1979). They presented subjects with a list of words followed by a probe word. Their subjects had to decide whether or not the probe word was physically identical with one of the words on the list they had been presented or whether the probe word belonged to the same semantic category as one of the categories of words presented in the list. Extraverts were able to reach a decision more rapidly than introverts under conditions of semantic matching. However, extraverts and introverts were equally rapid in their decisions when they were presented with a physical matching task in which they had to determine whether the probe word was identical to a previously appearing word on the list. These results, as well as other related studies, led M. W. Eysenck (1982) to suggest that introverts were inferior to extraverts in retrieving information from long-term memory store.

The Eysenck and Eysenck experiment and the results of the Hamilton, Hockey, and Rejman study illustrate the contemporary tendency to attempt to specify the cognitive processes that are affected by various attempts to manipulate arousal level. The effects of different sources of arousal are likely to be subtly different for different tasks, and the effects of any given source of arousal

Table 5.3

Task Conditions and Examples for the Hamilton, Hockey, and Rejman Study[a]

Storage instruction Store	Process instruction			
	Add 1		Add 4	
	Stimulus	Response	Stimulus	Response
0	F	G	F	J
3	FBRJ	GCSK	FBRJ	JFVN

[a]Based on Hamilton, Hockey, and Rejman (1977).

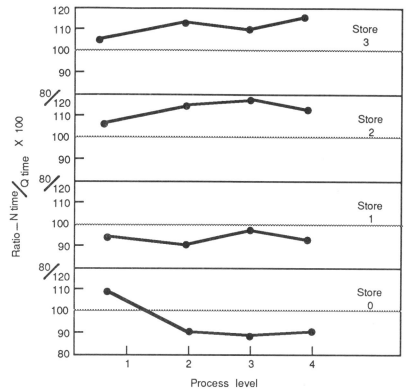

Figure 5.9   Performance in noise expressed as a function of time, taken under quiet conditions. (Based on Hamilton, Hockey, and Rejman, 1977.)

on a task cannot be adequately summarized by a statement of the effects of arousal on overall task performance. Therefore, a theory about individual differences in arousal no longer provides the basis for the development of predictions relating personality to performance in diverse tasks at a level that is of interest to the contemporary cognitive psychologist.

We have argued that arousal theory is no longer an adequate representation of individual differences in neurophysiological, psychophysiological, and cognitive experimental contexts. As a result, it can be argued that Eysenck's theory of the physiological basis of extraversion no longer has a firm foundation in contemporary biological and experimental psychology.

Despite its somewhat dated quality, the theory is important as an example of a systematic effort to develop a hypothetico-deductive model of personality that relates individual differences in personality to a biological theory that can be used to derive aspects of the social behavior of individuals, as well as the behavior of individuals in diverse experimental tasks. And while it can be argued that Eysenck's theory appears to be increasingly inadequate and out of touch with contemporary research developments, it is still the case that no other personality theorist has attempted to develop a biologically based theory with comparable rigor and scope. Fifteen years ago I noted that Eysenck's theory encountered several empirical and conceptual difficulties and that the theory, while satisfying a number of desiderata with respect to the form of an adequate personality theory, should not be considered as an empirically satisfactory account of the several phenomena presumably encompassed by its boundary conditions (Brody, 1972). I see no reason to change this judgement today, some 15 years later. In the past 15 years the empirical inadequacies of Eysenck's biological theory have become more manifest, but it is still the case that there are virtually no competing theories of comparable scope.[1]

Gray's Theory

Explication: The Behavioral Inhibition Theory

Gray has presented a neurophysiological theory of anxiety. Although his theory shares with Eysenck's theory the attempt to relate personality characteristics to a theory of brain functioning, the theory differs from Eysenck's both with respect to the specific neural mechanisms that are presumed to be related to certain dimensions of personality and with respect to the procedures used to develop the theory. Eysenck's theory is quite clearly based on studies of human personality. The dimensional analysis of personality he presented preceded the attempt to describe a biological source for variations in personality. Although Eysenck has discussed the congruence between his personality dimensions and individual differences in other species, including rats (see Eysenck and Eysenck, 1985; Sevilla, 1984), it is clearly the case that the overwhelming preponderance of research designed to test Eysenck's theories has used human subjects. By contrast, as we shall see, Gray's theory is based extensively on research with animal subjects—usually rats.

Gray's theory derives initially from an investigation of the effects of different drugs that are assumed to reduce states of high anxiety in human beings. Gray indicates that the class of such drugs includes the benzodiazepines (including drugs commercially named Librium and Valium), barbiturates (Sodium Amytal), and alcohol. Gray notes that the members of this class of drugs are chemically

---

[1]It is interesting to note that Eysenck's descriptive theories, particularly with respect to the existence of extraversion and neuroticism, as well as his theories of their genetic basis, have been amply supported by contemporary research.

differentiated and have somewhat different behavioral effects. However, since they all are clinically considered to reduce anxiety Gray assumes that they have a common behavioral and neurophysiological impact. Gray's theory may be construed as a detailed specification for the behavioral and neural effects of these drugs. The theory is based on an extensive and subtly detailed specification of the common effects of these drugs on the behavior of animals and the neurophysiological effects of this class of drugs. Gray attempts to show that stimulation of the rat brain and lesions of certain parts of the brain may mimic the effects of drugs on behavior. Because the data base for the theory rests extensively on animal studies, Gray is able to test his theory using direct brain interventions. The use of animals permits Gray to develop a model of brain functioning that is presumed to relate to human personality and that is more detailed and more closely allied to experimental results than is provided by the rather general model of brain funtioning presented by Eysenck. Of course, it should be noted that the specificity exists on the animal level and, as we shall see, Gray's theory has not been tested extensively with human subjects. However, Gray has extrapolated the theory to an analysis of such psychopathological conditions as phobias, obsessive–compulsive disorders, and neurotic depression. He views each of these types of pathology as being related to his conception of anxiety. Thus, Gray's theory deals with drug effects in both clinical and animal populations.

It is beyond the scope of this book to present Gray's theory in detail. His full presentation of the theory requires a 500-page book with detailed presentations of empirical results and neuroanatomical and neurochemical specification (see Gray, 1982). In what follows I shall present a sketch of the theory, indicating some of the empirical bases of the theory. and I shall discuss Gray's extrapolations of his theory to explain psychopathological states. This will be followed by a discussion of the empirical support for the theory in research dealing with human beings.

Gray relates anxiety to what he calls "the behavioral inhibition system." Gray assumes that the system is activated by four different types of inputs— signals of punishment, signals of nonreward, novel stimuli that are of importance to the organism, and a class of innate fear stimuli that, as a result of evolution, have an innate capacity to elicit fear even though the organism has had minimal or no previous encounters with the stimuli. Each of these types of stimuli is presumed to influence common neural structures. Since the neural structures influenced by these stimuli are identical, they are assumed to have common behavioral outputs, including behavioral inhibition, an increase in arousal, and increased attention to the environment. Anxiety is defined as the activation of the behavioral inhibition system. Anti-anxiety drugs are assumed to reduce the activity of the system.

In order to get a better understanding of the empirical basis of Gray's theory, we shall consider research on passive avoidance. In passive avoidance an organism can avoid receiving punishment by not performing a given action. Gray distinguishes this type of avoidance from an active-avoidance situation in which punishment can be avoided if an organism performs a given action. The behavioral-inhibition system is assumed to increase passive avoidance and to be unrelated to active avoidance. To use a somewhat more evocative language than is preferred by Gray, the behavioral-inhibition system alerts the organism to possible danger in the environment, inhibits action, and leads the organism to pay attention to the environment. The system is not involved, however, in the control of instrumental actions that might assist the organism to avoid punishment. That is, anxiety, or, for Gray's purpose, its theoretical equivalent—the behavioral-inhibition system—increases an organism's awareness or concern about potential dangers in the environment and is capable of inhibiting actions that might result in punishment, but is not involved in the selection of an effective response to potential punishment.

Passive avoidance can be demonstrated by observing the behavior of a rat in a Skinner box after it receives electric shock, which occurs whenever the bar in the box is depressed. In this type of experiment, prior to the use of shock, bar pressing was rewarded. The introduction of punishment (electric shock) for the previously rewarded response leads to a suppression of bar pressing. The response suppression associated with punishment is an example of passive-avoidance behavior. The class of anti-anxiety drugs reduces the suppression of bar pressing as well as other forms of passive-avoidance behavior.

Although anti-anxiety drugs influence passive-avoidance behavior, they do not influence active-avoidance behavior involving the response to punishment. The anti-anxiety drugs have little or no effects on the actual response to a painful or aversive stimulus. Thus, they do not influence the threshold for jumping or flinching in response to an electric shock in the rat. Anti-anxiety drugs do not influence the tendency of a rat to escape shock. For example, a rat can learn to make a particular response to terminate shock. Anti-anxiety drugs do not influence the rat's ability to acquire such responses, or to learn new avoidance responses. For example, a rat can be given shock at the start of a straight alley if it remains at the start of the alley for a designated period of time. If the rat runs to the end of the alley within a given time period, the animal can avoid the shock. Anti-anxiety drugs do not influence the rat's behavior in this situation. This suggests that such drugs do not influence the ability of the rat to anticipate punishment. Their effect appears specific to the inhibition of actions that have the potential to produce aversive states.

A clear example of the distinction between active and passive avoidance is provided by an experiment cited by Gray, which was performed by Waddington and Olley (1977). In their experiment, a rat received electric shock if it stepped down from an elevated platform onto an electrified grid. In one condition, the rat was removed from the apparatus after being shocked and later returned to the platform. In the second condition, the rat was shocked until it returned of its own accord to the platform. If anti-anxiety drugs affect passive avoidance, we would expect that they would reduce the avoidance behavior of the rats in the first condition. That is, where the rat has been removed from the apparatus after being shocked, the suppression of responses by behavioral inhibition is sufficient to avoid the shock. In the latter condition, the rat must acquire an escape response to avoid shock. Waddington and Olley found that chlordiazepoxide (a benzodiazepine) reduced the avoidance behavior of the rat in the passive-avoidance-conditioning situation and had no effect on the behavior of rats in the second situation.

Anti-anxiety drugs also influence the response of animals to situations in which a reward is omitted following a response in a situation in which the response had previously been rewarded, or in which a reward for the response was anticipated. Gray assumes that the effects of nonreward where it had been anticipated are functionally equivalent to punishment. The psychological state instantiated by the occurrence of such nonrewards is called *frustration*. Thus, Gray assumes that the behavioral-inhibition system inhibits responses that may lead to frustration.

Several demonstrations of the influence of nonreward can be obtained by studying the behavior of rats in a Skinner box. Extinction occurs when a previously reinforced or rewarded response, such as the delivery of a pellet of food for a hungry rat following bar pressing, is no longer reinforced. The rat's tendency to cease responding is, in part, a reflection of the effects of omitting a reward for a previously rewarded response. Gray suggests that the behavioral-inhibition system influences the response to nonrewarded behavior and inhibits responses that might lead to nonreward. Thus, anti-anxiety drugs that reduce the activity of the behavioral-inhibition system might be expected to reduce the rate of extinction, and Gray indicates that sodium amylobarbitone and the benzodiazepines have this effect.

There are also a number of other effects of anti-anxiety drugs on behaviors following the omission of reward in a Skinner box. For example, in a fixed-interval schedule of reinforcement the occurrence of a rewarded response is followed by a fixed interval during which responses are not rewarded. Thus, the occurrence of a reward becomes a signal for the occurrence of nonreward. Rats typically suppress responses following rewards on this schedule and then demonstrate an increase in responding as the specified interval elapses. Anti-anxiety drugs reduce the response-suppression effects at the beginning of the interval. In variable-interval schedules of reinforcement the period of time that elapses following reinforcement, when responses are nonrewarded, is variable and the effects of reward are no longer an adequate signal of the occurrence of nonreward. The anti-anxiety drugs do not influence behavior in these situations. Thus, the system is activated only when the organism anticipates the omission of reward following a response.

Although the behavioral inhibition system leads to a reduction of responses in situations in which responses are expected to lead to nonreward, it does not influence the occurrence of responses whose probability of occurrence is increased following frustrative nonreward. For example, in a double-runway experiment in which reward is invariably present in one runway and is only sporadically present in the second runway, running speed in the first runway is increased following the omission of reward in the second runway. The "frustration" of not receiving reward leads the animal to respond more rapidly. Anti-anxiety drugs do not influence behavior in this experimental situation. It is also possible to distinguish between the effects of anti-anxiety drugs on the responses that are decreased following the omission of reward and responses that are increased following the omission of reward. Soubrie, Thiebot, and Jobert (1978) studied the response of rats to the removal of water from their water bottle. Following the restoration of water in the water bottle, there was an increase in water intake. The increased water intake may be interpreted as a response that increased following the omission of a reward. Anti-anxiety drugs did not influence this response. Soubrie, Thiebot, Simon, & Boissier (1978) also studied the response of rats in this situation to the omission of water in the water bottle. The reduction of responses (extinction) following the omission of the water was influenced by the administration of benzodiazepines, meprobamate, and sodium amylobarbitone. These drugs increased resistance to extinction, or, put another way, they led to a reduction in the tendency to omit responding when responses were likely to produce nonreward.

This review of the behavioral effects of anti-anxiety drugs suggests that they counteract tendencies to reduce responses that are likely to lead to punishment or to nonreward of a previously rewarded response. They do not affect responses whose probability of occurrence is increased following nonreward or following punishment. It is the anticipation of negative affect, rather than the response to negative affects, that are affected by the behavioral inhibition system, and anti-anxiety drugs that are assumed to counteract the behavioral-inhibition system.

Gray asserts that the behavioral effects of anti-anxiety drugs are comparable in many different species. He explains this by assuming that the drugs affect common brain structures that are phylogenetically old and are, as a result, represented in the brains of all mammalian species. He identifies these structures as the septohippocampal system, and he assumes that this includes the hippocampal formation, the septal area, the "Papez circuit" neocortical inputs to the system from the entorhinal area and the prefrontal cortex, ascending noradrenergic and serotonergic inputs to the system, dopaminergic ascending inputs to the prefrontal cortex, ascending cholinergic input, noradrenergic innervation of the hypothalamus, and descending noradrenergic fibers of the locus coeruleus. Somewhat different functions are assigned to these different neuroanatomical structures, and they are assumed to control different components of the system. Evidence for their involvement in the functioning of the system derives from studies in which the effects of electrical stimulation of the brain or brain lesions are investigated.

Gray indicates that lesions of either the septal or hippocampal areas in the rat impair passive-avoidance conditioning. This result is congruent with Gray's analysis of the anatomical locus of the behavioral-inhibition system. Gray would expect that the destruction of the anatomical structures that are the basis for the system would reduce the functioning of the behavioral-inhibition system. Therefore, the effects of lesions to the septal and hippocampal areas would be similar to the effects of anti-anxiety drugs.

Septal and hippocampal lesions also affect the response of animals to the frustrative effects of nonreward. Gray indicates that both kinds of lesions increase resistance to extinction. In experiments with fixed-interval reinforcement, septal lesions reduce the postreinforcement-response suppression in a manner that appears quite analogous to the effects of the anti-anxiety drugs. Hippocampal lesions do not appear to have as clear cut an effect in this type of experimental situation. Gray indicates that lesions to either the hippocampus or septal area tend to mimic the effects of anti-anxiety drugs. However, the data are not invariably in perfect agreement, and there are occasional discrepancies reasonably attributable to the somewhat diffuse effects of lesioning parts of the brain.

Gray's detailed specifications of the neurophysiological basis of the behavioral-inhibition system led him to develop a more refined theory of the psychological functioning of the system. Gray assigns to the system the task of monitoring the environment in order to ascertain whether the events encountered by the organism are congruent with its expectations. If there is a mismatch between expected outcomes and what is actually encountered, or if the event one encounters is aversive, the system acts to interrupt or inhibit ongoing motor activities or actions.

Extensions to Personality

Gray's analysis of the behavioral-inhibition system extends to an explication of the behavior of neurotic and normal individuals. Gray assumes that individuals who are high in anxiety are prone to the development of anxiety neuroses, phobias, and obsessive–compulsive neuroses. These individuals are assumed by him to be those who score high on neuroticism and low on extraversion as Eysenck defines these dimensions. Thus, they are introverted neurotics.

Gray views phobias and obsessive–compulsive behaviors as symptoms of anxiety. Gray begins his analysis of phobias by noting that the stimuli that elicit phobias are not a random sample of dangerous events that are encountered by an individual. Also, phobias typically have their onset in early adult life. Gray argues that these features of phobias can be accommodated by a theory that assumes that there are species-specific innate fears that appear at a given ontogenetic stage of development. The onset of the fear is "prepared" by an evolutionary process and does not necessarily require a history of previous traumatic encounters with the phobic stimulus. While such a history might lead to a specific phobia, it is not a necessary condition for the development of phobias. Gray notes that, in many animal species, stimuli that arise in the course of social interaction are among the most important sources of innate fears. Among the most common, and most disabling, phobias in humans are agoraphobia and social phobia. Gray views these phobias as arising out of innate fears deriving from social interactions. Anxious individuals who are assumed to have overdeveloped behavioral-inhibition systems are prone to have that system activated by innate fear stimuli. The activation of the system leads to passive avoidance and the development of phobias. The behavioral inhibition and avoidance of actions that lead to the encounter of the phobic objects are expected outcomes of the activation of the behavioral-activation system.

Gray also has a theoretical explanation for obsessive–compulsive behaviors. He notes that cross-cultural investigations of obsessive–compulsive rituals suggest that there is a continuity of the kinds of obsessional thoughts and rituals that are a feature of this type of neurosis (Akhtar, Wig, Varma, Pershad, and Verma, 1975; Rachman, 1978). He notes that an obsessional preoccupation with dirt, disease, and contamination are the most common obsessions. Behavioral rituals (compulsions) are frequently concerned with actions designed to attend to or to remove potential sources of dirt and contamination from the environment. Gray's analysis of the behavioral-inhibition system provides a way of understanding the persistent features of obsessive–compulsive actions. A hyperreactive behavioral-inhibition system might lead someone to become excessively preoccupied with potential environmental threats. The concern with dirt might represent an evolutionary byproduct of an innate fear. Once activated, the system is assumed to heighten attentional awareness and to focus on potential threats. Obsessional thoughts involving fears of internal impulses are influenced by a system acting to scan motor programs and potential sources of action, in order to ascertain whether or not they are likely to lead to actions that will provide negative affect. Compulsions are explained by Gray as responses designed to check the environment for potential threats. They are viewed as the outcome of an excessive preoccupation with potential dangers that requires the individual to monitor the environment constantly. Gray's theory attempts to explain the virtually paradoxical preoccupation with thoughts and rituals that elicit anxiety, and that would appear to provide the individual engaged in these behaviors with relatively little relief from fears, by postulating a system that is preoccupied with potential threats in the environment and that is triggered by such threats. The system is not presumed to mediate or control effective action or to help the organism avoid threats. Hence it does not remove danger or provide an effective course of action. That is, it is not related to active-avoidance behavior. Rather, it leads to a preoccupation with potential threats.

Gray has also related his theory to individual differences in personality. Gray view individuals who are anxious as being both introverted and neurotic. Thus, the behavioral inhibition system that is the center of his theoretical investigations is located in a two-dimensional space defined by the traits of neuroticism and extraversion that is diagonal to the horizontal and vertical axes of the space. Gray's representation of the two-dimensional space is presented in Figure 5.10. Note that neurotic introverts and stable extraverts define opposite ends of the continuum of potential activation of the behavioral-inhibition system defined primarily in terms of the potential concern with negative affect. Largely for reasons of symmetry, Gray postulates the existence of a personality dimension that is independent, or orthogonal, to the anxiety dimension he calls impulsivity,

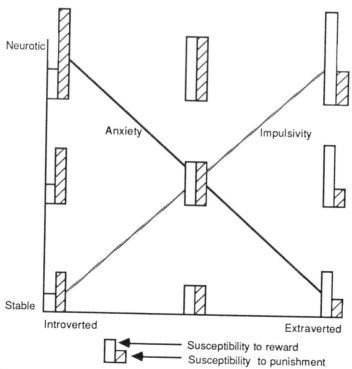

Figure 5.10   Gray's rotation of Eysenck's dimensions. (Based on Gray, 1982.)

which he assumes is defined by sensitivity to potential sources of positive affect. It is anchored at its extremes by extraverted neurotics and stable introverts.

Evaluation of Gray's Theory

Gray's theory has a number of virtues. It is based on an explicit well-developed contemporary conception of neural functioning with an extensive empirical foundation in contemporary neurochemistry and neuroanatomy. The theory deals with a wide-ranging set of phenomena including drug effects and psychopathological states. The theory presents an extensive psychological analysis of anxiety that provides a rationale for the occurrence of what, on the surface, appears to be a puzzling and nonfunctional state. Gray's theory is arguably the most detailed and sophisticated biological theory of a dimension of personality that is currently available.

Although Gray's theory has many obvious virtues, it is also limited in many ways. The detailed empirical basis for the theory is overwhelmingly present in animal research. In large measure, the theory remains untested at the human level other than in general observations of the effects of anti-anxiety drugs. I do not have the expertise to present a detailed critique of the neuroanatomical and neurochemical aspects of Gray's theory. The brief explication of the theory presented here has largely omitted this aspect of his theory. What I shall concentrate on in this critique is the relevance of his theory to understanding individual differences in personality at the human level. While I do not intend to discuss animal research, I should say parenthetically that I count it a virtue that a biological theory is able to encompass research on animals as well as humans.

It is difficult to reach a clear understanding of the adequacy of Gray's theory, with respect to understanding individual differences in personality, for the simple reason that the theory has not been systematically tested at this level.

Perhaps the most radical aspect of Gray's theory, with respect to understanding personality, is his suggestion of a new way of defining the relationship between neuroticism and extraversion. Gray's attempt to define the dimension of anxiety as being a combination of neuroticism and introversion may be criticized on empirical grounds. There are several self-report measures of anxiety. Correlational studies of the relationship between these measures and measures of neuroticism and extraversion generally indicate that they are more closely related to neuroticism than to extraversion. The correlations that are reported between anxiety measures and neuroticism are usually between .6 and .7, and the correlations between these measures and measures of extraversion are generally between $-.2$ and $-.3$ (see Eysenck and Eysenck, 1985). These data imply that anxiety is more closely related to neuroticism than to extraversion.

If anxiety is defined by the combination of neuroticism and extraversion, then one would expect that, in the vast array of studies that attempt to relate individual differences in personality to behavior in various experimental settings, most of the relationships would occur not between each of the dimensions and performance but only for the relevant combination of the dimensions and performance—in technical terms, statistical interactions between personality dimensions would be the typical finding, rather than main effects. In general, studies in which measures of both personality dimensions are used tend to report relationships between scores on one of the dimensions and performance more frequently than they report interactions between the dimensions and performance on the task. One could object that this argument, based as it is on a general impression of the literature, is not critical since it does not differentiate among the tasks studied to select those that are most germane to Gray's theory. Even here, however, such literature as does exist is not always precisely supportive of Gray's realignment of the personality dimensions of neuroticism and extraversion. For example, Gray briefly cites a study by McCord and Wakefield (1981) as being supportive of his theory. They studied individual differences in learning in classroom situations. They observed five different elementary school classrooms and obtained a measure of the extent to which teachers relied on positive rewards or punishments in their interactions with their pupils. McCord and Wakefield found that extraverts had higher scores on a test of arithmetic achievement in classrooms where teachers emphasized rewards rather than punishments. Introverts performed better in classrooms where teachers were more likely to rely on punishments. Gray would argue that these data fit his theoretical analysis of the fundamental distinction between introverts and extraverts. The former are more responsive to punishment, the latter are more responsive to rewards (see Figure 5.10.). However, this analysis is rather superficial. Even if we accept Gray's analysis of the basis for the distinction between introverts and extraverts, we still must assume that responsiveness to rewards and punishments will influence the rate at which an individual will learn. This latter expectation may appear to involve an almost trivial deduction from the theory. That is, one learns best and performs best in those situations in which one is more responsive to the kinds of rewards and punishments used to motivate learning. While this trivial deduction appears to be theoretically innocuous, it should be noted that Gray finds in his detailed explication of the behavioral-inhibition system in animals that it is not, in general, related to an organism's ability to learn about its environment. It may change attentional patterns or inhibit behavior, but it is by no means obvious that the system is related to the quality of performance on an arithmetic test. If introverts are more responsive to punishments than extraverts, one would expect that they would be more aware of potential punishments in the classroom and perhaps would be more likely to act in such a way that they would avoid those actions likely to lead to punishment (passive avoidance). It is by no means clear that they would learn more in a classroom in which punishment is frequently used. In fact, M. W. Eysenck (1982), in his extensive review of the relationship between anxiety and learning at the human level, asserts that the typical outcome of such studies is that there are relatively small or nonexistent effects of anxiety on the measure of performance. Typically, one must search for the effects of anxiety at a more subtle or componential level of analysis. That is, anxiety is likely to relate to the way in which an individual learns and to certain more refined measures of performance on components of learning rather than to affect the overall quality of performance (see Brody, 1983a, Chapter 2).

Even if we accept the assumption that individual differences in what is learned in a classroom provide an adequate outcome measure to assess Gray's theory of personality, the results of the McCord and Wakefield study pose a more fundamental challenge to Gray's theory. His theory implies that the differences between introverts and extraverts with respect to their responsiveness to positive and negative affects are likely to be present in their most dramatic form for individuals who are highly neurotic. Thus, his theory would apparently imply that there would be an interaction between extraversion and neuroticism in determining learning in classrooms differing in reward. McCord and Wakefield did study the relationship between neuroticism and psychoticism and performance in their study, and they did not obtain evidence of the kind of interactions one would expect based on Gray's theory. In fact, they reported an interaction between extraversion and psychoticism. Superior learning occurred for introverts in classrooms where teachers relied on punishment, and superior learning for extraverts occurred when teachers relied on rewards only for those introverts and extraverts whose score on psychoticism was low or average. The interaction between extraversion and psychoticism is not readily explicated using Gray's theory, and thus the results of the McCord and Wakefield study provide, at best, tangential support for the theory.

There is some research that is directly relevant to Gray's suggested realignment of the two-dimensional space defined by neuroticism and extraversion. Tellegen (undated) has studied the relationship between mood states and self-report personality questionnaires. Factor analyses of mood states for individual subjects indicates the presence of two independent dimensions of moods, defined by a tendency to experience positive mood states and a tendency to experience negative mood states. Tellegen has reported the correlations between measures of moods and scores on the Differential Personality Questionnaire. Factor analyses of the Differential Personality Questionnaire and scores on the Eysenck Personality Questionnaire indicate that the higher-order factors derived from the former test are highly related to the three dimensions measured in the latter test. In his factor analysis of personality questionnaires, Tellegen was able to define a factor on which the Eysenck measure of extraversion loaded .79 and .76 in females and males, respectively. The Differential Personality Questionnaire measure of the trait he calls "positive affectivity" had loadings on this factor of .67 and .80 in females and males, respectively. A second factor obtained in this study was related to the Eysenck measure of neuroticism. The loadings of the neuroticism score from the Eysenck test on this factor were .68 and .70 in female and male subjects, respectively. The loadings on the trait measure Tellegen calls "negative affectivity," derived from the Differential Personality Questionnaire on this latter factor, were .81 and .78 in female and male subjects, respectively. These data clearly demonstrate that the traits Tellegen calls negative and positive affectivity are substantially related to, if not identical with, the traits of neuroticism and extraversion as measured by the Eysenck questionnaires. As indicated by the choice of names for these dimensions, positive and negative affectivity are related to the tendency to experience positive and negative affect. Table 5.4 presents Tellegen's data relating positive and negative affect mood scores to positive and negative affectivity trait scores, as defined by the Differential Personality Questionnaire. Table 5.4 clearly indicates that the reported tendency to experience either positive or negative moods is substantially related to responses to the personality questionnaire.

The Tellegen study provides us with information that is directly relevant to Gray's theory. The tendency to experience either positive or negative mood states is substantially related to personality dimensions that are themselves virtually identical with extraversion and neuroticism. However, the relationships are not those that are postulated by Gray's theory. The tendency to experience negative affect is related to neuroticism, and the tendency to experience positive affect is related to extraversion. Tellegen also considers the trait of anxiety to be a component of negative affectivity. These data suggest that it is inappropriate to redefine the two-dimensional space formed by this independent relationship between extraversion and neuroticism. On this analysis extraversion is defined *interalia* by a susceptibility to experience positive moods, and neuroticism is defined by a susceptibility to experience negative moods.

It is possible to argue that Tellegen's data does not provide strong evidence

Table 5.4

Correlations between Differential Personality Questionnaire Scores and Mood Factors Scores[a]

Mood	Sex[b]	Positive affectivity	Negative affectivity
Positive affect	Females	.50	−.09
	Males	.42	−.24
Negative affect	Females	−.20	.53
	Males	−.17	.50

[a]Based on Tellegen (undated).
[b]N for females = 222, N for males = 168.

against Gray's theory. Gray's theory deals with individual differences in response to situations that have the capacity to activate the behavioral-inhibition system. The theory cannot derive assertions of the frequency of arousal of the system independent of knowledge of the characteristic situations to which an individual has been exposed. Measures of mood aggregated over many days provide an index that reflects both the influence of the characteristic response of individuals to various situations and the characteristic situations that are encountered.

This analysis is compatible with a *post hoc* attempt to reconcile Gray's analysis of affect and personality with the data obtained by Tellegen. Assume that Gray is correct. Individuals who are introverted are more likely to experience negative affect in comparable situations than extraverts. Individuals who are stable introverts may be successful in selecting environments that are unlikely to confront them with situations that are likely to arouse the behavioral inhibition system, or that are likely to lead to the experience of negative affect. Neurotic introverts, by contrast, may be less successful in controlling their environments and thus may be susceptible to frequent experiences of negative affects. Thus, Gray's assumption that introverts have a higher potential for the experience of negative affect than extraverts may be correct. The existing data based on responses to the same situations does provide some support for Gray's theory. Thus, Tellegen's failure to find a relationship between extraversion and the reported frequency of negative moods may reflect the successful ability of stable introverts to avoid those situations that are likely to elicit negative affect.

There are other data that also pose difficulties for the identification of Gray's anxiety dimension with introversion. Gray notes that anti-anxiety drugs do not influence the behavioral response of animals to actual aversive stimulation. As we have seen, he notes that the threshold response for flinching in response to electric stimulation is not affected by anti-anxiety drugs. Similarly, he notes that septal and hippocampal lesions do not, in general, influence flinching thresholds or the actual response to aversive stimuli. The closest analogue to this type of experiment for human subjects is the response to painful stimulation. Recall that introverts have lower pain tolerance than extraverts and appear to find painful stimuli more aversive than extraverts. These results suggest that the behavior of introverts in response to painful stimuli is not related to the influence of the behavioral-inhibition system.

In addition to evidence that the behavioral effects of extraversion do not invariably fit Gray's conception of the behavioral-inhibition system, there are other data relating extraversion to behavior that Gray cites as being supportive of his theory that, on critical analysis, really do not fit his theory. Gray indicates that a crucial test for his revision of Eysenck's theory is obtained in studies of conditioning. He asserts that Eysenck's theory implies that introverts will condition more rapidly than extraverts. Gray asserts that his theory implies that introverts will condition better than extraverts in experimental situations in which aversive conditioning is used and extraverts will condition better than introverts in conditioning situations in which appetitive stimuli are used. Eysenck accepts Gray's theoretical analysis on this point (Eysenck and Eysenck, 1985). I shall argue that both Eysenck and Gray are incorrect in their analysis of the role of individual differences in conditioning in aversive and appetitive conditions.

Let us begin with the response to aversive conditioning. Gray asserts that his theory and Eysenck's both predict superior conditioning for introverts for this class of experiments. Gray's analysis is contradicted by his detailed discussion of the effects of anti-anxiety drugs on conditioning. Gray indicates that there is very little evidence that anti-anxiety drugs impair conditioning in aversive situations. In addition, the experimental situation that has been most often used to investigate the effects of individual differences in conditioning is classical eyeblink conditioning, in which a CS is followed by a UCS that is a puff of air to the eye. The puff of air is an unpleasant and aversive stimulus. The eyeblink response as a conditioned response may be assumed to be an avoidance response since it serves to reduce the aversive quality of the UCS. Gray asserts repeatedly that the behavioral-inhibition system does not influence active avoidance learning or behavior. If the CR in eyeblink conditioning is construed as a learned response that reduces the aversiveness of the UCS, then Gray's theory implies that individual differences in extraversion, in so far as they are attributable to variations in the activity of the behavioral-inhibition system, should not be related to the rate of conditioning in this situation.

Gray also suggests that extraversion should be positively related to conditioning in situations in which positive or appetitive reward is used. This deduction follows from the general assumption that extraversion is related to individual differences in response to reward and punishment. Again, this derivation is only weakly related to Gray's formal analysis of the behavioral inhibition system. Gray indicates that the anti-anxiety drugs do not influence the rate at which organisms acquire rewarded responses. Curiously, Gray cites Gupta and Nagpal's (1978) finding that extraverts exhibit more rapid operant conditioning than introverts in a verbal-conditioning experiment in which subjects were rewarded for choosing a particular verbal response. This experimental situation appears, at least on the surface, to be a direct analogue of the experimental situations involving operant conditioning in which rats are presented with rewards (a pellet of food) each time they bar press. If the behavioral-inhibition system is not involved in the acquisition of rewarded responses in the rat, it ought not to be involved in the acquisition of operantly conditioned verbal responses in introverts and extraverts (see Gupta, 1976; Gupta and Nagpal, 1978; Nagpal and Gupta, 1979).

The revision of Gray's theory suggested here is compatible with the results of studies indicating that extraverts condition better than introverts in appetitive conditioning situations. That is, if individual differences in extraversion are defined as arising, in part, from positive affectivity, we should expect that extraverts are likely to be more responsive to rewarding situations and are likely to be more influenced by them. The available data on conditioning studies, while rather sparse, are generally supportive of this assertion. For example, Kantorowitz (1978) reported a correlation of .88 between extraversion and the rate of conditioning of the conditioned penile response to slides of female nudes in male subjects.[2]

Although the results of the conditioning studies appear to be only tangentially relevant to Gray's theory, there are studies that are explicitly designed to test concepts derived from Gray's theory. Newman and his associates have recently reported a series of studies relating individual differences in extraversion to experimental situations designed to reflect the effects of the behavioral-inhibition system (Gorenstein and Newman, 1980; Newman, Widom, and Nathan, 1985; Pearce-McCall and Newman, 1986).

Newman, Widom, and Nathan (1985) studies an experimental situation that was designed to obtain a measure of passive-avoidance conditioning. They studied the responses of their subjects to a learning situation in which the subjects were presented one at a time with one of eight 2-digit numbers. Half of the numbers were arbitrarily designated as correct (S+) and half were incorrect (S−). Subjects were given the option of responding or not responding. If they chose not to respond, they neither won nor lost money. If they responded, they won 5¢ if they were correct, and they lost 5¢ if they were wrong.

In a second version of this task (task 2) rewards were omitted. Subjects lost money if they did not respond when the stimulus was an S+, and they lost money when they responded incorrectly to a stimulus that was an S−. For task 2, subjects were provided with an initial sum of money. Subjects assigned to both tasks ended the experiment with an equal amount of money.

In this type of experimental task, two errors are possible. An error of omission consists of the failure to respond in the presence of S+. Passive-avoidance errors consist of the failure to inhibit a response to S−.

Newman, Widom, and Nathan assumed that passive-avoidance errors in task 1 would be related to the behavioral-inhibition system. In this task subjects have a choice of responding or not responding. Responding does, on occasion, lead to reward, and also to punishment (the loss of money). The failure to respond always removes the potential for punishment. In the second task, both choices, responding and not responding, could lead to punishment. Thus the subject is not given a passive-avoidance response guaranteed to omit punishment. Newman, Widom, and Nathan assumed that passive-avoidance errors would reflect the operation of the behavioral-inhibition system in the first task. They predicted that

---

[2]The value of the correlation obtained should be accepted cautiously in view of the small sample used in the Kantorowitz (1978) study ($N = 8$).

extraverts would have a weaker behavioral-inhibition system than introverts, and thus they assumed that extraverts would be more likely to make passive-avoidance errors in the first task than introverts.

Their results were exactly in line with their predictions. There were no differences between introverts and extraverts in either kind of error in the second task, and there were no differences between these two types of subjects in the numbers of errors of omission in the first task (i.e., the failure to respond in the presence of S+). Extraverts were more likely than introverts to make passive-avoidance errors in the first task. Apparently, when a response might lead to a reward, or to punishment, extraverts were more likely to respond even where they might not have been certain about the outcome of their response. Introverts were more likely to exhibit passive-avoidance response—that is a failure to respond if that response might lead to punishment. These results are precisely congruent with theoretical assumptions derivable from Gray's analysis of the behavioral-inhibition system. Although the Newman, Widom, and Nathan study does provide empirical support for Gray's theory, the study does leave two additional issues unresolved. First, Newman, Widom, and Nathan did not obtain measures of neuroticism in this study, and thus the joint contribution of the two personality dimensions that Gray assumes are involved in the behavioral-inhibition system cannot be assessed. Second, the measure of passive-avoidance behavior obtained in this study reflects the joint effects of both rewards and punishments. Perhaps, as has been argued previously, extraversion is related to differential responsiveness to positive affect (not to negative affect). If extraverts are more attuned to the possibility of obtaining a reward, they might be willing to respond in any situation in which rewards are potentially present. That is, the passive-avoidance behavior of introverts might reflect either a relative fear of potential punishment or an indifference to potential reward, or both. Extraverts, by contrast, might be motivated by reward, they might be indifferent to punishment, or both. Thus, it is not possible to distinguish the relative importance of rewards and punishments in the Newman, Widom, and Nathan study.

Nichols and Newman (1986) reported the results of another study designed to investigate the behavioral-inhibition system. In this study the subjects were assigned a pattern-matching task in which they were presented with two patterns and had to decide whether the patterns were the same or not. The subjects performed this task under either a reward or a punishment condition. In the reward-only condition the subjects won 10¢ whenever they were correct, and did not lose money when they were wrong. In the punishment-only condition subjects were given $4 and lost 10¢ whenever they were incorrect. They did not receive money for being correct. Both groups of subjects ended the experiment with the same amount of money.

Nichols and Newman measured the speed of response as an index of the effects of the behavioral-inhibition system. Presumably, the activation of the behavioral-inhibition system should lead to a decrease in response speed in situations in which the response might be punished. Nichols and Newman obtained their subjects' scores on both neuroticism and extraversion and formed four groups of subjects by combining scores on both personality dimensions. If Gray's theory is correct, one would expect that neurotic introverts would behave differently from stable extraverts. Neurotic introverts would tend to exhibit relatively slow responses in a situation in which incorrect responding could lead to punishment (i.e., loss of money). Table 5.5 presents the response speeds for the four groups of subjects defined by personality measures in reward-only or punishment-only situations. An examination of Table 5.5 indicates that the pattern of results is not precisely congruent with hypotheses derivable from Gray's theory. Both neurotic extraverts and stable extraverts respond more rapidly in reward-only than in punishment-only conditions. These results suggest that extraverts are more attuned to reward conditions and are either more aroused or more eager to respond when a response has the potential to lead to a reward. These results buttress the theoretical suggestion developed here that the extraversion dimension is related to a sensitivity to potential positive affects. By extension and extrapolation it is possible to interpret the results of the Newman, Widom, and Nathan experiment in the same way—namely, in terms of variations in the response to potential positive affects.

We have not considered the role of neuroticism in the Nichols and Newman study. There is very little indication that neuroticism is related to differential responsiveness to reward and punishment conditions. There is another way to look at their data that suggests a role for neuroticism. Consider each of the experimental conditions separately. Under reward-only conditions the largest differences in response times are exhibited by stable introverts and neurotic extraverts. Note that these groups define Gray's impulsivity dimension that is

Table 5.5

Mean Response Speeds (in msec) for Four Types of Individuals
in Reward-Only and Punishment-Only Conditions[a]

Personality type	Condition	
	Reward only	Punishment only
Stable		
introvert	1953.0	1808.3
extravert	1554.0	1908.8
Neurotic		
introvert	1689.3	1687.6
extravert	1424.7	1813.4

[a]Based on Nichols and Newman (1986). (Copyright 1986 by the American Psychological Association. Adapted by permission of the publisher and author.)

assumed to be responsive to rewards. Note that the assumed high responsivity to rewards results in more rapid responding for the neurotic extravert. Consider the punishment condition. The largest differences in response times are obtained for stable extraverts and neurotic introverts. These groups define the end points of Gray's anxiety dimension. The assumed sensitivity to negative affect leads to more rapid response times for the neurotic introvert under punishment conditions. On this analysis, the Nichols and Newman data are remarkably congruent with Gray's theory. However, there is one difficulty with this way of looking at the data. The behavioral-inhibition system is assumed to stop action and to lead to a more intense investigation of the environment. Therefore, it is difficult to argue that the system could be responsible for a more rapid execution of responses. One could argue, as Nichols and Newman do, that the arousal created by the activation of the system tends to reduce response times. However, it should be noted that, while Gray assumes that arousal does accompany the activation of the behavioral-inhibition system, he does not imply that the diffuse arousal serves to activate motor responses. Rather, the system, as is implied by its name, is assumed to lead to a cessation of response and an increased attention to environmental events. For this reason, I am inclined to interpret the results of the Nichols and Newman study as being supportive of the assertion that extraverts are more responsive than introverts to situations in which reward is present.

Pearce-McCall and Newman (1986) have studied the response of introverts and extraverts to a situation in which they were presented with a task that they could not successfully perform. Following a period of unsuccessful experiences with a task, they were presented with a potential to win or lose money by their performance on the task. In a reward-only condition subjects received 25¢ each time they succeeded. In a punishment-only condition subjects lost 25¢ from an initial sum of $5 each time they failed the task. Both groups ended the task with the same amount of money. Pearce-McCall and Newman obtained different measures of the optimism exhibited by their subjects. These included measures of the change in their expectancy for success at the task and measures of the amount they would be willing to bet on the task. Table 5.6 presents their results for each of these measures for extraverts and introverts under reward-only and punishment-only conditions. Pearce-McCall and Newman indicated that neuroticism had little or no effect on behavior in this context. Table 5.6 indicates that there is very little difference on the measures between extraverts and introverts under reward-only conditions following a period of failure on the task. However, extraverts differ from introverts in the punishment-only condition. Note that extraverts exhibit greater optimism and hope for success when they are faced with a potential loss of money on each trial. One might argue that extraverts, relative to introverts, appear indifferent to the potential loss of money in the task. In this experiment, in contrast to the Nichols and Newman study, extraverts differ from introverts most profoundly under punishment conditions. Of course

Table 5.6

Expectancy Change and Betting Level in Extraverts
and Introverts Following Reward
and Punishment Pretreatments[a]

Personality type	Expectancy change	Betting level
	Punishment	Pretreatment
Extravert	6.24	32.14
Introvert	−1.52	24.36
	Reward	Pretreatment
Extravert	.40	29.10
Introvert	3.20	28.56

[a]Based on Pearce-McCall and Newman (1986). (Copyright 1986 by the American Psychological Association. Adapted by permission of the publisher and author.)

the behavioral indices are quite different in the two experiments—response speed versus responses that are indices of optimism following failure.

The results of the studies reported by Newman and his associates indicate both that Gray's theory can be tested on the human level and that it contains a rich source of potential, testable hypotheses. Also, these studies provide support for the theory, although on detailed analysis they are not invariably in accord with the theory.

Eysenck and Gray Combined

The research we have reviewed, designed to test Eysenck's arousal theory and Gray's behavioral-inhibition theory, provides a number of useful suggestions about extraversion, and, perhaps less coherently, about neuroticism. Gray's emphasis on affect and Eysenck's emphasis on arousal both provide overlapping, and occasionally reinforcing, conceptions of the nature of extraversion. Introverts apparently dislike highly stimulating situations and perform poorly in situations in which they are exposed to intense stimuli, noise, or arousing drugs. They have low-pain tolerance. In general they perform best in, and apparently prefer, situations that are low in stimulation. They are less likely to experience positive affect and appear to be less responsive than extraverts to situations in which there is a large potential for reward. Introverts appear to be more responsive to potential punishments.

This brief gloss of some of the features of extraversion appears to provide a basis for understanding the differences in the social behaviors of individuals who differ in extraversion. Other human beings are a source of both positive and negative affects and are, as well, a source of potential arousal. On several grounds we would expect extraverts to seek the behavior of others more than introverts. The high-arousal potential created by the presence of others should lead introverts to avoid such situations more than extraverts. Large groups of individuals, or parties in which many people are present, are likely to be noisy and highly arousing. As such, they might appeal more to extraverts than introverts. The potential positive affects attainable from social interactions would also be of greater appeal to extraverts than introverts. And, the potentially punishing or negative affects derivable from social interactions might lead introverts to avoid such situations. Thus, the social behaviors of introverts and extraverts might be part of more general response dispositions to be responsive to highly stimulating situations, to prefer situations with high potential for positive affects. and to avoid situations with high potentials for negative affects.

The role of individual differences in neuroticism in this analysis is more problematic, in part because differences in neuroticism have been less consistently related to situations differing in arousal potential or potential affects. It is possible to relate individual differences in extraversion to their neurotic counterparts. Introverted neurotics may be characterized by a neurotic shyness and a self-conscious preoccupation with the potentially aversive effects of social interactions (Eysenck and Eysenck, 1985). Neurotic extraverts may be prone to a reckless indifference to potential punishments and to a narcissistic pursuit of gratification at the expense of others. Psychopathy may be related to neurotic extraverted patterns of behavior.

This analysis leaves the precise behavioral consequences of neuroticism relatively unexplicated. Neuroticism may be related to the amplification of affective responses. Diener, Laresn, Levine, and Emmons, (1985) have indicated that affective experiences have an intensity dimension. They note that individuals do not report positive and negative experiences at the same time. Yet when we obtain a correlation for positive and for negative affects over time, the dimensions are uncorrelated. The substantial independence of positive and negative affects is attributable to a tendency of individuals to consistently report intense experiences irrespective of whether they are positive or negative in tone. Diener et al. obtained repeated measures of their subjects' mood states and correlated their characteristic positive and negative moods, removing[3] the influence of intensity. They found in three separate samples that positive mood scores were substantially inversely related to negative mood scores: $r = -.46, -.76,$ and $-.86$, respectively. These results indicate that there is an important intensity dimension to affective states. It may be that neuroticism acts as an emotional amplification system. This is, of course, a view of neuroticism that is quite congruent with Gray's general position (see Figure 5.10) and of Eysenck's view of neuroticism as well. It is also congruent with some of the results of the Nichols

---

[3]The "removal" involved the use of a partial correlation.

Table 5.7

Verbal Conditioning in Reward and Punishment
Conditions Related to Personality[a]

| | Conditioned responses | |
Personality	Reward	Punishment
Neurotic		
Extravert	4.7	-2.6
Introvert	2.8	-4.3
Normal		
Extravert	2.6	-2.4
Introvert	2.7	-3.1

[a]Based on Gupta and Nagpal (1978).

and Newman (1986) study and of the conditioning experiment of Gupta and
Nagpal (1978). They studied verbal operant conditioning in an experimental
situation in which subjects were rewarded or punished for choosing a member of
one of two classes of words. Table 5.7 presents the effects of rewards and
punishments (mild electric shocks) for correct choices for subjects classified into
four groups on the basis of their scores on neuroticism and extraversion. Table
5.7 indicates that for subjects who are low in neuroticism, rewards and punishments have relatively little differential effect on the behavior of introverts and
extraverts. For subjects who are high in neuroticism, there are clear differences
between introverts and extraverts in response to rewards and punishments. Introverts are highly responsive to punishment and learn to avoid the choice of the
punished responses. Extraverts are highly responsive to rewards and learn to
choose the rewarded response. In this experimental situation, individual differences in neuroticism appear to amplify or make more salient the affective
dimensions of rewards and punishments among introverts and extraverts. If this
analysis is correct, neuroticism ought to be related to the intensity dimension of
mood assessed by Diener and his colleagues.

Zuckerman's Theory of Sensation Seeking

Sensation Seeking as a Trait

Zuckerman's theory derives from an attempt to study individual differences in
response to sensory deprivation (Zuckerman, Kolin, Price, and Zoob 1964). This
led him to develop a self-report measure of personality that is alleged to measure
a trait he calls "sensation seeking". The most recent form of the scale permits
one to derive a summary score on the test and to derive measures for each of four

components, or more narrowly specified traits, that collectively define the global trait (Zuckerman, 1979). The four components of sensation seeking are described as follows:

1. *Thrill and Adventure Seeking (TAS):* the seeking of sensation through risky but exciting sports and other activities, such as fast driving
2. *Experience Seeking (ES):* seeking sensation through the mind and the senses and through a nonconforming life-style
3. *Disinhibition (Dis):* the seeking of sensation through social stimulation and of disinhibition through social drinking
4. *Boredom Susceptibility (BS):* an aversion to monotonous, invariant situations and restlessness when exposed to such situations

These four dimensions of the trait are correlated with each other. The correlations among the subscales range from .3 to .6 (see Zuckerman, 1979). Sensation seeking as a trait has properties that are characteristic of many other trait measures. Among them are the following:

1. A score derived from the self-report measure of the trait correlates positively with ratings of an individual made by informed observers. Caril (1980, as cited in Zuckerman, 1984a) obtained correlations of .55 between peer-ratings and the summary score on the Sensation-Seeking Scale.

2. The trait is influenced by gentoypes. Fulker, Eysenck, and Zuckerman (1980), have reported a twin study of sensation seeking. Their behavior-genetic analysis indicates that 58% of the variance in the trait scores is attributable to genetic variance and that the environmental variance in the trait is attributable to within-family, rather than between-family influences.

3. The trait is related to other trait dimensions of personality. Summary scores on the Sensation-Seeking scale correlate positively with scores on extraversion and psychoticism as measured by the Eysenck questionnaires. The typical correlations obtained are about .3 (see Zuckerman, 1979). The thrill-and adventure-seeking component of sensation seeking is more substantially correlated with extraversion than the other subscales.

The subscales of the scale tend to correlate more highly with each other than they do with either extraversion or psychoticism. Zuckerman (1984b) argues that this finding supports his decision to consider the trait of sensation seeking as a trait that has a status that is independent of the general traits of extraversion and psychoticism, although the trait is related to both of these general traits. Thus one could assert that individuals who score high on the Eysenck measures of extraversion and psychoticism are more likely to be sensation seekers as defined by Zuckerman than individuals who score low on the trait. However, sensation seeking as a trait is not reducible to the traits of psychoticism and extraversion.

Summary scores on sensation seeking are positively correlated with a variety of heterosexual activities. Zuckerman (1978) reports correlations between sensation seeking and self-report measures of sexual activity of .51 and .39 in two separate male samples and .15 and .29 in two separate female samples. The summary score on the scale correlates .42 and .36 with a measure of the use of illegal drugs in males and females, respectively (Zuckerman, 1972). Kish and Donnenwerth (1972) found correlations ranging between .26 and .36 between sensation-seeking scores and a measure of preference for spicy, sour, and crunchy foods, rather than for bland, sweet, and soft foods. Sensation seeking is related to an interest in dangerous and risky activities. Individuals engaged in dangerous occupations usually have high scores on the sensation-seeking scale. For example, skydivers, firemen, riot-squad policemen, and race-car drivers have been found to score higher on sensation seeking than control groups of individuals not engaged in risky occupations (see Hymbaugh and Garrett, 1974; Kusyszyn, Steinberg, and Eliot 1973; Zuckerman, 1978).

In addition to relationships with self-reported interests and activities, the scale relates to such behaviors as volunteering for participation as a subject in psychological experiments—particularly in experiments involving unusual experiences, such as hypnosis or sensory-deprivation experiments. Also, in sensory-deprivation experiments, individuals who are high in sensation seeking are more likely to press a button to receive sensory stimulation than individuals who were low in sensation seeking (Lambert and Levy, 1972).

Biological Theory of Sensation Seeking

Zuckerman has developed a biological theory of individual differences in the trait of sensation seeking. The theory is based on obtained relationships between sensation seeking and psychophysiological and neurochemical measures, as well as on some animal research.

Sensation seeking has been related to a psychophysiological measure of augmentation and reduction of responses to intense stimulation. The usual procedure in these studies is to present intense stimuli to subjects and to record changes in the cortical-evoked response to the stimuli. There is an initial peak positive response to stimulation, occurring as approximately 100 msec after stimulus onset (P_1), followed by a negative response, at approximately 140 msec after stimulus onset (N_1). The difference between these initial responses ($P_1 - N_1$) may be taken as an index of the cortical response to stimulation. Changes in the $P_1 - N_1$ response may be plotted as a function of changes in stimulus intensity. Augmentation is defined as a positive slope of $P_1 - N_1$ as stimulus intensity increases. A negative slope for $P_1 - N_1$ as stimulus intensity increases is an index of the reducing tendency.

Zuckerman (1984a) has summarized the findings of several studies indicating a positive relationship between sensation seeking—particularly for the disinhibition subscale of the total measure—and augmentation. Figure 5.11 presents data reported by Zuckerman, Murtaugh, and Siegel (1974) indicating augmentation of

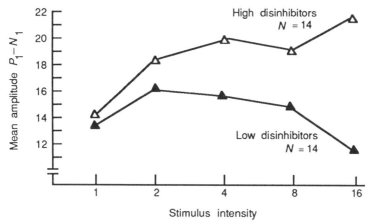

Figure 5.11   Evoked potential amplitudes $(P_1 - N_1)$ as a function of stimulus intensity and sensation seeking. (Based on Zuckerman, Murtaugh, and Siegel, 1974.)

cortical-evoked responses for individuals who score high on the disinhibition scale and the reduction of cortical-evoked responses for individuals who scored low on the disinhibition scale.

Sensation seeking has also been related to gonadal hormones and to mono-amine oxidase (MAO). For the purposes of Zuckerman's biological theory, the latter relationship is critical. Scores on the sensation scales have been negatively related to MAO measured in blood platelets. Negative correlations of .45 and .52 between scores on sensation seeking and MAO in two samples of male subjects have been reported by Murphy et al. (1977) and Schooler, Zahn, Mur-phy, and Buchsbaum (1978). The comparable correlations for female subjects were $+.17$ and $-.43$ in two different samples, respectively. Von Knorring, Oreland, and Winblad (1983), using a sample of 1129 draftees, reported a significant negative relationship between MAO levels and scores on a Swedish translation of the sensation-seeking scale. In addition, they found MAO levels related to alcohol and marijuana use.

Monoamine oxidase is an enzyme that degrades various monoamine neuro-transmitters in the brain. Monoamine oxidase should therefore be inversely relat-ed to the levels of several neurotransmitters. There is some data that suggests that sensation seeking is negatively related to various indices of neurotransmitters whose activity is inhibited by MAO. Umberkoman-Wiita, Vogel, and Wiita (1981) reported negative correlations between MAO levels and dopamine-beta-hydroxylase, an enzyme that converts dopamine to norepinephrine in the brain. Zuckerman, et al. (1983) reported a correlation of $-.51$ between levels of norepinephrine obtained from cerebrospinal fluid and sensation seeking. The direction of these relationships is unexpected given the findings of an inverse relationship between MAO and sensation seeking. That is, in the brain MAO acts as an inhibitor of monoamine neurotransmitters. If the peripheral relationships were congruent with a simple model of activity of the norepinephrine system, one would expect that sensation seeking would be positively, rather than negatively, related to norepinephrine levels, given the negative relationship between MAO and sensation seeking obtained from blood platelet levels.

Zuckerman's current theory (1984a) relates sensation seeking to the level of activity of the norepinephrine system. He assumes that individuals who are high in sensation seeking have either chronically low levels of norepinephrine activity or have a norepinephrine system that is hypoarousable. Such individuals are assumed to seek high levels of activity and stimulation to compensate for a level of activity in the norepinephrine system that is below optimal level.

More generally, Zuckerman proposes that sensation seeking is linked to an optimal level of arousal in a catecholamine activity system. Figure 5.12 presents a summary of this theory. Sensation seekers are likely to be at the low end of the activity of the catecholamine system, and thus they seek intense stimulation to raise them to optimal levels of stimulation. Low-sensation seekers, who are more likely to be at intermediate levels of the system, are likely to avoid intense stimulation. Such stimulation is assumed to lead to the hyperactivity in the system and a variety of associated psychopathological conditions. Thus, low-sensation seekers are likely to find intense stimulation aversive.

Evaluation of Zuckerman's Theory

Zuckerman's theory is an ambitious attempt to integrate data and theory deriving from several different research traditions. In effect, it proposes a link between neurochemical activities at the cellular level and complex human social behavior. Not surprisingly, given the scope of the theory and its ambitious integrative nature, it is subject to criticisms at several different levels. The most recent and comprehensive presentation of Zuckerman's theory is contained in an article published in the journal, *Behavioral and Brain Sciences,* that elicits peer commentary from several individuals in response to each "target" article (Zuckerman, 1984a). My evaluation of Zuckerman's theory has been substantially influenced by the accompanying peer commentary to his presentation of the theory.

Zuckerman has presented a persuasive case for the existence of the trait of sensation seeking. The general trait appears to relate to a diverse set of behaviors. In addition, the set of behaviors and relationships that collectively help to define the trait are relatively comprehensible, and the designation of sensation seeking as a first approximation for a theoretical description of the trait appears justified. The relationship between the narrower trait components of the general trait is somewhat more problematic. Correlations between the trait and biological, physiological, and behavioral indices are sometimes reported with the gen-

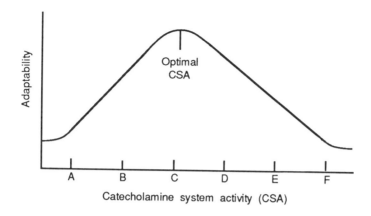

MOOD	1. Depression 2. Anxiety	Boredom, Apathy	Positive Feelings	Euphoria	1. Anxiety 2. Depression	Panic
ACTIVITY	Minimal	Limited	Active	Hyperactive	Aimless Limited	Stereotyped
SOCIAL INTERACTION	Withdrawn or hostile	Introverted (state)	Sociable	Hypersociable	Unsociable	Aggressive - Hostile Interactive
CLINICAL CONDITION	Major depression	Normal	Normal	Cyclothymic Hypomanic	Anxiety Disorder	Paranoid Disorder

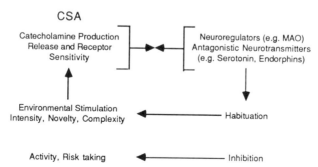

Figure 5.12   A model for the relationship of mood, activity, social interaction, and clinical conditions to catecholamine system activity. (Based on Zuckerman, 1984a.)

eral-trait summary score and sometimes with one of the narrower components—
for example, the disinhibition scale is often found to be more substantially
related to biological markers of the trait than other components. Wohlwill
(1984), in his critical commentary on Zuckerman's paper, notes that the subscales appear to measure psychologically separable aspects of the response to
stimulation—a preference or interest in novel and complex stimuli and a preference for stimuli that are intense. Zuckerman notes that the data relating sensation
seeking to augmenting and reducing indicates that sensation seeking moderates
the response to stimulus intensity, as well as the response to novelty. However,
the relationship between the general and specific components of the trait needs to
be specified with greater precision. The correlations among the narrow traits
fully justifies the postulation of a general trait. However, further specification of
the biological substrates may require clearer distinctions among the components
of the general trait.

   While sensation seeking as a trait appears relatively well grounded at the
personality level, the attempt to relate the trait to a biological theory is subject to
several difficulties. The theory has a strong foundation in the study of animals
that has not been dealt with here. Zuckerman draws on extensive animal research
to relate the functioning of the catecholamine system to behaviors. One difficulty
with this approach is that there is no clear-cut analogue at the animal level to
sensation seeking. Zuckerman's theory is, in this respect, less advantaged than
Gray's theory. Gray's theory has a firm empirical foundation in the study of
behavioral paradigms used in animal research. By contrast, Zuckerman relies on
a biological model developed on the basis of animal research without a clear-cut
model of the behavioral analogue of the sensation-seeking trait at the animal
level. For example, Zuckerman discusses research relating catecholamines to the
response of rats to an open field. Different strains of rats differ with respect to
their tendency to leave their cage and explore an open field. Exploratory tendencies in this situation are generally thought of as being influenced by fear, as well
as the positive response to novelty. Sensation seeking is relatively independent of
fear-like responses. Thus, the animal behavior is not precisely identical with the
human behavior. This is not an argument against comparative research per se.
Rather, it indicates that for the particular trait investigated, animal parallels are
somewhat less precise than they might be for other traits, such as those related to
fear and anxiety.

   Zuckerman's theory encounters increasing difficulty as it deals with increasingly more fundamental biological processes. At the psychophysiological
level, the best established result, based on several investigations, is that of the
relationship between sensation seeking and augmentation of the evoked response. However, even this relationship is subject to a number of qualifications.
It is apparently dependent on the use of very high levels of stimulus intensity and
is not present at lower levels of intensity. In addition, augmentation of evoked

responses to auditory stimulation is related to sensation seeking only under conditions of long-interstimulus intervals between stimulus presentations (see Zuckerman, 1984a). This does not constitute a great difficulty for the theory. However, the fact does not follow in any deductive sense from the theory. It merely stands outside of the body of empirical support for the theory. It is of course, in principle, possible to develop some hypothesis that would explain why sensation seeking is related to augmentation of visual stimuli at short-interstimulus intervals but not to augmentation of auditory stimuli at these same intervals. The example indicates that when one examines the details of pyscho-physiological data relevant to sensation seeking, one encounters complexities and details that do not fit neatly into the general theory. That is, the theory provides a general sketch of relationships, rather than a detailed explication of empirical results.

The most controversial aspect of Zuckerman's theory is the attempt to relate a personality trait to neurochemistry. The difficulties involved in this attempt are formidable. The neurochemical interactions allegedly responsible for trait-like variations in behavior are not observed, although they are observable, in princi-ple, with new techniques that have not been used in this context. Thus, most of the research reported by Zuckerman relates chemical measures obtained in the blood or cerebrospinal fluid to personality. The relationship between such pe-ripheral concentrations and brain neurochemistry is not always clear. Moreover, MAO may have different effects on different neurotransmitters at different loci of the brain. There are innumerable interactions, and both inhibitory and excit-atory relationships, among different neurochemical reactions that may collec-tively influence the final level of a chemical present in the periphery. Thus, in large measure, the neurochemical processes postulated to determine sensation seeking occur at a level that is quite remote from that studied by Zuckerman. The correlations reported by Zuckerman probably provide a reasonable basis for the assumption that some aspects of the catecholamine system are related to sensa-tion seeking. But a precise statement of the way in which various neurotransmit-ters combine to influence the trait cannot be made. In this respect I believe that Zuckerman's theory suffers from a difficulty that is endemic in most, if not all, current attempts to relate personality traits to biological models. Our understand-ing of the biological basis of behavior is in considerable flux, not least with respect to new discoveries about neurotransmitters. We know relatively little about many of these transmitters and the way in which they influence behavior. Even where there is a relatively clear conception of a dimension of personality it may be difficult to relate it to its alleged biological substratum simply because our conception of the biological foundation of many behaviors is so uncertain.

Zuckerman's espousal of an optimal level of arousal theory creates additional problems for his theory. Results indicating both positive and negative rela-tionships with various enzymes are difficult to reconcile with the theory. The theory postulates a complex feedback system in which stable levels of MAO determine the rate or magnitude of response to stimulation. Neurotransmitter levels are presumably influenced by both the level of MAO and by an individual's actions that affect the level of various transmitters. In order to study the actions of such systems on the neurochemical level, one needs a procedure to monitor changes in neurotransmitter levels in response to various stimulus conditions. The only neurochemical measures currently used in research provide measurement of the levels of a chemical substance at a single moment in time. Thus, the neurochemistry measures are ill suited to study a system that is presumed to be responsive to feedback from behavior and external stimuli.

Quite apart from the failure to use measures that monitor changes in neurochemical events, optimal-level theories are subject to several other difficulties. In order to clearly test such theories, it is necessary to distinguish among several different respects in which individuals may differ in the level of a variable that is assumed to have an optimal level. Individuals may differ in the characteristic level of the variable. They may differ in the response to events that increase or decrease the level of the variable, and they may differ with respect to the preferred or optimal level of the variable. In principle, it is possible to obtain information with respect to each of these potential components of individual differences in the level of a neurochemical system. However, such research has not been undertaken and, as a result, an appeal to a biologically based, optimal-level theory to explain individual differences in sensation seeking is largely an unsubstantiated conjecture.

Conclusion

Claridge (1986) has suggested that none of the biologically based theories of personality dimensions currently available provides a completely satisfactory account of the biological basis of personality. There are no theories that purport to account for each of the three traits postulated by Eysenck, or of each of the five traits postulated by Norman. Moreover, none of the biological theories of traits has received consistent and unambiguous research support. Despite this somewhat pessimistic assessment of our current knowledge, I believe that the study of the biological basis of personality dimensions is of fundamental importance. There are at least five justifications for this belief.

First, as indicated earlier, the evidence for a genotypic influence on personality leads ineluctably to a search for the biological basis of that influence. Genotypic influences must influence some aspect of the biological structure of the organism. Of course, to assert this is not to assert that we are in a position to describe and understand the influence of genotypes on biological structures—nor is it to assert that whatever understanding of this nature that is attained will be relevant to the understanding of personality. The assertion merely indicates that the search for those biological structures that are influenced by genotypes that influence personality is a search for something that must exist.

Second, while a completely adequate account of the biological basis of a particular personality trait may not exist, it is not true that there are no demonstrable relationships between the personality traits and the biological characteristics of the organism. There are, for example, relationships between the monoamines and sensation seeking. There are anti-anxiety drugs, and Gray has summarized a good deal of what is known about their common biological effects. And, research based on Eysenck's theory has clearly demonstrated psychophysiological and behavioral differences in the response of introverts and extraverts to stimuli that differ in arousal potential. There is a body of research and data that adds to our sense of the range and scope of individual differences.

Third, the search for the biological basis of personality has the salutary effect of integrating personality psychology with experimental psychology, and with physiological psychology. Personality research becomes an interstitial field with roots simultaneously in the biological and experimental aspects of psychology, as well as in social psychology. It is interesting to note that in American psychology, the study of personality is aligned with the study of social psychology. Division 8 of the Americal Psychological Association is called the division of Personality and Social Psychology, and the most important journal publishing research in personality is called the *Journal of Personality and Social Psychology*. Personality psychology is quite properly related to social psychology, but, I would argue, no more so than it is related to other, more biological and experimental, aspects of psychology.

Fourth, the study of the biological basis of personality has led to the development of concepts that, at the least, provide suggestive evidence of the relationship between biological characteristics of individuals and their responses to stimuli that differ in arousal potential, and in potential to elicit affective responses that provide insights into the social behavior of individuals. Thus, the available research literature provides at least a beginning sense of the breadth and coherence of individual difference dimensions. It is no longer possible to attain a complete understanding of what it means to be introverted or extraverted without reference to the fundamental psychophysiological aspects of the behavior of such individuals.

Fifth, the development of biologically based theories of personality dimensions is compatible with and, indeed, has been supportive of a specification of the relationship between personality traits and situations. That is, such theories often lead to the precise specification of the situations that are likely to elicit trait-relevant behaviors. There are, for example, many reasonably precise deductions that can be obtained from Gray's analysis of the behavioral-inhibition system that specify the expected behavior of individuals who differ in personality dimensions in a variety of experimental contexts. Such theories add both a hypothetico-deductive quality to personality research and a precision to the specifications of the characteristics of situations that will elicit particular kinds of behaviors in particular classes of individuals.

For the above reasons I believe that the study of the biological foundations of personality is important.

6

Conscious and Unconscious
Influences

Introduction

In this chapter we shall consider conscious and unconscious influences on behavior. The topics to be dealt with appear, superficially, to involve a transition from the trait-theoretical issues that have been the focus of Chapters 1–5 of this book. In part, the material to be dealt with here constitutes an addendum to the issues discussed previously that, in my judgment, is necessary for a complete understanding of personality. In part, the issues to be discussed here deal indirectly with aspects of personality that are implicit or submerged within a trait-theoretical approach.

Trait theory assumes a kind of "rough-and-ready" sense of self-awareness and understanding of human behavior. Traits, as we have noted, derive initially from self-descriptions that are subsequently buttressed by congruent observations by observers. Both observers and individuals engaged in the act of self-description may be assumed to be more or less veridical reporters of their actions. The state of awareness and knowledge of human action that is assumed to exist for the purposes of trait description is rendered non problematic by the ultimate behavioral referents of trait descriptors. Whether one is inclined to be alone, or to be impulsive, or to be friendly, or the like is, for the most part, a matter of behavioral observation that may be made without training or the need for the refinement of introspective skills. With the possible exception of the role of self-reports about mood states that are related to personality traits, the implicit assumption that we are aware of our actions plays little or no formal role in trait theory. At the explanatory level, as we have seen in Chapters 3 and 5, trait theory has an affinity with biological explanations that are, for the most part, non phenomenal—that is that do not deal with the state of awareness of the human being—and thus do not assume the existence of a "ghost in the machine."

In a curious way trait theory has been ignored by personality theorists who emphasize either conscious influences on behavior, or unconscious influences. Many personality psychologists have assumed that human thoughts, beliefs, and self-conceptions lie at the heart of an understanding of personality. Such theorists as Bandura (1986) and Kelly (1955) would agree, for somewhat different reasons, that one cannot understand personality without understanding the thoughts and beliefs of an individual. For such theorists, trait theory is incomplete and unsatisfactory because it fails to do justice to the thoughts and beliefs that may be assumed to accompany actions and that may provide a rationale for actions.

Psychodynamic theorists and Freudians would find the trait theorists' emphasis on behavioral acts as a superficial analysis of personality. They would insist that the true reasons for human actions are to be found in unconscious influences and that a focus on what human beings do misses what is essential to understand human personality—namely, the unconscious reasons that explain individual differences in behavior.

It is interesting to note that the psychoanalytic and the cognitive, or phenomenal, theorists' rejections of trait theories share several features. Both groups of theorists believe that the concentration on behavioral acts provides a limited and incomplete account of personality. Both groups of theorists emphasize the importance of an analysis of the reasons for human actions. Both groups of theorists assume that the reasons are to be found in beliefs about the world and in the influence of thoughts on actions. Both groups of theorists postulate the existence of a rich mental life that provides the focus for their attempts to understand personality. However, the theorists differ with respect to whether the mental events that are critical are assumed to be conscious or unconscious.

The Unconscious

Definition of the Unconscious

We begin with a discussion of unconscious influences. In order to define an unconscious influence, it is necessary to define conscious influences. It appears obvious that at any moment in time we are capable of being aware of mental events. Clearly, what is unconscious is that of which we are not aware. But this definition is too broad. We are not in the normal course of events aware of our genes—yet, as we have seen, there is considerable evidence that genes influence our behavior. It is usual in consideration of unconscious influences on behavior to restrict investigations to various stimuli of which one could be aware, but of which one is not. An unconscious influence may be defined as an influence of some stimulus that could be in awareness that is, for any of a variety of reasons, not in awareness.

In order to establish that a particular stimulus is not in awareness, it is useful to distinguish between a state of awareness and our awareness of our state of awareness. It is a commonplace observation of research on unconscious processes that individuals are often aware of stimuli that they are not aware of being aware of. Subjects will, for example, deny that they saw a tachistoscopically presented stimulus and assert that they have no knowledge of the stimulus. However, subjects will be able to make judgments about the stimulus with better than chance accuracy. In a recently completed experiment, Brody, Goodman, Halm, Krinzman, and Sebrechts, (in press), my colleagues and I used a tachistoscope to present words with either positive or negative affective meaning to subjects. The subjects were required to judge whether the stimuli they encountered were positive or negative. We wanted to find a duration of stimulus presentation that would lead subjects to be approximately 75% correct in their responses (*N.B.*, 50% would represent chance responding in this task). In our pre testing we discovered that subjects would typically report that they had no information about the stimulus and did not "see" it when the stimulus was presented for durations at or below 50 msec. The level of stimulus duration that produced 75% accurate judgements occurred at 2 or 3 msec for different subjects. These results are congruent with results that have been repeatedly obtained in research on unconscious processes and demonstrate that a simple verbal report about whether a subject has seen or not seen some stimulus does not provide a veridical index of the subject's knowledge of a stimulus.

Since subjects' reports about their level of awareness of a stimulus are not veridical, it is necessary to use a more rigorous experimental procedure to assess the status of a subject's awareness of a stimulus. The usual procedure involves the use of some type of discrimination task that involves the use of forced-choice procedures. The semantic priming paradigm may be used to illustrate procedures for assessing the level of awareness of a stimulus. Meyer and Schvaneveldt (1971) pioneered the use of a lexical decision task to measure semantic priming. In this task subjects are required to decide whether a string of letters constitutes a word in English or is merely a meaningless compilation of letters. The time required to reach this decision is noted. If a string of letters constituting a word is preceded by a word that is semantically related to the "target" word, the time required to reach the decision is shorter than if the word preceding the target word is semantically unrelated to the target word. Thus, subjects are able to decide that the word *ship* is a word more rapidly when it is preceded by the word *boat* than when it is preceded by the word *face*. In this example the word boat acts as a semantic prime. Marcel (1980) argued that words that were out of awareness could act as semantic primes. He used a pattern-masking procedure to prevent subjects from being aware of the prime. In this procedure the prime stimulus was followed by the presentation of a stimulus, called a mask, consisting of a series of letters in different orientations that was assumed to prevent subjects from being aware of the prime stimulus. How could one demonstrate that subjects were unaware of the prime in this type of experiment? Let us consider several possible procedures that might be used to ascertain the subject's awareness of the prime stimulus.

1. We could ask the subject if he or she "saw" the prime. If we assume that the subject has provided an honest and accurate report, the subjects assertion that he or she is not aware of the stimulus could be taken as *prima facie* evidence for its unconscious status. However, such a procedure could at best establish that the subject is not aware of being aware of the stimulus. The subject could be aware of the stimulus but be unaware of his or her state of awareness.

2. We could test the subject's state of awareness of the stimulus by presenting either the word boat or the word face to the subject on many random trials, holding constant all other conditions of stimulus presentation. Subjects could then be required to guess after each presentation whether the stimulus was the word boat or the word face. If the subject's guesses were no better than chance (i.e., correct 50% of the time) we could infer that the subject was not aware of the stimulus.

The criterion described in 2 above is probably too rigorous. One could argue that any stimulus presented to a subject, irrespective of the extent to which it is degraded, is likely to add a minimal amount of signal or information to a background of noise.[1] If one presents an extremely large number of trials, it is likely that subjects will acquire some minimal information about the stimulus that will increase the probability that subjects will be able to detect the presence of the stimulus with better than chance accuracy—although for stimuli that are very degraded, the probability of being correct may be only vanishingly better than .50. In the limiting case, it may approach .50. This stochastic or probabilistic detection is compatible with the assertion that subjects have acquired a minimal level of information about the stimulus—or, perhaps equivalently, that their state of awareness is different following the presentation of a particular stimulus. If the true probability of correct detection of a stimulus using forced-choice procedures is very close to chance (say, .5001 in our example), it may be impossible to empirically demonstrate that subjects are aware of the stimulus without presenting an indefinitely large number of trials. Indeed, there may be no practical way to demonstrate such a minimal level of awareness. However, it might also be true that such a minimal level of awareness has no functional

---

[1]This analysis is obviously based on signal detectability theory (see Swets, Tanner, and Birdsall, 1961). I am not, however, presenting a full explication of the theory here.

significance. The assumption that all stimuli engender minimal awareness may be taken as a fundamental premise.

Irrespective of whether or not one assumes that all stimuli that are presented to an individual engender some minimal change in the awareness of a subject, a serviceable definition of awareness may be derived by the use of forced-choice procedures. If subjects are not able to demonstrate better than chance discrimination after a reasonably adequate number of trials in which they are asked to discriminate between stimuli that are presented to them, it may be assumed that the stimuli are out of awareness.

Priming Studies

Are there unconscious influences on behavior? We shall present several different kinds of studies designed to answer this question. We begin with a presentation of semantic priming studies. Several researchers, beginning with Marcel (1980), have reported evidence of semantic priming of stimuli that are not in awareness (see Balota, 1983; Fowler, Wolford, Slade, and Tassinary, 1981; Marcel, 1980, 1983a, b). The typical procedure used in this research involves the presentation of a prime stimulus (usually a word) followed by the presentation of a pattern mask that is presumed to interfere with the recognition or awareness of the prime followed by the target stimulus. The allegedly subliminal prime reduces the time required to process the target stimulus. On occasion, the magnitude of the priming effect attributable to the prime stimulus that is masked and is, as a result, not in awareness is comparable to the effect of unmasked primes that are clearly recognizable and are in awareness.

Holender (1986) has recently presented a comprehensive critique of these and related studies. Holender accepts the evidence for the existence of priming for stimuli that are masked. He and several individuals who commented on his article further agree that stimuli that are masked and that are reported by subjects to be out of awareness can prime target stimuli.

Although Holender accepts the existence of priming for primes that subjects report they are not aware of, he is quite skeptical of claims for the existence of priming effects for stimuli that cannot be consciously identified. Holender argues that there are flaws in the demonstration that subjects are not able to consciously identify the stimuli. He indicates that rigorous procedures to establish that stimuli are not in awareness have not been used. Such procedures involve the use of modern techniques of threshold determination involving many presentations of the stimuli and the use of statistical procedures contained in signal detectability theory. Demonstrations that stimuli that are presented infrequently (e.g., 20 times) cannot be correctly distinguished from blank stimuli or other words at better than chance accuracy do not provide a sensitive test of the possibility that subjects might be able to make above-chance discriminations of the stimuli if they were presented for many trials. In addition, it is possible that subjects may have a shifting state of awareness for stimuli that are close to a detection threshold and thus might be aware of the prime stimulus on some trials. However, demonstrations that the magnitude of the priming effect obtained with masked stimuli are, on occasion, comparable to the effects obtained with unmasked stimuli that are clearly in consciousness argues against an interpretation of masked priming as being attributable to an infrequent presence of an above-threshold detection of the prime (see Fowler et al., 1981, for a demonstration of priming effects that are comparable for allegedly unconscious and conscious prime stimuli).

Holender does note that there are demonstrations of semantic priming even where experiments have presented prime stimuli that their subjects were not able to detect with greater than chance accuracy in some types of a forced-choice tasks. Even if the procedures used in these studies were not sufficient to demonstrate that subjects had absolutely no information or awareness of the stimuli, the procedures were clearly sufficient to demonstrate relatively minimal and, perhaps, near zero awareness of the stimuli. Holender argues that many of these studies contained a fundamental methodological flaw. He notes that the levels of dark adaptation and the levels of light present during the determination of the threshold for the prime were different than the levels of light and dark adaptation present during the priming phase of the experiment. In the threshold-determination phase, subjects typically were in a dark or dimly illuminated room and presented with a brief prime stimulus followed by a mask. During the priming phase of the experiment, the subjects were presented with the same stimulus displays under the same conditions as in the threshold-determination phase with the addition of a brightly illuminated target stimulus that changed the level of dark adaptation of the subjects. The effect of the additional light, present during the priming phase of the experiment, is likely to improve the subject's ability to detect the prime stimulus. Thus, Holender argues that the failure to assess the subject's threshold for the prime stimuli, under stimulus conditions that were comparable to those that were present during the priming phase of the experiment, is compatible with the possibility that subjects were aware of the masked prime.

Hollender's critique cannot account for all of the evidence for semantic priming in the absence of conscious identification of the prime. There are several studies in the literature in which threshold determinations for the prime stimuli were made under stimulus conditions that were comparable to those that were used during the priming phase of the experiment. Brody et al. (in press, Experiment 3) obtained semantic priming for positive and negative masked prime words in an experimental situation in which subjects had to decide whether the target words were either positive or negative in meaning. In their experiment the prime stimuli were presented for either 10, 30, or 60 msec. Subjects were clearly aware of the 60 msec duration primes and had no difficulty in recognizing them.

Subjects reported they were not aware of seeing the 10 msec prime stimuli. In addition, in a post-test recognition task in which the 10 msec prime and target stimuli were presented under viewing conditions that were identical to those used in the priming experiment proper, the subjects were not able to discriminate with above-chance accuracy whether the prime stimuli were positive or negative in meaning. No subject tested attained better than 12 out of 20 correct responses on this task, and for 8 subjects tested for 20 trials (160 trials in all) the subjects were correct on 51% of the trials. Since the determination of the subliminal character of the 10 msec prime was obtained under identical viewing conditions to those used in the experiment proper, the results cannot be attributable to differential light adaptation. Brody et al. found that the effects of the 10 msec prime were equivalent to the effects of a 60 msec prime.

Dagenbach and Carr (1986) used a lexical-decision task to study semantic priming. They determined a detection threshold for the prime stimuli they used in their experiment. The detection threshold was the level of stimulus onset asynchrony between the onset of a 10 msec prime stimulus and the onset of a pattern mask stimulus at which the subject's ability to discriminate between a blank stimulus and the prime fell below 12 out of 20 responses correct. The threshold value was rechecked after the priming experiment, and those subjects who on retesting were correct more than 12 out of 20 trials were eliminated from the analysis. The remaining subjects still exhibited a priming effect leading to faster lexical decisions when the target stimulus was primed by a semantically relevant prime.

Marcel (1983a, Experiment 5) demonstrated priming with stimuli that could not be recognized in a design wherein he mixed trials in which subjects were required to identify the target with trials in which subjects were asked to identify the prime. Since judgments of the prime occurred during the same time period and under the same conditions of stimulus presentations used to determine the effects of the prime on the target, the prime was equally visible during threshold determination and during the priming phase of the experiment. Thus, the subliminal priming effects in this experiment could not be attributable to differential dark adaptation.

Bargh, Bond, Lombardi, and Tota (1986) presented subjects with words in the parafoveal region (i.e., in a part of the visual field that is removed from a central fixation point where visual acuity is reduced) followed by a pattern mask. They presented 100 words to their subjects, 80 of which were relevant to *shy* characteristics and 80 of which were relevant to *kind* characteristics of a person. Subjects who were exposed to either of these kinds of words then had to rate the personal characteristics of an individual described to them. The priming stimuli influenced the ratings assigned to the person in a direction congruent with the content of the prime words. In order to establish that the words presented were subliminal, Bargh et al. designed a discrimination task in which they presented the 100 prime words under the same conditions used in the experiment, followed by the presentation of three words including the prime word presented. After each presentation of the prime, the subjects had to select the correct word presented to them from the list of three words. A control group presented with blank prime stimuli was given the same selection task. The control group was correct 33.8% of the trials, and the group actually presented with a prime word was correct on 34.5% of the trials. These percentages are not significantly different, and the mean correct percentage of 34.5% is virtually indistinguishable from an expected value of 33.3% correct by chance. These data suggest that subjects were not aware of the prime stimuli. However, these prime stimuli were nevertheless capable of coloring the subsequent judgments of the ambiguous-stimulus person described to the subjects. It is interesting to note that the effects of the prime stimulus were delayed in time because the judgment task was presented as a second task, independent of the first. Thus, the influence of the stimulus out of awareness can extend over a period of time that is longer than the duration used in the subliminal semantic priming literature, where the effects occur with delays between the presentation of the prime and the target stimulus that are characteristically measured in milliseconds.

The experiments cited above may be construed as constituting evidence opposing Holender's skeptical view that semantic priming in the absence of conscious awareness does not exist. These results cannot be attributed to methodological artifacts involving differences in stimulus conditions and dark adaptation during the threshold-determination phase and the priming phase of the experiment. It is also true that the forced-choice recognition procedures used in these experiments imply that subjects have, at best, extremely limited awareness of the prime stimuli. However, it is possible that subjects might have some limited awareness of the prime and that a more rigorous assessment procedure of their ability to detect the presence or absence of the prime or the difference between one of two kinds of primes using a large number of trials might indicate some minimal degree of improvement over chance detection of the prime.[2] One could assert that these experiments demonstrate that stimuli that subjects are not aware of being aware of and that may result in very limited states of awareness or, perhaps, that are totally out of awareness can nevertheless influence subsequent information processing and judgment.

The experiments that are briefly reviewed above leave a number of additional questions unsettled. Are the effects of subliminal priming equivalent to the effects of supraliminal priming by stimuli of which subjects are aware? With respect to the quantitative effects of such primes, the data are inconclusive. For example, in the Brody et al. study the effects of subliminal priming were equivalent to those of priming with stimuli that were clearly recognizable. In the

[2]In signal detectability terms, $d' > .00$.

Dagenbach and Carr (1986) study semantically related subliminal prime stimuli reduced lexical decision times by 20 msec, and semantically related supraliminal prime stimuli reduced lexical decisions by 75 msec. Chessman and Merikle (1984; see also Merikle, 1982) presented subliminal stimuli in a study of the *Stroop phenomenon* in which color names prime color patches. When the name describes the color patch, the time taken to describe the patch is reduced. When the color word is at variance with the color of the visual stimulus, interference occurs. Chessman and Merikle found evidence for Stroop effects for semantic word primes below their subjects' reported subjective thresholds (i.e., the threshold where subjects claimed they could no longer see the prime stimulus) and above their subjects' thresholds for detection of the prime at no better than chance levels. However, for prime presentations at a threshold level they reported no effects of the prime. Thus, in their study of Stroop effects, priming effects occurred only where the prime was supraliminal. It is apparent from this beief review that subliminal priming effects are occasionally weaker and occasionally equivalent to the effects of supraliminal prime stimuli.

A more interesting issue, and one that is clearly relevant to the role of the unconscious influences on actions and behavior relevant to an understanding of personality, is the possibility that unconscious prime stimuli may have effects on cognitive processes that are qualitatively different from the effects of conscious stimuli. One of the more interesting claims of qualitatively different effects is provided in a study reported by Marcel (1980). Marcel's study is based on a priming paradigm originally studied supraliminally by Schvaneveldt, Meyer, and Becker (1976), who studied the priming of polysemous words (i.e., words having two, clearly distinct meanings), in an experiment in which they presented sequences of three words to their subjects. The polysemous word was the second word in the sequence, and the first word primed either a relevant or an irrelevant meaning of the polysemous word. If the first word in the sequence primed a relevant meaning of the polysemous word, the processing of the third or target word was facilitated. If the first word primed an irrelevant meaning of the polysemous word, the processing of the third target word was not facilitated. Thus, money would be more rapidly processed in a lexical-decision task if subjects were presented with the sequence—save, bank, money. However, the processing of the word *money* was not facilitated if subjects were presented with the sequence—river, bank, money. Marcel found that the priming effects of polysemous words in this paradigm depended upon whether subjects were or were not aware of the content of the polysemous word. If the polysemous word was followed by a pattern mask, preventing the subjects from becoming aware of the polysemous word and prohibiting them from making better than chance discriminations about the content of the word, the polysemous word facilitated the processing of the target word even if the polysemous word was itself primed by an initial word in the sequence that primed an irrelevant meaning of the word.

If the polysemous word was not followed by a mask, thereby permitting subjects to be aware of the content of the word, processing of the target word was facilitated only if the relevant meaning of the polysemous word was primed. Marcel explains these results by appealing to a theory of the selective role of consciousness. He suggests that in a preconscious state all of the meanings of a word are present and activated. Consciousness serves to select and restrict meaning and focuses on one of several possible meanings present. As a result, only the meaning of the polysemous word that has been primed is made available to consciousness, and the restricted meaning is capable of influencing the processing of the target word. As long as the stimulus is out of consciousness, Marcel asserts that all of its potential meanings remain salient and capable of acting as prime for the target. Marcel's hypothesis implies that the rules that define and govern preconscious or unconscious processing of information are different from the rules that govern conscious processing of information.

Psychophysiological Indices of Unconscious Processes

In the above studies we have reviewed evidence for the influence of unconscious processing derived from a judgment or verbal report about a stimulus. There are several different paradigms for the study of unconscious influences that rely on some form of psychophysiological index that is presumed to provide evidence of a response to a stimulus that is out of awareness. Öhman's (1986) studies of the conditioning of fear-inducing stimuli provide an example in which masks are used to prevent subjects from being aware of the stimuli. Öhman uses a two-stage conditioning paradigm in which emotional faces are associated with electrical shock which leads to the development of a conditioned skin response to the presentation of the conditioned stimulus. In the second phase of the experiment, an angry face (now functioning as a conditioned fear stimulus) is presented to the subject in the absence of electric shock. Under conditions in which a mask is used to prevent subjects from being able to discriminate the presence or absence of the conditioned face stimulus with better than chance accuracy, subjects exhibit greater skin conductance responses to the presentation of a conditioned stimulus than to the presentation of a stimulus not previously associated with shock. Öhman's studies demonstrate the presence of an emotional response to a stimulus that subjects cannot recognize and that is presumably out of awareness.

Psychophysiological indices of emotional responses have been used to demonstrate the influence of stimuli out of awareness using dichotic listening procedures. In these experiments subjects are presented with different verbal materials to each ear with instructions to attend to material presented in one of the two ears. Subjects are usually required to report or repeat the content of material presented to one of their ears—(that is, to "shadow" the material). The experimental manipulation of attention to material presented to one of the two ears is assumed to prevent the awareness of material presented to the unattended ear.

Corteen and Wood (1972; Corteen and Dunn, 1974) used a conditioning paradigm to demonstrate the influence of emotional stimuli presented to the unattended channel. They first conditioned their subjects by associating words with electrical shock. In the second phase of the experiment the shock-related words were presented to the unattended ear, while subjects shadowed material presented to the other ear. They found that subjects exhibited conditioned, electrodermal responses to the emotional stimuli presented to the unattended ear. Corteen and Wood reported that at the end of the experiment subjects asserted that they were not aware of the conditioned emotional stimuli. In addition, in the Corteen and Dunn study subjects were asked to press a buzzer during the experiment whenever they thought that an emotionally significant word was presented to them. Subjects did not press the buzzer. It should be noted that the assessment of the subjects' level of awareness in these studies was not as rigorous as the assessments that were used in the priming studies. That is, subjects were not presented with forced-choice procedures in which they were required to guess at random moments wherein the stimulus presented to their unattended ear was, or was not, an emotionally relevant stimulus.

The Corteen studies have been controversial. Wardlaw and Kroll (1976) reported a failure to replicate. In addition, Corteen (1986) has indicated that it is difficult to prevent momentary shifts of attention to the unattended ear, thus resulting in a momentary awareness of the conditioned stimulus. Dawson and Schell (1982) have performed the best-controlled study using the dichotic listening task to demonstrate conditioned responses to stimuli presented to an unattended channel. They used three procedures to demonstrate that subjects were not aware of the stimuli presented to the unattended ear. Subjects were asked if they heard the stimuli at the end of the experiment—a weak test. Subjects were instructed to press a buzzer during the experiment if their attention momentarily shifted to the unattended channel. Finally, subjects were required to continuously shadow (i.e., verbally report) the contents of the material presented to the attended ear. They found that subjects were more likely to be incorrect in their shadowing responses following the presentation of a shock-associated word to the unattended ear than following a previously presented word not associated with shock. Since subjects were more likely to make shadowing errors following the presentation of a shock-associated stimulus to the unattended ear, they reasoned that these errors could be considered as an indirect index of the level of awareness of the stimulus. Therefore, they excluded all trials in which an error was made. They found that most of the electrodermal responses indicative of a conditioned emotional response to shock stimuli occurred when subjects were momentarily aware of the shock stimuli, as indicated by their buzzer responses or by the occurrence of an error in shadowing. However, there was a small set of conditioned emotional responses that occurred on trials in which subjects gave no indication that they were aware of the conditioned stimuli. These responses occurred only if the shock stimuli were presented to the left ear, and the material to be shadowed was presented to the right ear. Corteen (1986), has indicated that he also found in his original studies with Wood, which utilized the dichotic listening task, evidence for conditioned emotional responses without awareness occurred primarily for conditioned stimuli that were presented to the left ear.

The Dawson and Schell study provides suggestive evidence for the occurrence of conditioned emotional responses in the absence of awareness of the conditioned stimulus. It should be noted that the methods used for the assessment of awareness in this study are not quite as rigorous as those used in the priming studies. Forced-choice discriminations were not used to establish that subjects' awareness of the stimuli would not result in discriminations between shock-related and nonshock-related words that were better than chance. It is possible, in principle, to ask subjects, at randomly selected times, to guess which of several words had been presented to them. Such a procedure would provide a more rigorous demonstration of conditioned emotional responding in the absence of awareness of the conditioned stimuli.

Laterality and the Unconscious

Dawson and Schell's finding that conditioned emotional response in the absence of awareness was restricted to left-ear presentations of the conditioned stimuli suggests that the phenomenon is related to differences in functioning of the left and right hemispheres. The principle pathways between the ears and the transduction of stimulation to the hemispheres are contralateral (for a comprehensive discussion of research on laterality see Bryden, 1982). In right-handed individuals the left hemisphere controls speech. Dawson and Schell reason that the left hemisphere's involvement with speech occupies the left hemisphere with the shadowing task during left-ear presentations of the conditioned emotional stimulus, leaving the right hemisphere free to mediate conditioned emotional responses. If the emotional stimuli are presented to the right ear, the left hemisphere is not free to mediate a conditioned emotional response to the stimuli because it is preoccupied with shadowing material. The right hemisphere does not normally control speech, and thus the left hemisphere must be involved in the shadowing task.

An alternative explanation of the results of the Dawson and Schell study involving hemispheric specialization is possible. There is a body of evidence (see Bryden, 1982) that indicates that the right hemisphere is specialized for the processing of the emotional content of stimuli. If this is correct, then emotional stimuli presented to the left ear would be predominantly projected to the right hemisphere and would apparently be more accurately or comprehensively processed than emotional information presented to the right ear and hence to the left hemisphere. In addition, the mute non verbal characteristics of the right hemisphere might leave the individual with only limited ability to signal or specify the level of awareness of the stimuli presented to it in a situation in which the left hemisphere is preoccupied with the task of shadowing verbal information.

The existence of specialized verbal and emotional functions of the right and left hemispheres provides a neuropsychological model and a spatial metaphor for the separation of affect and verbal report that appears to be central to many clinical references to unconscious processes.

Ley and Bryden (1982, see also Bryden and Ley, 1983) have obtained data that supports the hypothesis of a neurologically independent locus of processing of the affective and the semantic content of stimuli in a dichotic listening task. In their experiment, subjects were presented with sentences that were read in various tones of voice (happy, sad, angry, and neutral). Subjects were more accurate in identifying the emotional content of the material when attending to left-ear presentations. Subjects were more accurate in identifying the content of the passages they heard when attending to the right ear. These data provide relatively direct evidence for the notion that the hemispheres are differentially specialized for processing affective and semantic contents.

Brody et al. (in press) studied the processing of affective stimuli that were out of awareness and that were presented to either the right or left hemisphere. In their study, the effects of prime stimuli that subjects were not able to recognize with better than chance accuracy were comparable to the effects of prime stimuli that were clearly recognizable. They used prime words with obvious positive and negative affective meaning, and schematic faces with the mouth line turned up or down to represent positive and negative affective prime stimuli. These stimuli were followed by the presentation of a target stimulus that was either a positive or negative affective word. Their subjects were required to judge whether the target words were either positive or negative. The prime stimuli and the target stimuli were both lateralized (i.e., tachistoscopically presented to either the right or left visual field.) Table 6.1 presents data indicating the presence of semantic priming effects for positive-prime stimuli. Note that Table 6.1 indicates that semantic priming effects are different for various prime and target locations. The

Table 6.1

Semantic Prime Scores for Positive Primes Presented to the Right
and Left Hemisphere Followed by Targets Presented
to the Right and Left Hemisphere[a]

	Target location	
Prime location	Right hemisphere	Left hemisphere
Right hemisphere	26.8	−2.9
Left hemisphere	7.2	12.9

[a]Based on Brody et al., in press.

clearest evidence for semantic priming effects in which positive affective primes improve the accuracy of judgment of positive affective target stimuli and decrease the accuracy of negative affective target stimuli relative to neutral-prime stimuli occurs when both the prime and target stimuli are presented to the right hemisphere. This aspect of the data is congruent with the hypothesis that the right hemisphere is specialized for the processing of affective stimuli. However, if the prime stimulus is presented to the right hemisphere and the target is presented to the left hemisphere there is no evidence of semantic priming effects. These data suggest that information about the affective sign of positive affective stimuli is not transferred from the right to the left hemisphere under the conditions of stimulus presentations used in this experiment. Brody et al. also found that these effects were virtually identical for prime stimuli that their subjects could not identify with better than chance accuracy and for prime stimuli that were clearly recognizable.

If the positive affective prime stimulus and the target were both presented to the left hemisphere, there was a significant semantic priming effect—although it was of smaller magnitude than the effect of right-hemisphere primes of right-hemisphere targets. However, left-hemisphere primes do have a semantic priming effect on right-hemisphere targets. These data suggest that information about the affective content of positive-prime stimuli presented to the left hemisphere does transfer to the right hemisphere and is capable of influencing the processing of right-hemisphere targets.

The data on semantic priming obtained by Brody et al. suggests that the interactive relationship between the hemispheres with respect to the processing of positive affective stimuli is nonsymmetric. The right hemisphere need not inform the left hemisphere about positive affective stimuli, and the left hemisphere does transfer such information to the right hemisphere. Brody et al. explain these results by appealing to studies of the affective responses to left- and right-hemisphere brain damage. Left-hemisphere brain damage is associated with depressive and negative affective states (see Heilman, Bowers, and Valenstein, 1985). Brody et al. suggest that the left hemisphere may be responsible for signaling the presence of positive affective states. Whether this speculative hypothesis is correct or not, the Brody et al. study does provide evidence for independent states of awareness of the affective meaning of stimuli at different loci of the brain. And, the study suggests, at least under the somewhat constrained and possibly ecologically nonrepresentative situation of brief tachistoscopic stimulis presentations, that information available to one part of the brain need not be transferred to other parts of the brain. This study, as well as the Dawson and Schell (1982) study, provides a structural basis on what is known about neurophysiological processes that helps to explain dissociation between different kinds of information that is fundamental to many demonstrations of unconscious influences of behavior. Of course, the extent to which such pro-cesses occur in non laboratory contexts remains problematic.

Independence of Content and Affect

The independent processing of information about the content and affective mean-ing of stimuli has been studied in a paradigm involving memory for stimuli that are presented briefly by Kunst-Wilson and Zajonc (1980; see also Wilson, 1979; Zajonc, 1980, 1984). These studies attempted to extend research demonstrating that subjects develop preferences for stimuli they are familiar with—"the mere-exposure" effect—to demonstrations that subjects develop preferences for stim-uli they had been exposed to but were unaware of having previously encoun-tered. Several times subjects were presented with different polygons in a random order. Researchers used a tachistoscope to present the stimuli at durations that were alleged to be too rapid to permit conscious recognition of the stimuli. In the second phase of the experiment, subjects were presented with a task in which each of the polygons they had previously encountered was paired with a polygon they had not previously seen. One group of subjects was asked to identify the polygon they had previously seen. The subjects were not able to perform this task with greater than chance accuracy. The second group of subjects was asked to choose the polygon they liked. Subjects tended to prefer the polygons they had previously encountered, even though they were not able to identify them as polygons that they had previously encountered. Apparently, subjects develop a preference or liking for stimuli they have encountered without knowing that these stimuli had previously been presented.

Seamon and his colleagues have replicated the basic phenomenon reported by Kunst-Wilson and Zajonc several times (see Seamon, Brody, and Kauff, 1983a, b; Seamon, Marsh, and Brody, 1984). Seamon, Brody, and Kauff (1983b) found that the development of a preference for previously seen polygons that subjects were unaware of having seen was present even when the test for preference and recognition occured 1 week after initial stimulus presentation. These findings suggest that the affective responses to the stimuli endure through time.

In his theoretical analysis of this phenomenon, Zajonc (1984) suggests that the processing of affective components of a stimulus occurs in a different manner than the processing of those components that are the basis of the recognition of the stimulus. He suggests that affective responses to a stimulus occur with a preferred channel prior to the processing of the components of a stimulus that permit adequate classification and response to the stimulus. Seamon, Brody, and Kauff (1983a) suggest that research demonstrating the development of prefer-ences for stimuli that subjects are not aware of having previously encountered may be interpreted in a different way. They note that the phenomenon that is studied is based on long-term memory. That is, subjects are not required immediately after stimulus presentation to judge whether they prefer or whether they are aware of which of two stimuli shown to them has been presented previously. In these experiments the subjects are presented with 10 different, non-easily-distinguished stimuli, and it is only after the entire sequence of stimulus presentations has ended that judgments of preference and previous encounter are obtained.

Seamon, Brody, and Kauff suggest that the form of the questions addressed to subjects might change the retrieval processes used by the subjects. If a subject is asked which of two stimuli has been previously presented, it is necessary for the subject to engage in a search of his or her memory traces for the set of polygons. Since the stimuli are presented under degraded conditions and, are, in addition, not easily discriminable, the extended search of memory traces required for correct judgments about the stimuli is a difficult task that is likely to produce errors. Judgments about whether one likes or does not like a particular stimulus do not require the subject to search through his or her memory traces of the stimuli. Such judgments might well be made indirectly on the basis of a vague sense of familiarity with the stimulus that might trigger a preference for the stimulus. Whether Zajonc's interpretation of this phenomenon or the alternative interpretation involving the way in which information is retrieved from memory is correct, the phenomenon does indicate that individuals can develop preferences for stimuli without being aware of the processes that lead to the development of a preference.

Libet's Analysis of Action

The studies we have reviewed provide support for the influence of stimuli that are out of awareness on judgments of stimuli made under constrained circumstances. These studies do not provide us with very much information about the influence of the unconscious on behavior in ordinary social contexts. Next, I shall review research that attempts to demonstrate unconscious influences on human actions other than judgments about stimuli.

Libet (1985) has presented data that indicate that the occurrence of simple motor acts is preceded by neurophysiological triggers that precede the awarensss of the intention to act. In his studies subjects were asked to perform a simple motor act, such as moving their fingers whenever they felt the urge to perform this act. They were required to signal their awarensss of the intention to act by pointing to the position of a light on a cathode ray tube. This light acts like a clock and signals when subjects first become aware of their intention or desire to act. The reported awareness of the intention to act precedes the action by approximately 200 msec. Libet monitored the subjects' physiological responses using an electromyogram. He reported that voluntary muscle movements were invariably preceded by a pattern of electromyographic change called a *readiness potential* that occurs approximately 550 msec before the allegedly voluntary motor act.

Since the readiness potential preceded the awareness of the intention to act, Libet argued that the origins of the intention are present neurologically before the phenomenal intention that the person believes controls the act. These data suggest that the awareness of the intention to act is epiphenomenal. That is, subjects may believe that it is conscious intention that triggers their voluntary acts. However, Libet would argue that the intention to act, as signaled by the occurrence of a neurologically defined readiness potential, is present preconsciously. The conscious intention merely signals the occurrence of an intention that is already in progress.

There is an obvious flaw in Libet's reasoning as we have presented it. The determination of the time (in msec) before an action takes place that a readiness potential is occurring involves the timing of the occurrence of an electrical event. The "response latency" of the apparatus is negligible because it is determined by the speed of transmission of an electrical impulse. The determination of the time at which the awareness of an intention to act occurs involves an unspecified time lag that requires subjects to report when they are aware of a mental event. If there is a time lag in the subject's ability to report the mental event, it is possible that the mental event might occur at some unspecified, earlier time—perhaps even at a time that precedes the occurrence of the neurologically defined readiness potential. Libet has used two procedures to circumvent this objection. First, he does not ask subjects to perform some motor response (e.g., pressing a button) to index their awareness of their intention. Such a procedure would clearly involve the interpolation of a time-to-respond component between the awareness of the intention and the time taken to signal the awareness of the intention. The use of a clock with a moving light on a cathode ray tube merely requires the subject to indicate the position of the light (or clock) when the awareness of the intention is first manifest. Thus, the subject must determine his or her experience of a light that occurs simultaneously with his or her awareness of an intentional experience. This procedure does not include an obvious component of motor response time.

It could still be argued that there is an inevitable delay between the awareness of a mental event (in this case an intention) and an awareness of a moving light and, as a result, subjects are inclined to report that the mental event occurred at a time that is later than it actually occurs. In order to circumvent this criticism, Libet (1985) designed a control experiment in which he asked subjects to indicate when they were first aware of a stimulus applied to the skin. He found, using the judged position of the light technique, that the awareness of the stimulus actually preceded the occurrence of the physical stimulus. This result does not mean that subjects are aware of a stimulus prior to its presentation. Rather, the results indicate that the procedure of judging the simultaneity of a mental event (perceived awareness of a tactile stimulus) and the judged position of a light is likely to introduce a bias into the judged time of occurrence of the internal mental event (the awareness of the tactile stimulus) that results in the determination that it has occurred earlier than its actual occurrence. These data appear to support Libet's assertion that the awareness of the intention must occur at a time that is close to, or perhaps even slightly later than, that which is indicated. In order to argue that the procedure used to determine the timing of the intention is somehow responsible for the finding that the awareness follows by over 300 msec the physical event that invariably triggers the intention, it is necessary to argue that the timing procedure introduces a time bias for the awareness of intentions that is quite different from the time bias introduced by the procedure when it is used to measure the time when subjects are aware of the sensation accompanying a tactile event. I do not see any obvious reason why the time taken to be aware of an intention should be fundamentally different than the time taken to be aware of a sensation. This suggests that Libet's analysis of the time relations between readiness potentials, intentions, and actions is correct.

Libet claims that physically defined readiness potentials serve as necessary conditions for the occurrence of voluntary motor acts. That is, such acts do not occur in the absence of a readiness potential. Näätänen (1985) attempted to circumvent the influence of a readiness potential. He tried to perform motor acts "spontaneously"—that is by willed creation of the phenomental state of spontaneous actions. He found, however, that actions that appeared to be virtually spontaneous and with minimal involvement of willed intention were nevertheless preceded invariably by a readiness potential.

Does the readiness potential serve as a sufficient, as well as a necessary, precedent for action? Libet suggests that in the normal course of events willed motor acts occur invariably if they are preceded by a readiness potential. This suggests that readiness potentials are both necessary and sufficient causes for acts. However, Libet also suggests that the conscious intention to act may interrupt or cancel the physically based intention to act signaled by a readiness potential. Thus, in his analysis, conscious processes could not initiate action, but they could serve to cancel or to prevent actions during the time period of some 300 msec or more in which the awareness of the intention precedes the occurrence of the act. Libet's suggestion of the existence of a consciously triggered cancellation program for actions is not based on a clear empirical demonstration of such events. Rather, at this stage of his research, it is to be construed as a relatively unsubstantiated hypothesis that preserves a role for conscious processes in the control of actions. It should also be noted that it is theoretically possible that the occurrence of a conscious intention to cancel an action might itself be preceded by the occurrence of a physically defined potential—that is, a potential that signals the cancellation of a readiness potential. Such a hypothetical, physically defined cancellation potential would still leave the awareness of the intention as an epiphenomenal event that accompanies voluntary action that may precede such actions, but that has little or no influence on the actual occurrence of the act.

It might be argued that Libet's research does not really establish that the conscious intention is epiphenomenal. Libet argues that the awareness of an intention always follows the readiness potential. Readiness potentials do not occur in the absence of a subsequent occurrence of a reported awareness of the intention to act. Since the two occur together, it might be argued that the readiness potential has, as a necessary component of its effect, the occurrence of a conscious state. If readiness potentials leading to actions occurred in the absence of a subsequently experienced intention to act, we would be more inclined to think that the awareness of the intention was epiphenomenal, and not critically involved in the occurrence of the action. Although Libet asserts that the awareness of intentions to act always follows the occurrence of readiness potentials, we can think of examples where actions occur in the absence of our intention to act. For example, males may develop penile erections in the absence of an intention to become erect. Such erections may occur at awkward times and be distinctly unwelcome. It might be objected that this example is not really critical since erections are not, in the normal course of events, under voluntary control. However, there are examples of motor actions in the absence of intentions to act that appear to occur for actions that are under voluntary control. I may, for example, be aware of my intention to sit down and write several pages of this manuscript, but I am not normally aware of the way in which I form letters on the page. Thus, many of the motor acts that are subsumed by actions preceded by an intention of which a person is aware may not be preceded by an awareness of the intention to perform each component motor act. Programs of motor actions that are well practiced apparently unfold with little or no sense of conscious direction. Thus actions that are under potential voluntary control may occur in the absence of an awareness of the intention to act. If Libet's results are paradigmatic for all actions, then possibly all actions are preceded by a physical event that is out of awareness and that triggers the occurrence of the act. Of course, this is an extraordinary extrapolation of Libet's results. Whether the particular pattern of results he finds for simple motor acts will generalize to apparently voluntary social actions that extend over relatively long periods of time remains to be ascertained.

Libet's research establishes that, at least for a class of simple voluntary motor acts, the events that trigger an act are physical events that are out of awareness and that precede the awareness of the intention to act. Although his results indicate that subjects are not aware of being aware of events that trigger their acts, they do not indicate that subjects have no awareness of such events. Consider the following thought experiment. Suppose subjects were asked to state the probability that they would perform a simple voluntary motor act some time in the next 200 msec. Would subjects be more likely to judge that they would perform the act in the 300 msec following the onset of a readiness potential prior to their reported awareness of the intention to act than in a time period in which a readiness potential had not previously occurred indicating that the action was imminent? This type of experiment has not been done—partly because it is difficult to determine when a readiness potential has occurred in the absence of a process of data analysis and aggregation that occurs after the experimental data are collected. However, such a study would provide evidence of whether or not subjects are aware of their intention to act even though they are not aware of being aware of such intentions. Since the readiness potential occurs over 300 msec prior to the reported awareness of the intention, it is unlikely that subjects would be aware of their intention to act shortly after the onset of the readiness potential. However, that remains to be demonstrated. In any case it does appear that the subject's awareness of being aware occurs much later than the event that signals the subsequent occurrence of the act.

Social Behavior and the Unconscious

Libet's demonstrations of unconscious influences on actions is confined to a simple motor act. There are also alleged demonstrations of unconscious influences on everyday social actions. Langer (1978) has argued that many social actions are undertaken with minimal attention and awareness of the reasons for one's actions. They are carried out as a result of a learned script that prescribes the appropriate action to be taken with minimal attention or conscious monitoring of behavior. Langer, Blank, and Chanowitz (1978) have performed a study that provides a particularly clear example of such a phenomenon. In their study, subjects who were using a Xerox machine and who were not aware that they were participating in an experiment were approached by confederates of the experimenter who asked the subjects if they could interrupt their copying and use the machine. The confederates indicated either that they wished to make a small number of copies (5) or a relatively large number of copies (20). These requests were accompanied by one of three types of justifications for the use of the machine. The confederates either failed to provide a reason for the interruption, presented a rational (real) reason—I am in a hurry, or provided what Langer and her colleagues considered a "placebic" or nonsensible justification for the interruption—I have to make copies. The percentage of times that the interruption was permitted under each of these six request conditions is presented in Table 6.2. The data indicate that when the request involves a brief interruption (5 copies) the subject is much more likely to respond favorably if the request is accompanied by a reason for the interruption. However, the reason need not be a sensible one or provide any realistic information. However, if the request is for a longer interruption, a subject's willingness to comply with the requested interruption is dependent upon the nature of the reason that is presented to the subject.

Table 6.2

The Proportion of Subjects Who Agreed to Let the Experimenter
Use the Copier[a]

Interruption	Reason		
	No information	Placebic information	Real information
Small (5 copies)	.60	.93	.94
Big (20 copies)	.24	.24	.42

[a]Based on Langer, Blank, and Chanowitz, 1978. (Copyright 1978 by the American Psychological Association. Adapted by permission of the publisher and author.)

If the reason does not appear sensible, then the subject is less likely to comply with the request.

The Langer, Blank, and Chanowitz study suggests that attention to the information presented to the subject and the depth of information processing engaged in by a person is variable in different social and motivational contexts. If compliance with a request involves minimal effort and is, consequently, of little importance to an individual, relatively little attention is paid to the request, and individuals appear to act with relatively little thought given to the reasons for their action. They follow a rather general social script or rule that specifies compliance with requests under conditions where some reason for the request is provided. Where an action requires a more profound commitment, individuals are likely to attend to the request and to consider more thoughtfully the reasons for their actions.

The Langer, Blank, and Chanowitz study does not provide a clear assessment of the level of awareness of the subjects. Presumably subjects were aware of the request and might even be assumed to be aware of the reasons for their actions. That is, the subjects might assert that they complied with the request because the person had asked in an appropriate way or had provided a reason for the interruption. However, the functional equivalence of both forms of request with reasons, under conditions where a small interruption was requested, suggests that subjects were either not aware, or only minimally aware, of the actual content of the reasons given for the interruption. Note that where the request is for a longer interruption (20 copies), the subjects did attend to the reasons given and responded differently to the two reasons. In the absence of a more rigorous assessment of the awareness of subjects in this type of experiment, we cannot be sure of their level of awareness. However, the data do suggest that some differential level of awareness of the reasons for the request did occur under conditions that differed with respect to the importance of compliance to the individual.

Lewicki (1986, Experiment 7.8) has reported evidence for the influence of an allegedly subliminal event on a social action. In his experiment, subjects first encountered a female experimenter who asked them two innocuous questions and then asked them the question "What is your birth order?" The subjects in this experiment were not familiar with the term birth order and responded with a request for information about the question. The female experimenter either responded negatively, in an irritated manner, to the requested clarification of the question or neutrally. In the second phase of the experiment, the subjects were sent to another room and told to choose whichever of two experimenters was free to administer the experiment to them. One of the two experimenters resembled the first experimenter. Both female experimenters were free to administer the experiment and subjects were, therefore, forced to choose the experimenter they wanted to administer the experiment to them. Lewicki found that 80.0% of the subjects in two similar studies who experienced an unpleasant encounter with the first experimenter avoided the experimenter who resembled her. By contrast, 42.9% of the subjects who did not have an unpleasant encounter with the first experimenter avoided the experimenter who resembled her.

In what sense were subjects unaware of the events that influenced their behavior in the Lewicki study. Lewicki presented his subjects with a questionnaire (see Table 6.3) indicating nine possible reasons for the choice of an action. Virtually all of the subjects endorsed item E, "My choice was completely random," as the primary reason for their action. Subjects who had an unpleasant encounter with the first experimenter did not differ in any way in their rank ordering of the reasons for their action from subjects who did not have an unpleasant encounter with the first experimenter. These data suggest that subjects were not aware of the reasons for their actions and did not associate the initial experience with the first experimenter with their subsequent reaction to the new experimenters. The data suggest that subjects had engaged in a process of unconscious inference that influenced their subsequent actions.

Table 6.3

Postexperimental Questionnaire[a]

A. One of them looked slightly more friendly.

B. One of them was slightly similar to a certain person I know and I like.

C. One of them was slightly similar to a certain person I know and I dislike.

D. I usually choose left (or right) in cases like that.

E. My choice was completely random.

F. One of them was slightly similar to the first experimenter, whom I liked.

G. One of them was slightly similar to the first experimenter, whom I disliked.

H. One of the experimenters looked at me when I entered the room.

I. Other.

---

[a]Based on Lewicki, 1986.

The assessment of the subject's state of awareness in the Lewicki study leaves several issues regarding awareness of the critical event unresolved. Among them are the following: Did subjects classify their intial experiences with the first experimenter as unpleasant? Were subjects aware of the resemblance between the first experimenter and one of the two experimenters in the second phase of the study? If subjects who had an unpleasant encounter with the first experimenter were asked to choose which of the two experimenters they would be likely to find unpleasant, would they select the experimenter who resembled the first experimenter with greater than chance probability? The Lewicki study does not provide a definitive assessment of the subject's level of awareness of the events that influence their actions. The study does indicate that subjects were not aware of why they acted as they did—although if presented with forced-choice alternatives, they might be aware of a slight negative reaction to one of the two experimenters without necessarily knowing why they had experienced that affect. Alternatively, it is possible that they were not even aware of the negative reaction that apparently controlled their response.

Nisbett and Wilson (1977) have presented a comprehensive analysis of the extent to which human beings understand the reasons for their actions. They argue that people rarely know why they act as they do. For example, they discussed research on bystander interventions in which each subject was provided with an opportunity to assist someone in distress. Studies of this phenomenon by Latané and Darley (1970) have indicated that the probability that one will assist someone in distress decreases as a function of the number of other people available to help the distressed person. However, when subjects who have participated in these studies are interviewed at the conclusion of the study and asked to explain the reasons for their decisions to assist the distressed persons, they almost never report that their decisions were influenced by the number of other people who could potentially have assisted the distressed persons. Moreover, when presented with this explanation, they usually vigorously denied that this was an appropriate explanation of their behavior. Yet, clearly, it must be the appropriate explanation for some of the subjects because the independent manipulation of the variable influences the outcome of the experiment. Nisbett and Wilson argue that the discrepancy between the true reasons for social actions and the reasons that are reported by subjects is endemic. They argue that subjects rarely know why they do what they do.

Nisbett and Wilson's paper presents an original account of a series of studies that purport to demonstrate the influence of thought processes on human action. They argue that in many situations individuals are unaware of the thought processes that influence their behavior. For example, they discuss research dealing with cognitive dissonance. According to dissonance theory, individuals are motivated to eliminate inconsistencies in their beliefs. Thus, if a person is aware that he or she smokes and also believes that smoking is harmful, the person is in a state of dissonance that could be eliminated by changing his or her beliefs (see

Festinger, 1957). Zimbardo (1969) reported the results of a series of studies dealing with the application of dissonance theory to motivation. In one of these studies dealing with the application of dissonance theory to motivation. In one of these studies Zimbardo, Cohen, Weisenberg, Dworkin, and Firestone (1969) attempted to manipulate pain induced by electric shock. In this experiment subjects who had received a series of shocks were given an opportunity to remain in the experiment. Subjects in a low-dissonance condition were given what was assumed to be adequate reasons to continue in the experiment—they were well paid for their services, and they were told that the results of the experiment were important. The decision to continue to participate in the experiment, even though it was assumed to involve additional pain, was not expected to create a state of high dissonance since the subject's knowledge that he or she had agreed to continue to participate would be balanced by his or her knowledge that there were valid reasons for participation. Subjects assigned to a high-dissonance condition were not provided with persuasive reasons for their continued participation in the experiment. Thus, their knowledge that they had agreed to continue to participate led to a state of dissonance. Zimbardo et al. reasoned that subjects could eliminate their dissonance if they did not find the shocks painful. The prediction in this and related studies is that subjects in a high-dissonance condition who are not given persuasive reasons to endure unpleasant motivational experiences are likely to reduce dissonance by decreasing the unpleasant motivational state.

Using a variety of different measures, Zimbardo was able to demonstrate that subjects assigned to high-dissonance conditions did eliminate their unpleasant motivational experiences. These results apparently demonstrate that reasoning and thought processes can change motivation. Indeed, Zimbardo entitled his book *Cognitive Control of Motivation*. Although thought processes are invoked as explanations of the results of these and related experiments, little attention has been given to the nature of thought processes whose occurrence serves as a putative explanation of the phenomenon of cognitive control of motivation. Nisbett and Wilson analyzed dissonance studies and noted three aspects of the results that had not been previously discussed. First, they mentioned that subjects had not been able to reproduce the pattern of reasoning they had allegedly engaged in when questioned in postexperimental interviews. Indeed, the subjects in these experiments denied that the thought processes invoked by dissonance theory in an attempt to explain this type of behavior did actually explain their own behavior. Second, Nisbett and Wilson emphasized the results of a series of studies in which behavioral and/or psychophysiological indices of changes in the level of motivation were obtained. In addition, verbal reports about the level of motivation experienced by the subjects were given. For example, in the Zimbardo et al. experiment, data on a learning task where pain and electrical shock had interfered with learning were obtained, as well as several different psychophysiological indices of the response to pain. Also, subjects were asked to rate the level of pain they had experienced in response to the shocks they had received. Nisbett and Wilson's survey of this and other related studies showed that the magnitude of the decrease in indices of motivational change was larger for non verbal indices than for verbal indices. They found in several studies that there were reductions in behavioral and physiological indices of motivation in the high-dissonance condition, but there were no changes in verbal reports about motivation. Thus, for example, they classified the Zimbardo et al. study of pain as one in which there were significant differences between the high- and low-dissonance groups, indicating a reduction in pain, on several psycho-physiological and behavioral indices, for subjects assigned to the high-dissonance condition but no significant differences between the dissonance groups verbal reports of the painfulness of the electric shocks. This finding is somewhat counterintuitive since the elimination of pain by a process of cognitive manipulation was more clearly manifest on nonverbal than on verbal responses. Third, Nisbett and Wilson reported that the correlation between changes in verbal and non verbal indices of motivational states tends to be close to zero in these experiments. Thus, the processes leading to a change in motivational states by cognitive manipulations appear to exert an independent influence on behavioral and verbal manifestations of the state.

Nisbett and Wilson used these three aspects of the data obtained in studies involving the cognitive manipulation of motivational states to reach the conclusion that individuals are not aware of the thought processes that they are engaged in in situations in which their behavior and actions are determined by reasoning. It is as if subjects were engaged in unconscious thoughts that changed their behaviors.

The conclusions reached by Nisbett and Wilson are controversial (see Ericcson and Simon, 1980; Quattrone, 1985; Smith and Miller, 1978). In his critique of the Nisbett and Wilson paper, Quattrone argued that there is a large body of attributional and dissonance studies that rely on verbal-report dependent variables. Thus, he asserts that it is not the case that dissonance-induced changes in psychological states cannot be indexed by changes in verbal reports. Moreover, Quattrone takes issue with Nisbett and Wilson's interpretation of the Zimbardo et al. study, and other related studies, indicating that changes in the behavioral indices of psychological states occur in the absence of changes in verbal reports. He indicates that such results are either anomalous, attributable to inappropriate verbal-report indices, reflect effects of behavioral dependent variables on subsequent measures of verbal reports that, in effect, contaminate the verbal reports, or are based on a failure to thoroughly examine the details of the quantitative changes in both sets of measures. In this connection Quattrone notes that in the Zimbardo et al. study the subjects in the high-dissonance condition do exhibit reductions in their verbal reports of pain relative to the subjects in the low-dissonance condition. However, the changes are not quite statistically significant at the conventional .05 level. The fact that the changes in several behavioral indices are statistically different does not establish that the difference between high- and low-dissonance groups between behavioral and verbal indices is statistically significant. The existence of a statistically significant difference and the absence of a statistically significant difference do not imply that the difference between the differences is statistically different.

In order to understand the import of the Zimbardo et al. study for a resolution of the issues addressed by Quattrone, and Nisbett and Wilson, it will be necessary to examine their data more carefully. Table 6.4 presents the actual verbal report data obtained in the Zimbardo et al. study. An examination of the data reported in Table 6.4 does indicate, in agreement with Quattrone, that there is some evidence that subjects in the high-dissonance group do exhibit larger decreases in their reported pain than subjects in the low-dissonance group (−9 vs. −2). What is not discussed by Quattrone, or Nisbett and Wilson, is the difference in magnitude of reduction of verbal reports exhibited by subjects in the high-dissonance group and subjects in the high-moderate control group who are exposed to shocks of the same intensity during the pretest period and are then exposed to shocks of lower intensity during the posttest period in the absence of an intervening choice to continue in the experiment. Not surprisingly, the control subjects respond to the reduction in the intensity of the shocks they experience by reporting that they have lower levels of pain. Also, the reduction in pain reported by subjects in the control group is clearly larger in magnitude than the reduction in pain reported by subjects in the high-dissonance group (−26 vs. −9).

Although the reduction in magnitude of reported pain is larger in the high-moderate control group than in the high-dissonance group, there is little or no difference between these groups on several behavioral indices of pain. These two groups exhibit approximately equal magnitudes of change in learning tasks in which pain tends to increase the number of trials to criterion and in physiological

Table 6.4

Mean Perceived Pain and Physical Shock Level of Sample Shocks[a]

Group	Mean shock		Perceived pain		
	N[b]	Volts	Precommitment	Postcommitment	Difference
Control:					
High–moderate	15	45–22	46	20	−26
High–high	15	44	50	47	−3
Dissonance:					
Low	20	38	49	47	−2
High	20	49	46	37	−9

[a]Based on Zimbardo et al., 1969.

[b]N = Number of trials.

indices of pain. These results indicate that subjects in the high-dissonance condition exhibit changes in verbal reports that are clearly of smaller magnitude than those of subjects in the high-moderate control group who experience shocks of lower intensity. However, the behavioral indices of pain support the inference that the magnitude of pain present is the same in subjects in the high-dissonance condition and in the high–moderate control group.

Quattrone has an additional criticism of the Nisbett and Wilson analysis of the Zimbardo et al. experiment. He claims that the analysis is logically untenable because of the ambiguity of the relationship between the experience of pain and the behavioral manifestations of pain. He argues as follows:

> When GSR (galvanic skin response) data are used to infer an individual's experienced pain, it is not assumed that the experience of pain directly mediated or caused the GSR. . . . Because pain does not directly mediate the GSR, why should differences in inferred pain, produced by manipulations of choice and justification, be expected to lead to differences in the GSR? In other words, if one subscribed to the theory that dogs bark before an earthquake, can a city be razed by exciting its kennels? . . . Yet a choice and justification manipulation designed to affect inferred pain (analogous to "exciting the kennels") was hypothesized and found to affect the GSR (analagous to "razing a city"; Zimbardo, Cohen, Weisenberg, Dworkin, & Firestone, 1969), and it is nothing more than pretense to claim to understand how the effect was obtained. (Quattrone, 1985, 20–21)

Quattrone's critique rests on the assumption that the psychological state that was manipulated in the Zimbardo et al. experiment must be a phenomenal state because the putative explanation of the change in the state of pain involves an appeal to processes of thought that could occur phenomenally. However, the Nisbett and Wilson analysis directly challenges the centrality of phenomenal states in the causal network surrounding this type of experiment. In effect, Quattrone's argument attacks a straw man. It is he who assumes that the state of pain that must be influenced by dissonance manipulations is the experience of pain. A more plausible interpretation of the results of this experiment that is more in line with Nisbett and Wilson's (1977) position is that the dissonance manipulation does not influence the experience of pain but influences a pain state whose meaning is not isomorphic with or exhausted by its phenomenal representations. Moreover, there is ample empirical justification, in part developed in the original Zimbardo et al. report, for the particular behavioral manifestations of the state of pain used as dependent variables in their experiment. One can interpret the results of their experiment by arguing that the dissonance manipulations induced a pattern of reasoning in subjects that they were not aware of that, in turn, produced a change in the level of pain that subjects were not aware of, that, in turn, led to a series of diverse changes in the behavioral manifestations of pain. This analysis of the Zimbardo et al. study supports a general conclusion that the processes of cognitive reasoning that influence various psychological states that are capable of influencing human action appear to exist outside of conscious awareness.

Psychoanalysis and the Unconscious

Evidence in support of unconscious influences on behavior is at least super-ficially congruent with psychoanalytic explanations that emphasize the influence of unconscious processes on human action. None of the studies considered has been conducted to test psychoanalytic hypotheses, nor have we considered the bearing of psychoanalytic thinking on the research we have discussed. I have not considered the voluminous psychoanalytic writings on unconscious phenomena; in part, because most of this literature assumes the existence of unconscious phenomena without providing direct empirical support for the existence of such phenomena. In most Freudian interpretations of various symptoms, dreams, and other assumed behavioral manifestations of the unconscious, the existence of unconscious influences is given the status of an unquestioned axiom. In psycho-analytic explanations, one assumes that unconscious influences exist and then uses this assumption to explain the various phenomena under investigation. The status of the unconscious itself is rarely the subject of direct investigation or test. Virtually the only direct evidence for the influence of unconscious processes on behavior discussed by Freud was his observation of hypnotic phenomena (Freud, 1915). Freud believed that hypnosis permitted direct access to unconscious states. He noted that subjects given posthypnotic suggestions to behave in partic-ular ways would, in their waking states, act in response to those suggestions without any awareness of the reasons for their actions. He believed that such demonstrations provided direct evidence for the existence of unconscious influ-ences on human behavior.

    The interpretation of the meaning of hypnosis and its bearing on the existence of unconscious influences on behavior has been the subject of intense debate. Theorists, such as Barber, Sarbin, and Spanos, have argued that the behavior of subjects under hypnosis is to be understood in terms of ordinary social psycho-logical principles essentially involving an attempt to cope with the various de-mand characteristics of the hypnosis. (see, for example, Barber, 1969, 1979; Sarbin, 1950; Sarbin and Coe, 1972; Spanos, 1986). Other theorists have argued that hypnosis induces a special state that provides direct eivdence for the exis-tence of special psychological processes that may provide evidence for uncon-scious processes or special experiences not normally accessible to our everyday conscious life (see, for example, Hilgard, 1977, 1979; Orne, 1959, 1979). It is beyond the scope of this book to consider this literature in detail. I shall briefly consider research on the "hidden observer" and hypnotic analgesia to illustrate current differences in interpretation of hypnotic phenomena and also to consider Hilgard's theory of dissociation and its bearing on the existence of unconscious influences on behavior. Hilgard has presented a dissociation theory of hypnosis. According to him, subjects who are "highly hypnotizable" (from 5 to 15% of the population) are capable of undergoing a dissociative experience in hypnosis in which they are able to relegate certain experiences to an unconscious part of the mind. The dissociated experiences coexist with a conscious part of the mind that has no direct access to the unconscious dissociated realm of experience. Thus, to him, hypnotic suggestions, given to the subset of individuals capable of being deeply hypnotized, create a split, or dissociated, consciousness that mimics the existence of conscious and unconscious processes within individuals in ordinary waking states. Hilgard has used his theory of dissociation to explain findings related to hypnotically induced analgesia. The most dramatic evidence in favor of this theory is presented in studies of the "hidden observer" (Hilgard, Morgan, and McDonald, 1975). In these studies, subjects are presented with painful stimuli, and they are told that a "hidden part" of themselves will remain aware of the pain, but that they will not experience the pain in their hypnotized mental state. They are further informed that the hypnotist will be capable of contacting their hidden or unconscious state. Subjects exposed to these instructions usually report relatively complete analgesia in response to the pain stimulus. In addition, they also indicate when the hidden or unconscious observer is queried that they are in fact in pain.

Spanos (1986) has presented a comprehensive review of this and related research and has offered a social–psychological analysis of these phenomena. He argues that subjects' performances in these studies are to be understood in terms of their responses to the various suggestions they received in the instructions provided to them. Good hypnotic subjects are, virtually by definition, subjects who are good at accepting the instructions of the experimenter or hypnotist. In Hilgard's experiments, subjects are told that they will be unaware of pain and that there is another, hidden part of themselves that will be aware of the pain. When queried, subjects report experiences that are precisely congruent with the implicit or explicit instructions they have received. Spanos and Hewitt (1980) obtained results that were congruent with this theoretical analysis. They presented hidden observer instructions to their hypnotic subjects that were similar to those used by Hilgard. A second group of hypnotic subjects was told that their hidden observer was so deeply hidden or suppressed that it would experience a level of pain that was even lower than that experienced by ordinary consciousness during the hypnotically induced analgesia. They found that subjects assigned to this latter condition reported lower hidden pain than overt pain, and subjects assigned to the former condition reported higher pain levels when their hidden observer was contacted. These results suggest that the dissociation or divided consciousness reported by subjects in the hidden observer experiments is, in effect, created by the subject's attempts to comply with the demands created by the instructions that were given by the hypnotist.

Spanos indicates that this analysis does not imply that subjects are faking or distorting their reports of a dual level of experience. He suggests that subjects might use devices, such as a shift of attention to the pain stimulus, to create different levels of awareness of the pain. Shifting levels of pain experienced then lead the subject to believe, in agreement with the suggestions provided by the hypnotist, that he or she does in fact have a dual level of consciousness.

This brief analysis of the controversy surrounding hypnotic experiences was undertaken in order to demonstrate a problematic status with respect to demonstrations of the influence of unconscious processes on behavior.

Is there any direct evidence of unconscious processes that is congruent with psychoanalytic hypotheses? Silverman (1976, 1983; Silverman and Weinberger, 1985) and his colleagues and students have presented the most extensive and rigorous attempt to test hypotheses derived from psychoanalytic theory in laboratory settings. The research reported by Silverman and his students, as well as the many independent attempts to replicate and extend these findings, could well be the subject of a chapter or a book in its own right. Therefore, I do not propose to present a comprehensive review of this research. Rather, I shall sketch the aims of the research program, present some of the results of representative studies, and attempt to provide an evaluation of this body of research.

Silverman has used subliminal stimulus presentations as a way to circumvent conscious defense processes and directly arouse unconscious processes. He views the subliminal character of the stimuli as fundamental to demonstrating their subsequent influence. Thus, for him, supraliminal stimuli do not directly influence unconscious processes and their influences are qualitatively different from those of subliminal stimuli. Subliminal stimuli may be used either to arouse unconscious conflicts or to ameliorate them. In both cases, Silverman claims that appropriately selected subliminal stimuli are capable of changing the behavior of individuals.

Silverman attempted to create unconscious conflicts in stutterers and male homosexuals. Using hypotheses derived from psychoanalytic theory, Silverman, Bronstein, and Mendelsohn (1976) suggest that stutterers are likely to have conflicts about anality. Male homosexuals are likely to have Oedipal conflicts. On the basis of these assumptions, Silverman et al. reason that the presentation of subliminal stimuli that are designed to arouse Oedipal conflicts will increase homosexual tendencies among male homosexuals and that the presentation to stutterers of subliminal material designed to arouse conflicts about anality will increase stuttering behavior. If the same stimuli are presented supraliminally, they would not lead to behavioral change. In addition, Silverman et al. argue that the effects of the subliminal stimuli are dependent upon the use of stimuli that are matched to the appropriate unconscious conflicts of different groups of individuals. Thus, the presentation of subliminal stimuli designed to arouse Oedipal conflicts in individuals who are stutterers would not be expected to increase stuttering behavior.

Silverman et al. obtained data in support of these assumptions in a series of studies in which stutterers and male homosexuals were exposed to tachistoscopically presented stimuli that they could not discriminate with greater than chance accuracy. In order to arouse anal conflicts, they presented a picture of a dog defecating with the words, "go shit" written on the stimulus. In order to arouse Oedipal conflicts, they presented a somewhat brooding picture of an older woman embracing a younger man with the words "fuck Mommy" superimposed on the stimulus. In order to assess the behavioral effects of these subliminal presentations, they had observers, who were unaware of the stimuli being presented, rate the subjects stuttering behavior. In order to observe changes in homosexual tendencies, they presented their male homosexuals with pictures of male nudes and asked them to rate the attractiveness of the individuals pictured. They found that homosexuals rated male nudes as more attractive after they were presented with subliminal stimuli designed to arouse Oedipal conflicts. Subliminal stimuli designed to arouse anal conflicts did not have an equivalent effect on subjects' behaviors. Stutterers exposed to subliminal stimuli that were designed to arouse anal conflicts exhibited an increase in stuttering. Subliminal stimuli designed to arouse Oedipal conflicts did not have comparable effects on stutterers.

Silverman has also used subliminal stimulus presentations to reduce unconscious conflicts and, thus, change behavior. In one set of studies he presented the subliminal stimulus, "It's OK to beat Dad", to college students (Silverman, Ross, Adler, and Lustig, 1980). He assumed that many males suffer from unconscious conflicts about performing better than their fathers. If this stimulus is capable of ameliorating the conflict, then individuals exposed to the stimulus would exhibit improved performance in competitive situations where the unconscious conflict might have impeded their performance. Silverman et al. used a dart-throwing game to demonstrate that individuals who received subliminal presentations of the stimulus, "It's OK to beat Dad," did in fact perform better in a dart-throwing task than individuals who received a variety of neutral stimuli.

Silverman and his associates have also studied subliminal presentations of the stimuli, "Mommy and I are one," (see Silverman and Weinberger, 1985). Silverman assumes that this stimulus is capable of arousing a feeling of a child-like symbiotic relationship with mother that serves to comfort individuals and to ameliorate unconscious conflicts and feelings of anxiety. Silverman and Weinberger have summarized a series of studies demonstrating that the subliminal presentations of the "Mommy and I are one" stimulus has changed behavior in a variety of situations. For example, it has been used to decrease phobic behaviors, to enhance the effectiveness of behavior therapy treatments, to reduce weight, and to change the behavior of schizophrenics.

The studies performed by Silverman and his colleagues constitute a body of evidence that provide direct empirical support for propositions that are central to psychoanalytic theory. If these data are accepted at face value, they imply that subliminal stimuli influence behavior in qualitatively different ways than supraliminal stimuli. In addition, these data suggest that unconscious conflicts do exert an influence on behavior. Moreover, they provide support for a conception of the contents of unconscious conflicts that are congruent with those specified by psychoanalytic theory.

In order to evaluate these conclusions, it will be necessary to consider a subset of the available data bearing on these issues in greater detail. We shall consider the following issues: (1) Are the stimuli used by Silverman in his studies out of awareness? (2) Are the effects of these stimuli different when they are presented subliminally and supraliminally? (3) Are the results of the studies conducted by Silverman and his associates in accord with the hypotheses that are tested? and (4) Are the findings replicable?

Let us consider the issue of the subliminality of the stimuli used in these studies. Silverman and his colleagues use tachistoscopic presentations to ensure very rapid stimulus presentations that serve to degrade the stimuli that are presented. In many of these studies, subjects are presented with forced-choice discrimination tasks requiring them to distinguish between a critical stimulus and a control stimulus not designed to arouse or alleviate unconscious conflicts. The subjects typically are not able with greater than chance accuracy to distinguish between the stimuli in trials that typically extend for 20 trials. Thus, while the number of trials is not sufficient to rule out with absolute certainty the possibility that subjects may, on occasion, have some extremely minimal awareness of the stimuli and the frequent replications over subjects and over studies of at, or near, chance performance on forced-choice discrimination tests of these stimuli imply that the degree of awareness of the contents of these stimuli is at, or close to, zero in these experiments. Thus, there is little doubt that Silverman's studies involve subliminal stimulus presentations that are, for all practical purposes, out of awareness.

Are the behavioral effects of the stimuli used by Silverman contingent on their subliminal state? In most of the studies, Silverman does not contrast a supraliminal with a subliminal presentation. However, he has, on occasion, made such comparisons and reported that stimuli do not influence behavior in the same ways when they are presented subliminally and supraliminally. In one of the studies relevant to this issue, Silverman and Spiro (1968) contrasted a subliminal and a supraliminal presentation of a stimulus designed to arouse unconscious conflicts in schizophrenic patients. The picture presented was that of a charging lion with bared teeth. The subliminal status of the stimulus was ascertained by the subject's inability to discriminate between different stimuli with better than chance accuracy under the viewing conditions used in the experiment. An additional stimulus condition was used in the experiment—the presentation of the stimulus supraliminally with the additional requirement that subjects verbally describe the stimulus. Following exposure to the stimuli, the experimenters obtained a number of measures of the psychopathological state of their subjects. Among the indices of psychopathological states that they observed were word-associate behavior, pathological overt behaviors, reports of pathological body experiences, and accuracy of story recall. The subjects exposed to the subliminal

Table 6.5

Changes in Pathology in Schizophrenics Following Subliminal and Supraliminal
Stimulus Presentations[a]

Measures	Subliminal	Supraliminal	Supraliminal & vocalization
Word association pathology	+2.09	−.28	2.12
Story recall	1.47	−1.00	.47
Pathological body experience	2.15	2.38	1.88
Pathological overt behavior	2.90	1.41	2.94
Faces test projection	.57	1.28	1.57
Story recall accuracy[b]	−1.14	−.21	−5.43

[a]Based on Silverman and Spiro, 1968.
[b]For this measure, lower scores indicate higher pathology.

stimulus tended to exhibit increases in psychopathology relative to the subjects
exposed to the supraliminal stimulus on several indices of psychopathology (see
Table 6.5). An examination of Table 6.5 indicates that subjects, who were
exposed to a supraliminal stimulus with the requirement that they verbally describe the stimulus, exhibited the same magnitude of increase in psychopathology as they did under conditions in which they were exposed to the stimuli
subliminally.

The Silverman and Spiro study was designed to demonstrate the importance
of unconscious conflicts on behavior. Paradoxically, it demonstrates that the
influence of unconscious states is parallel to the influence of conscious states if
the conscious states are made salient. Evidently, under conditions of supra-
liminal-stimulus presentation without instructions to vocalize, the schizophrenic
subjects simply ignore, or do not attend to, the stimulus.

These data suggest that the subliminal status of the stimulus is not a necessary
condition for its ability to arouse conflict. Silverman has not used the procedure
of having subjects verbally describe the supraliminal stimulus presented to them
in other studies. Therefore, it is difficult to know whether this phenomenon is or
is not pervasive.

Are the results obtained in Silverman's research in agreement with theoretical
expectations? A close examination of the data obtained in Silverman's research
indicates that the results are not invariably, completely consistent, and in agreement with theoretical expectations. Many of the published studies have small
samples, use dubious statistics, and often contain data that provide only partial
support for the hypotheses under investigation. It should also be noted that there
are also several studies providing clear-cut support for the hypotheses under
investigation.

The assertions about these studies summarized above can be exemplified by a
consideration of the details of specific studies.

Among the studies in this body of literature that use somewhat dubious statistical procedures are a study by Silverman, Frank, and Dachinger (1974) and a study by Ariam and Siller (1982). Silverman, Frank, and Dachinger studied subjects who exhibited phobic responses to bugs. They presented subjects with one of two subliminal stimuli, "Mommy and I are one," or "People are walking." The subjects were then tested for their level of phobic response to bugs. Ratings of phobic behavior were made by observers who were unaware of the stimuli presented to the subjects. They noted actual phobic behaviors, ratings of anxiety, and overall levels of phobic behavior. They reported that subjects who were presented with the subliminal stimulus, "Mommy and I are one," exhibited less phobic behavior on some of their measures. However, the results were statistically significant at the conventional .05 level only if a one-tailed test of significance was used. It is usually considered that one-tailed tests are not legitimate. I do not wish to prevent a general discussion of the legitimacy of one-tailed tests in this manuscript. I do wish to make a more general point. The study exemplifies a pattern of statistical analysis and data analysis in this body of research that occasionally fails to meet the most rigorous standards of inference used in psychology.

Ariam and Siller (1982) used two different Hebrew versions of the subliminal stimulus, "Mommy and I are one," and two control stimuli, "My teacher and I are one," and "People are walking in the street," in a study performed with Israeli school children. They wished to discover whether or not the subliminal stimuli designed to alleviate unconscious conflicts would improve academic performance. They obtained data for their four groups of subjects on three math exams obtained after 2, 4, or 6 weeks of subliminal presentations of stimuli. In the standard statistical analysis that is suggested by the design of this experiment, one would use an analysis of variance to determine whether or not the performance averaged over all three tests differed among the four groups. This test indicated that, when averaged over the three tests, the groups were not significantly different. Ariam and Siller argue that the benefits of subliminal stimuli might be more apparent as the treatment extends through time. This line of reasoning could be tested by using an analysis of variance test for the significance of the Group X Test-occasion interaction. The expected result would be one in which the groups presented with the critical stimuli would exhibit increased superiority over the other groups on each succeeding test. The data did in fact exhibit this expected pattern of results, but the relevant interaction of groups by test occasions was not statistically significant. Arian and Siller did report that the groups presented with the critical stimuli did, in point of fact, score significantly higher on the last exam than the other two groups. This result is theoretically coherent, but it should be realized that the statistical procedure is actually a posthoc test and that the appropriate direct tests of the hypotheses were not statistically significant. Again, the statistical procedures used are less than optimally rigorous.

Table 6.6

Mean Grades on Examinations for Groups Exposed to Subliminal Messages[a]

Group	Exams			
	First	Midterm	Final	Follow-up
Mommy and I are one	75.95	88.95	90.40	82.00
Prof and I are one	72.85	86.00	88.35	82.10
Control	72.70	83.05	82.70	74.35

[a]Based on Parker (1982). (Copyright 1982 by the American Psychological Association. Adapted by permission of the publisher and author.)

Among the studies in which the pattern of results is not precisely as expected are studies by Parker (1982) and by Linehan and O'Toole (1982). Parker presented groups of law students with one of three subliminal stimuli, "Mommy and I are one," "Prof and I are one," and "People are walking." These students were given four exams. Table 6.6 presents the results obtained by Parker. Note that both the groups presented with the stimuli referring to "oneness" obtained higher scores on the final and follow-up exam than subjects assigned to the control group who received the control stimulus, "People are walking." These data are not in accord with the psychoanalytic reasoning that led Silverman to attribute particular emotive significance to the stimulus, "Mommy and I are one."

Linehan and O'Toole (1982) subliminally presented the stimuli, "Mommy and I are one," and "People are walking," to groups of women in counseling. They obtained ratings of the self-disclosure behavior of their subjects after 0, 4, and 8 weeks of treatment. Table 6.7 presents their results. Note that subjects exposed to the subliminal stimulus, "Mommy and I are one," exhibited more

Table 6.7

Mean Subject Self-disclosure as a Function of Counselor
Self-disclosures and Subliminal Exposure[a]

Group	Number of counselor self-disclosures for each treatment period (weeks)		
	0	4	8
Subliminal	14.89	8.11	12.89
Control	8.94	8.33	7.89

[a]Based on Linehan and O'Toole (1982). (Copyright 1982 by the American Psychological Association. Adapted by permission of the publisher and author.)

self-disclosure than subjects exposed to the subliminal stimulus, "People are walking," at the beginning of the counseling sessions and after 8 weeks of counseling. However, after 4 weeks of counseling there were no differences in self-disclosures. There is no obvious explanation for these results. The results of the Parker, and Linehan and O'Toole studies both indicate that the pattern of results obtained in studies designed to test hypotheses derived from Silverman's theoretical analyses are not invariably in accord with theoretical predictions.

I have selected a very small subset of the available studies relating to Silverman's theories that for one reason or another do not provide clear-cut support for his theories. I do not wish to leave the impression that all members of the total set of studies are similarly problematic. There are studies that appear to provide clear support for Silverman's theories. For example, Bryant-Tuckett and Silverman (1984) studied the effect of subliminal presentations of "Mommy and I are one" and "people are walking" on the academic performance of a group of emotionally disturbed students. They found that the students given subliminal presentations of "Mommy and I are one" performed better on a math test than students given the subliminal stimulus "people are walking."

Silverman, Martin, Ungaro, and Mendelsohn (1978) studied the effects of subliminal presentation of the same stimuli on women in a weight-reduction program. They found in the first study that women presented with the stimulus, "Mommy and I are one," had lower weight at a follow-up exam after the end of treatment. Thus, they were able to maintain their weight loss. Then they designed a replication experiment and obtained the same results. At the end of 24 weeks after treatment, women presented with the subliminal stimulus, "Mommy and I are one," weighed 15 pounds less than their initial weight, and women presented with the subliminal stimulus, "People are walking," weighed 6 pounds less than their pretreatment weight. These differences were significantly different. The Bryant-Tucker and Silverman study, and the Silverman et al. study described above both indicate that there are studies in the literature that provide clear support for Silverman's theories.

The evaluation of Silverman's research is further complicated by the existence of several reported failures to replicate his findings in research that appears to be carefully conducted. For example, Oliver and Burkham (1982) failed to replicate the results obtained by Nissenfield (1979) in a study in which he presented subliminal stimuli including the "Mommy and I are one" stimulus to female depressive patients. Oliver and Burkham failed to find any evidence of the amelioration of depressive symptoms on any of several indices of depressive behavior including measures, such as an adjective checklist of mood, the contents of a thematic apperception test, measures of self-esteem, and measures of nonverbal behavior presumed to be reflective of depression.

Condon and Allen (1980) failed to replicate results obtained by Silverman,

Frank, and Dachinger (1974) in their study of the effects of subliminal stimulus presentations of "Mommy and I are one" to students who were presumed to be bug phobic. Condon and Allen's study was, if anything, more carefully conducted than the Silverman et al. (1974) study that was replicated. They demonstrated that the observations of the phobic responses of their subjects were reliable, that is, different observers agreed in their ratings. They used change-score measures to index differences in response to the phobic situation before and after treatment, and they include a psychophysiological measure of response to the phobic situation. Despite the use of these methodological refinements, they found no evidence of a change as a result of being exposed to different subliminal stimuli. In addition, the magnitude of behavioral change obtained was unrelated to the number of subliminal presentations of the stimulus.

Heilbrun (1980) has reported a failure to replicate results obtained by Silverman et al. (1980). Silverman et al. found that the subliminal presentation of the stimulus, "Beating Dad is OK," improved the performance of college students in a dart-throwing experiment. In their original report of their research, Silverman et al. indicate that they were able to obtain this result in several independent studies. However, Heilbrun reported that he was unable to obtain this effect in three separate attempts to replicate these results including efforts on his part to match the conditions of the original studies as carefully as possible.

The reports of the failure to replicate reported findings makes the evaluation of Silverman's research difficult. Many of the studies cited by Silverman as supporting his research are unpublished doctoral dissertations or were performed by Silverman and his associates and students. Silverman and Weinberger (1985) discussed the issue of the replicability of Silverman's findings by independent investigators. They reported that an unpublished meta-analysis aggregating the results of all of the studies conducted that are germane to Silverman's psychoanalytically based research programs indicates that the magnitude of effects obtained by independent investigators in this research is approximately equivalent to the magnitude of effects obtained by Silverman and his students and associates. These findings suggest that the findings obtained by Silverman and his colleagues and students are similar to those obtained by independent investigators. Since the meta-analysis on which this conclusion is based has not, as far as I know, been published, it is difficult to evaluate the conclusions reached in the analysis. Even if one grants that Silverman's findings are not dramatically different from those obtained by independent investigators, the existence of several reported nonreplications is disturbing. At the very least, these results suggest that the phenomena obtained by Silverman are contingent upon the existence of variables that are not reported or noted in the original research reports. Whether such variables include subtle aspects of the relationship between the experimenter and his or her subjects, the social or physical atmosphere of the experimental context, or any of an indefinitely large number of possible critical variables that may expand our imaginative resources even to contemplate remains to be determined.

In an additional discussion of the replicability issue, Silverman (1985) reported that approximately 20% of the time his results do not replicate. Thus, in his own view, the occasional reported failure to replicate his findings does not indicate that studies demonstrating subliminal activation effects germane to psychoanalytic theory are not replicable.

In his commentary on reported failures to replicate his work, he specifically discussed two reported failures to replicate—Oliver and Burkham's (1982) failure to replicate results obtained by Nissenfeld (1979), and a study of Porterfield and Golding (1985) who failed to replicate research findings indicating that aggressive subliminal stimuli presented to schizophrenics increase schizophrenic symptoms (see Silverman and Spiro, 1968). With respect to Oliver and Burkham's research, he noted that Nissenfeld's research provided only tentative support for the notion that the subliminal presentation of the stimulus, "Mommy and I are one," influenced the level of depression in women. In addition, he reported that Dauber (1984) also failed to find clear cut evidence of an influence of this stimulus on the level of depression of college women. Silverman also indicated that this stimulus is less effective for women than for men. In effect, Silverman has modified his theory, and he now indicates that the subliminal stimulus, "Mommy and I are one," has little or no effect on female depressives. Thus, Oliver and Burkham's results are not in fundamental disagreement with other results in the literature.

Silverman also discussed Porterfield and Golding's (1985) failure to find an effect of subliminal presentations of the stimulus. "Tiger eats persons," on a variety of measures of the cognitive processes of schizophrenia. Silverman revealed that Porterfield and Golding did not include a composite measure of the behavior of schizophrenics that had been used in previous research that indicated that subliminal aggressive stimuli increased pathological behavior in schizophrenics. Silverman implied that his hypothesis about the subliminal presentation of aggressive stimuli to schizophrenics is that such presentations will increase pathologies of thought *or* behavior in schizophrenics. Since Porterfield and Golding did not include the composite behavioral measure used in previous research, Silverman asserted that their results constitute neither a failure to replicate nor a critical test of Silverman's hypothesis about the effects of the presentation of subliminal aggressive stimuli to schizophrenics. With reference to the latter claim, Silverman's arguments seem a bit strained. Silverman and Spiro did find that the presentation of subliminal aggresive stimuli led to an increase in several cognitive measures of psychopathology in schizophrenics. Porterfield and Golding's failure to include a behavioral measure appears to support Silverman's assertion that they did not conduct an exact replication of earlier research. However, they certainly failed to replicate aspects of previously reported research.

Silverman's attempts to critically evaluate reported failures to replicate still leaves unexplained repeated reports of failures to replicate his results in the literature. The appeal to post hoc changes in his theory will not, for example, explain the recent failure to replicate his reports of the effects of subliminal presentations of the stimuli, "Beating Dad is Wrong," and "Beating Dad is OK," on the behavior of subjects in a dart-throwing task reported by Fisher, Glenwick, and Blumenthal (1986). Silverman would presumably argue that this and related studies fall into the category of 20% nonreplications that would be expected on the basis of past research on subliminal psychodynamic activation. However, it is my impression that many of the studies presumably falling into the 80% support category are themselves flawed in that they occasionally use inappropriate statistical procedures, or obtain a pattern of results that is only partially congruent with theoretical expectations. Thus, the balance of research relevant to hypotheses germane to the overall theory of subliminal psychodynamic activation cannot be neatly summarized by the assertion that 80% of the time studies testing these hypotheses provide positive support.

In the final analysis, the evaluation of Silverman's research rests largely on the preexistent belief structures of the evaluator. Many psychologists, who are skeptical of Freudian theoretical positions, are inclined to find claims that subliminal presentations of the stimulus, "Mommy and I are one," are capable of having a dramatic long-term effect on behavior inherently improbable. Such individuals would require completely convincing empirical evidence before giving credence to such claims. Other psychologists, with stronger convictions about the role of unconscious processes in controlling behavior and a greater commitment to the logic of psychoanalytic reasoning, are less skeptical of such claims and are probably inclined to find the results obtained by Silverman as plausible. Thus, they are likely to be less skeptical or concerned about reported failures of replication. It is a well-known secret of the rules of scientific inference that judgment of the truth value of any scientific proposition is dependent upon the a priori probability that the proposition is true. The a priori probability is itself a function of a complex set of beliefs and theories that are accorded various truth values. Since psychologists differ among themselves with respect to the validity of propositions based on psychoanalytic reasoning, they are likely to begin the evaluation of Silverman's claims with different a priori beliefs and are thus likely to reach different conclusions about this research. My own conclusion, based on a lack of prior commitment to psychoanalytic theory, is that the evidence obtained by Silverman and his colleagues and other researchers is not completely convincing. I do not dismiss it, but I think we need additional compelling evidence to accord to unconscious processes the kinds of influences that Silverman claims can be obtained by subliminal presentations of stimuli.

Conscious Influences on Behavior

Before attempting to reach conclusions about unconscious influences on behavior we shall consider research purporting to demonstrate the influence of conscious states on behavior, In particular, we shall review research germane to Bandura's theory of efficacy and Carver and Scheier's (1981) research on "phenomenal enhancement" effects.

Bandura's Theory of Efficacy

Bandura's theory of efficacy is a theory that emphasizes the role of conscious processes in the control of behavior (see Bandura, 1977, 1982, 1986). Bandura has attempted to interpret a number of studies dealing with attempts to change behavior by appeal to the influence of a phenomenal state called *efficacy*. Efficacy is a belief held by an individual with respect to his or her ability to perform a given action.

Bandura makes a number of assumptions about efficacy beliefs. The most fundamental is that efficacy beliefs and actions are congruent. That is, if a person believes that he or she is capable of performing an act, then he or she is likely to be able to perform that act. And, if a person believes that he or she is not able to perform an act (the person has low-efficacy), then the person will not be able to perform the act.

Methods of inducing behavior change are effective if they are able to induce changes in efficacy that are then assumed to influence behavior. Bandura and his associates have demonstrated that the magnitude of behavior change produced by a procedure is correlated with the magnitude of changes in efficacy produced by the procedure.

Schunk and Hanson (1985) have obtained data that supports this assumption. They studied the effects of observing peer models and adult teachers' demonstrations of methods of solving math problems (see also Schunk, 1982, 1984). They found that children who observed peer models solving problems developed a greater sense of efficacy than children who were exposed to adult models. Schunk and Hanson reasoned that children exposed to peer models are more likely to infer that they too are capable of performing in an analogous manner. They also found that the level of efficacy attained by the children (i.e., their belief in their ability to solve various problems) was correlated with various measures of the children's ability to solve math problems.

Bandura assumes that efficacious beliefs, although correlated with the effectiveness of behavior change induced by some procedures, are not perfectly correlated with such changes. That is, efficacious beliefs are assumed to have an independent status. They are assumed to be predictive of future behavior. Indeed, Bandura argues that efficacious beliefs are more predictive of future behavior in new situations than previous behaviors. For example, Bandura, Adams, and Beyer (1977) used several techniques to decrease phobic responses in a group of snake-phobic subjects. After initial experiences with snakes, subjects were presented with snakes with an obviously different appearance, and these researchers attempted to predict the behaviors that would be exhibited by their subjects under these conditions. They indicate that behaviors in the new, or generalization, task could be predicted on the basis of a subject's performance with the first snake without any consideration given to the stated efficacy beliefs of their subjects. Alternatively, one could attempt to predict the behavior of the subjects in the novel task by reference to the stated efficacy beliefs of the subjects. Bandura, Adams, and Beyer found that predictions based on efficacy beliefs were more accurate than predictions based on the behaviors attained by their subjects in response to the first snake. For example, they found that in 52% of the cases those who were able to perform all of the required actions with the original snake were not able to perform all of the required actions with the new snake. Of the subjects who made maximal efficacy assertions about their ability to perform the required actions with the original snake, 24% were not able to perform all of the required activities with the new snake. These data suggest that efficacy beliefs are not merely a reflection of induced behavioral change. Such beliefs contain information that is apparently independent of measures of behavioral change.

Efficacy beliefs have been found to be predictive not only of the overall level of performance of individuals but also of what Bandura calls the "microstructure of behavior." For example, Bandura, Reese, and Adams (1982) studied the degree of congruence expressed by snake-phobic subjects beween stated efficacy beliefs after treatment about the capability of performing specific actions with a new snake, and they found that the efficacy beliefs were congruent with the actions that were actually performed in 83% of the cases. Predictions based on the identical behaviors exhibited by subjects with the first snake were congruent in 73% of the cases. These differences were significant indicating that efficacy beliefs are more predictive of behavior than measures of the behavior of subjects obtained in similar situations.

Candiotte and Lichtenstein (1981) obtained efficacy beliefs in conjunction with an evaluation of various treatments designed to eliminate smoking behavior. They found that efficacy beliefs were correlated .57 with a measure of relapse after treatment and .68 with the time to relapse. Thus, subjects who had a strong efficacy belief were more likely to continue to avoid smoking and were likely to take longer to exhibit relapse behavior. Efficacy beliefs were also highly congruent with predictions about the kinds of situations that are likely to trigger relapse behavior. They asked subjects to state their efficacy beliefs about their ability to avoid smoking in various situations. Efficacy beliefs were highly congruent with the actual situations likely to trigger relapse behavior. They found a correlation of .89 between efficacy beliefs for particular situations and the likelihood of relapse in that situation for a particular subject.

Bandura also argued that efficacy beliefs are likely to determine the psychophysiological response to fear-inducing situations. He assumes that the fear experienced by an individual in response to a phobic situation and the psychophysiological indices of fear are determined by efficacy beliefs. Bandura, Reese, and Adams (1982) found that they were able to predict the changes in blood pressure and heart rate of subjects with spider phobias who were presented with various tasks involving spiders from a knowledge of specific efficacy beliefs held by these subjects with respect to their performance on that task. They found particularly marked elevations of blood pressure and increased cardiac accelerations when their subjects were required to perform actions for which their efficacy beliefs were low. Similarly Bandura, Taylor, Williams, Medford, and Barchas (1985) obtained catecholamine measures of the response to stress for women who were phobic for spiders. They found increased levels of catecholamine secretions occurred when their subjects were confronted with tasks for which they had low-efficacy.

Do efficacy beliefs influence behavior? On the surface the answer to this question would appear to be "yes." However, a more critical examination of these data leaves the status of efficacy beliefs as an independent causal influence on behavior somewhat vexed. Bandura indicates that changes in efficacy are correlated with changes in behavior, yet efficacy exerts an independent influence on future behavior. This implies that efficacy beliefs themselves must be based on something other than the observations of behavior made by the experimenter who has obtained a measure of behavior change. Where do efficacy beliefs come from? One could argue that efficacy beliefs reflect the subject's observations of his or her behavioral and psychophysiological responses to situations. There may be conditions of observation in which the subject may be aware of components of his or her behavior that are not contained in the psychologist's measures of behavior. Consider, for example, the behavior of a subject in a snake-phobic situation. The psychologist may note whether or not a subject performs a given action in response to the snake. This behavioral observation is then used to predict the behavior of the subject in response to a snake. The subject may be aware of his or her own psychophysiological responses when performing a given action, the level of fear he or she experiences and the ease or general difficulty of performing the act. If the subject monitors a larger and somewhat independent set of behavioral dimensions, the subject's judgments about the likelihood of performing that or a related action in a new situation may be more accurate than generalizations based merely on whether or not a given act was performed. If the psychologist had included additional behavioral measures of a subject's response to the original snake, it is conceivable that predictions to a new situation based solely on behavioral measures might equal or exceed those based on efficacy beliefs. In these studies psychophysiological measures of the response to each behavior are usually not included in the behavioral prediction equation. Also, measures of latency and other measures of the quantitative details of the actual performance are not obtained. This argument raises the possibility that efficacy beliefs might be epiphenomenal. That is, they might reflect a more accurate assessment of behavior than the assessment of behavior used by the psychologist.

There is additional evidence that suggests that efficacy beliefs might, in the limiting case, reflect nothing more than an accurate assessment of a subject's behavior in a particular situation. Biran and Wilson (1981) compared two methods of treating phobias—guided exposures by a therapist in which subjects were permitted to perform various actions in response to the phobic stimulus or cognitive restructuring designed to eliminate irrational beliefs (see Meichenbaum. 1977). They found that guided-exposure methods were more effective than cognitive-restructuring methods in eliminating fear as assessed by psychophysiological responses. Guided-exposure methods also produced greater congruence between efficacy beliefs and behavior in the presence of familiar and novel phobic stimuli. The congruence measures for the subjects given guided-exposure treatments in these two situations were 96 and 92%, respectively. The comparable data for subjects given cognitive-restructuring therapy were 71 and 64%, respectively. These data may be interpreted as indicating that the congruence between efficacy and subsequent behavior is itself a function of the extent to which the efficacy beliefs of subjects are based on observations of their own behavior in relevant situations. Subjects who were given cognitive-restructuring therapy had little or no opportunity to observe their behavior in response to the phobic stimulus and, thus, their efficacy beliefs were not well-founded and were, as a result, less predictive of their subsequent behavior.

Bandura's theory assigns a privileged causal influence to efficacy beliefs. However, the theory begs the question of the origins of efficacy beliefs in the first instance. It is possible that phobic behaviors and their accompanying beliefs of low-efficacy to perform various actions in the presence of phobic stimuli may derive from psychophysiological and behavioral responses to the phobic stimuli. These tendencies may even reflect the influence of genetically based effects thay may in part be mediated by psychophysiological responses. This suggests that efficacy beliefs may be as much a reflection of past actions as a cause of actions. Once developed, they may acquire an independent causal influence and may come to control behavioral and psychophysiological responses. Biran and Wilson's finding that efficacy beliefs that are not derived from behavioral observations are not completely congruent with actions suggests that behavior is not determined solely by one's beliefs. More generally, the relation between efficacy and action is stochastic. Behavior is never precisely congruent with efficacy. A person may believe that he or she is capable of performing an action and find, to his or her surprise, that he or she is not capable of performing the action. Conversely, a person may believe that he or she is not capable of performing an action and discover, to his or her surprise, that he or she is capable of performing the action.

Not only is it possible for belief and action to be incongruent, it is also true that there can be discrepancies between efficacy beliefs and psychophysiology. Consider Epstein's research on parachute jumping (see Epstein, 1967). Epstein studied sports parachutists. He found that individuals developed an ability to master their fears of bodily harm as they had increasing experiences with parachute jumping. Both psychophysiological measures of fear and phenomenal reports of fear decreased as subjects had more experiences with parachuting from planes. Epstein's research was performed in the 1960s before the development of Bandura's theory of efficacy. However, the behavioral and psychophysiological changes accompanying increased experiences with parachute jumping are compatible with the assertion that subjects were developing increased efficacy in their ability to master their fears and anxieties about potential bodily harm with increased experiences in parachute jumping.

While the general finding of a reduction in fear and anxiety with repeated exposure to a fear-inducing situation may be compatible with an efficacy analysis, there are other findings obtained by Epstein that are not compatible with this sort of analysis. Epstein found that with increasing experience there was an increased tendency of subjects to experience physiological arousal indicative of fear and to experience fear at times that were remote from the actual jump. Figure 6.1 presents data indicative of the temporal displacement of fear to times both earlier than and later than the jump as a function of experience. The displacement of fear does not appear to be related to efficacy beliefs. A person who has conquered his or her fear may well develop a sense of efficacy that, in turn, leads to further reduction in fear in response to a particular fear-inducing situation. However, an efficacy belief that reduces fear ought not to result in a displacement of fear and its increased presence in other situations. This analysis of Epstein's research suggests that efficacy beliefs do not completely determine and control the responses they influence.

Whether or not one grants that efficacy beliefs reflect judgments that are partially autonomous, or independent, of the previous observations of one's own behaviors that constitute the foundation for their content, it does appear that once instantiated such beliefs do exert an influence on subsequent behavior and action. Thus, this body of research does provide support for the influence of conscious states on action. At the same time, our analysis suggests that this influence may be rather limited and that it is, in any case, not the sole determinant of behavioral responses to phobic fear-inducing situations.

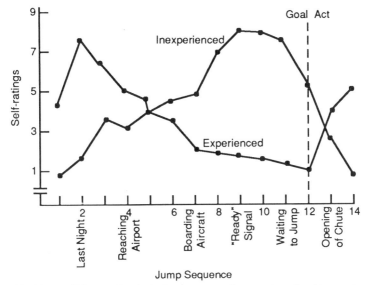

Figure 6.1   Fear at different points in the jump sequence for experienced and inexperienced para-chutists. (Reprinted by permission of Elsevier Science Publishing Co., Inc. from *Psychosomatic Medicine,* Vol. 29, p. 33. Copyright 1967 by the American Psychosomatic Society, Inc.)

Phenomenal Enhancement Effects

One reason that it is difficult to determine the precise character of the indepen-dent influence of efficacy on behavior is that experimental manipulations that change efficacy are likely to change behavior as well. This reciprocal influence makes it difficult to determine the influence of phenomenal events that are independent of typically covarying behavioral events. If one could manipulate phenomenal events without simultaneously manipulating behavior, it might be possible to obtain a somewhat clearer understanding of the independent role of such events. Carver and Scheier (1981) have reported the results of an extensive series of studies designed to demonstrate the influence of enhanced awareness of one's psychological states. The shift of attention to one's experiences and thoughts is assumed to enhance the influence of the phenomenal states. Their research is based on the assumption that subjects are influenced by the presence of mirrors in a variety of experimental situations. The mirrors are usually a relatively unobtrusive component of the experimental arrangements. They are, however, placed in a position that enables the subject to view himself or herself. Carver and Scheier claim that the mirror tends to make their subjects self-conscious and to lead them to focus their attention on their inner experiences. In most of the studies, the influence of the mirror is compared with its absence. The usual effects of the mirror mimic and parallel the effects of an individual difference variable assessed by a self-report questionnaire called "The Self-Consciousness Scale" (see Fenigstine, Scheier, and Buss, 1975). This scale is assumed to measure a component of self-awareness described as private self-consciousness, referring to the awareness of one's inner experiences. Individuals who endorse such items as, "I am generally attentive to my inner feelings," tend to score high on private self-consciousness. In their research, Carver and Scheier frequently find that individual differences in self-consciousness have effects that are similar to those induced by the presence or absence of a mirror.

Scheier (1976) has obtained data in a study of aggressive behavior that demonstrates the parallel influence of individual differences in private self-consciousness and the presence and absence of a mirror. In his study, subjects who were either low or high in the measure of private self-consciousness were assigned to either a mirror-present or a mirror-absent condition. In addition, some of the subjects in each of these four groups were assigned to a condition designed to elicit anger. Anger was manipulated by presenting the subject with a difficult problem that he or she had to solve alone but in the presence of a second person, who was actually an agent of the experimenter. In the anger condition, the agent insulted the subject and criticized his or her problem-solving ability. In the anger-absent condition, the agent remained silent. After subjects had worked on the problem-solving task, they acted as teachers in an experimental situation in which they were instructed to deliver a shock whenever an incorrect response was made by a learner or "victim," who was the experimental agent present during the first phase of the experiment. The subject could choose the level of shock that he wished to deliver to the victim by choosing buttons clearly labeled to indicate different intensities of shock. The principal dependent variable was the level of shock intensity chosen by the subject.

Scheier had relatively clear-cut theoretical expectations for the outcome of the experiment. First, he assumed that the effects of private self-consciousness would parallel the effects of the mirror manipulation. Second, he assumed that both of these variables would enhance the influence of the anger manipulation. Third, he assumed that the intensification of the awareness of the state of anger would result in an increase in the expression of aggression as indexed by the level of shock intensity chosen by the subject. Table 6.8 presents the principal results of this experiment and indicates that the results are in accord with theoretical expectations. Note that the intensity of shock selected increases following an anger-induction experience. Subjects who scored high on the dispositional measure of self-consciousness delivered higher levels of shock to their victims if they had been angered. No such difference was present among the nonangered subjects. Similarly, those who were angered and who performed the task in the presence of the mirror gave higher intensities of shock than subjects who did not perform the task in the presence of the mirror.

Scheier also found that subjects who were angered in the presence of the

Table 6.8

Mean Shock Intensities Delivered by Subjects in Each Treatment Group[a]

Disposition	No anger		Anger	
	No mirror	Mirror	No mirror	Mirror
High self-conscious	2.9	2.7	4.1	4.9
Low self-conscious	3.0	2.5	3.3	3.9

[a]Based on Scheier, 1976 (© 1977 Duke University Press).

mirror were more aware of their anger than subjects who were angered to the absence of a mirror. There were no differences in the awareness of anger in the *anger* and *no-anger* condition in the absence of a mirror (see Table 6.9).

Carver, Blaney, and Scheier (1979a, b) studied the interaction between changes in phenomenal states and beliefs about the likelihood of successful completion of a behavioral sequence on the performance of that sequence. In the first of these studies Carver, Blaney, and Scheier (1979a) studied the influence of a mirror-present and a mirror-absent condition on responses to a moderately fearful stimulus. In this experiment subjects were presented with the task of reaching into a cage and picking up a boa constrictor. All of the subjects chosen for this study were moderately fearful of snakes. On the basis of their responses to a pretest questionnaire, subjects were classified as belonging to a group that was doubtful of their ability to perform the act and a group who were at least moderately confident of their ability to perform the task. The experimenters assumed that these differences in outcome expectancy would interact with self-focusing manipulations to determine the performances of subjects on the assigned task. Specifically, they reasoned that a self-focusing condition would lead subjects who had feelings of inadequacy and anxiety to become aware of these feelings and, as a result, would lead them to withdraw from the task, and to have more difficulty completing the task than subjects who were doubtful, but who

Table 6.9

Mean Anger Ratings Collapsed across Levels
of Self-consciousness[a]

Condition	Condition		
	No anger	Anger	M[b]
Mirror	2.0	4.1	3.1
No mirror	2.5	2.6	2.6
M[b]	2.3	3.4	2.9

[a]Based on Scheier, 1976 (© 1977 Duke University Press).
[b]M = mean value.

had not been assigned to the self-focusing condition. The effects of a self-focusing condition were expected to be different for subjects who were relatively confident about their ability to complete the assigned task. Although they might be expected to experience a phenomenal enhancement of their anxiety states in the presence of the mirror, they would also experience, in an enhanced way, their awareness of the goal and, perhaps as well, of their beliefs in their ability to attain the goal. Presumably the mirror would lead these subjects to focus upon whatever cognitive influences were present that led them to believe that they would attain the goal in the first place. Tables 6.10 and 6.11 present the results of this study. An examination of the data indicates that the initial confidence in the ability to complete the assigned task interacted with the presence of the mirror to influence actual goal attainment. Confident subjects exhibited a slight, but insignificant, increase in their approach behavior in the presence of the mirror. Doubtful subjects exhibited a significant decrease in their approach behavior in the presence of the mirror. An analysis of the postexperimental questionnaire data indicates that the presence of the mirror changed retrospective reports about the phenomenal events that transpired during the experiment. Doubtful subjects reported increases in anxiety, a sense of inadequacy, an awareness of chronic levels of fearfulness, and a decrease in awareness of the discrepancy between behavioral attainments and the attainment of the goal.

Subjects who expressed confidence also reported an increase in their awareness of their fear and anxiety in the presence of the mirror, but the level of

Table 6.10

Self-Reported Anxiety Experienced in the Presence of the Snake, Self-Reported Momentary Sense of Inadequacy and Fearfulness during the Approach Task, and Actual Level of Approach toward the Snake[a]

Group	Condition	
	Mirror present	Mirror absent
	Self-reported anxiety[b]	
Confident	4.33	3.46
Doubtful	5.25	3.56
	Self-reported sense of inadequacy[b]	
Confident	4.20	3.85
Doubtful	5.38	3.63
	Approach behavior[c]	
Confident	8.47	8.23
Doubtful	6.38	8.31

[a]Based on Carver, Blaney and Scheier (1979). (Copyright 1979 by the American Psychological Association. Adapted by permission of the publisher and author.)

[b]Larger numbers indicate greater anxiety and felt inadequacy.

[c]Larger numbers indicate greater approach.

Table 6.11

Self-reports of Attention Paid to Chronic Level of Fearfulness,
Self-assessment of Bodily Arousal, and Behavior–Goal Comparison[a]

Group	Mirror present	Mirror absent
	Chronic level of fearfulness	
Confident	4.67	4.23
Doubtful	4.81	3.56
	Assessing degree of bodily arousal	
Confident	3.60	4.69
Doubtful	4.31	3.13
	Behavior–goal comparison	
Confident	5.93	5.62
Doubtful	5.06	6.06

[a]Based on Carver, Blaney and Scheier (1979). (Copyright 1979 by the
American Psychological Association. Adapted by permission of the publisher
and author.)

increase was less extreme for these subjects. In addition, this increase was also
accompanied by an increase in the awareness of the goal state. It is as if the
presence of the mirror led doubtful subjects to focus upon the factors that determined their inability to complete the task and confident subjects to counter-
balance this increase in their doubts and anxieties with a renewed focus on the
goals of their behavior.

The Carver, Blaney, and Scheier study suggests that there is an interaction
between expectations for success and failure at a task and manipulations of
phenomenal enhancement effects. Carver, Antoni, and Scheier (1985) have obtained data that suggest that individuals who differ in private self-consciousness
may differ in their desire to acquire information about their potential success or
failure at a task following a previous success or failure at a task following a
previous success or failure experience in a similar situation. This suggests that
states of private self-consciousness may not only influence the salience of one's
private experiences, but the kinds of experiences available to private scrutiny. In
their study, they permitted subjects to select items that provided or did not
provide information about the quality of their performance on a task. Figure 6.2
presents the results of their study. Note that Figure 6.2 indicates that subjects
who were high in self-consciousness seek information about the quality of their
performance after success and decrease their tendency to seek information about
their performance after a previous failure. Thus, whether individuals want to be
aware of characteristics of their behavior may vary as a function of their personality and of their previous experiences.

The research of Carver and Scheier provides clear evidence that phenomenal
events influence action and behavior. The mirror manipulation appears to act in a
way that is parallel to the influence of individual differences in private self-

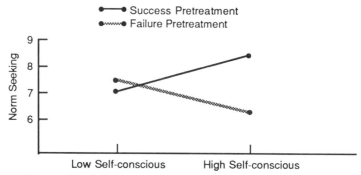

Figure 6.2   Norm-seeking in high- and low-self-conscious subjects following success and failure.
(Based on Carver, Antoni, and Scheier, 1985.)

consciousness and creates an enhanced influence of the role of inner experiences
and phenomenal states on behavior.

Conclusion: Conscious and Unconscious Processes Compared

We have presented evidence both for the influence of conscious and unconscious
processes on behavior. It should be noted that much of the evidence for conscious and unconscious influences on behavior suggests that the effects of such
influences are often parallel and comparable. Consider some examples. In studies designed to demonstrate the influence of phenomenal states on behavior, it is
frequently possible to show that psychological states that are out of awareness
may exert comparable influences on behavior. Consider, the results of Scheier's
study of aggression. He found that subjects in the presence of a mirror were more
likely to be aware of their anger and that this increased awareness of anger led to
an increase in the behavioral expression of anger. However, subjects who were
not in the mirror condition did not differ in their experience of anger (see Table
6.9). However, even though there were no differences in the phenomenal reports
about the experience of anger between subjects who were and were not angered
in the nonmirror condition, these subjects differed in their tendency to express
anger (see Table 6.8). Those subjects who were angered did increase their
behavioral expression of anger even though they reported that they were not
angry. If we accept these results at face value, they suggest that it is not necessary to be aware of one's anger in order to behave in an angry manner.

Berkowitz (1978) has also found that subjects who were not aware of their
anger could nevertheless behave aggressively. In his study, subjects were required to peddle a stationary bicycle at either high- or low-levels of speed. Half
the subjects assigned to each of these peddling conditions were assigned to a

frustration condition. Frustration was induced by informing subjects that they would receive a prize if they were able to match the peddling speed of a fictitious partner whose peddling speed was indicated to them by signal lights. Subjects were frustrated by the introduction of a sudden change in the signaled peddling speed towards the end of the experimental session, thus depriving subjects of an opportunity to receive the prize. They were provided with a plausible explanation for the arousal that they might have experienced. They were led to believe that their arousal was a result of exercise.

In a second phase of this experiment. subjects were permitted to deliver rewards or punishments to their fictitious partner in the first phase of the experiment while the partner worked on a game. Berkowitz obtained self-reports from the subjects about their mood states. He reported that subjects who were frustrated and those who were not frustrated reported comparable moods. There were no differences between these groups with respect to their reported frustration, anger, or irritation. Presumably the information about the exercise-induced arousal led subjects to attribute any frustration-induced arousal to the influence of the exercise. However, frustrated and nonfrustrated subjects differed with respect to their behavior in the second phase of the experiment. Berkowitz reported that those assigned to the frustration condition were more likely to be punitive to their partners and were less likely to reward the partner. In addition, those subjects who were most aroused physiologically by virtue of having been assigned to the groups required to peddle rapidly were more likely to deliver punishments to the partner if they had been frustrated.

Berkowitz argued that his experiment implies that subjects need not have labeled their psychological state as one of anger in order to have behaved in an angry manner following frustration. In Berkowitz's experiment, a state of frustration-induced anger continued to determine the behavior of an individual even though the individual had been induced into relabeling and reinterpreting the motivational state as one of exercise-induced physiological arousal.

There are some other respects in which the Carver and Scheier research on the effects of mirrors provides support for the influence of unconscious processes on behavior. Carver and Scheier placed the mirror in an unobtrusive location in their studies. While subjects may be aware of the presence of the mirror, it is unlikely that they are aware of the influence of the mirror on their experiences. Moreover, they are probably not aware of the influence of their changed state of awareness on their subsequent behavior. One might say that the Carver and Scheier studies demonstrate that subjects may be made aware of their inner states without knowing why they are aware of them. The changed awareness of these states may influence behavior, but subjects may not be aware of this influence. Thus, in several respects the results of the Carver and Scheier studies may be congruent with the position taken by Nisbett and Wilson with respect to the limitations of the influence of phenomenal states on behavior.

There are other studies in the literature that purport to demonstrate the influence of conscious processes on behavior that also provide evidence for the influence of states outside of awareness on behavior. For example, Pittman, Cooper, and Smith (1977) studied the overjustification effect. This effect occurs when subjects who are provided with an extrinsic reward for performing a task appear to lose interest in performing that task (see Deci, 1975). This phenomenon is usually explained by reference to a change in cognition. Subjects who are rewarded for engaging in a particular task are assumed to form a cognition that indicates to them that their interest in the task was extrinsic rather than intrinsic. When subjects who have received tangible rewards for performing the task are subsequently given an opportunity to perform the task on their own, they usually choose not to engage in the previously rewarded activity. Pittman, et al. attempted to manipulate the cognitions of intrinsic and extrinsic interest in the task directly. In addition to the usual reward and no-reward conditions included in these studies, subjects were also assigned to conditions in which they received false physiological feedback and were informed that their physiological responses indicated a pattern of response characteristics of intrinsic interest in the task or extrinsic interest in the task. Table 6.12 presents subjects' self-reports about their interest in playing the game and indicates that the manipulations were effective. Note that subjects led to believe that their physiological patterns were indicative of intrinsic interest in the game did indeed express the highest intrinsic interest. Note further that subjects who received tangible rewards for their performances on the task expressed decreased intrinsic interest in the task relative to those who had not received extrinsic rewards.

A reduction in intrinsic interest was measured by a reduced tendency to engage in the task during a free-choice period in which the experimenter is out of the room. Table 6.13 presents the results of the measure of the tendency to engage in the task under free-choice conditions. Note that manipulations of cognitions, as indexed by verbal reports, did influence the behavior of subjects in this experimental situation. Those who had been led to believe that they were intrinsically interested in the task did choose to play the game in the absence of

Table 6.12

Mean Amount of Arousal Attributed to Interest in the Game[a,b]

No reward, no cue	Reward, no cue	Reward, extrinsic cue	Reward, intrinsic cue
$47.30_{1,2}$	$40.15_{1,2}$	35.95_2	55.25_1

[a]Based on Pittman, Cooper, and Smith, 1977.
[b]Means not sharing a common subscript are significantly different from each other.

Table 6.13

Mean Number of Trials on the Task during
the 5-Min-Free-Choice Period[a,b]

No reward, no cue	Reward, no cue	Reward, extrinsic cue	Reward, intrinsic cue
18.15_1	4.15_3	2.40_3	10.45_2

[a]Based on Pittman, Cooper, and Smith, 1977.

[b]Means not sharing a common subscript are significantly different from each other.

the experimenter more than subjects who were led to believe that they had only an extrinsic interest in the game. However, what is of some interest, and is not discussed by Pittman, Cooper, and Smith, is the difference between subjects assigned to the *intrinsic-cue* condition and those in the traditional *no-reward–no-cue* condition. Subjects who had not received a reward for task performance during the first phase of the experiment exhibited the largest behavioral interest in the task during the second phase of the experiment. They were more likely to play the game than those given a reward, who were led to believe that their pattern of physiological response was indicative of intrinsic interest in the game. However, the *reward–intrinsic cue* subjects had slightly, but nonsignificantly higher, self-reported intrinsic interest in the game. This pattern of results permits us to suggest some tentative resolution of the apparent paradoxical results suggesting that phenomenal states do and do not mediate cognitive influences on motivation. The use of direct manipulations that change subject's beliefs about the reasons for their actions can result in a change in their verbal reports about their phenomenal states and, also one may assume, in the underlying phenomenal state that is indexed by the report. However, the change does not account for the total motivational influence.

Just as studies of phenomenal states on behavior provide evidence of the influence of states that are outside of awareness on action, it is also the case that studies designed to demonstrate the influence of unconscious processes on behavior may occasionally provide evidence for the influence of conscious processes. Consider an example. Silverman and Spiro found that the influence of subliminal stimuli that were designed to arouse unconscious conflicts among schizophrenics was paralleled by the influence of verbally described supraliminal stimuli. Brody et al. (in press) found that information presented to one hemisphere of the brain might not influence the processing of targets presented to the other hemisphere. These studies provide support for the notion of assymetrical information transmission from the right to the left hemisphere and vice versa. However, the suggested dissociations created by this paradigm occurred in comparable ways for prime stimuli that were in awareness and for subliminal prime stimuli. Thus, the transfer of information from one hemisphere to the other is not a function of the phenomenal status of the information.

Even studies that purport to demonstrate differential influences of sub- and supra-liminal stimuli appear to provide relatively restricted support for such an influence. Consider, for example, Marcel's (1983a, b) finding of the differences in the influence of a polysemous prime word on a target word as a function of whether or not the prime word is in awareness. Recall that Marcel found that the influence of the polysemous prime, such as the word *palm* on the target word *tree* when the word palm was preceded by the word wrist, was different if the word palm was in awareness than if the word was not in awareness. Marcel argued that his results supported a view of preconscious processing that emphasized the existence of multiple meanings and a view of consciousness that emphasized its selective and restricting influence on the range of meanings of a stimulus. However, even if Marcel's analysis is correct and if consciousness acts in a selective and restrictive manner, it can be argued that these effects of conscious processes can be overcome by the mere expedient of informing the subject that the word *palm* can refer both to a tree and to a part of the human anatomy. Thus, we can be made aware of the multiplicity of meanings of a stimulus. In this connection it is possible to entertain the notion that we might, perhaps even in a manner suggested by psychoanalytic reasoning, be influenced by unconscious thoughts and meanings of events that are not in our awareness. However, to assert this is not to assert that the influence of such events would be fundamentally different if they were out of awareness rather than if they were in awareness. While there are many examples of such alleged special influences of unconscious processes on behavior in the clinical literature, I have seen few convincing demonstrations of fundamentally different influences on the behavior of conscious and unconscious processes in the recent experimental literature dealing with this topic.

Our discussion of conscious and unconscious influences suggests that a complete understanding of personality requires that we consider both conscious and unconscious processes. An individual's ability to observe his or her own behavior and mood states may provide an adequate descriptive understanding of his or her actions to provide veridical reports about traits. Moreover, an individual's sense of his or her own abilities and behavioral tendencies may exert an influence on subsequent behavior and action. The research we have reviewed provides reasonable support for the rejection of an epiphenomenalist position that assumes that conscious processes do not exert an independent influence on behavior. Thus, a complete understanding of an individual's personality will require an assessment of his or her phenomenal states.

The research we have reviewed also provides ample evidence for the limitations of a phenomenally based psychology of personality. We may be influenced by events of which we are not aware. The ways in which we are influenced and even the thought processes whose occurrence is assumed to explain some of our actions may occur outside of our awareness. An explanation of phenomenal states may not provide an adequate explanation of human action. People may be better reporting what they do and what they think and feel when they do something than why they do what they do. Thus, a complete understanding of the reasons for actions may require dealing with processes that are out of awareness.

Epilogue

After completing this book it has become clear to me that I have been led by my review of some aspects of the empirical literature in personality to an awareness of certain orienting ideas about personality. In this epilogue I propose to state these ideas explicitly.

In Chapters 1–5 of this book I have reviewed research and theory that supports a trait-theoretical view of personality that is based on the assumption that personality is to be described in terms of enduring, relatively invariant dispositions that derive in part from genotypes that influence the structure of the nervous system of individuals. In Chapter 6 I have reviewed research that emphasizes unconscious influences on behavior. There is a sense in which there is an affinity between the ideas espoused in Chapters 1–5 and in Chapter 6. The orienting ideas implicit in these chapters are compatible with a particular view of the meaning of change in personality and of the meaning of self-understanding.

If we are usually not aware of the reasons for our actions and if many of our actions are influenced by unconscious processes, then changes in our understanding of ourselves may be of only limited utility in changing our behavior. Thus, an emphasis on the importance of unconscious processes is compatible with a trait theoretical view of personality that emphasizes enduring, relatively invariant dispositions. Self-understanding from this position is not so much a matter of understanding why one behaves in a particular way, but of understanding how one is likely to behave in a particular situation. So too, conscious awareness may often derive from observations of one's own actions that may be initiated by processes that are only dimly understood, or are not in awareness. Both the

James–Lange theory of emotion as the awareness of a physiological response to a situation that has preceded the awareness and Libet's analysis of voluntary motor acts as deriving from a physiologically defined readiness potential that precedes the awareness of the intention to act may be generally paradigmatic of social action.

If personality characteristics endure and if our phenomenal understandings of our actions do not in general control our behaviors, how is personality to be changed? In order to address this question we need to have an understanding of the relationship between personality and situations. I believe that there is a limited role in personality psychology for an interactionist approach that attempts to derive predictions about the characteristic behavior of individuals with different personality dispositions in different situations. I believe that such an interactionist position is likely to be most successful in circumstances in which the situations studied are likely to be nonecologically valid for an understanding of ordinary social action. That is, under conditions in which the situation that is studied is in a laboratory setting with reasonably rigorous controls over extraneous variables, it is possible to study the way in which personality interacts with various situations. The research reviewed in Chapter 5 that derives from various attempts to test hypotheses derived from biologically based theories of traits is paradigmatic of this type of research. However, hypotheses relating personality to variables, such as the augmentation and reduction of evoked potential responses, may strike many personality psychologists as dealing with situations that are relatively remote from the understanding of social action that appears to be at the center of our concern with an understanding of individual lives. As we deal with more ecologically valid and complex social situations, I believe that the role of hypotheses describing interactions between personality and situations will become more limited. In such situations, there is more scope for the individual to shape the situation and to express idiosyncratic personal dispositions. That is, the situation is more likely to become noncommensurate in the dispositions that it elicits in different individuals. If personality dispositions endure, and if they in effect serve to define and change the meaning of situations that are encountered in everyday life, is it possible to change personality? I am inclined to answer this question in the negative. However, this negative answer does not lead to a completely negative view of our potential for the amelioration of psychological distress attributable to undesirable personal dispositions. If we can understand the potential range of social actions available to an individual in a given environment with a defined set of personal dispositions, it is possible to contemplate radical changes in the environment that, in effect, will limit the potential for the behavioral manifestations of various personal dispositions. An apt example of the model of personality change contemplated here can be found in the treatment of alcoholics provided by Alcoholics Anonymous. This treatment is based on the assumption that the personal tendency toward alcoholism is an invariant characteristic of individuals, and the treatment is not directed toward its removal. Rather the treatment aims, by the provision of social supports, to provide an environment that will minimize the opportunity of an individual to imbibe alcohol. Paradoxically, a commitment to personality as a relatively invariant disposition directs one's attention to the potential for restructuring our environments in ways that will change the opportunities provided to express various personal dispositions. I suspect that our current technologies and therapies used to change personality may be of limited validity, in part, because they emphasize the attempt to change the individual. And, our efforts to create psychologically healthy environments may be of limited succes in part because they assume that such environments will be beneficial to virtually all individuals. I think that we will be able to intervene successfully in a person's life when we learn how to restructure, in rather radical ways, the environmental options available to a person.

References

Ahern, F. M., Johnson, R. C., Wilson, J. R., McClearn G. E., & Vanderberg, S. G. (1982). Family resemblances in personality. *Behavior Genetics, 12,* 261–280.

Akhtar, S., Wig, N., Varma, O., Pershad, D., & Verma, S. (1975). A phenomenological analysis of symptoms in obsessive compulsive neurosis. *British Journal of Psychology, 127,* 342–348.

Allport, G. W. (1961). Pattern and growth in personality. New York: Holt, Rinehart, & Winston.

Allport, G. W., & Odbert, H. S. (1936). Trait names: A psycholexical study. *Psychological Monographs, 47,* 171.

Amelang, M., & Borkenau, P. (1984). Versuche einer Differenzierung des Eigenschaftskonzepts: Apekte intraindividueller Variabilitat and differentieller Vorhersagbarkeit. [Efforts to differentiate the trait construct: Aspects of intra-individual variability and differential predictability.] In M. Amelang & H. J. Ahrens (Eds.), *Brennpunkte der persona lichkeitsforschung.* Gottingen: Hogrefe.

Amelang, M., Kobelt, C., & Frasch, A. (1984). Auf der Suche nach Personen mit Eigenschaften: Untersuchungen zur Restriktion des Eigenschaftsmodells auf Untergruppen von Personen, Verhaltensweisen und Situationen. [On the search for persons with traits: Investigations on restrictions of the trait model to subgroups of individuals, behaviors and situations.] In: D. Albert (Ed.), *Bericht uber den 34.* Kongress der Deutschen Gesellschaft fur Psychologie in Wien 1984. Gottingen: Hogrefe.

Ariam, S., & Siller, J. (1982). Effects of subliminal oneness stimuli in Hebrew on academic performance of Israeli high school students: Further evidence of the adaptation-enhancing effects of symbiotic fantasies in another culture using another language. *Journal of Abnormal Psychology, 91,* 343–349.

Aries, E. J., Gold, C., & Weigel, R. H. (1983). Dispositional and situational influences on dominance behavior in small groups. *Journal of Personality and Social Psychology, 44,* 779–786.

Backteman, G., & Magnusson, D. (1981). Longitudinal stability of personality characteristics. *Journal of Personality, 49,* 148–160.

Balota, D. (1983). Automatic semantic activation and episodic memory encoding. *Journal of Verbal Learning and Verbal Behavior, 22,* 88–104.

Baltes, P. B., & Schaie, K. W. (1976). On the plasticity of intelligence in adulthood and old age: Where Horn and Donaldson fail. *American Psychologist, 31*, 720–725.

Bandura, A. (1977). Self-efficacy: Toward a unifying theory of behavioral change. *Psychological Review, 84*, 191–215.

Bandura, A. (1982). Self-efficacy mechanism in human agency. *American Psychologist, 37*, 122–147.

Bandura, A. (1986). *Social foundations of thought and action: A social cognitive theory.* Englewood Cliffs, NJ: Prentice-Hall.

Bandura, A., Adams, N. E., & Beyer, J. (1977). Cognitive processes mediating behavioral change. *Journal of Personality and Social Psychology, 35*, 125–139.

Bandura, A., Reese, L., & Adams, N. E. (1982). Micro-analysis of action and fear arousal as a function of differential levels of perceived self-efficacy. *Journal of Personality and Social Psychology, 43*, 5–21.

Bandura, A., Taylor, C. B., Williams, S. L., Medford. I. N., & Barchas, J. D. (1985). Catecholamine secretion as a function of perceived coping self-efficacy. *Journal of Consulting and Clinical Psychology, 53*, 406–414.

Bandura, A., & Walters, R. (1963). *Social learning and personality development* New York: Holt, Rinehart, & Winston.

Barber, T. X. (1969). *Hypnosis: A scientific approach.* New York: Van Nostrand & Rinehold Co.

Barber, T. X. (1979). Suggested ("hypnotic") behavior: The trance paradigm versus an alternative paradigm. In E. Fromm & R. E. Shor (Eds.), *Hypnosis: Developments in research and new perspectives* Chicago: Aldine-Atherton.

Bargh, J. A., Bond, R. N., Lombardi, W. J., & Tota, M. E. (1986). The additive nature of chronic and temporary sources of construct accessibility. *Journal of Personality and Social Psychology, 50*, 869–878.

Barnes, G. (1975). Extraversion and pain. *British Journal of Social and Clinical Psychology, 14*, 303–308.

Bartol, C. R., & Costello, N. (1976). Extraversion as a function of temporal duration of electric shock: An exploratory study. *Perceptual and Motor Skills, 42*, 1174.

Bell, R. Q. (1968). A reinterpretation of the direction of effects in studies of socialization. *Psychological Review, 75*, 81–95.

Beller E. K. (1979). Early intervention programs. In J. D. Osofsky (Ed.), *Handbook of infant development.* New York: Wiley.

Bem, D. J. (1983). Further dejá vu in the search for cross-situational consistency: A response to Mischel and Peake. *Psychological Review, 90*, 390–393.

Bem, D. J., & Allen, A. (1974). On predicting some of the people some of the time: The search for cross-situational consistencies in behavior. *Psychological Review, 81*, 506–520.

Benson, V. E. (1942). The intelligence and later scholastic success of sixth grade pupils. *School and Society, 55*, 163–167.

Berkowitz, L. (1978). Whatever happened to the frustration–aggression hypothesis? *American Behavioral Scientist, 21*, 691–708

Biran, M., & Wilson, G. T. (1981). Treatment of phobic disorders using cognitive and exposure methods: A self-efficacy analysis. *Journal of Counseling and Clinical Psychology, 49*, 886–899.

Blake, M. J. F. (1967). Relationship between circadian rhythm of body temperature and introversion–extraversion. *Nature, 215*, 896–897.

Block, J., & Block, J. H. (1980a). *California Child Q-set.* Palo Alto, CA: Consulting Psychologists Press.

Block, J., & Block, J. H. (1980b). The role of ego-control and ego-resiliency in the organization of behavior. In W. A. Collins (Ed.), *Development of Cognition, Affect, and Social Relations: The Minnesota Symposium on Child Psychology.* (Vol. 13). Hillsdale, NJ: Erlbaum.

Block, J., & Gjerde, P. F. (1985). Distinguishing between antisocial behavior and undercontrol. In D. Olweus, J. Block, & M. Radke-Yarrow (Eds.), *Development of antisocial and prosocial behavior: Research theories and issues.* New York: Academic Press.

Block, J., Weiss, D. S., & Thorne, A. (1979). How relevant is a semantic similarity interpretation of personality ratings? *Journal of Personality and Social Psychology, 37,* 1055–1074.

Bloom, B. S. (1974). Time and learning. American Psychologist, 29, 682–688.

Bouchard, T.J. (1985). Twins reared together and apart: What they tell us about human diversity. In S. W. Fox (Ed.), *The chemical and biological basis of individuality.* New York: Plenum.

Bowers, K. S. (1973). Situationism in psychology: An analysis and critique. *Psychological Review, 80,* 307–336.

Bowles, S., & Gintis, H. (1976). *Schooling in capitalist America.* New York: Basic Books.

Brill, N. Q., Koegler, R. R., Epstein, L. J., & Forgy, E. W. (1964). Controlled study of psychiatric outpatient treatment. *Archives of General Psychiatry, 10,* 581–95.

Brody, E. B., & Brody, N. (1976). *Intelligence: Nature, determinants, and consequences.* New York: Academic Press.

Brody, N. (1972). *Personality: Research and theory.* New York: Academic Press.

Brody, N. (1980). Social motivation. *Annual Review of Psychology, 31,* 143–168.

Brody, N. (1983a). *Human motivation. Commentary on goal-directed action.* New York: Academic Press.

Brody, N. (1983b). Where are the emperor's clothes? *Behavioral and Brain Sciences, 6,* 303–310.

Brody, N. (1985a). Is psychotherapy better than a placebo? *Behavioral and Brain Sciences, 7,* 758–762.

Brody, N. (1985b). The construct validity of tests of intelligence. In B. Wolman (Ed.)., *Handbook of intelligence.* New York: Wiley.

Brody, N., Goodman, S. E., Halm, E., Krinzman, S., & Sebrechts, M. (in press). Lateralized affective priming of lateralized affectively valued target words. *Neuropsychologia.*

Bronfenbrenner, U. (1975). Is early intervention effective? Some studies of early education in familial and extrafamilial settings. In A. Montagu (Ed.), *Race and IQ.* New York: Oxford University Press.

Brookover, W., Beady, C., Flood, P., Schweitzer, J., & Wisenbaker, J. (1979). *School social systems and student achievement: Schools can make a difference.* New York: Praeger.

Bryant-Tucker, R., & Silverman, L. H. (1984). Effects of the subliminal stimulation of symbiotic fantasies on the academic performance of emotionaly handicapped students. *Journal of Counseling Psychology, 31,* 295–306.

Bryden, M. P. (1982). *Laterality: Functional asymmetry in the intact brain.* New York: Academic Press.

Bryden, M. P., & Ley, R. G. (1983). Right-hemispheric involvement in the perception and expression of emotion in normal humans. In K. M. Heilman & P. Satz (Eds.), *Neuropsychology of human emotion.* New York: Guilford.

Burgess, L. S. (1973). Recovery from the effects of somatosensory stimulation. Unpublished doctoral dissertation, University of Ottowa, Ottowa.

Buss, A. H., & Plomin, R. (1984). *Temperament: Early developing personality traits.* Hillsdale, NJ: Erlbaum.

Buss, D. M., & Craik, K. H. (1980). The frequency concept of disposition: Dominance and prototypically dominant acts. *Journal of Personality, 48,* 379–392.

Buss, D. M., & Craik, K. H. (1985). Why *not* measure that trait? Alternative criteria for identifying important dispositions. *Journal of Personality and Social Psychology, 48,* 934–946.

Caldwell, B. M., & Bradley, R. H. (1978). *Home Observation for Measurement of the Environment.* Little Rock: University of Arkansas.

Candiotte, M. M., & Lichtenstein, E. (1981). Self-efficacy and relapse in smoking cessation programs. *Journal of Consulting and Clinical Psychology, 49,* 648–658.

Caril, L. R. (1980). Assertiveness: A construct validity study. Doctoral dissertation, University of Delaware.

Carver, C. S., Blaney, P. H., & Scheier, M. F. (1979a). Focus of attention, chronic expectancy, and responses to a feared stimulus. *Journal of Personality and Social Psychology, 37,* 1186–1195.

Carver, C. S., Blaney, P. H., & Scheier, M. F. (1979b). Reassertion and giving up: The interactive role of self-directed attention and outcome expectancy. *Journal of Personality and Social Psychology, 37,* 1859–1870.

Carver, C. S., & Scheier, M. F. (1981). *Attention and self-regulation: A control approach to human behavior.* New York: Springer-Verlag.

Carver, C. S., Antoni, M., & Scheier, M. F. (1985). Self-consciousness and self-assessment. *Journal of Personality and Social Psychology, 49,* 117–124.

Cattell, R. B. (1943). The description of personality: Basic traits resolved into clusters. *Journal of Abnormal and Social Psychology, 38,* 476–506.

Cattell, R. B. (1952). P-technique factorization and the determination of individual dynamic structure. *Journal of Clinical Psychology, 8,* 5–10.

Cattell, R. B. (1971). *Abilities: Their structure, growth, and action.* Boston: Houghton Mifflin Co.

Cattell, R. B., Eber, H. W., & Tatsouka, M. W. (1970). *Handbook for the Sixteen Personality Factor Questionnaire (16PF).* Champaign, IL: Institute for Personality and Ability Testing.

Chaplin, W. F., & Goldberg, L. R. (1985). A failure to replicate the Bem and Allen study of individual differences in cross-situational consistency. *Journal of Personality and Social Psychology, 47,* 2075–2060.

Cheek, J. M. (1982). Aggregation, moderator variables, and the validity of personality tests: A peer-rating study. *Journal of Personality and Social Psychology, 43,* 1254–1269.

Chessman, J., & Merikle, P. M. (1984). Priming with and without awareness. *Perception and Psychophysics, 36,* 387–395.

Christiansen, K. O. (1977). A review of studies of criminality among twins. In S. A. Mednick & K. O. Christiansen (Eds.), *Biosocial bases of criminal behavior.* New York: Gardner.

Christie, R., & Geis, F. L. (Eds.). (1970). *Studies in Machiavellianism.* New York: Academic Press.

Claridge, D. S. (1981). Psychoticism. In R. Lynn (Ed.), *Dimensions of personality.* London: Pergamon Press.

Claridge, D. S. (1986). Eysenck's contribution to the psychology of personality. In S. Modgil & C. Modgil (Eds.), *Hans Eysenck: Consensus and controversy.* Philadelphia: Falmer.

Claridge, G. S., & Birchall, P. (1978). Bishop, Eysenck, Berck and psychoticism. *Journal of Abnormal Psychology, 87,* 664–668.

Claridge, G. S., Donald, J. R., & Birchall, P. M. (1981). Drug tolerance and personality: Some implications for Eysenck's theory. *Personality and Individual Differences, 2,* 153–166.

Clarke, A. M., & Clarke, A. D. B. (1976). *Early experience: Myth and evidence.* New York: The Free Press.

Condon, T. J., & Allen, G. J. (1980). The role of psychoanalytic merging fantasies in systematic desensitization: A rigorous methodological examination. *Journal of Abnormal Psychology, 89,* 437–443.

Conley, J. J. (1984a). Relation of longitudinal stability and cross-situational consistency in personality: Comment on the Mischel-Epstein debate. *Psychological Review, 91,* 491–496.

Conley, J. J. (1984b). The hierarchy of consistency: A review and model of longitudinal findings on adult individual differences in intelligence, personality, and self-opinion. *Personality and Individual Differences, 5,* 11–26.

Conley, J. J. (1985). Longitudinal stability of personality traits: A multitrait–multimethod–multioc-casion analysis. *Journal of Personality and Social Psychology, 49,* 1266–1282.

Conley, J. J., & Angelides, M. (in press). Personality antecedents of emotional disorders and alcohol abuse in men: Results of a forty-five year prospective study. *Journal of Personality and Social Psychology.*

Corteen, R. S. (1986). Electrodermal responses to words in an irrelevant message: A partial reap-praisal. *Behavioral and Brain Sciences, 9,* 27–28.

Corteen, R. S., & Dunn, D. (1974). Shock-associated words in a nonattended message: A test for momentary awareness. *Journal of Experimental Psychology, 102,* 1143–1144.

Corteen, R. S., & Wood, B. (1972). Automatic responses to shock-associated words in an unat-tended channel. *Journal of Experimental Psychology, 94,* 308–313.

Costa, P. T., Jr., & McRae, R. R. (1980). Still stable after all these years: Personality as a key to some issues in adulthood and old age. In P. B. Baltes & O. G. Brim, Jr. (Eds.), *Life span development and behavior.* New York: Academic Press.

Costa, P. T., Jr., & McRae, R. R. (1985). Comparison of EPI and psychoticism scales with measures of the five-factor model of personality. *Personality and Individual Differences, 6,* 587–597.

Cronbach, L. J., & Snow, R. E. (1977). *Aptitudes and instructional methods.* New York: Irvington.

Dagenbach, D., & Carr, T. H. (1986). Awarensss, attention, and automaticity in perceptual encod-ing: Conscious influences on unconscious perception. Unpublished manuscript. Michigan State University, East Lansing.

D'Andrade, R. G. (1965). Trait psychology and componential analysis. *American Anthropologist, 67,* 215–228.

D'Andrade, R. G. (1974). Memory and the assessment of behavior. In T. Blalock (Ed.), *Measure-ment in the social sciences.* Chicago: Aldine-Atherton.

Daniels, D., & Plomin, R. (1985). Differential experience of siblings in the same family. *Develop-mental Psychology, 21,* 747–760.

Dauber, R. B. (1984). Subliminal psychodynamic activation in depression: On the role of autonomy issues in depressed college women. *Journal of Abnormal Psychology, 93,* 9–18.

Dawson, M. E., & Schell, A. M. (1982). Electrodermal responses to attended and unattended significant stimuli during dichotic listening. *Journal of Experimental Psychology: Human Per-ception and Performance, 8,* 315–324.

Deci, E. L. (1975). *Intrinsic motivation.* New York: Plenum.

DePaulo, B. M., Kenny, D. A. Hoover C., Webb, W., & Oliver, P. V. (1985). Accuracy in person perception: Do people know what kind of impressions they convey? Unpublished paper, Univer-sity of Virginia.

Diener, E., & Larsen, R. J. (1984). Temporal stability and cross-situational consistency of affective, behavioral, and cognitive responses. *Journal of Personality and Social Psychology, 47,* 871–883.

Diener, E., Larsen, R. J., Levine, S., & Emmons, R. A. (1985). Intensity and frequency: Dimen-sions underlying positive and negative affect. *Journal of Personality and Social Psychology, 48,* 1253–1265.

Digman, J. M., & Inouye, J. (1986). Further specification of the five robust factors of personality. *Journal of Personality and Social Psychology, 50,* 116–123.

Duffy, E. (1962). *Activation and behavior.* New York: Wiley.

Duncan, O. D., Featherman, D. L., & Duncan. B. (1968). Socioeconomic background and occupa-tional achievement: Extension of a basic model. Washington, DC: U. S. Office of Education, Bureau of Research, Final Report, Project No. 5–0074 (EO–191).

Dworkin, R. H. (1978). Genetic influences on cross-situational consistency. In W. E. Nance, G. Allen, & P. Parisi (Eds.), *Twin research: Psychology and methodology.* New York: Liss.

Dworkin, R. H. (1979). Genetic and environmental influences on person–situation interactions. *Journal of Research in Personality, 13,* 279–293.

Easterbrook, J. A. (1959). The effect of emotion on cue-utilization and the organization of behavior. *Psychological Review, 66,* 183–201.

Eaves, L. J., & Eysenck, H. J. (1975). The nature of extraversion: A genetical analysis. *Journal of Personality and Social Psychology, 32,* 102–112.

Eaves, L. J., & Young, P. A. (1981). Genetical theory and personality differences. In R. Lynn (Ed.), *Dimensions of personality.* London: Pergamon Press.

Ekehammer, B. (1974). Interactionism in personality from a historical perspective. *Psychological Bulletin, 81,* 1026–1048.

Endler, N. S. (1982). Situational aspects of interactional psychology. In D. Magnusson (Ed.), *Toward a psychology of situations: An interactional perspective.* Hillsdale, NJ: Erlbaum.

Endler, N. S., & Hunt, J. McV. (1966). Sources of behavioral variance as measured by the S–R inventory of anxiousness. *Psychological Bulletin, 65,* 336–346.

Endler, N. S., & Okada, M. (1975). A multidimensional measure of trait anxiety. The S–R inventory of general trait anxiousness. *Journal of Consulting and Clinical Psychology, 43,* 319–329.

Epstein, S. (1967). Toward a unified theory of anxiety. In B. Maher (Ed.), *Progress in experimental personality research* (Vol. 4). New York: Academic Press.

Epstein, S. (1977). Traits are alive and well. In D. Magnusson & N. S. Endler (Eds.), *Personality at the crossroads: Current issues in interactional psychology.* Hillsdale, NJ: Erlbaum.

Epstein, S. (1979a). The stability of behavior: I. On predicting most of the people much of the time. *Journal of Personality and Social Psychology, 37,* 1097–1126.

Epstein, S. (1979b). Explorations in personality today and tomorrow: A tribute to Henry A. Murray. *American Psychologist, 34,* 649–653.

Epstein, S. (1983a). The stability of behavior across time and situations. In R. Zucker, J. Aronoff, & A. I. Rabin (Eds.), *Personality and the prediction of behavior.* San Diego, CA: Academic Press.

Epstein, S. (1983b). The stability of confusion: A reply to Mischel and Peake. *Psychological Review, 90,* 179–184.

Epstein, S. (1983c). Aggregation and beyond: Some basic issues on the prediction of behavior. *Journal of Personality, 51,* 360–392.

Epstein, S. (1983d). A research paradigm for the study of personality and emotions. In M. M. Page (Ed.), *Personality—Current Theory & Research: 1982 Nebraska Symposium on Motivation.* Lincoln: University of Nebraska Press.

Ericcson, K. A., & Simon, H. A. (1980). Verbal reports as data. *Psychological Review, 87,* 215–251.

Eysenck, H. J. (1947). *Dimensions of personality.* London: Routledge & Kegan Paul.

Eysenck, H. J. (1952). The effects of psychotherapy: An evaluation. *Journal of Consulting Psychology, 16,* 319–324.

Eysenck, H. J. (1953). *The scientific study of personality.* London: Routledge & Kegan Paul.

Eysenck, H. J. (1957). *The dynamics of anxiety and hysteria.* London: Routledge & Kegan Paul.

Eysenck, H. J. (1967). *The biological basis of personality.* Springfield, IL: Charles C. Thomas.

Eysenck, H. J. (1973). *Eysenck on extraversion.* London: Granada.

Eysenck, H. J., & Eysenck, M. W. (1985). *Personality and individual differences: A natural science approach.* New York: Plenum.

Eysenck, H. J., & Eysenck, S. B. G. (1983). Recent advances: The cross-cultural study of personality. In C. D. Spielberger & J. N. Butcher (Eds.), *Advances in personality assessment* (Vol. 2). Hillsdale, NJ: Erlbaum.

Eysenck, H. J., & Levey, A. B. (1967). Konditionierung, Introversion–Extraversion und die Starke des Nervensystems. [Conditioning, introversion–extraversion and the strength of the nervous system.] *Zeitschrift fur Psychologie*, 1967, *174*, 96–106.

Eysenck, H. J., & Prell, D. B. (1951). The inheritance of neuroticism. *Journal of Mental Science*, *97*, 441–465.

Eysenck, H. J., & Prell, D. B. (1956). The inheritance of introversion–extraversion. *Acta Psychologica, 12*, 95–110.

Eysenck, M. W. (1982). *Attention and arousal: Cognition and performance.* Berlin: Springer.

Eysenck, M. W., & Eysenck, M. C. (1979). Memory, scanning, introversion–extraversion, and levels of processing. *Journal of Research in Personality, 13*, 305–315.

Eysenck, M. W., & Folkard, S. (1980). Personality, time of day, and caffeine: Some theoretical and conceptual problems in Revelle, et al. *Journal of Experimental Psychology: General, 109*, 32–41.

Eysenck, S. B. G., & Eysenck, H. J. (1967). Salivary response to lemon juice as a measure of introversion. *Perceptual and Motor Skill, 24*, 1047–1051.

Eysenck, S. B. G., Pearson, P. R., Easting, G., & Allsopp, J. F. (1985). Age norms for impulsiveness, venturesomeness and empathy in adults. *Personality and Individual Difference, 6*, 613–619.

Fagan, J. F., III, & McGrath, S. K. (1981). Infant recognition memory and later intelligence. *Intelligence, 15*, 121–130.

Fenigstein, A., Scheier, M. F., & Buss, A. H. (1975). Public and private self-consciousness: Assessment and theory. *Journal of Consulting and Clinical Psychology, 43*, 522–527.

Festinger, L. (1957). *A theory of cognitive dissonance.* Stanford, CA: Stanford University Press.

Fisher, C. B., Glenwick, D. S., & Blumental, R. S. (1986). Subliminal Oedipal stimuli and competitive performance: An investigation of between-group effects and mediating subject variables. *Journal of Abnormal Psychology, 95*, 292–294.

Floderus-Myrhed, B., Pedersen, N., & Rasmuson, S. (1980). Assessment of heritability for personality based on a short form of the Eysenck Personality Inventory. *Behavior Genetics, 10*, 153–162.

Flood, M., & Endler, N. S. (1980). The interactional model of anxiety: Am empirical test in an athletic competition situation. *Journal of Research in Personality, 14*, 329–339.

Flynn, J. F. (1984). The mean IQ of Americans: Massive gains 1932–1978. *Psychological Bulletin, 95*, 29–51.

Folkard, S. (1975). The nature of diurnal variations in performance and their implications for shift work studies. In P. Colquhoun, S. Folkard, P. Knauth, & J. Rutenkrary (Eds.), *Experimental studies of shift work.* Opladen: Westdeutsche Verlag.

Fowler, C. A., Wolford, A., Slade, R., & Tassinary, L. (1981). Lexical access with and without awareness. *Journal of Experimental Psychology: General, 110*, 341–362.

Freud, S. (1956). The unconscious. In S. Freud *Collected papers*, Vol. IV. London: Hogarth. (Original work published in 1915)

Frith, C. D. (1977, August). Habituation of the pupil size and light responses to sound. Paper presented at the American Psychological Association, San Francisco.

Fulker, D. W., Eysenck, H. J., & Zuckerman, M. (1980). A genetic and environmental analysis of sensation seeking. *Journal of Research in Personality, 14*, 261–281.

Funder, D. L. (1983). Three issues in predicting more of the people: A reply to Mischel and Peake. *Psychological Review, 90*, 283–289.

Funder, D. C., Block, J. H., & Block, J. (1983). Delay of gratification: Some long-term correlates. *Journal of Personality and Social Psychology, 44*, 1198–1213.

Furnham, A. (1981). Personality and activity preference. *British Journal of Social Psychology, 20*, 57–68.

Furnham, A. (1986). Interactionism in psychology: A critical analysis of the S–R Inventories. In A. Furham (Ed.), *Social behavior in context*. Boston: Allyn & Bacon.

Gale, A. (1973). The psychophysiology of individual differences: Studies of extraversion and the EEG. In P. Kline (Ed.), *New approaches in psychological measurement*. New York: Wiley.

Gale, A. (1983). Electroencephalographic studies of extraversion–introversion. A case study in the psychophysiology of individual difference. *Personality and Individual Differences, 4*, 371–380.

Galton, F. (1883). *Inquiries into human faculty and its development*. London: McMillan.

Geen, R. G. (1984). Preferred stimulation levels in introverts and extraverts: Effects on arousal and performance. *Journal of Personality and Social Psychology, 46*, 1303–1312.

Geen, R. G., McCown, D. J., & Broyles, J. W. (1985). Effects of noise on sensitivity of introverts and extraverts to signals in a vigilance task. *Personality and Individual Differences, 6*, 237–241.

Gilbert, D. G., & Hagen, R. L. (1985). Electrodermal responses to noise stressors: Nicotine extraversion interactions. *Personality and Individual Differences, 6*, 573–578.

Gillan, P., & Rachman, S. (1974). An experimental investigation of desensitization and phobic patients. *British Journal of Psychiatry, 124*, 392–401.

Goldberg, L. R. (1982). From ace to zombie: Some explorations in the language of personality. In C. D. Spieberger & J. N. Butcher (Eds.), *Advances in personality assessment*. Vol. 1). Hillsdale, NJ: Erlbaum.

Goldsmith, H. H., & Gottesman, I. I. (1981). Origins of variations in behavioral styles: A longitudinal study of temperament in young twins. *Child Development, 52*, 91–103.

Gorenstein, E. E., & Newman, J. P. (1980). Disinhibitory psychopathology: A new perspective and a model for research. *Psychological Review, 87*, 301–315.

Gottesman, I. I., & Shields, J. (1972). *Schizophrenia and genetics: A twin study vantage point*. New York: Academic Press.

Gottesman, I. I., & Shields, J. (1982). *Schizophrenia, the epigenetic puzzle*. New York: Cambridge University Press.

Gottfried, A. E., & Gottfried, A. W. (1984). Home environment and mental development in middle-class children in the first three years. In A. W. Gottfried (Ed.), *Home environment and early cognitive development: Longitudinal research*. New York: Academic Press.

Gottfried, A. W., & Brody, N. (1975). Interrelationships between and correlates of Psychometric and Piagetian scales of sensorimotor intelligence. *Developmental Psychology, 11*, 379–387.

Gray, J. A. (1982). *The neuropsychology of anxiety: An inquiry into the functions of the septo-hippocampal system*. Oxford, Clarendon.

Green, B. F. (1978). In defense of measurement. *American Psychologist, 33*, 664–679.

Guilford, J. P. (1964). Zero intercorrelations among tests of intellectual abilities. *Psychological Bulletin, 61*, 401–404.

Guilford, J. P. (1967). *The nature of human intelligence*. New York: McGraw-Hill.

Guilford, J. P., & Hoepfner, R. (1971). *The analysis of intelligence*. New York: McGraw-Hill.

Gupta, B. S., & Nagpal, M. (1978). Impulsivity/sociability and reinforcement in verbal operant condition. *British Journal of Psychology, 69*, 203–206.

Haan, N. (1981) Common dimensions of personality development: Early adolescence to middle life. In D. H. Eichorn, J. A. Clausen, N. Haan, M. P. Honzik, & P. H. Mussen (Eds.), *Present and past in middle life*. New York: Academic Press.

Haier, R. J. (1984). Sensation seeking and augmenting–reducing: Does a nerve have a nerve? *Behavioral and Brain Sciences, 7*, 441.

Hamilton, P., Hockey, P., & Rejman, M. (1977). The place of the concept of activation in human information processing. In S. Dornic (Ed.), *Attention and performance, VI*. New York: Wiley.

Hampson, S. E. (1982). *The construction of personality: An introduction*. London: Routledge & Kegan Paul.

Harnquist, K. (1968a). Relative changes in intelligence from 13–18. I. Background and methodology. *Scandinavian Journal of Psychology, 5,* 50–64.

Harnquist, K. (1968b). Relative changes in intelligence from 13–18. II. Results. *Scandinavian Journal of Psychology, 9,* 65–82.

Harrington, D. M., Block, J., & Block, J. H. (1983). Predicting creativity in preadolescence from divergent thinking in early childhood. *Journal of Personality and Social Psychology, 45* 609–623.

Hartshorne, H., & May, M. A. (1928). *Studies in deceit.* New York: Macmillan.

Hartshorne, H., & May, M. A. (1929). *Studies in service and self-control.* New York: Macmillan.

Heber, R., & Garber, H. (1970). An experiment in the prevention of cultural-familial mental retardation. Paper presented at the Second Congress of the International Association for the Scientific Study of Mental Deficiency, Warsaw, Poland.

Heilbrun, K. (1980). Silverman's subliminal psychodynamic activation method: A failure to replicate. *Journal of Abnormal Psychology, 89,* 560–566.

Heilman, K. E., Bowers, D., & Valenstein, E. (1985). Emotional disorders associated with neurological diseases. In K. M. Heilman & E. Valenstein (Eds.), *Clinical neuropsychology* 2nd ed.). New York: Oxford.

Henderson, N. D. (1982). Human behavior genetics. *Annual Review of Psychology, 33,* 403–440.

Heston, L. L. (1966). Psychiatric disorders in foster home reared children of schizophrenic mothers. *British Journal of Psychiatry, 112,* 819–825.

Hilgard, E. R. (1977). *Divided consciousness.* New York: Wiley.

Hilgard, E. R. (1979). Divided consciousness in hypnosis: The implications of the hidden observer. In E. Fromm & R. E. Shor (Eds.), *Hypnosis: Developments in research and new perspectives* (2nd ed.). New York: Aldine.

Hilgard, E. R., Morgan, A. H., & McDonald, H. (1975). Pain and dissociation in the cold pressor test. A study of hypnotic analgesia with "hidden reports" through automatic key-pressing and automatic talking. *Journal of Abnormal Psychology, 84,* 280–289.

Holender, D. (1986). Semantic activation without conscious identification in dichotic listening, parafoveal vision, and visual masking: A survey and appraisal. *Behavioral and Brain Sciences, 9,* 1–66.

Hormouth, S. E. (1986). The sampling of experiences *in situ. Journal of Personality, 54,* 262–293.

Hutchings, B., & Mednick, S. A. (1977). Criminality in adoptees and their adoptive and biological parents: A pilot study. In S. A. Mednick & K. O. Christiansen, (Eds.), *Biosocial bases of criminal behavior.* New York: Gardner.

Hymbaugh, K., & Garrett, J. (1974). Sensation seeking among skydivers. *Perceptual and Motor Skills, 38,* 118.

Insel, P. (1974). Maternal effects in personality. *Behavior Genetics, 4,* 133–143.

Jackson, D. N., & Paunonen, S. V. (1985). Construct validity and the predictability of behavior. *Journal of Personality and Social Psychology, 49,* 544–570.

Jacobsen, L. L., Berger, S. M., Bergman, R. L., Millham, J., & Greeson, L. E. (1971). Effects of age, sex, systematic conceptual learning sets and programmed social interaction on the intellectual and conceptual development of pre-school children from poverty backgrounds. *Child Development, 42,* 1399–1415.

Jencks, C. (1972). *Inequality: A reassessment of the effect of family and schooling in America.* New York: Basic Books.

Jensen, A. R. (1977). Cumulative deficit in IQ of blacks in the rural south. *Developmental Psychology, 13,* 184–191.

Jensen, A. R. (1980). *Bias in mental testing.* New York: Free Press.

Jensen, A. R. (1985). The nature of the black–white difference on various psychometric tests: Spearman's hypothesis. *Behavioral and Brain Sciences, 8,* 192–264.

Jones, E. E. (1979). The rocky road from acts to dispositions. *American Psychologist, 34,* 107–117.

Jones, E. E., & Nisbett, R. E. (1972). *The actor and the observer: Divergent perceptions of the causes of behavior.* New York: General Learning Press.

Kantorowitz, D. A. (1978). Personality and conditioning of tumescence and detumescence. *Behavior Research and Therapy, 16,* 117–128.

Kelly, E. L., & Conley, J. J. (1987). Personality and compatibility: A prospective analysis of marital stability and marital satisfaction. *Journal of Personality and Social Psychology, 52,* 27–41.

Kelly, G. A. (1955). *The psychology of personal constructs.* New York: Norton.

Kendall, P. C. (1978). Anxiety: States, traits–situations. *Journal of Consulting and Clinical Psychology, 46,* 280–287.

Kenrick, D. T., & Braver, S. L. (1982). Personality: Idiographic and Nomothetic! A rejoinder. *Psychological Review, 89,* 182–186.

Kenrick, D. T., & Stringfield, D. O. (1980). Personality traits and the eye of the beholder: Crossing some traditional philosophical boundaries in the search for consistency in all of the people. *Psychological Review, 87,* 88–104.

Kety, S. S., Rosenthal, D., Wender, P. H., Schulsinger, F., & Jacobsen, B. (1978). The biological and adoptive families of adopted individuals who become schizophrenic: Prevalence of mental illness and other characteristics. In L. C. Wynne, R. L. Cromwell, & S. Matthysse (Eds.), *The nature of schizophrenia: New approaches to research and treatment.* New York: Wiley.

Kipnis, D. (1971). *Character structure and impulsiveness.* New York: Academic Press.

Kish, G. B., & Donnenwerth, G. V. (1972). Sex differences in the correlates of stimulus seeking. *Journal of Consulting and Clinical Psychology, 38,* 42–49.

Knorring, L. von, Oreland, L., & Winblad, B. (1983). Personality traits related to monoamine oxidase (MAO) activity in platelets. Unpublished paper cited in Zuckerman, M. (1984a). Sensation seeking: A comparative approach to a human trait. *Behavioral and Brain Sciences, 7,* 413–471.

Kobasa, S., Maddi, S. R., & Kahn, S. (1982). Hardiness and health: A prospective study. *Journal of Personality and Social Psychology, 42,* 168–197.

Kunst-Wilson, W. R., & Zajonc, R. (1980). Affective discrimination of stimuli that cannot be recognized. *Science, 207,* 557–558.

Kusyszyn, I., Steinberg, P., & Eliot, B. (1973). Arousal seeking, physical risk taking and personality. Unpublished manuscript cited in Zuckerman, M. (1979). *Sensation seeking: Beyond the optimal level of arousal.* Hillsdale, NJ: Erlbaum.

Lambert, W., & Levy, L. M. (1972). Sensation-seeking and short-term sensory isolation. *Journal of Personality and Social Psychology, 24,* 46–52.

Lamiell, J. T. (1981). Toward an idiothetic psychology of personality. *American Psychologist, 36,* 276–289.

Lamiell, J. T. (1982). The case for an idiothetic psychology of personality: A Conceptual and empirical foundation. In B. A. Maher & W. B. Maher (Eds.), *Progress in experimental personality* (Vol. 11). New York: Academic Press.

Langer, E. J. (1978). Rethinking the role of thought in social interaction. In J. M. Harvey, W. I. Ickes, & R. F. Kidd (Eds.), *New directions in attribution research* (Vol. 2). Hillsdale, NJ: Erlbaum.

Langer, E. J., Blank, A., & Chanowitz, B. (1978). The mindlessness of ostensibly thoughtful action: The role of "placebic" information in interpersonal interaction. *Journal of Personality and Social Psychology, 36,* 635–642.

Langinvainio, H., Kaprio, J., Koskenvuo, M., & Lohnquist, J. (1983, June). *Finnish twins reared apart: II. Personality factors.* Paper presented at the Fourth International Congress on Twin Studies, London, England.

Larsen, R. J. (1985). Individual differences in circadian activity rhythm and personality. *Personality and Individual Differences, 6,* 305–311.

Latané, B., & Darley, J. M. (1970). *The unresponsive bystander: Why doesn't he help?* New York: Appleton-Century-Crofts.

Lavin, D. E. (1965). *The prediction of academic performance: A theoretical analysis and review of research.* New York: Russell Sage Foundation.

Leon, G. R., Gillum, B., Gillum, R., & Gouze, M. (1979). Personality stability and change over a 30-year period—middle to old age. *Journal of Consulting and Clinical Psychology, 47,* 517–524.

Levinson, O. J., Darrow, C. N., Klein, E. B., Levinson, M. H., & McKee, B. (1978). *The seasons of man's life.* New York: Knopf.

Lewicki, P. (1986). *Nonconscious social information processing.* New York: Academic Press.

Lewis, M., & Brooke-Gunn, J. (1981). Visual attention at three months as a predictor of cognitive functioning at two years of age. *Intelligence, 5,* 131–140.

Ley, R. G., & Bryden, M. P. (1982). A dissociation of right and left hemispheric effects for recognizing emotional tone and verbal content. *Brain and Cognition, 1,* 3–9.

Libet, B. (1985). Unconscious cerebral initiative and the role of conscious will in voluntary action. *Behavioral and Brain Sciences, 8,* 529–566.

Lindsley, G. (1957). Psychophysiology and motivation. In M. R. Jones (Ed.), *Nebraska symposium in motivation* (Vol. 5). Lincoln: University of Nebraska Press.

Lindsley, E., & O'Toole, J. (1982). The effect of subliminal stimulation of symbiotic fantasy on college students' self-disclosures in group counseling. *Journal of Counseling Psychology, 29,* 151–157.

Loehlin, J. (1986). H. J. Eysenck and behaviour genetics: A critical view. In S. Modgil & C. Modgil (Eds.), *Hans Eysenck: Consensus and controversy.* Philadelphia: Falmer.

Loehlin, J. C., Horn, J. M., & Willerman, L. (1981). Personality resemblances in adoptive families. *Behavioral Genetics, 11,* 309–330.

Loehlin, J. C., & Nichols, R. C. (1976). *Heredity and environment and personality: A study of 850 sets of twins.* Austin: University of Texas Press.

Loehlin, J. C., Willerman, L., & Horn, J. M. (1985). Personality resemblances in adoptive families when the children are late-adolescent or adult. *Journal of Personality and Social Psychology, 48,* 376–392.

Longstreth, L. E., Davis, B., Carter, L., Flint, D., Owen, J., Rickert, M., & Taylor, E. (1981). Separation of home intellectual environment and maternal IQ as determinants of child IQ. *Developmental Psychology, 17,* 532–541.

Lorr, M., McNair, D. M., Weinstein, G. J. (1963). Early effects of chlordiazepoxide (Librium) used with psychotherapy. *Journal of Psychiatric Research, 1,* 257–270.

Lykken, D. T. (1982). Research with twins: The concept of emergenesis. *Psychophysiology, 19,* 361–373.

Malloy, T. E., & Kenny, D. A. (1986). The social relations model: An integrative method for personality research. *Journal of Personality, 54,* 199–225.

Marcel, A. J. (1980). Explaining selective effects of prior context on perception: The need to distinguish conscious and pre-conscious processes. In J. Requin (Ed.), *Anticipation and behaviour.* Paris: Centre National de la Recherche Scientifique.

Marcel, A. J. (1983a). Conscious and unconscious perception: Experiments on visual masking and word recognition. *Cognitive Psychology, 15,* 197–237.

Marcel, A. J. (1983b). Conscious and unconscious perception: An approach to the relations between phenomenal experience and perceptual processes. *Cognitive Psychology, 15,* 238–300.

Markus, H. (1978). The effect of mere presence on social facilitation: An unobtrusive test. *Journal of Experimental Social Psychology, 14,* 384–397.

Martin, N., & Jardine, R. (1986). Eysenck's contributions to behaviour genetics. In S. Modgil & C. Modgil (Eds.), *Hans Eysenck: Consensus and controversy*. Philadelphia: Falmer.

Matarazzo, J. D. (1972). *Wechsler's measurement and appraisal of adult intelligence* (5th ed.). Baltimore: Williams & Wilkins.

Matheny, A. P., Jr. (1980). Bayley's Infant Behavior Record: Behavioral components and twin analyses. *Child Development, 51*, 1156–1167.

Matheny, A. P., Jr., Dolan, A. B., & Wilson, R. S. (1976). Twins with academic learning problems. *American Journal of Orthopsychiatry, 46*, 464–469.

McCall, R. B. (1979). The development of intellectual functioning in infancy and the prediction of later IQ. In J. D. Osofsky (Ed.), *Handbook of development*. New York: Wiley.

McCall, R. B. (1981). Early predictors of later IQ: The search continues. *Intelligence, 5*, 141–147.

McCord, R. R., & Wakefield, J. A., Jr. (1981). Arithmetic achievement as a function of introversion–extraversion and teacher-presented reward and punishment. *Personality and Individual Differences, 2*, 145–152.

McLean, P. D., & Hakstian, A. R. (1979). Clinical depression: Comparative efficacy of outpatient treatments. *Journal of Consulting and Clinical Psychology, 47*, 818–836.

McRae, R. R. & Costa, P. J., Jr. (1982). Self-concept and the stability of personality. Cross-sectional comparison of self-reports and ratings. *Journal of Personality and Social Psychology, 43*, 1282–1291.

Meehl, P. (1956). *Clinical vs. statistical prediction*. Minneapolis: University of Minnesota Press.

Meehl, P. E. (1972). A critical afterword. In I. I. Gottesman and J. Shields, *Schizophrenia and genetics: A twin study vantage point*. New York: Academic Press.

Meichenbaum, D. H. (1977). *Cognitive-behavior modification: An integrative approach*. New York: Plenum.

Meltzoff, J., & Kornreich, M. (1970). *Research in psychotherapy*. New York: Aldine-Atherton.

Merikle, P. M. (1982). Unconscious perception revisited. *Perception and Psychophysics, 31*, 298–301.

Messick, S., & Jungeblut, A. (1981). Time and method and coaching for the SAT. *Psychological Bulletin, 89*, 191–216.

Meyer, D. E., & Schvaneveldt, R. W. (1971). Facilitation in recognizing parts of words: Evidence of a dependence between retrieval operations. *Journal of Experimental Psychology, 90*, 227–234.

Milgram, S. (1974). *Obedience to authority*. New York: Harper & Row.

Miller, L. L., Berg, J. H., & Archer, R. L. (1983). Openers: Individuals who elicit intimate self-disclosure. *Journal of Personality and Social Psychology, 44*, 1234–1244.

Mischel, W. (1968). *Personality and assessment*. New York: Wiley.

Mischel, W. (1973). Toward a cognitive social learning reconceptualization of personality. *Psychological Review, 80*, 252–283.

Mischel, W. (1979). On the interface of cognition and personality: Beyond the person–situation debate. *American Psychologist, 34*, 740–754.

Mischel, W., & Peake, P. K. (1982). Beyond *déjà vu* in the search for cross-situational consistency. *Psychological Review, 89*, 730–755.

Mischel, W., & Peake, P. K. (1983). Some facets of consistency: Replies to Epstein, Funder and Bem. *Psychological Review, 90*, 394–402.

Monson, T. H., Hesley, J. W., & Chernik, L. (1982). Specifying when personality traits can and cannot predict behavior: An alternative to abandoning the attempt to predict single-act criteria. *Journal of Personality and Social Psychology, 43*, 385–399.

Moruzzi, G., & Magoun, H. W. (1949). Brain stem reticular formation and activation of the EEG. *EEG Clinical Neurophysiology, 1*, 455–473.

Moskowitz, D. S. (1982). Coherence and cross-situational generality in personality: A new analysis of old problems. *Journal of Personality and Social Psychology, 47*, 754–768.

Moskowitz, D. S., & Schwarz, J. D. (1982). Validity comparison of behavior counts and ratings by knowledgeable informants. *Journal of Personality and Social Psychology, 42,* 518–528.

Murphy, D. L., Belmaker, R. H., Buchsbaum, M. S., Martin, N. F., Ciagnello, R., & Wyatt, R. J. (1977). Biogenic amine related enzymes and personality variations in normals. *Psychological Medicine, 7,* 149–157.

Mussen, P., Eichorn, D. H., Honzik, M. P., Bieher, S. L., & Meredith, W. (1980). Continuity and change in women's characteristics over four decades. *International Journal of Behavioral Development, 3,* 333–347.

Näätänen, C. (1985). Brain physiology and the unconscious initiation of movements. *Behavioral and Brain Sciences, 8,* 549.

Nagpal, M., & Gupta, B. S. (1979). Personality, reinforcement, and verbal operant conditioning. *British Journal of Psychology, 70,* 471–476.

Nesselroade, J. R., & Baltes, P. B. (1974). Adolescent personality development and historical change: 1970–1972. *Monographs of the Society for Research in Child Development, 39,* (Whole No. 154), 1–79.

Newman, J., Freeman, F., & Holzinger, K. (1937). *Twins: A study of heredity and environment.* Chicago: University of Chicago Press.

Newman, J. P., Widom, C. S., & Nathan, S. (1985). Passive avoidance in syndromes of disinhibition: Psychopathy and extraversion. *Journal of Personality and Social Psychology, 48,* 1316–1327.

Nichols, S., & Newman, J. P. (1986). Effects of punishment on response latency in extraverts. *Journal of Personality and Social Psychology, 50,* 624–630.

Nisbett, R. E., & Wilson, T. D. (1977). Telling more than we can know: Verbal reports on mental processes. *Psychological Review, 84,* 231–259.

Nissenfeld, S. (1979). *The effects of four types of subliminal stimuli on female depressives.* Unpublished doctoral dissertation, Yeshiva University, New York.

Norman, W. T. (1963). Toward an adequate taxonomy of personality attributes: Replicated factor structure in peer nomination personality ratings. *Journal of Abnormal and Social Psychology, 66,* 574–583.

Norman, W. T. (1967). *Personality trait descriptors: Normative operating characteristics for a University population.* Department of Psychology, University of Michigan.

Norman, W. T., & Goldberg, L. R. (1966). Raters, ratees, and randomness in personality structure. *Journal of Personality and Social Psychology, 4,* 681–691.

Notterman, J. M. (1959). Force emission during bar pressing. *Journal of Experimental Psychology, 58,* 341–347.

O'Gorman, J. G. (1977). Individual differences in habituation of human physiological responses: A review of theory, methods and findings in the study of personality correlates in non-clinical populations. *Biological Psychology, 5,* 257–318.

Öhman, A. (1986). Face the beast and fear the face: Animal and social fears as prototypes for evolutionary analyses of emotion. *Psychophysiology, 23,* 123–145.

Oliver, J. M., & Burkham, R. (1982). Subliminal psychodynamic activation in depression: A failure to replicate. *Journal of Abnormal Psychology, 91,* 337–342.

Olweus, D. (1978). *Bullies and whipping boys.* Washington. DC: Hemisphere.

Olweus, E. (1979). The stability of aggressive reaction pattern in human males: A review. *Psychological Bulletin, 86,* 852–875.

Orne, M. T. (1959). The nature of hypnosis: Artifact and essence. *Journal of Abnormal and Social Psychology, 58,* 277–299.

Orne, M. T. (1979). On the simulating subject as a quasi-control group in hypnosis research: What, why and how. In E. Fromm & R. E. Shor (Eds.), *Hypnosis: Developments in research and new perspectives* (2nd ed.). New York: Aldine.

Page, E. G. (1975). Miracle in Milwaukee: Raising the IQ. In B. Z. Friedlander, G. M. Sterritt, & G. E. Kirk (Eds.), *The exceptional infant*. New York: Brunner/Mazel.

Parker, K. A. (1982). Effects of subliminal symbiotic stimulation on academic performance: Further evidence of the adaptation enhancing effects of oneness fantasies. *Journal of Counseling Psychology, 29,* 19–28.

Passini, F. T., & Norman, W. T. (1966). A universal conception of personality structure. *Journal of Personality and Social Psychology, 4,* 44–49.

Peake, P. K. (1982). *Searching for consistency: The Carelton Student Behavior Study*. Unpublished doctoral dissertation, Stanford University, Palo Alto, CA.

Peake, P. K., & Mischel, W. (1984). Getting lost in the search for large coefficients: Reply to Conley. *Psychological Review, 91,* 497–501.

Pearce-McCall, D., & Newman, J. P. (1986). Expectation of success following noncontingent punishment in introverts and extraverts. *Journal of Personality and Social Psychology, 50,* 439–446.

Pedersen, J. J., Friberg, L., Floderus Myrhed, B., McClearn. G. E., & Plomin, R. (1983, June). *Swedish early separated twins: Identification and characterization*. Paper presented at the Fourth International Congress on Twin Studies. London, England.

Pinneau, S. R. (1961). *Changes in intelligence quotient: Infancy to maturity*. Boston: Houghton-Mifflin.

Pittman, T. S., Cooper, E. E., & Smith, T. W. (1977). Attribution to causality and the overjustification effect. *Personality and Social Psychology Bulletin, 3,* 280–283.

Plomin, R., & Daniels, D. (1984). The interaction between temperament and environment: Methodological considerations. *Merrill-Palmer Quarterly, 30,* 149–162.

Plomin, R., & DeFries, J. D. (1985). *Origins of individual differences in infancy: The Colorado Adoption Project*. New York: Academic Press.

Plomin, R., Loehlin, J. D., & DeFries, J. C. (1985). Genetic and environmental components of "environmental" influences. *Developmental Psychology, 21,* 91–402.

Porterfield, A. L., & Golding, S. L. (1985). A failure to find an effect of subliminal psychodynamic activation upon cognitive measures of pathology in schizophrenia. *Journal of Abnormal Psychology, 94,* 630–639.

Prioleau, L., & Murdock, M., & Brody, N. (1983). An analysis of psychotherapy versus placebo studies. *Behavioral and Brain Sciences, 6,* 275–310.

Quattrone, G. E. (1985). On the congruity between internal states and action. *Psychological Bulletin, 98,* 3–40.

Rachman, S. (1978). An anatomy of obsessions. *Behavioral Analysis and Modification, 2,* 253–278.

Ramey, C. T., & Haskins, R. (1981a). The modification of intelligence through early experience. *Intelligence, 5,* 5–19.

Ramey, C. T., & Haskins, R. (1981b). Early education, intellectual development, and school performance: A reply to Arthur Jensen and J. McVicker Hunt. *Intelligence, 5,* 41–48.

Rehberg, R. A., & Rosenthal, E. R. (1978). *Class and merit in the American high school*. New York: Longman.

Revelle, W., Humphreys, M. S., Simon, L., & Gilliland, K. (1980). The interactive effect of personality, time of day and caffeine: A test of the arousal model. *Journal of Experimental Psychology: General, 109,* 1–31.

Romer, D., & Revelle, W. (1984). Personality traits: Fact or fiction? *Journal of Personality and Social Psychology, 47,* 1028–1042.

Rosenthal, D., Wender, P. H., Kety, S. S., Schulsinger, F., Welner. J., & Ostersand, L. (1968). Schizophrenics offspring reared in adoptive homes. In D. Rosenthal and S. S. Kety (Eds.), *The transmission of schizophrenia*. Oxford: Pergamon Press.

Rosenthal, D., Wender, P. H., Kety, S. S., Schulsinger, F., Welner, J., & Rieder, R. (1975).

Parent–child relationships and psychopathological disorder in the child. *Archives of General Psychiatry, 32,* 466–476.

Routtenberg, A. (1968). The two-arousal hypothesis: Reticular formation and limbic system. *Psychological Review, 75,* 51–80.

Rowe, D. C., & Plomin, R. (1981). The importance of nonshared environmental influences in behavior development. *Developmental Psychology, 17,* 517–531.

Rushton, J. P., Brainerd, C. J., & Pressley, M. (1983). Behavioral development and construct validity: The principle of aggregation. *Psychological Bulletin, 94,* 18–38.

Rushton, J. P., Fulker, D. W., Neule, M. C., Blizard, R. A., & Eysenck, H. J. (in press). Altruism and genetics. *Acta Genetical et Gemelliologiae: Twin Research.*

Rust, J. (1975). Cortical evoked potential, personality and intelligence. *Journal of Comparative and Physiological Psychology, 89,* 1220–1226.

Rutter, M. (1983). School effects on pupil progress: Research findings and policy implications. *Child Development, 54,* 1–29.

Sarbin. R. T. (1950). Contributions to role-taking theory: 1. Hypnotic behavior. *Psychological Review, 57,* 255–270.

Sarbin, T. R., Coe, W. C. (1981). Hypnosis: A social-psychological analysis of influence communication. New York: Holt, Rinehart & Winston.

Scarr, S. (1981). *Race, social class and individual differences, new studies of old problems.* Hillsdale, NJ: Erlbaum.

Scarr, S., & Carter-Saltzman, L. (1979). Twin method: Defense of a critical assumption. *Behavior Genetics. 9,* 527–542.

Scarr, S., & McCartney, K. (1983). How people make their own environments: A theory of genotype environment effects. *Child Development, 54,* 424–435.

Scarr, S., Webber, P. L., Weinberg, R. A., & Wittig, M. A. (1981). Personality resemblance among adolescents and their parents in biologically related and adoptive families. *Journal of Personality and Social Psychology, 40,* 885–858.

Scarr, S., & Weinberg, R. A. (1976). IQ test performance of black children adopted by white families. *American Psychologist, 31,* 726–739.

Schaie, K. W., & Strother, C. R. (1968). A cross-sequential study of age changes in cognitive behavior. *Psychological Bulletin, 70,* 671–680.

Scheier, M. F. (1976). Self-awareness, self-consciousness, and angry aggression. *Journal of Personality, 44,* 627–644.

Scheier, M. F., Buss, A. H., & Buss, D. M. (1978). Self-consciousness, self-report of aggressiveness, and aggression. *Journal of Research in Personality, 12,* 133–140.

Schiff, M., Duyme, M., Dumaret, A., Stewart, J., Tomkiewica, S., & Feingold, Jr. (1978). Intellectual status of working-class children adopted early into upper-middle class families. *Science. 200,* 1503–1504.

Schooler, C., Zahn, P., Murphy, D. L., & Buchsbaum, M. S. (1978). Psychological correlates of monoamine oxidase in normals. *Journal of Nervous and Mental Disease, 166,* 177–186.

Schunk, D. H. (1982). Effects of attributional feedback on children's perceived self-efficacy and achievement. *Journal of Educational Psychology, 74,* 548–556.

Schunk, D. H. (1984). Sequential attributional feedback and children's achievement behaviors. *Journal of Educational Psychology, 76,* 1159–1169.

Schunk, D. H., & Hanson, A. R. (1985). Peer models: Influence on children's self-efficacy and achievement. *Journal of Educational Psychology, 77,* 313–322.

Schvaneveldt, R. W., Meyer, D. E., & Becker, C. A. (1976). Lexical ambiguity, semantic context and visual word recognition. *Journal of Experimental Psychology: Human Perception and Performance, 2,* 243–256.

Seamon, J., Brody, N., & Kauff, D. (1983a). Affective discrimination of stimuli that are not recognized: Effects of shadowing, masking, and cerebral laterality. *Journal of Experimental Psychology: Learning, Memory and Cognition, 9,* 544–555.

Seamon, J. G., Brody, N., & Kauff, D. M. (1983b). Affective discrimination of stimuli that are not recognized: II. Effect of delay between study and test. *Bulletin of the Psychonomic Society, 21,* 187–189.

Seamon, J. G., Marsh, R. L., & Brody, N. (1984). Critical importance of exposure duration for affective discrimination of stimuli that are not recognized. *Journal of Experimental Psychology: Learning, Memory, and Cognition, 10,* 465–469.

Sevilla, L. G. (1984). Extraversion and neuroticism in rats. *Personality and Individual Differences, 5,* 511–532.

Shields, J. (1962). *Monozygotic twins brought up apart and brought up together.* London: Oxford University Press.

Shigehisa, T., & Symons, J. R. (1973). Effects of intensity of visual stimulation on auditory sensitivity in relation to personality. *British Journal of Psychology, 64,* 205–213.

Shweder, R. A. (1975). How relevant is an individual difference theory of personality? *Journal of Personality, 43,* 455–484.

Shweder, R. A. (1977). Likeness and likelihood in everyday thought: Magical thinking in judgments about personality. *Current Anthropology, 18,* 637–658.

Shweder, R. A. (1982). Fact and artifact in trait perception: The systematic distortion hypothesis. In B. A. Maher & W. B. Maher (Eds.), *Progress in experimental personality research* (Vol. 11). New York: Academic Press.

Shweder, R. A., & D'Andrade, R. G. (1980). The systematic distortion hypothesis. In R. A. Shweder (Ed.), *New directions for methodology of social and behavioral science. Vol. 4 Fallible judgment in behavior research.* San Francisco: Josey-Bass.

Silverman, L. H. (1976). Psychoanalytic theory. The reports of my death are greatly exaggerated. *American Psychologist, 31,* 621–637.

Silverman, L. H. (1983). *The search for oneness.* New York: International Universities Press.

Silverman, L. H. (1985). Comments on three recent subliminal psychodynamic activation investigations. *Journal of Abnormal Psychology, 94,* 640–643.

Silverman, L. H., Bronstein, A., & Mendelsohn, E. (1976). The further use of subliminal psychodynamic activation method for the clinical theory of psychoanalysis. *Psychotherapy: Theory, Research and Practice, 13,* 2–16.

Silverman, L. H., Frank, S., & Dachinger, P. (1974). Psychoanalytic reinterpretation of the effectiveness of systematic desensitization: Experimental data bearing on the role of merging fantasies. *Journal of Abnormal Psychology, 83,* 313–318.

Silverman, L. H., Martin, A., Ungaro, R., & Mendelsohn, N. E. (1978). Effect of subliminal stimulation of symbiotic fantasies on behavior modification treatment of obesity. *Journal of Consulting and Clinical Psychology, 46,* 432–441.

Silverman, L. H., Ross, D. L., Adler, J. M., & Lustig, D. A. (1980). Simple research paradigm for demonstrating subliminal psychodynamic activation. Effects of oedipal stimuli on dart-throwing accuracy in college males. *Journal of Abnormal Psychology, 87,* 341–357.

Silverman, L., & Spiro, R. H. (1968). The effects of subliminal, supraliminal and vocalized aggression on the ego functioning of schizophrenics. *Journal of Nervous and Mental Disease, 146,* 50–61.

Silverman, L. H., & Weinberger, J. (1985). Mommy and I are one. Implications for psychotherapy. *American Psychologist, 40,* 1296–1308.

Skinner, B. F. (1938). *The behavior of organisms.* New York: Appleton-Century Crofts.

Small, S. A., Zeldin, S., & Savin-Williams, R. C. (1983). In search of personality traits: A multimethod analysis of naturally occurring prosocial and dominance behavior. *Journal of Personality and Social Psychology, 51,* 1–16.

Smith, B. D. (1983). Extraversion and electrodermal activity: Arousability and the inverted-U. *Personality and Individual Differences, 4,* 411–419.

Smith, B. D., Rypma, C. B., & Wilson, R. J. (1981). Dishabituation and spontaneous recovery of the electrodermal orienting response: Effects of extraversion, impulsivity, sociability and caffeine. *Journal of Research in Personality, 15,* 233–240.

Smith, B. D., Wilson, R. J., & Davidson, R. (1984). Electrodermal activity and extraversion: Caffeine, preparatory signal and stimulus intensity effects. *Personality and Individual Differences, 5,* 59–65.

Smith, E. R., & Miller, F. D. (1978). Limits on perception of cognitive processes: A reply to Nisbett and Wilson. *Psychological Review, 85,* 355–362.

Smith, G. M. (1967). Usefulness of peer ratings of personality in educational research. *Educational and Psychological Measurement, 27,* 967–984.

Smith, M. L., Glass, G. V., & Miller, T. I. (1980). *The benefits of psychotherapy.* Baltimore: Johns Hopkins University Press.

Smith, R. T. (1965). A comparison of socioenvironmental factors in monozygotic and dyzgotic twins, testing an assumption. In S. G. Vandenberg (Ed.), *Methods and goals in human behavior genetics.* New York: Academic Press.

Snow, R. E., & Yalow, E. (1982). Education and intelligence. In R. Sternberg (Ed.), *Handbook of human intelligence.* Cambridge: Cambridge University Press.

Snyder, M., & Ickes, W. (1985). Personality and social behavior. In G. Lindzey & E. Aronson (Eds.), *Handbook of Social Psychology,* Vol. 2, (3rd ed.). New York: Random House.

Sommer, R., & Sommer, B. A. (1983). Mystery in Milwaukee: Early intervention, IQ, and psychology textbooks. *American Psychologist, 38,* 982–985.

Soubrie, P., Thiebot, M. H., & Jobert, A. (1978). Picrotoxin-diazepan interaction in a behavioural schedule of differential reinforcement of low rates. *Experientia, 34,* 1621–1622.

Soubrie, P., Thiebot, M. H., Simon, P., & Boissier, J. R. (1978). Benzodiazepines and behavioral effects of reward (water) omission. *Psychopharmacology, 59,* 95–100.

Spanos, N. P. (1986). Hypnotic behavior: A social psychological interpretation of amnesia, analgesia, and "trance logice". *Behavioral and Brain Sciences, 9,* 449–502.

Spanos, N. P., & Hewitt, E. G. (1980). The hidden observer in hypnotic analgesia: Discovery or experimental creation? *Journal of Personality and Social Psychology, 39,* 1201–1214.

Spearman, C. (1904). General intelligence, objectively determined and measured. *American Journal of Psychology, 15,* 201–293.

Spearman, C. (1927). *The abilities of man.* New York: Macmillan.

Stelmack, R. M. (1981). The psychophysiology of extraversion and neuroticism. In H. J. Eysenck (Ed.), *A model for personality.* Berlin: Springer.

Stelmack, R. M., & Mandelzys, N. (1975). Extraversion and pupillary response to affective and taboo words. *Psychophysiology, 12,* 536–540.

Sternberg, R. J. (1977). *Intelligence, information processing and analogical reasoning: The componential analysis of human abilities.* Hillsdale, NJ: Erlbaum.

Sternberg, R. J. (1985). *Beyond IQ: A triarchic theory of intelligence.* Cambridge: Cambridge University Press.

Sternberg, R. J., & Weil, E. M. (1980). An aptitude-strategy interaction in linear syllogistic reasoning. *Journal of Educational Psychology, 72,* 226–234.

Swets, J. A. (Ed.). (1964). *Signal detection and recognition by human observers.* New York: Wiley.

Swets, J. A., Tanner, W., & Birdsall, T. G. (1961). Decision processes in perception. *Psychological Review, 68,* 301–340.

Tellegen, A. (undated). The Differential Personality Questionnaire. Unpublished manuscript.

Thurstone, L. L. (1938). *Primary mental abilities.* Chicago: Chicago University Press.

Tupes, E. C., & Christal, R. E. (1961). Recurrent personality factors based on trait ratings. *USAF ASD Technical Report,* Report No. 61–97.

Umberkoman-Wiita, B., Vogel, W. H., & Wiita, P. J. (1981). Some biochemical and behavioral (sensation seeking) correlates in healthy adults. *Research Communications in Psychology, Psychiatry and Behavior, 6,* 303–316.

Vernon, P. E. (1961). *The structure of human abilities* (2nd ed.). London: Methuen.

Waddington, J. L., & Olley, J. E. (1977). Dissociation of the anti-punishment activities of chlordiazepoxide and atropine using two heterogeneous avoidance tasks. *Psychopharmacology, 52,* 93–96.

Wardlaw, K. A., & Kroll, N. E. A. (1976). Automatic responses to shock-associated words in a nonattended message: A failure to replicate. *Journal of Experimental Psychology: Human Perception and Performance, 2,* 357–360.

Wechsler, D. (1958). *The measurement and appraisal of adult intelligence.* Baltimore: Williams & Wilkins.

Weikart, D. P. (1967). *Preschool intervention: A preliminary report of the Perry preschool project.* Ann Arbor, MI: Campus Publishers.

Whimbey, A. (1975). *Intelligence can be taught.* New York: Dutton.

Wiggins, J. S. (1973). *Personality and prediction: Principles of personality assessment.* Reading, MA: Addison-Wesley.

Wigglesworth, M. J., & Smith, B. D. (1976). Habituation and dishabituation of the electrodermal orienting reflex in relation to extraversion and neuroticism. *Journal of Research in Personality, 10,* 437–445.

Wilson, G. T., & Rachman, S. (1982). Meta-analysis and the evaluation of psychotherapy outcome: Limitations and liabilities. *Journal of Consulting and Clinical Psychology, 51,* 54–64.

Wilson, R. S. (1983). The Louisville Twin Study: Developmental synchronies in behavior. *Child Development, 42,* 1381–1398.

Wilson, R. S., & Matheny, A. P., Jr. (1986). Behavior-genetics research in infant temperament: The Louisville Twin Study, In R. Plomin & J. Dunn (Eds.), *The study of temperament: Changes, continuities and challenges.* Hillsdale, NJ: Erlbaum.

Wilson, W. R. (1979). Feeling more than we can know: Exposure affects without learning. *Journal of Personality and Social Psychology, 37,* 811–831.

Wohlwill, J. F. (1984). What are sensation seekers seeking? *Behavioral and Brain Sciences, 7,* 453.

Yerkes, R. M., & Dodson, J. O. (1908). The relation of strength of stimulus to rapidity of habit formation. *Journal of Comparitive Neurology and Psychology, 18,* 459–482.

Zajonc, R. B. (1965). Social facilitation. *Science, 149,* 269–274.

Zajonc, R. B. (1980). Feeling and thinking: Preferences need no inferences. *American Psychologist, 35,* 151–175.

Zajonc, R. B. (1984). On the primacy of affect. *American Psychologist, 39,* 117–123.

Zevon, M. A., & Tellegen, A. (1982). The structure of mood change: An idiographic/nomothetic analysis. *Journal of Personality and Social Psychology, 43,* 111–122.

Zigler, E., Abelson, W. D., & Seitz, V. (1973). Motivational factors in the performance of economically disadvantaged children on the Peabody Picture Vocabulary Test. *Child Development, 44,* 295–303.

Zigler, E., & Seitz, C. (1982). Social policy and intelligence. In R. J. Sternberg (Ed.), *Handbook of human intelligence.* Cambridge: Cambridge University Press.

Zigler, E., & Valentine, J. (Eds.). (1979). *Project Head Start: A legacy of the war on poverty.* New York: Free Press.

Zimbardo, P. G. (1969). *The cognitive control of motivation.* Glenville, IL: Scott, Foresman & Co.

Zimbardo, P. G., Cohen, A., Weisenberg, M., Dworkin, L., & Firestone, I. (1969). The control of experimental pain. In P. G. Zimbardo (Ed.), *The cognitive control of motivation*. Glenville, IL: Scott, Foresman & Co.

Zuckerman, M. (1972). Drug usage as one manifestation of a "sensation seeking" trait. In W. Keup (Ed.), *Drug abuse: Current concepts and research*. Springfield, IL: Charles C. Thomas.

Zuckerman, M. (1978). Sensation seeking. In H. London & J. Exner (Eds.), *Dimensions of personality*. New York: Wiley.

Zuckerman, M. (1979). *Sensation seeking: Beyond the optimal level of arousal*. Hillsdale, NJ: Erlbaum.

Zuckerman, M. (1984a). Sensation seeking: A comparative approach to a human trait. *Behavioral and Brain Sciences, 7*, 413–471.

Zuckerman, M. (1984b). Home from a perilous journey. *Behavioral and Brain Sciences, 7*, 453–465.

Zuckerman, M., Ballenger, J. C., Jimerson, D. C., Murphy, D. L., & Post, R. M. (1983). A correlational test in humans of the biological models of sensation seeking, impulsivity and anxiety. In M. Zuckerman (Ed.), *Biological bases of sensation seeking, impulsivity and anxiety*. Hillsdale, NJ: Erlbaum.

Zuckerman, M., Kolin, E. A., Price, L., & Zoob, I. (1964). Development of a sensation seeking scale. *Journal of Consulting Psychology, 28*, 477–482.

Zuckerman, M., Murtaugh, T. T., & Siegel, J. (1974). Sensation-seeking and cortical augmentation-reducing. Psychophysiology, 11, 534–542.

Index